Toasts & Sentiments.

Music.

THE QUEEN.
Proposed by His Excellency The Governor.

"God Save the Queen."

THE PRINCE OF WALES & THE ROYAL FAMILY.
Proposed by His Excellency The Governor.

"God Bless the Prince of Wales."

THE GOVERNORS OF THE OTHER AUSTRALASIAN COLONIES.
Proposed by His Excellency The Governor.
Responded to by the Governors.

"Rule Britannia."

AUSTRALASIA: HER TRIALS AND TRIUMPHS IN THE PAST; HER UNION AND PROGRESS IN THE FUTURE.
Proposed by the Hon. Sir Henry Parkes, K.C.M.G.

"Home! Sweet Home!"

THE HONOURED GUESTS OF THE MOTHER COLONY.
Proposed by His Honor Sir Frederick Darley, Knt.C.J.
Responded to by The Right Hon. the Earl of Carnarvon and the Premiers of the neighbouring Colonies.

"Auld Lang Syne."

THE AUSTRALASIAN PRESS AND AUSTRALASIAN LIBERTY.
Proposed by Sir John Robertson, K.C.M.G.
Responded to by The Hon. A. Deakin, Chief Secretary of Victoria.

"Australian Anthem."

THE LADIES OF AUSTRALASIA.
Proposed by D. O'Connor, Esq., M.P.

"A Health to all Good Lasses."

THE CHAIRMAN—HIS EXCELLENCY THE GOVERNOR.
Proposed by The Hon. Sir John Hay, K.C.M.G., President of the Legislative Council.

"Rule Britannia."

"God Save the Queen."

Menu of State banquet, Sydney, January 26, 1888

ONE CONTINUOUS PICNIC

Cheval & Poehlman's Café Restaurant, Sydney, 1854

Michael Symons

ONE CONTINUOUS PICNIC
*A history of eating
in Australia*

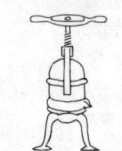

Adelaide   DUCK PRESS   1982

Duck Press, Adelaide
(PO Uraidla, South Australia 5142)
First published 1982

© Michael Symons
All rights reserved

Set in 11/13 Garamond
Typeset by ProComp Productions Pty Ltd, Adelaide
Printed at Griffin Press Limited, Netley, South Australia.

National Library of Australia
Cataloguing-in-Publication data

Symons, Michael, 1945–
  One continuous picnic.

  Bibliography.
  Includes index.
  ISBN 0 9593047 0 3.

  1. Food—History. 2. Cookery, Australian—
History. 3. Food habits—Australia—History.
I. Title.

641.3'00994

To my mother

Contents

	Preface	1
	Introduction *The uncultivated continent*	5
PART I	**HISTORY WITHOUT PEASANTS** *The sailing ship era (1780s–1860s)*	
1	The English heritage *The rations of an ocean-going empire—salt meat, flour, sugar and tea—formed our assumptions about food. Meals had to be convenient and transportable, rarely fresh*	15
	The taste for home	24
2	Meat three times a day *With the success of grazing, bush workers ate meat, damper and billy-tea at every meal. The small "Dungaree" settlers on the Hawkesbury, attempting the peasant alternative, were harrassed and ridiculed*	27
	Eating and drinking in 1839	39
3	The Aristologist *Australia's first cookery book, published in 1864, showed the wonderful variety of foods possible, but emphasised the isolation of the gourmet*	42
	The next cookery books	52
PART II	**FEEDING THE CITY** *The age of the railways (1850s–1930s)*	
	How we entertained a prince	57
4	Metropolitan paradise *After toasting the goldrush in champagne, our expanding cities adopted inventions like stoves and ice-chests, and revelled in the world's cheapest living*	60
	The city markets	70

5	**The Chinese exception**	74
	The goldrush Chinese stayed on as market gardeners, an early immigrant group destined to grow and serve the fresh fruit and vegetables that factories could not offer	
	The tea and scones of Quong Tart	82
6	**The tyranny of transport**	85
	Some Australian farms might have been the havens of children's storybooks, but most were producers of durable foods to be rushed by train to the cities and the world	
	Granny Smith	96
7	**The first food factories**	98
	The packaging and advertising of processed foods — epitomised by the refined white flour of giant roller mills — created household names like Arnott's, Rosella and Foster's	
	Mr MacRobertson	106
8	**Bohemian restaurants**	110
	Rapid innovation in food processing in the late nineteenth century also brought interesting times for the gourmet. Some restaurants would stand up well against today's best	
	Let's go to Fasoli's	120
9	**Family goodness**	124
	The austerities of the Great War killed off restaurant society, leaving the workers of tomorrow to be built up with fads for orange juice, milk, cornflakes and processed cheese	
	Vegemite	132
10	**Dainty cooks and sudden drinkers**	135
	Between the world wars, men took rations to work and drank quickly till 6 o'clock closing, while women were encouraged to "civilise" the society with sweet fantasies	
	The pavlova	147
PART III	**FRESH FROM THE FREEZER** *The automobile ascendancy (1940s–1970s)*	
	Sliced white	155

11	The first munition	162
	With World War II, American agricultural and processing experts arrived to show how to mass produce more varied but still portable rations	
	Coca-Colonisation	173
12	Carpark shopping	177
	With an obsession for cheapness, plus a new love of cars and refrigerators, Australians embraced the nationally-distributed and standardised foods of the supermarket	
	Golden Circle pineapple	188
13	The industrial kitchen	194
	Identifying gaps on the supermarket shelves, large food corporations shaped, coloured, flavoured and marketed food to fit	
	Frozen food	207

PART IV THE COMING OF THE QUICHE
Where we think we reached (1970s–1980s)

	The great wine dinner	215
14	Oh, for a French wife!	221
	Theories for the gourmet boom from the 1960s included immigration, increased overseas travel, bulging household budgets—but the most likely explanation was the food industry's shake-up of cooking	
	Chefs to the court of Whitlam	233
15	Hard tomatoes for hard times	242
	The sacrifice of family farms to agribusiness left us to eat hard tomatoes, pale eggs and stale apples cosmetically coated with wax	
	A fresh start	251
16	The art of eating in Australia	254
	Not left to establish agrarian roots, Australians have suffered the world's worst cuisine. The hope is a consumer revolt towards fresh, local produce	
	Select bibliography	263
	Notes on sources	266
	Index	268

Illustrations

Menu of State banquet, Sydney, January 26, 1888 (State Library of SA)	Endpapers
Cheval & Poehlman's Café-Restaurant, Sydney (*Illustrated Sydney News*, Feb 11, 1854)	Frontispiece
Emigrants at dinner (*Illustrated London News*, April 13, 1844)	13
Richmond looking West (*Landscape Scenery Illustrating Sydney*, Sydney, 1855)	24
The Fruit Market, Sydney (*Landscape Scenery*, 1855)	39
Edward Abbott (Allport Library & Museum, Hobart)	43
The burst of Australian cookery books in the 1890s (the author)	52
S. T. Gill, *Premises of Samuel Henderson*, Footscray, c. 1870 (La Trobe Library)	55
Eastern market, Melbourne (*Australasian Sketcher*, January 17, 1880, courtesy *A'asian Post*)	70
Quong Tart (John Fairfax & Sons)	82
Chinese costermonger (*Illustrated Australian News*, Oct 27, 1866)	82
Maria Ann Smith (Apple & Pear Corporation)	96
One of the "Old Gold" dipping departments (MacRobertson, 1921)	106
Robertson & Lord Leverhulme, Melbourne, 1924	109
George Dick Meudell (Mitchell Library)	117
Fasoli's (Alex Sass in William Moore, *City Sketches*, 1905)	120
Vegemite advertisement, 1920s	132
Herbert Sachse and pavlova (West Australian Newspapers)	147
Coles New World supermarket, Dandenong 1963 (G. J. Coles)	153
Have a Coke (*Women's Weekly*, June 2, 1945)	173
Coke sticker on shop, Norwood Parade, SA (the author)	176
Golden Circle recipe booklet, c. 1958	188
Charles Frater in his Sydney Tower restaurant (John Fairfax & Sons)	213
Gay & Tony Bilson at the Bon Goût, Sydney, 1974 (Gay Bilson)	233
Gil Wahlquist at future Botobolar vineyard, Mudgee 1971 (Gil Wahlquist)	251

Preface

Tell me what you eat, and I shall tell you what you are.

Brillat-Savarin,
La Physiologie du Goût, 1825

It requires the tongue and the pen of a Brillat-Savarin to give flavour to a Barmecide's feast; but as victualling is as necessary a condition of existence here as anywhere else, I must do my best to enlighten you as to our situation in this respect. May you never have practical experience thereof!

Richard Twopenny,
Town Life in Australia, 1883

IN APRIL, 1977, I set off with Jennifer Hillier to live in Italy with an intention of eating well and also in some vague expectation of understanding why Australian society seemed culturally impoverished. Not quickly finding jobs and apartment in Rome or Bologna, we followed the more economical dream of locating a village with a house with geraniums in every window. And so it was that at Radda-in-Chianti we started gardening, we discovered how sublime food could be, we understood Australia's deprivation and I began writing this book.

From this Tuscan base, we became agritourists in Europe, finding our way according to the stars in restaurant guidebooks, judging towns by their markets, appreciating the weekend allotments encircling cities, and marvelling at the extraordinary range of vine trellises—from rocky craters in Yugoslavia to wires strung high between trees near Naples. Between trips, I researched Australian food history—by talking to visitors, by writing letters back home, by ordering books and by visiting the libraries at the old British Institute in Florence and the FAO headquarters in Rome.

Thinking of moving into the business, we took the opportunity to become partners briefly in a small restaurant on a vineyard at Bacchereto, outside Florence. We liked the idea of a restaurant being a bridge between town and country, and so decided to set up in a market gardening area near an Australian city. It made returning to Sydney difficult, and, besides, I had an aversion to the Centrepoint tower. We chose Adelaide's still beautiful Piccadilly Valley. We found a century-old building with a little land at Uraidla. In April,

1981, we opened the Uraidla Aristologist, the reason for the name made clear in this book.

Our aim to use local produce has been hampered by increasing industrialisation of crops. In place of the once balanced income from fruit, vegetables, cows, pigs, fowls and bees, local growers have resorted to high overdrafts and semi-trailers to send brussels sprouts interstate. However, we've found a few gardeners with top fruit and vegetables. We have our own free-range eggs, a few salad vegetables and loads of raspberries. And we discovered that the Hills climate is becoming important for wine.

In researching this book, I was interested to find out about dampers, Foster's lager and the pavlova. I was pleased to unearth stories about the Dungaree settlers, author Edward Abbott and some great nineteenth-century restaurants. I decided that if we understood the more recent history of supermarket food, we could improve our daily lives. But I only sustained these efforts for five years through the conviction that a study of eating reveals Australia's uniqueness.

This is the only land which has never enjoyed agrarian society. Our history is without peasants. We've had hunter-gatherers and then industrial civilisation. It means we've been either conservationists or developers, without appreciating the cultivated landscape. We've not made a permanent home, even using refrigeration to pretend we live somewhere else.

I submit that a gastronomic history of Australia disposes of such clichés as the "Englishness" of our eating (the English used to be more concerned about eating than we've supposed—think how often nursery rhymes refer to food). It offers other explanations than immigration for the recent "Europeanisation" of dining. And it alters our broader self-image—the impression, for example, that we are "too young for true culture". Our eating shows us to be a singularly working-class society, whose food had to be portable and profitable.

The book is divided into four parts, broadly reflecting changes in transport and also the steps in the industrialisation of food—of the garden, pantry and then kitchen, plus a discussion of the present position. Each chapter is divided into two sections, the second being an illustrative "case history".

I wish to acknowledge Jennifer Hillier's contribution to the ideas in this book, and also to permitting my work on our restaurant being part-time to the present. I thank Lenna Symons for doing much library research. I thank my partners in Duck Press, Angie and Gabriel Gaté and David Dale, who was also editor. I wish to list Darce Cassidy, Barrie Dyster, Julie Rigg, Barbara Santich and Richard White among the others who helped.

Michael Symons,
Uraidla, South Australia
September, 1982

ONE CONTINUOUS PICNIC

*Did Trollope have to foot it through the Paroo's heavy sand,
With his "one continuous picnic" in Australia's happy land?*

Tibbs' Popular Song Book
Sydney, *c.* 1887

Introduction

The uncultivated continent

THE BRITISH government exploded a handful of nuclear bombs at Maralinga and Woomera in South Australia between 1953 and 1957 and fired various missiles into the 1960s. The British chose central Australia because they considered it was so arid that few pastoral stations, let alone towns, blocked their path. Nevertheless, they had to despatch patrols to round up remnants of the 10,000 or more Aborigines who once roamed the Western desert. Deposited in the care of mission stations and government settlements and no longer permitted to wander the distances necessary to find food and water, the refugees soon picked the nearby desert clean. Dependent on White rations, they began to lose the complicated skills and culture which had sustained them perhaps 40,000 years in apparently inhospitable conditions. And so, Australia's last completely self-sufficient hunter-gatherers were brought into the fringe of industrial society.

Studying the last of the tribes in 1966–67, anthropologist Dr Richard Gould gave a glimpse of how food was consumed in Australia before the arrival of the Europeans. He found that these Aborigines covered the greatest distance of any nomads—walks of 400 and 550 km were not unusual, particularly in times of drought. Groups shifted camp as many as nine times in three months, foraging over roughly 2,500 square km, he said. Moving typically in groups of 10 to 30, they came together in groups of 100 or more when food was plentiful.

The monotonous Western desert of long, low sandhills and gravel knolls lacked real seasons, making food unpredictable. Yet with 38 edible plants and 47 varieties of meats available to them, the Aborigines considered food less a problem than the terrifying lack of water. The rains averaged about 250 mm annually, but that figure is misleading since many years came with scarcely a drop. There were no freshwater lakes, flowing rivers or permanent springs in the desert, and the Warburton-Musgrave and Rawlinson-Petermann ranges were landmarks without streams. Instead, the Aborigines relied on occasional shaded pools in rocky areas or sub-surface water tables, the so-called "native wells", where they dug. Dr Gould, who happened to visit in the last months of a record drought, summed this habitat up as the world's "most unreliable and impoverished". Yet these Australians lived a healthy, contented and fulfilled life. They survived not so much through great physical endurance as through knowledge—their "cognitive map" of where to find food and, especially, water.

The women sought the berries, seeds, leaves, bulbs, roots and fruits which made up the bulk of the primarily vegetarian diet. The main daily staple was about 1·5 kg each of desert tomatoes. Good rain would bring wild figs. Drought meant relying more on dried fruit, like quandong desiccated on the tree. Some dried fruit was preserved in balls. The women and children also caught small game, such as goannas, mice, birds, grubs and, more recently, rabbits and cats. Yet the food quest did not require more than four or five hours of work for each woman daily, and generally less. Even in drought, two or three hours' collecting could be sufficient. The women's work, in a sense, freed the men for their longer hours of more chancy hunting. As with the women, they collected small game but also hoped for a feast like a kangaroo or emu. It still left plenty of time for people to rest, gossip and make tools and artworks. Their adaptation was an "impressive human achievement," Dr Gould concluded. Ironically, the tough environment protected the desert nomads nearly two centuries longer than their amply-provided coastal counterparts, as European invasion reduced an estimated 314,500 Aboriginal population to one-fifth by the 1930s.

The first Europeans to penetrate the Western desert were explorers who sought overland stock routes and grazing lands as relatively recently as 1872 and 1876. The immense and arid terrain frustrated them. In 1892 gold was discovered at Coolgardie and the following year at Kalgoorlie, on the fringe of the desert. Sheep grazing gained footholds in the early years of this century, work kept up on the transcontinental railway through the 1920s, the missions brought Christianity in the 1930s, missile recovery roads were graded across the desert in the 1950s and, more recently, mineral explorers tried their luck. But none of these visits or settlements was self-sustaining. They required a 565-km water pipeline to the goldfields, trucks from railheads at Leonora and Meekatharra and planes from Alice Springs and Kalgoorlie.

The Aborigines drifted into the mining settlements, stations and coastal towns attracted by curiosity, companionship, food and permanent water. They stopped walking and instead sat around, day after day, perhaps playing cards amid a squalor described long ago by Daisy Bates. The women were sexually exploited and the elders became demoralised. From a state of complete economic independence, the desert Aborigines became tragically dependent. The typical diet became white flour for damper, white sugar for tea, camp pie, salt and beer: the combination which we will recognise as the classic nutritional disaster of industrialisation.

The diet particularly lacked fresh fruit and vegetables, something which the desert had provided but which government rations and then the stores found hard to supply. When Richard Gould and his wife were there, the desert's Aboriginal population, guessed originally at between 10,000 and 18,000, had fallen to 3,200. Whites had killed some and many died of introduced diseases, exacerbated by malnutrition. The more natural ways of the self-sufficient hunter-gatherers had been replaced by the "relatively unsuccessful and unstable" adaptations of the Europeans and Europeanised Aborigines. The records of Aboriginal eating would fill a book, and I mention the last of the tribes really only to highlight our own profoundly novel way of feeding. Yet, despite the dramatic difference between the Aborigines' respect for the immediate environment and the invaders' indifference, we both would leave the continent uncultivated.

Modern Australians

Australians in the 1980s drive the car once a week to a supermarket. There, we push a trolley down long lines of packages crying to be pulled off the shelf. It might be a dozen eggs with thin shells, pale yolks and watery whites. It might be a carton containing a white liquid derived from scalding and chilling stainless-steel pipes connected to a cow. It might be a packet containing slices of spongy dough factory-baked to a scientific formula for bread. Whatever it is, it will be brightly displayed, it will be transported long distances, it could well be a health risk, and it probably won't look much like its original, if we happen to remember what that was.

We push our way to the check-out queue, where we pay what retailers call the "tape", an amount which need not be questioned since it is electronically-determined. Having never needed to speak to the young, female and thus cheap "checker", we drive straight home so that the peas won't defrost or the block of icecream melt. Between trips, we may visit separate shops for fresh fruit and vegetables, looking plump and attractively unblemished, thanks to better breeding and the planned application of commercial formulations, although the taste has faded. The same with meat, which the butcher might still cut, although he no longer slaughters the beast and the pork appears to have been frozen.

Not very many people join the meal anymore. Grandmother is looked after by matron and Uncle Bob is fed by Meals on Wheels. At night, most of the family watch television, where their appetites are constantly reminded of the food industry's menu. Lunch is a pie or sandwich away from home. Breakfast is taken in relays. So, on the rare occasions when it sits down together, the "tribe" now numbers four. The shopper has chosen foods that the family might like and since the children are so important these days, they dictate fare that seemed so much more exciting on colour television. Nutritious old staples like potatoes get eaten because they are now "crinkle-cut". The kids need never die of thirst because they can grab an aluminium can from the refrigerator and call in for regular iceblocks. The way to have a real family outing, somehow so important in childhood memories, is to drive the car to the local copy of the American takeaway barn. When the adults get together for a candle-lit evening with friends, the cook nervously ventures into a strange "gourmet" world charted in part-French by glossy recipe books. The wines are selected like products at a supermarket and end with a proud port. And, after it's all over, the council truck collects the bags of garbage, food mixed with glass and plastic. The process by which wastes disappear is as magic as those which bring water, electricity and the foods themselves.

The only chance we might have to glimpse the outside world is when we go to work. It's a long week, necessary to keep a family. Indeed, paying the bills increasingly requires joint husband-and-wife efforts, which apparently leaves less and less time actually to prepare foods. We slave for eight hours on the production line or at the desk. Food is our biggest industry. We work to feed ourselves and feed to work. We would get off the treadmill, if it were not for the kids, who will probably thus never hear the cry of the "rabbit-oh", the "ping" of the milk separator, never smell genuine bread or never know what a fowlyard looks like. Food technologists tell each other this old joke: "A boy, visiting the country for the first time, sees a pile of empty condensed milk cans and says, 'Look, Mum, a cow's nest'."

Tuscan peasants
This book was partly inspired by the recognition that there is another style of eating, quite different from the present-day Australian and not a return to the original, testing paradise of the Aborigine. I realised this while spending two and a half years in the Tuscan countryside. While industrialisation has made great inroads in Italy, many people—still partly peasant—retain close contact with the soil, preserve their own foods and cook them in appropriate ways, perfected over the centuries. I'd never managed to eat or drink like it.

For a year we lived in an ancient water-mill surrounded by woods, which provided strawberries in spring, blackberries in summer and chestnuts in autumn. We cooked the chestnuts as soup, fried them in marsala, puréed them with whipped cream and called it Monte Bianco and, perhaps best of all, simply roasted them on the open fire. There was an old apple tree at the backdoor, various figs, grapes and olive trees, which even provided a little oil when combined with the neighbour's harvest. The house grew rosemary, sage, thyme, marjoram and parsley. And it taught an amazing fact, something which had been known to virtually everyone who had ever existed, that if you put seeds into soil and then water them they produce a bounty. We had staggering crops of peas, lettuces, cabbages and three types of beans—those eaten raw with cheese, those cooked whole and, best of all, those *fagioli* taken from the pod and simmered, either fresh or dried, in a Tuscan pot. Not to forget the tomatoes weighing down the plants, the garlic to be plaited into strings and the zucchini.

The red wines of the Chianti region were still largely made on semi-feudal estates owned by rich families from the cities and operated by teams of "contadini" (peasants). Most of the wine was made from the surrounding vineyards and by largely natural methods in old stone cellars, which were built to last. The slopes unsuitable for grapes grew olives for some of the world's best oil. The farm labourers, dwindling in number under the competition of capitalism, lived on the estates or in nearby villages. They and their now factory-working neighbours managed to use, rent or share-farm land for their own grapes, oil, fruit, vegetables, fowls, rabbits and pigs, slaughtered ritually each winter.

While the men did the growing, the women had left the fields and commanded the kitchens. The midday break was usually of four hours and the lunch huge, starting with spaghetti and other pasta. There was a meat dish, a vegetable and then cheese, fruit and coffee. And red wine and thick slices of the morning's bread. The people remembered baking bread in the large brick ovens alongside every farmhouse. Declining with the extended family, it was now done by a village baker. There was a general store almost as handy as a bar, and the butcher too, who slaughtered his own beast and hung it for a day's dismantling in the middle of the shop.

The annual cycle of dishes gave food social meaning—with, to take one instance, the festivities of carnevale ("farewell to meat") leading to Lent and then the pleasures of Easter lamb. While national accounts don't show Italy as a particularly wealthy country, economists neglect the intangible treasures of superb stone farmhouses, traditions of winemaking and food grown in your own garden. At least as much as works of art, the cuisine contributes to the richness of Italian culture, a caricature of which is only seen in our own versions of Italian restaurants.

No-one would recommend feudalism for Australia; indeed, many Tuscans looked forward to running the estates as communist cooperatives. No-one would recommend that work should be divided along sex lines. No-one would imagine transplanting the way of life to Australia, even if city Italians talk about returning to the country. Yet my Tuscan experience flavours this book.

History without peasants

In terms of food, there are three main types of society: represented by the Aboriginal, the disappearing Tuscan and the modern Australian. The first, that of the hunter-gatherer, scarcely disturbs the pre-historic world in search of nourishment. Nuts and fruits are plucked from the trees, animals are captured, a little preservation is practised and collecting is a communal, daily activity. Preparation with simple implements and fires tends to leave the food much as in the original. While individuals and tribes may suffer the whims of nature, this way of life could sustain a relatively small population for thousands upon thousands of years.

The second type is agrarian. The family stays fixed in a house, planting crops and keeping animals—in a creative interplay with the environment domesticating grains, vegetables, fruit trees, goats and cows. Preservation is by cooking, cooling, drying, smoking, pickling, syruping, salting and fermenting—giving such products as ham, cheese, yoghurt, wine and beer. Cooking is still done on a fire, but often in pots and usually with supplementary chopping, mixing and shaping and serving in appealing combinations. This type of food supply, the product of the neolithic revolution about 10,000 years ago, still sustains the majority of the world's population, and gives us our impression of what food should be, whether it is "country garden freshness" or "grannie's apple pie".

The third type is the industrial. Agriculture is mechanised, chemicalised and rationalised. Preservation and much cooking is done in factories, separating consumers from producers, and an enormous range of foods is distributed, obliterating geographic and seasonal variation. The system is distinguished by the fact that it is heavily dependent on non-renewable resources, especially petroleum for fuels and fertilisers. It thus has struck some people as a relatively temporary food supply.

Of course, the divisions are not firmly fenced. The recognition that Aborigines used fire to clear grasslands allows them more husbandry than we've previously accepted. But having agreed that there are essentially three approaches to food supply it is possible to recognise the single most important fact which distinguishes food in Australia from that in any other country. This is the only continent which has not supported an agrarian society. It has recent experience of hunter-gatherers. Then it switched to an industrialised food supply. Our land missed that fertile period when agriculture and cooking were created. There has never been the creative interplay between society and the soil. Almost no food has ever been grown by the person who eats it, almost no food has been preserved in the home and, indeed, very little preparation is now done by a family cook. This is the uncultivated continent. Our history is without peasants.

By way of contrast, take North America. There, the Indians were agricultural

—collecting, cultivating and cooking maize, potatoes, sweet potatoes, haricot beans, pumpkin and 2,000 other plant foods. The Indians provided many classic American dishes—such as roast turkey, roasted peanuts, clam chowder, steamed lobster, spoon bread and cranberry sauce. An Indian is even said to have treated the first Thanksgiving in 1621 with popcorn. Two centuries before the First Fleet, the Pilgrim Fathers set off with entirely agrarian expections. In 1815, two million people just west of America's Appalachian mountains (which still didn't put them very far west) were largely self-sufficient and only peripherally connected to the market economy. An American historian, Carter Goodrich, wrote in the *Economic Record* in 1928 that: "The United States owes its individualism largely to its small man's frontier; I think it is not fanciful to suggest that Australia owes much of its collectivism to the fact that its frontier was hospitable to the large man instead." Putting that in terms of food, while Americans have traditionally enjoyed the smallholders' chicken and pig, we have relied on the graziers' sheep and cattle.

European seafarers discovered the "last" continent's agrarian gap and passed on. Confronted with Australia, Captain Cook noted on Thursday, August 23, 1770: "The Land naturly produces hardly anything fit for man to eat and the Natives know nothing of Cultivation." Europeans would have not "one Inch of Cultivated land" to adapt, purchase or plunder, as they had done around the rest of the globe. Australia would have to be settled not for the old imperialist motives of plunder, slavery and trade, but as a quarry and a dump. For this, the British had to carry rations and then hew out cash crops. It meant a new kind of mission, a profitable equivalent of sending an expedition to the moon. It could be argued that opening up the country required a form of peasant living, but most arrivals settled in towns, were fed by massive imports of food, and squatters kept down the number of small holdings. Certainly, we failed to incorporate a single indigenous food into anything resembling an agriculture and cooking appropriate to the environment. This country became the world's earliest truly urban nation, in which many of us could no longer even recognise a tomato plant.

Are we really "too young"?

> *If true culture is the product of a deep and intimate relationship between a people and the soil where they have lived for centuries, then clearly Australia has none and could have none . . . The white man still seems an incongruous invader, huddling in cities, on the edge of this time-worn continent, building the wrong houses, wearing the wrong clothes, eating the wrong food.*

I can agree with the above statement by my old newspaper editor, John Douglas Pringle, in his book *Australian Accent* (1958). However, the three fullstops in the middle of the quotation replace the brief sentence, "There has not been time." Pringle was wrong here. Like others, he explained Australia's lack of "culture", "civilisation" and "identity" in terms of its newness. So many times I've heard the same about a "national" food, that "Australia is too young." But massive culinary shifts have occurred in much less than eight generations. European settlement of Australia is older than stoves, restaurants and Anglo-Saxon acceptance of the tomato. It took only one generation for us to forget the pleasures of bêche-de-mer, turtle soup and native turkey and another generation to regard the pavlova as a most traditional accomplishment. Nor, given another two centuries could our present way of life produce a "cuisine" in any traditional sense. It's not our youth but the persistent temporariness of our industrial society, its lack of links with the land.

The historian Keith Hancock was closer to the mark in his passionate *Australia* (1930), when he said all our history came after the French and industrial revolutions, affecting our political and economic relations respectively. He wrote of Australia: "She has not inherited a village civilisation nor love of the soil, but she has inherited factories and factory farms and the class-war." While historians have interpreted for us our political fate, they have usually overlooked this factory feeding. Otherwise, we have easily recognised that we are not "too young" for a rich national culture, but too industrial.

So far, great cuisines have arisen from peasant societies, even if recognised by elites and refined by professionals. The rigours of survival have given the peasant a proper respect for cultivation and cooking, have demonstrated the advantages of tradition, have aroused the joys in the seasons, have enforced on-the-spot freshness. But Australians have put down peasants as ignorant, superstitious, inefficient and dirty. Continual attempts at closer settlement— from Governor King on—have been laughed at as installing a peasantry. The term of abuse, "peasant", is used by industrial Australians to assert superiority. Yet the lack of a peasant experience—or, conversely, our total history of industrialisation—explains why we have traditionally cared less about food than any other people in history.

It has been as if we were sent—in a description credited to novelist Anthony Trollope—on "one continuous picnic". We brought our food with us and we have been kept well-supplied with portable provisions. We called our spot the "working-man's paradise" last century and the "lucky country" this. But we have invariably consumed preserved, packaged fare. We have sometimes feared ourselves to be intruders. At the end of an often tiring journey, we've not felt at home.

PART I
History without peasants
The sailing-ship era (1780s–1860s)

Emigrants at dinner, *Illustrated London News*, April 13, 1844

1
The English heritage

*The rations of an ocean-going empire—
salt meat, flour, sugar and tea—formed our
assumptions about food. Meals had to be
convenient and transportable, rarely fresh*

THE WEEKLY rations for the marines during the First Fleet's 8½-month voyage were:

7 lb bread; 2 lb salt pork; 4 lb salt beef; 2 lb peas; 3 lb oatmeal; 6 oz butter; ¾ lb cheese; ½ pt vinegar;

along with three quarts of water daily. The convicts were to receive two-thirds of this, since they were meant to be enjoying a less arduous voyage.

The list of rations, which would soon be shortened and modified under the harsh conditions, reveals something of eighteenth-century English eating. The bread, oatmeal and cheese represented the core of the peasant diet, but without the supplementary fresh meat, milk, fruit and vegetables of the countryside. Salt meat, ships' biscuits and dried peas were common preserved foods handy on ships. The vinegar was erroneously thought to keep away scurvy, but good sailors recognised the need for fresh food. Conscious of the hardships ahead, Captain Phillip tried to feed his charges well, stopping at Tenerife and lingering a month each at Rio de Janeiro and Table Bay to supplement the salt rations with fresh. Only a couple of dozen convicts died on the voyage.

Arriving in January, 1788, the ships quickly abandoned Botany Bay as lacking fresh water and settled instead on Port Jackson. In the first year Phillip tried to allow adults a weekly ration of:

7 lb flour; 7 lb beef or 4 lb pork; 3 pt peas; 6 oz butter; ½ lb rice.

We can take it that rations were reduced both because the newcomers expected to find and grow supplementary fresh food and because the stores on this bold mission were diminishing. Provisions were meant to last two years, but, as the later colonial figure John Dunmore Lang observed, "every ounce of food for civilised man" had to be imported, and stock brought for breeding had to be slaughtered to feed the starving. A female convict noted at the time:

> We are comforted with the hopes of a supply of tea from China, and flattered with getting riches when the settlement is complete, and the hemp which the place produces is brought to perfection. Our kingaroo [*sic*] rats are like mutton, but much leaner; and there is a kind of chickweed so much in taste like our spinach that no difference can be discerned. Something like ground ivy is used for tea; but a scarcity of salt and sugar makes our best meals insipid.

It seemed smart to bring food in and Phillip sent the *Sirius* off on a long food search in October, 1788. The *Sirius* circled the globe and returned the following May with supplies which only lasted four months. The supply-ship *Guardian* was wrecked off the Cape in December. When the peas "were all expended," in April, 1790, the weekly rations were reduced to:

2½ lb flour; 2 lb rice; 2 lb pork.

Brought from England, the rice was now infested and the salted pork so dry that it could not be boiled, but was toasted before the fire, the drops caught on a slice of bread or in a saucer of rice. The flour was good, having been brought on the *Sirius*, and instead of baking it, the soldiers and convicts often boiled it up with greens. By June 1790, when the Second Fleet began to straggle in, Phillip, who became famous for requesting guests to bring their own bread, noted that "we have not made that advance towards supporting ourselves which may have been expected."

Great efforts were made to supplement the rations with hunting and fishing parties. Kangaroos were often shot and fishermen out all night received a pound of uncleaned fish for breakfast. Within weeks of landing, Phillip had reported "wild celery, spinages [spinach], samphose [perhaps samphire, a cliff-face plant generally pickled], a small wild fig, and several berries which have proved most wholesome, particularly the leaves of a small shrub which is found in such plenty that it has not yet failed us as most of the others have done." Other plants reported include a "sweet tea", wild parsley and the leaves of the cabbage tree, considered a "rather pleasant substitute for vegetables" when found. There was a small white berry which tasted like a green gooseberry, which was found to prevent scurvy, but it was not in sufficient quantities. Three researchers of these "Hungry Years 1788–92", Lois Davey, Margaret MacPherson and F. W. Clements, concluded in 1947:

"Nearly three years of an unappetising diet, which sometimes was below subsistence level and at all times low in most vitamins, had led to marked emaciation of soldiers and convicts . . . it would be correct to assume that the settlers lost the will to work as well as the physical ability." But that assumption underestimates the drive, still not quite eliminated among even that dispossessed lot, to grow food.

The first agriculture

The early arrivals brought with them the "cultural baggage" of the British Isles. They spoke, thought, dressed and hoped to eat, as they were accustomed. That they might eventually become less dependent on outside supplies, their encumberances also included "agricultural baggage". The First Fleet decks were crowded with pens of sheep, hogs, goats, kids, turkeys, geese, ducks, chickens, pigeons, dogs and cats. More livestock was taken on at the Cape and one list gives: 1 bull, 1 bull-calf, 7 cows, 1 stallion, 3 mares and 3 colts, 44 sheep, 4 goats, 28 boars and breeding sows. They had set out with peas, beans, potatoes and turnips and at Rio and then the Cape they purchased a tremendous range of possibilities: coffee, cocoa beans in the nut, bananas, oranges, lemons, tamarinds, guava-seed, prickly-pear, fig trees, sugar-cane, vines, quinces, apples, pears, strawberries, rice, wheat, barley, maize and more besides.

As well as the government farmyard, officers found room for private stock and stashed away seeds, plants and cuttings. Despite the preparations for a comfortable isolation, farming took painfully slow years to develop. Cattle died at sea or were sacrificed as fresh meat and, by the end of the first year, the remaining herd of two bulls and five cows wandered off into the bush. They were discovered in 1795, multiplying in a fertile area of the Nepean River later known as Cowpastures. Meanwhile, a fresh herd had not arrived for almost four years.

The first public plots were planted east of Sydney Cove (part of the Botanic Gardens is still known as Farm Cove). One of the senior officers, David Collins, recorded: "Some ground having been prepared near his Excellency's House . . . we had the satisfaction of seeing the grape, the fig and the orange, the pear and the apple, those delicious fruits of the old taking root and establishing themselves in the new world." Grain which escaped weevils and hungry mouths appeared and then withered in the poor sandstone soils. A good load of manure would have helped, but there were few animals to provide it. So Phillip took the government farms to a more promising locality, which he named Rose Hill, now Parramatta. "Most of the axes, spades and shovels were the worst that ever were seen," Phillip complained.

But perhaps the greatest handicap was that these were military personnel and city poor, two model groups of consumers. Of the just over one thousand persons landed, it is often said that only one was a farmer, although this undoubtedly undervalues the widespread pastoral and horticultural knowledge of the day.

The first settlement was brutal and ill-fed, bestial and despairingly alcoholic, a lonely and not terribly successful prison-farm. Yet there were pockets of hope, Governor Phillip keeping a vision of a new land before him, and some individuals finding solace in their gardens. The first clergyman, the Reverend Richard Johnson, is claimed to be the first farmer, or, as he referred to himself, "½ a farmer". He did not like the place. The first November he disclosed his "humble opinion" that the government "would act very wisely to send out another fleet and take us all back to England, or to some other place more likely to answer than this poor wretched country, where scarcely anything is to be seen but Rocks or eaten but Rats." But the 35-year-old Yorkshireman had already planted orange pips beside his family's cottage, near modern Bridge Street in central Sydney. He planted corn and vegetables and by the colony's first spring his "little garden" was flourishing.

By August, 1790, when his pips had reached two feet high and were "very promising" and his garden peas doing very well, he had cut two crops of wheat, barley, oats and Indian corn and had collected potatoes, at least a thousand cucumbers and many other vegetables. He revealed this in a letter to an English friend, to whom he remarked that strawberries, raised from a single root which Governor Phillip had brought, had become so abundant that there were scarcely any of the settlers "but who have them in their gardens". He promised his friend that if all went well he would soon drink his health in "a Bumper [brimming glass] of New Holland wine". He stayed on 12 years, acquiring more land and gardening against the gloom.

Phillip's relatively unproductive public farms, using slave labour, were not long being overtaken by individualistic enterprise. The Governor had been empowered to allocate land, and, in a despatch dated June 17, 1790, he reported: "In order to know in what time a man might be able to cultivate a sufficient quantity of ground to support himself, I last November ordered a hut to be built in a good situation, an acre of ground to be cleared, and, once turned up, it was put into the possession of a very industrious convict, who was told if he behaved well he would have thirty acres." James Ruse was paying his way by the next summer. By then, with free grants of 100 acres to officers and 50 acres to privates and other settlers and lesser grants to released convicts, a total of 950 acres had been cleared and cultivated about Sydney and Rose Hill.

By the end of the following year, 1791, 30 emancipists and three men still under sentence had been settled on blocks near Parramatta, modern Carlingford and north of Prospect Hill. Watkin Tench noted that while some of these first emancipists were "in a state of despondency, and predicted that they would starve", others were "tranquil and determined to persevere". On April 2, 1792, the new Lieutenant-Governor, Major Francis Grose, wrote home expressing his amazement. Instead of the bare rocks he had been expecting, he found himself amid gardens which produced all sorts of fruit and vegetables. All that was needed for the colony to become self-sufficient was a shipload of livestock and grain.

Though Phillip might regret that "the period at which this colony will supply its inhabitants with animal food is nearly as distant at present as when I first landed in this country," and have to send to Calcutta for supplies again, in 1792 there was no longer danger of starvation. Indian corn (maize) had been found more suitable than wheat, beginning the forgotten period of its triumph. Norfolk Island, which was highly fertile and easier to clear, had taken more than 1100 people from Port Jackson. In 1794, the rich Hawkesbury settlement was begun and in 1795 a plough was used for the first time. With Arthur Phillip now departed, agriculture was underway.

The first food industry

With the expectation of imported supplies, the food processing industry was slower in setting up. The majority of English people already valued the wheaten loaf, yet no large mill was sent in the early fleets. The 40 hand-mills proved unfit. On July 24, 1790, the Governor wrote to Under-Secretary Nepean: "Windmills will be wanted, and for the sending out of which I am to request that you, sir, will take the necessary steps . . ." A little over a year later, Phillip wrote home that "a windmill is now become absolutely necessary". Yet not until 1797 did Governor Hunter get one going, and Sydney soon clattered with windmills.

On landing, Governor Phillip emancipated James Wright as government baker. Wright supervised the urgent erection of a bakehouse, out of stone from a nearby quarry and with ovens and smokestack of English bricks. For 10 years he baked every sort of flour, frequently maize. The larger houses and first hotels had their own wells, fruit, vegetables, milk, brew houses and ovens. In 1803, the Union hotel was advertised for sale with—in addition to the "choicest fruit-trees"—an "excellent Bakehouse, a capital Oven and every utensil necessary to carry on the Baking Business".

The first beer was brewed by John Boston in 1796, from Indian corn "properly malted" and bittered with the Cape gooseberry. David Collins stated that "Mr Boston found this to succeed so well that he erected at some expense a building proper for the business and was . . . engaged in brewing from the above-mentioned materials." However, Boston's brewery failed after a short time. High consumption of spirits continued to worry early governors and they attempted several importations of hop plants. Soon after 1800, James Squire planted five acres of hops and began brewing, and again not very successfully. Sydney was not the right climate for good brewing.

Yet settlers sought tenaciously to keep food and drink familiar, to retain an Englishness for which we were long to apologise. And it is perhaps surprising how quickly they succeeded, at least to the minimum extent that makes, say, a holiday resort habitable. When Dr Joseph Arnold reached Sydney in 1810, he was enthusiastic. "Thirty years ago this place was entirely forest," he recorded, but "a person coming into Sydney Cove would think himself in the midst of a large city; if he dines on shore he finds all the luxury and elegance of the finest English tables."

Tea, the beverage of empire

After visiting Australia, Percy Rowland wrote in 1903: "Some wag has observed that a merciful Providence delayed the discovery of Australia till after that of tea had rendered it inhabitable." Perhaps this jest contained much truth, since tea was a portable, early "convenience" food, the sort our nation had to be built on. While the Dutch might have shipped in an Indonesian influence to our continent, the Spanish might have imported a food better adapted to Mediterranean latitudes and the French turned this into a gastronomic paradise, their ships had found no industrious peoples to plunder, no exotic potatoes or corn to carry home in triumph, no sugar or other spices to trade, nothing, and passed on. Colonisation of the uncultivated continent had to be supplied from without, like a space expedition. Such a "cold, broken and unnatural form of society" would require the emerging English approach to food.

Tea had arrived in England in the middle of the seventeenth century at the coffee houses of the well-to-do. The East India company ships brought prices down to popular levels, until Jonas Hanway complained in 1757 in his *Essay on Tea* that: "Your very *Chambermaids* have lost their bloom, I suppose, by *sipping tea* . . . What an *army* has *gin* and *tea* destroyed!" Immediately having dropped their charges in NSW, three First Fleet transports were contracted to return to England via China to pick up shipments of the drug of the day. In 1830, the rural romanticist William Cobbett deplored the deliberate replacement of good strong beer by tea, as a stimulant to excessive labour. It is little wonder that Australians, detached from English society at this period, became the world's heaviest tea drinkers. As an easily shipped treasure and tool of imperial expansion, it was singularly appropriate.

In 1748, a visiting Swede Pehr Kalm had remarked that the "art of cooking as practised by most Englishmen does not extend much beyond roast beef and plum pudding." But England expanded the empire not on Sunday dinners but on tea, sugar and flour. Its ships' providores foreshadowed the modern food industry, essentially the business of preserving food for those detached from the soil. The First Fleet carried traditionally-stored foods, like grain, dried peas, cheese and alcoholic beverages. But world trade boomed in such portable commodities as tea, coffee and sugar, products of colonial exploitation. These were joined by all sorts of attempts at extending what we later came to call "shelf-life". For instance, beer had been first bottled in

England in 1736 for export to India. In 1772, Captain Cook had taken the first cases of "portable soup", made by evaporating meat to a virtual glue. It was common on ships visiting Australia until about 1820, when it was dropped in favour of a very important development, tinned meats.

The secret of feeding those removed from the land was the overcoming of food's perishability, the elimination of freshness. The robbing of food's vitality rebounded in the curse of scurvy. It was the first of a list of modern nutritional hazards, which includes pellagra (over-reliance on maize), beri-beri, heart disease and cancers. Not only afflicting sailors, scurvy caused trouble when people shifted to cities—Gideon Harvey, the physician to Charles II, spoke of it as "the Disease of London". It became a common complaint with the highly unnatural diet of Australia, where it was called "Barcoo rot". Incidentally, the cure had been known all along to various medical people, ships' captains and whole nations, which survived frozen winters with herbs. Sensibly noting that the "Sea is naturall for Fishes, and the Land for Men", Sir Richard Hawkins in 1593 was glad to reach Santos, where he obtained fruit, a "certaine remedy for this infirmity". Captain Cook was also noted for conquering scurvy for the British Navy. But the confidence to feed our far-fetched paradise came from more than ships' stores; it came from industrialisation.

The industrialisation of England

In his *The Wealth of Nations* in 1776, the Scottish economist, Adam Smith, mapped out an industrial empire based on the division of labour, the free market and determined colonisation, a project fit for his "nation of shopkeepers". The new glories, it has been said, were inaugurated by the first iron bridge (1779) and the first steam engine (1780). But for the purpose of this book they were signalled by Thomas Robinson's patent (1780) for the first kitchen range—based on the principles of physicist Count Rumford and a firebox with cast-iron oven and boiler on either side. This was the world out of which, in 1787, the fleet of 11 ships had set without fuss.

During the 60 years of transportation, Australia's formative period, capitalism turned England upside down. By 1848, Marx and Engels hailed a feast of rational progress, which rescued people from the "idiocy of rural life". While capitalists had been "clearing whole continents for cultivation", finding new wants to be satisfied from distant climes and battering down Chinese walls with cheap prices, they had reduced culture to a "mere training to act as a machine". It was the Industrial Revolution.

England became the first developing nation by an organic explosion of population pressure, Protestantism and maritime might. During an "age of explorations" (1420–1620), European rivals sought spices and exotic foods and dispersed domestic species among all except the "last continent". The buccanneering British also became the oceans' greatest slave traders, transporting perhaps 4·5 million out of history's 15 million slaves. The scheme combined the immense labour-power of Africa with the seemingly inexhaustible soil of the Americas, where plantations supplied the motherland with tobacco, cotton and cheap sugar, the once rare "spice" of medieval grocers. Simultaneously, England received more reverse "foreign aid" by relieving India, and later China, of spices, cotton goods, silk, gems and tea. The same basic idea was still pushed for Australia—notably by one of Cook's crew, James Matra, and an editor of Adam Smith's works, E. G. Wakefield— only here English landowners took the place of planters, and convicts and assisted migrants replaced slaves.

Meanwhile, also to have a fundamental effect on the food supply, the British Isles had undergone what is termed the agricultural revolution—the industrial revolution of the countryside. The first wave of enclosures—big farmers fencing off the commons—made "fat sheep and lean people" in the thirteenth to sixteenth centuries, and then "hedges became the gravestones of the peasants" from the 1750s to 1820s. Large-scale farming was specialised, produced for distant markets and reduced land and labour to simple cash commodities. The bigger farms produced not just wool but mutton for the expanding cities. This application of capital to agriculture pushed peasants unwillingly off the land. With the social turmoil, a rigorous internal security program made 63 extra crimes into capital offences between 1760 and 1810 and not just petty theft, but primitive forms of industrial rebellion, like destroying a silk loom, throwing down a fence and firing a corn rick. Bread riots became common. Many of those hounded into city slums or arrested were then whisked off to New South Wales. The peak of looting and machine-smashing was reached in the winter of 1830–31, when nine labourers were hanged, about 400 sentences were commuted to imprisonment and 457 to transportation to Van Diemen's Land.

This amounted to the most massive social disruption in human experience. Instead of toiling together in fields, extended families were split up and forced into factories, domestic service, down mines or onto the roads. They lost the mutual aid of village communities and they lost land and old crafts; in other words, they lost access to the means of production. They became dependent on a wage. As for eating and drinking, they were robbed of the cottage diet based on bread, butter and cheese, supplemented with milk, oatmeal and various bits of meat, abundant herbs, plums, apples and cherries, cabbages, carrots and onions, as well as beer, sugar, and tea. The familiar tastes of the immediate countryside, the seasonal succession of tested dishes, the grandeur of peasant cuisine was updated with industrial fare. It took an industrial food to establish an industrial empire. Established at this moment in history, Australia never enjoyed the fruits of peasant society. Our continent was never to be cultivated as the old world had been.

For a glimpse of the new English life, listen to a workman arguing in a radical newspaper, the *Black Dwarf*, for sympathy with striking cotton spinners in Manchester in the year of Marx's birth, 1818:

> Let the advocates for obedience to his master take his stand in an avenue leading to a factory a little before five o'clock in the morning, and observe the squalid appearance of the little infants and their parents taken from their beds at so early an hour in all kinds of weather; let him examine the miserable pittance of food, chiefly composed of water gruel and oatcake broken into it, a little salt, sometimes coloured with a little milk, together with a few potatoes and a bit of bacon or fat for dinner . . . they are allowed no time, except three quarters of an hour at dinner in the whole day: whatever they eat at any other time must be as they work. The Negro slave in the West Indies, if he works under a scorching sun, has probably a little breeze of air sometimes to fan him, he has a space of ground, and time allowed to cultivate it. The English spinner slave has no enjoyment of the open atmosphere and breezes of heaven. Locked up in factories of eight stories high, he has no relaxation till the ponderous engine stops, and then he goes home to get refreshed for the next day; no time for sweet association with his family; they are all alike fatigued and exhausted.

The industrial revolution was partly financed by deliberately reduced living standards, particularly dietary, of the Dickensian working-class. The economic masters pushed potatoes as cheap and nutritious and set the wage so that employees would do with a little flour, potatoes and perhaps milk and pork. In the classic book, *The Englishman's Food* (1939 and 1957), Jack Drummond and Anne Wilbraham wrote: "One does not have to look far to find evidence that during the first 25 years of the nineteenth century the condition of the poorer people, both in town and country, went from bad to worse. Thousands driven to desperation by their terrible struggle for existence faced the horrors of the long voyage to Australia rather than endure the misery at home."

Fortunately, the city brought some pleasures. Take the case of oysters. For centuries oysters were so cheap in London that they were within reach of the poorest. In fact, they were associated with poverty. In Charles Dickens' *Pickwick Papers* (1837), Sam Weller describes Whitechapel: ". . . here's a oyster stall to every half-dozen houses. The street's lined vith 'em. Blessed if I don't think that ven a man's wery poor, he rushes out of his lodgings, and eats oysters in reg'lar desperation . . ." While the custom became impossible about 1850, owing to reckless dredging prompted by London's rapid growth, it survived in dozens of Sydney oyster bars and today Australians are still devoted. However, in general, grim industrialisation made English workers reliant on a crude food industry, the increasing sophistication of which is the subject of the rest of this book. From a "nation of shopkeepers", Australians would inherit a diet of flour, sugar and tea.

THE TASTE FOR HOME

Richmond looking west

MODERN Australians chuckle at attempts by early artists to depict the new land. They made it look so "English". And while some artists had trouble representing the strange flora and fauna, they were more accurate than we accept in portraying the rustic village life here, which seems foreign to our eyes. For, with a lingering taste for the disappearing European countryside, many settlers tried to civilise this continent with traditional comforts.

Alongside James Cook on the "Endeavour" was another very modern person, Joseph Banks, a sophisticated young botanist who had put up £10,000 for scientific equipment and assistants on the ship. He eventually became the influential president of the Royal Society, the centre of the scientific universe. He took a great interest in the continent and has been given the title, "The Father of Australia". He wrote from England to Governor Hunter on March 30, 1797: "In truth, my dear Sir, could it be done by Fortunatus's wishing cap, I have no doubt that I should this day remove myself and family to your quarters and ask for a grant of lands on the banks of the Hawkesbury". Never again setting foot on our soil, he was a distant hand who shaped the colony, especially in its all too slight agrarian ambitions.

He was consulted by government officials and by governors, in whose appointment he had a part. Governor King was his protégé and Bligh his nominee—two governors unusually interested in cultivation. Under Banks' advice, King brought with him the seeds of cabbage, cauliflower, rhubarb, lettuce, celery, melons, onions, radish, turnips, peas and beans. Among letters held by the Mitchell Library are two large volumes rich in correspondence between Banks and Bligh about botanical and horticultural matters. Banks provided the colony with gardeners, like George Suttor, whom he sent in March 1800 in charge of a consignment of plants. Suttor was given 186 acres at Baulkham Hills, which he named Chelsea Farm after his birthplace, built up a nursery and soon was sending oranges and lemons to Sydney.

Another Banks disciple, botanist and explorer Allan Cunningham was induced to become a "Johnny Appleseed" and, as John Dunmore Lang put it, "uniformly to carry along with him a small bag of peach-stones on his exploratory expeditions into the interior; and whenever he found a suitable piece of ground in the wilderness, to dig it up and plant a few of them in it in the hope that the future trees might one day afford a timely supply of food, either to the wandering native, or to Europeans who might accidentally lose their way into the pathless solitudes of the interior." So Joseph Banks, noted for his botanical explorations of this strange land, attempted—not the least by domesticating the country with introduced species—a not inconsiderable civilising task, neglected by the dominant capitalist ethos, but taken up by his associates and a proud tradition of acclimatisation societies and nurseries.

The surprisingly large catalogues of nineteenth-century plant nurseries indicates that such cultivating impulses should not be overlooked, despite the widespread poverty of our attitudes to food. An early Sydney nurseryman, Thomas Shepherd, who established his Darling Nursery on a 28½-acre grant from Governor Darling in 1827, soon offered 70 varieties of apple trees. Take the case of John Smith and Sons in the soon prosperous Mount Macedon area outside Melbourne. By 1869, this nursery advertised 71 kinds of dessert apple trees, of which only Cox's Orange Pippin and Northern Spy would still be familiar, 17 other varieties of English apples, 11 American varieties, 80 kinds of pears (nearly all with French names), not to forget the plums, cherries, nectarines, peaches, apricots and soft fruits. If we turned up the 1887 catalogue of nearby Taylor and Sangster, that nursery alone offered a surprising 70 varieties of gooseberries.

Catalogues, reports, newspapers, books and diaries store countless other cases of the transport of English comforts. One appealing anecdote is contained in the letters of Mary Thomas, who was among Adelaide's first settlers in 1836. She longed for the tastes of home, or even fresh vegetables, although for several weeks a black woman supplied a bunch of native watercress in return for a biscuit, and Mary collected a "sort of samphire" for excellent pickles, and the "leaves of the Hottentot fig", which were also very acceptable. After nearly two years, she was moved to write home to her brother, "It is only a childish whim, for I fancy I could relish a bit of Hampshire bacon more than anything to be got here, and if you can prevail on Mr Kinggate to pay you for two flitches out of my money from the bank interest I would be glad to have them." A month later, she wrote asking George to add four or six hams and a pot of good honey and "about five or six dozen of Isle of Wight cracknels, for which Southhampton is so famous ... You will perhaps think me very childish to send 16,000 miles for a pot of honey and a few biscuits, but I am so attached to my native country, and especially to my native county and its productions, that I fancy nothing like them."

By April the following year, she was describing the quickly maturing fruit in her orchard, which "brings me to mention a whim I have lately taken into my head . . . two or three bushels of apples . . . Further, six or eight dried chappers, a chapper being a part of a pig I am particularly fond of, especially when cut and smoked in the Hampshire fashion . . ." and, finally, for she had nearly forgotten one thing, slips of apple and pear trees for her orchard . . . "Likewise, I want a root of rhubarb . . . You will think me very silly, but I cannot help it, for I have such a desire for something English that nothing else gives me any pleasure." Here she was, ordering more delicacies, before the first shipment arrived.

Ten months after the original letter, Mary Thomas explained to her brother that—following a drought, several months without vegetables, the cattle driven beyond the mountains for feed and generally high prices—"you will realise housekeeping is no joke here." She still had no kitchen, using the outdoor fire for cooking, and, by the way, she hoped the apples had been shipped, "for, I assure you, I long to taste them, not having touched fruit, except melons for more than three years."

Waiting was a tremendous strain. As she eventually revealed to her brother, "I really long so much to hear from you that when an English ship comes in it makes me quite nervous till the mail arrives, and when I find myself disappointed of a letter I am almost ready to cry." However, on March 15, 1840, after waiting exactly one year and a half, she wrote an excited postscript: "We have received the bacon and hams, and excellent they are; such a treat as I, at least, have not had since I have been in the colony. The cracknels were as fresh as if they were just out of the oven, but the pot of honey, I am sorry to say, was broken." By scraping it up and clarifying it, she "saved about a pound of as fine honey as I ever saw", and immediately ordered yet another hamper of everything.

Mary Thomas had described the first Christmas Day in Adelaide, three days even before the colony was proclaimed. "We kept up the old custom . . . as far as having a plum pudding for dinner, likewise a ham and a parrot pie . . ." she recorded. And she later discovered one of her neighbours actually had enjoyed roast beef, "though we were not aware at the time that any fresh meat was to be had in the colony". The fact was that Captain Duff's cow had fallen into a lagoon and was so injured it was expedient to kill her. The continuation of a quite unseasonal feast—"plum pudding at 100 degrees in the shade"—is perhaps the most oft-remarked Australian food oddity. After devoting a chapter of his *Australian Colonists* (1974) to the habit, the historian K. S. Inglis remarked, "It would long be an Australian tradition to enjoy both the heavy Christmas dinner and the absurdity of it." More than a joke, it was clear evidence that we had not made a home here.

2
Meat three times a day

With the success of grazing, bush workers ate meat, damper and billy-tea at every meal. The small "Dungaree" settlers on the Hawkesbury, attempting the peasant alternative, were harrassed and ridiculed

IF JOHN MACARTHUR is to be credited for starting Australia's ride on the sheep's back, then he ought also to be blamed for putting us on the road to appalling cuisine. He was ringleader of the opportunist syndicate surrounding the NSW Corps, which overthrew a governor and whose activities stunted the colony's economy and agriculture. Macarthur and other budding capitalists pioneered an industry which had profitably replaced peasants in Britain—grazing. After the 1813 crossing of the Blue Mountains and encouragement from Commissioner Bigge's report for the British government in 1822, the rich adventurers bought stock, acquired a small complement of shepherds from the largely male, rootless population, and squatted on land "further out". Ironically, the grasslands had been created by burning-off by the Aborigines, who thus hastened their own downfall.

Grazing's success turned us into a nation of meat eaters, an impossible dream back home. More profoundly, the maintenance and, indeed, glorification of the drifting, shiftless way of life prevented the food supply from ever really out-growing the convict stage. The itinerant workforce, the founders of so many working-class traditions, were paid in rations. Handed out on Saturday nights in unreliable measures and supplemented by spirits and a final cheque, their food eventually earned the name, "Ten, Ten, Two & a Quarter", because it usually was:

10 lb flour; 10 lb meat; 2 lb sugar; ¼ lb tea; salt.

This became the characteristic and monotonous diet for Australia's first century. Contemporary accounts, job advertisements and political debates referred again and again to the rations, whether on land or sea. They dominated life like no other foods before or since. Milk was no use since it quickly went off. Butter and cheese, which had been methods for keeping cream through the northern hemisphere winter, were no better, even with over-salting. Fresh fruit and vegetables needed good water, a modicum of stability and effort. The starkness of a limited, year-round fare suited the all-male, brutalised society.

Arriving by long sea voyage, Australians had to pass a curious form of fitness test—enduring the artificial fare of ship's rations. Historian Russel Ward has pointed out that 40 years after the First Fleet, 87 per cent of the population were either convicts, emancipists or "currency", who were generally the children of convicts. Even in 1851, 59 per cent came from the convict side. So the population was reared on prison rations. When they laboured on bond for settlers, they hoped for something approaching the same weekly sustenance. When they joined the great, wandering bush workforce, they received the same from the squatters. And if they worked along the coast in boats it was the same treatment. For instance, court records show that a gang of sealers signed on in 1804 by Simeon Lord, an emancipist turned entrepreneur, were to receive a weekly ration of seven pounds of meat, ten of flour or biscuit, one pound of sugar, together with ten bags of rice "for the voyage" and "tea or grain for coffee". The sealers were often stranded in the unknown oceans—becoming used to wallaby, mutton bird, seal flesh and oil, seaweed, birds' eggs and fish—and, if rescued, the men were compensated with 10 shillings for each week of exhausted rations.

Even when they went into business for themselves as timber-getters, they carried the same stocks. If setting up as settlers, they continued to import the same chests of China tea, bags of salt and sugar and kegs of rum from the capital. Only the biggest or most thorough installed a garden, let alone a bread oven. Although Australians would be among the first to install the new iron stoves, for the first 70 years at least, the dominant means of cooking was an open fire, whether at a campsite, or in a hut or cottage. With the necessary implements—a tomahawk, knife, quart-pot and frying-pan—the rations made:

A damper; a fry of meat; pots of tea.

The damper was flour and water, without leavening. The meat was salted pork, corned beef and then slaughtered mutton cooked without aging. The tea, though taken with plenty of sugar, generally lacked the refinement of milk. The rations became the source, as nutritionists might note, of today's dietary distortion, and, as gourmets might note, of gastronomic disaster.

The Reverend David Mackenzie wrote in the 1840s that "no personal

female attractions, however great, can long remain scatheless against beef-
steaks at breakfast, cold beef at noon lunch, roast and boiled beef at dinner and
cold beef at tea or supper." Equally discouraging, W. W. Dobie in 1856 talked
of the "muttonous" diet. A young Frenchman, Edmond Marin La Meslée,
concluded when the country had been conquered not quite a century: "It is
true to say that no other country on earth offers more of everything needed
to make a good meal, or offers it more cheaply, than Australia; but there is
no other country either where the cuisine is more elementary, not to say
abominable." "The average Australian takes no aesthetic pleasure in food,"
wrote Melbourne playwright Louis Esson in 1918. "This country was
pioneered on corned beef and damper," he said. "That is why the Australian
in general takes plain and heavy food, looking askance on anything exotic,
and why the general run of our restaurants lack enterprise and variety."

Early bush life

Not given the three Rs, the convict side rarely left the same historical
accounts as their superiors and few first-hand reports remain of the rations.
In the racy novel of around 1840, *The Adventures of Ralph Rashleigh*, the
author (probably James Tucker) showed our early fare to be the cause of
prison despair, murder by starving felons and moments of happiness.
Fortunately, too, a clergyman's son, Alexander Harris, fell into sufficiently
bad ways that he left a series of books, notably *Settlers and Convicts*, written
under the name of an "Emigrant Mechanic", with such a conscientious and
powerful record of ordinary bush life between 1826 and 1841 that they
helped create the mateship legend.

When first timber splitting in the Illawarra district, Harris appreciated the
permutations permitted by the rations. He wrote:

> We were up by day-break, worked for about two hours, and then had our
> breakfast, which was of damper, salt pork fried, and good tea—for tea and
> sugar are used among bushmen very prodigally. My mate and myself often
> used a pound of tea and six pounds of sugar between us in a week... After
> breakfast we pelted away until twelve o'clock, and then had dinner, which
> was damper, pork, and tea again, and laid down till the heat of the day was
> over, which was about three o'clock where we were. We then worked for
> another hour, had a lunch of damper, and tea, and pork, and knocked along
> till night. At about 8 pm we had our supper, pork, tea, and damper, and
> soon after 9 were under the blankets.

But this monotony didn't stop them employing a little art. Harris described
making a damper. After kneading the flour and water a couple of minutes, he
said the dough was flattened into a cake, not more than 1½ or 2 inches thick,
and any diameter as required. Then the ashes were pushed aside and, to take
up his story, "on the glowing smooth surface thus exposed the cake is lightly

deposited, by being held over it on the open hands, and the hands suddenly drawn from under it. The red ashes are then lightly turned back over the cake with the shovel. In the course of twenty minutes or half an hour on removing the ashes, the cake is found excellently baked; and with a light duster, or the tuft of a bullock's tail, every vestige of the ashes is switched off, and the cake, if the operations have been well conducted, comes to table as clean as a captain's biscuit from a pastry-cook's shop." The word "damper" was first recorded in 1827, according to student of Australian terms, S. J. Baker. Its derivation was long considered to be unknown, although modern scholars have asserted that it comes from an English word for a snack. It could refer to the damping of the flour, the fire, or, in this case, the appetite.

Harris found little other food. Of the native plants, he mentioned the cabbage tree, a lofty palm (*Livistona australis*) whose outer leaves expose a heart which he thought was "very similar when dressed to cabbage". It was a favourite food, but removal of the apical bud killed the tree. He also noted manna fallen from gum trees (actually exuded by feeding insects). He said a little was nice, but much nauseated. It sometimes replaced sugar in tea, being most palatable in tea made of the "pennyroyal" (mint creeper) which the shepherds were so fond of.

Beer wasn't easy to brew or transport for the first hot century; which left us to drink much more potent and thus portable spirits, particularly rum early on from Bengal. The bushmen coming together at the head station for the week's rations established the tradition of "work and burst" or, as the men said, they would "earn their money like horses and spend it like asses". At the end of a contract, the lump sum was blown at the nearest grog shanty or in the inns of the country township or, best of all, in the "big smoke". This was the "spree", which the Oxford dictionary says is a nineteenth-century word of unknown origin. Time and time again the more schooled observers of Australian life recorded, with scarcely concealed revulsion, the crude, brawling nights they heard through the thin walls of pubs. Harris was more sympathetic. He described a party of free men at a grog house (unlicensed but where police "helped the spree on"). With the full intention of having "only one half-pint" of rum before going, that one led to a second, the second to a third, and so on till the "count was lost in the unfathomable obscurities of a publican's conscience."

Arrivals found the Australian bush pretty terrifying, and so too did the lonely bushman. Harris escaped in smoking, singing, yarning and eating. An evening spent frying pancakes unusually "plentiful of eggs" led him to ask: "Who has not felt how agreeable it is sometimes to be thoughtless?" This was the legendary mateship. On the move, the custom was to share the floor, bedding, fire and food at the nearest bush hut. Long after these had evolved into grog shanties and pubs, often only richer travellers paid. "As full two-thirds of the labouring population of the country is in perpetual migration, the custom is a very proper one," Harris claimed. The men sharing damper, tea, meat, rum, tobacco, songs and stories worked out how to cook cockatoo: "Boil the bird with a boot. When it's done, throw away the bird and eat the boot." Or, "Roast the cockatoo stuffed with a handful of rocks. The bird's ready when the rocks are tender." Bullockies commemorated the terrible time when, as written in June 1859, "the dog sat on the tuckerbox, five miles from Gundagai." The word meant "shat", giving point to the story. The word "tucker" was not recorded until mid-century, presumably being a variation of an English word, "tuck", as in tuck-shop.

Nothing in Australian folklore carried more symbolic significance than "billy", declared historian Russel Ward when theorising about its origin. Previous guesses had put the derivation as the Aboriginal "billa" (for river or water, as in billabong), the French "bouilli" (from which also came "bully beef" and a common label on preserved meat tins commonly usurped for tea-making) and the Scottish "bally" (for milk-pail) and "billypot" (cooking utensil). They all sound convincing and Ward further confirmed human ingenuity by suggesting it was named after King William IV. His evidence came from James F. O'Connell's *A Residence of Eleven Years*, which referred to a big bush kettle as a "royal George". Ward proposed that when George IV died in 1830 this became a "royal William", after the new king, hence a "William" and hence "billy". Certainly, this name of our handy metal container with wire handle was not common enough to be recorded until about the time of G. B. Wilkinson's *Working Man's Handbook* of 1849.

Food provided lean pleasure in a lonely, brutal world, in which men, packed off to the end of the earth, were held on basic rations, were under the threat of flogging before the local magistrate and, in turn, poisoned the flour of difficult Aborigines. However, within this society was a group, neglected by both the historians of Macarthur's fabulous merino and the historians of mateship, and of great fascination to those interested in food.

The Dungaree settlers

When the author Alexander Harris reached Sydney in 1826, he found a scattered waterside town, and "if it be a breezy day the merry rattling pace of its manifold windmills, here and there perched on the high points, is no unpleasing sight." The relative abundance of hills over streams meant most millers employed wind over water, he explained. Strolling to the marketplace, an open area with rough stalls and near today's Market Street, he reported a novelty to him, that horsefeed was not hay but coarse green grass. He also found little wheat and much maize. He was surprised, too, to find vegetables arriving from the "Curryjong Mountains", 40 miles away, a very long day by bullock cart. Within good bowshot of the markets were the wharves where the great numbers of market boats unloaded produce from the Parramatta and Lane Cove Rivers and timber from up and down the coast. Foreign merchandise, subject to duty, landed at the King's wharf further seawards.

When he repaired to the Market House for a drink, instead of the "refreshing beer of Old England", he engaged in "that frightfully pernicious habit of the colony, drinking rum neat out of wine-glasses". And he found some intriguing companions. Mostly former convicts, a good many Englishmen and Irishmen, and here and there a woman, they boasted about their bullocks, the productiveness of their farms, and the amount of work they could perform. "There was no offensive intrusiveness about their civility; every man seemed to consider himself just on a level with all the rest," he noted. They wore all sorts of clothes: "the blue jacket and trousers of the English lagger, the short blue cotton smock-frock and trousers, the short woollen frock and trousers, fustian jacket and trousers, and so forth". Harris's description of their dress is pertinent, because these people—the small farmers bringing food to Sydney—had a name connected with their familiar blue garb. "From their frequently clothing themselves, their wives and children in that blue Indian manufacture of cotton", he said, they were known as the "Dungaree settlers".

The Dungarees farmed along the Hawkesbury, near Windsor and Richmond. By June, 1795, when more than 400 already lived in the seductive, fertile 50-km stretch of the river, they had been involved in the colony's first major clash with the natives, and in September the first of the serious floods hit them; there were to be a further six in the next 15 years. The first settlers had been convicts rewarded with 30 acres each for industrious habits. With little experience, no animals for manure or pulling ploughs, only five remained of the original 85 by 1805. Nevertheless, the desire for independence, and encouragement from agriculturally-inclined governors, especially Bligh, brought replacements, struggling to establish an historically identifiable way of life. They were real evidence in this otherwise largely untilled country that you can't quite stamp out gardeners.

Alexander Harris could not conceal his delight when he looked down about 1830 on the "fine expanse of rich cultivated ground" in the valley near Richmond:

> I felt at once I was in the land of the husbandman. Whichever way I looked I could see fields of the tall green Indian corn (maize), with its tassel tops, bending and waving under the fresh breeze that was sweeping over it. Here again a square of orchard loaded with splendid peaches broke the uniformity of the surface; there a piece of ground new ploughed or with the teams at work upon it, and here a square of wheat stubble on which a boy tended a herd of pigs as they picked up the scattered grain, still further varied the prospect—and every few fields apart some more or less simple edifice marked the homestead. In some places it was no more than the bark hut of a few feet area, with its own dungheap and stack; in others it was

the capacious and costly mansion surrounded by farm buildings of all sorts, and abundance of grain.

On making his way through this tract, he discovered all sorts of vegetables and fruit trees. There were:

excellent figs, gooseberries, currants, lemons, oranges, melons, peaches as large as a good sized breakfast cup and of the most exquisite flavour; potatoes, pumpkins as big as a large bucket, cabbages, radishes, onions, beans, pease; in short everything of the kind profusely produced and of the most superior quality. In one place I saw a whole cart-load of the most delicious peaches going along the road; and on asking the driver where he was taking them to market, he said they were for the pigs, and that all the season through they gathered a similar load every other day from under the trees in the orchard for the same purpose.

Later, he went on to find: "every house and hut had its wheaten or maize cake, its joint of pork or beef, and its fragrant pot of tea ready for the traveller. Occasionally a niggard or a helpless spendthrift was found; but such were the exceptions to the rule." The chief vegetable was the pumpkin, which he preferred to anything English; and the chief fruit was watermelons, "the size, the colour, and delicious refreshing coolness of which, eaten during the three hours of mid-day heat when most farming people pause for a time from their field labour, it would be impossible for me to describe by mere words." While elsewhere men far outnumbered women, the settled Hawkesbury families produced a balanced population, so that Harris was struck by the "very general prettiness of the native white girls".

For his part, "Ralph Rashleigh" too was spellbound by the women, and included mention of the tendency for women to dress as men, probably for safety. He was attracted by one honest family, including daughters, labouring in the fields. When he stopped over, he noticed hanging in the chimney pieces of salt beef and pork, pigs' heads, bags of cabbage and pumpkin seeds—everything that needed to be kept dry. Having, in his convict misery, at last found a neat, English-looking cottage, he sat down to the same food as most of the colonists ate, but "prepared with that care that bespeaks of a gentle character". The pork had been soaked to make it less salty, and the pumpkins, besides having been pared before boiling, had been steamed after they were done; the bread was leavened and baked in a great loaf under an inverted iron pot, making it more enticing than the ordinary damper. The Dungaree settlers, or their convict labourers, drove carts laden with grain, hay, vegetables, fruit and fowls twice weekly along the Great Western road to the Sydney market. Rashleigh found a woman drunk in her bullock cart, a small keg of rum on the floor, and also carrying home tobacco, sugar, tea, cotton shirts and one or two pairs of duck trousers.

Against Harris and Rashleigh's idyllic pictures, other contemporary descriptions of the Dungarees were surprisingly uncomplimentary. They presented them as "slovenly", "given to debauchery", "idle", "negligent", "improvident" and "drunken". Out of 149 persons in 1820 settled on their own properties at Windsor, Richmond, Wilberforce, Portland Head and Pitt Town, the Reverend Mr Cartwright could name only 83 whom he considered "industrious and well disposed, living upon their property and educating their children". James Atkinson, when describing NSW agriculture in 1826, said their farms exhibited "nothing but a scene of confusion, filth and poverty". But defending them against Atkinson, the *Sydney Gazette* published: "It is to the exertions of these very men that the Colony is indebted for almost everything."

In his study of the first 50 years of NSW agriculture, C. J. King decided in 1948 that the story of the small settler was a "very sad one—pathetic is perhaps the proper description". They were the "victims not alone of the elements and of a peculiarly harsh and forbidding country, but of monopolists who had preyed on their defencelessness". In the worst days of the rum traffic, the public stores were fixed so that they could not get the full value of their crops. An Impounding Act throttled all attempts at pig-raising, the only form of stock ownership open to them. They continued "miserably poor, living a hand-to-mouth existence, hundreds of them succeeding each other, three-fourths of them being probably bankrupted". The big farmers have continually overseen the ruin of the small person in Australia and the potential political explosiveness in those days is illustrated by a couple of incidents.

When the Irish convicts at Castle Hill revolted in 1804 (an event held by some to be more dramatic than Eureka), they set off unsuccessfully for the Hawkesbury, where they hoped to collect such a force that they might march on Sydney. Again, when Bligh was arrested in John Macarthur's Rum Rebellion of 1808, the Governor's only hope had been "my getting into the interior of the country adjacent to the Hawkesbury, where I knew the whole body would flock to my standard". This might have been optimistic, but Bligh, who had his own farm in the district, had done much to encourage, in his words, the "industrious settler-farmers" against those "who consider themselves of the superior class". Dressed in the antecedents of today's blue jeans, the Dungarees represent the nearest to an Australian peasantry. Those who oppose what Macarthur stood for should put these settlers into the history books, with their American-like, pioneer food of "Hawkesbury duck" (a roasted cob of maize), hominy, pork, pumpkin, peaches and water melons.

Civilising the bush

The Australian economy was founded on the proposition that a working-class would labour in the bush, offices and households under the direction of what was often called the middle-class. Various ploys were devised to raise and maintain the large and dependent workforce, especially for the dominant grazing industry. The convicts were ideal, but to keep up the labour supply, the authorities had to mount free emigration schemes, increasingly in the 1830s. These struck trouble since the country's natural wealth was too accessible and employees deserted for their own projects. So, E. G. Wakefield found support for his ideas of keeping land prices artificially high and out of reach of poorer immigrants—and the money from land sales paying their fares.

On the other hand, two notable colonists endeavoured to encourage a more "industrious" population, who might dot the wilderness with village steeples. The Presbyterian leader, the Reverend John Dunmore Lang, delighted in challenging the squatters and advocated replacing wool-growing (with its "semi-savage" population scattered over vast tracts of country and isolated from humanising influences) with cotton-growing, and its "beautiful picture of numerous rural communities . . . each with its long line of smiling cottages, its village church and its district school".

And the Catholic activist Caroline Chisholm, who arrived in 1838, wrote: "To give a poor man the chance of getting *good* land, is a proposal that has never been made; surely it can never be said that one of the strongest impediments in the way of emigration, is the dread that the poor would too soon become rich?" Short-sighted masters preferred single men, since they were cheaper to maintain and usually less anxious to get off the rations than men with "encumberances". Just as Lang repeatedly visited Europe to import entire communities, Caroline Chisholm sought to repair the "monstrous disparity" between the sexes by introducing women to the bush. She argued that employers must offer more than a single man's "10, 10, 2 & ¼" so that families might survive. For them, she asked a wage around the single person's level (£12 to £15 a year), but with a "generous weekly ration including 20 lbs meat, 20 lbs flour, 6 oz soap, milk of 2 cows, and a half an acre of ground for gardening".

She took caravans of immigrants through the countryside, finding them positions. "Stop! stop!" shouted a rough bushman, according to one report. "Are you Mrs Chisholm?" "Yes, what do you want?" "Want—want—why, what every man like me wants when he sees Mrs Chisholm. Come now, do look up that hill, and see that nice cottage and 40 acres under crop; and I have in it 20 hams and flitches of bacon, and a chest of tea, and bag of sugar; the land is paid for, and the three cows . . ." He pulled out character references. "Come now, Mrs Chisholm, do be a mother to me, and give me a wife."

To attract emigrants, especially eligible brides, she collected "voluntary information" from the people of NSW. The advertisements provide a believable picture of at least the luckiest of the little settlers. Her pitch was encapsulated in the title of a small booklet published in London in 1847. It was called *Comfort for the Poor! Meat Three Times a Day!!* In Statement No 25, John I ---, sent from Dublin in 1829, had told Chisholm: "Have tea and meat three times a day—I like a pot of tea to be handy by my fire for any body travelling by." The slogan "Meat Three Times a Day" became the boast of nineteenth-century Australia.

In attempts to make the settlers' life easier, Caroline Chisholm has occasionally been credited with publishing Australia's first recipe book. The only justification I've found is the short section on "Bush-Cookery" contained in Eneas Mackenzie's *Emigrants' Guide to Australia* (1853). The two pages were sub-headed, "From an unpublished MS. by Mrs Chisholm". It gave hints on how to vary the monotonous rations. The idea was to divide the flour into three parts (one for dumplings and pancakes and two for dampers) and to divide the meat into seven portions, one for each day. The best cut should be used on Sunday, when the men congregated. It was soaked on Saturday, then beaten with a rolling-pin and put into flour paste and boiled. This made a "very nice pudding", known in the bush as "Station-Jack". On Monday was recommended a stew put on top of a pancake and kept hot "until your husband comes home, and then he will have a palatable dish called 'The Queen's Nightcap'." Tuesday's "Trout Dumplings" were of mere flour and beef, so named because the only way to extract the dumplings from a boiling six-gallon iron pot was said to be with fishing tackle. Wednesday could bring a "Stewed Goose", a stew covered in crust. Thursday offered boiling beef and dumplings. Friday—"Beefsteak pudding, if Catholics, *fish* for your dinner." And finally, on Saturday the even shorter instruction was, "Beef à-la-mode", a common recipe for braising beef. Meat could prove a tiresome luxury.

In agrarian societies, industrialisation broke up the extended family. In Australia, it worked the other way, putting together the nuclear family in a country of lonely itinerants. Lang and Chisholm helped promote the potent ideal of the husband-and-wife team working its own land. However, the dominant economic force encouraged the basic social unit of wage-earner and unpaid housewife to remain dependent on industry for food.

The Irish influence

No group thrived in this landless role like the Irish, because they had long been viciously robbed of their agriculture. For a group who had learned to survive on the potato, the addition of beef and mutton in a new land must have seemed luxury indeed. They were unlikely to demand much variety or quality in their food. They were the prototypes of modern Australians.

The Irish famines of 1845–47 climaxed more than three centuries of English repression. In successive orgies of brutality, the invaders had slaughtered the population, burnt their houses, laid waste their crops and livestock, stamped out their language and religion and told jokes against them. After one early rampage in 1580, it was said that "the lowing of a cow, or the voice of the ploughman, was not to be heard that year from Dingle to the Rock of Cashel". It's a story documented in one of the greatest books on food, Redcliffe N. Salaman's *The History and Social Influence of the Potato* (1949). For, as he explains, the continual devastation reduced the Irish from a rich culture and agriculture to an impoverished life sustained by a single, safely-stored, nutritious arrival, the potato. It has been claimed that between 1645 and 1652 Oliver Cromwell's troops killed as many as five-sixths of the people—the remnants surviving on the new root. The result was like a painfully drawn-out agricultural revolution, with English landlords establishing their own estates for grazing and grains.

The resultant way of life repelled and dismayed many visitors, with families and their pig sharing both a simple hut and solitary item of furniture, the potato pot. In 1727, Jonathan Swift wrote his famous "A Modest Proposal", suggesting that Irish children should be fattened and eaten, solving both hunger and over-population. Swift had just toured the island, with heavy heart recording: "Whatever stranger took such a journey would be apt to think himself travelling in Lapland or Iceland rather than in a country so favoured by nature as ours. The miserable dress and diet and dwelling of the people, the families of farmers who pay great rents living in filth and nastiness upon buttermilk and potatoes, not a shoe or stocking to their feet, or a house so convenient as an English hog-sty to receive them". In the mid-nineteenth century, a Melbourne visitor to Ireland, Dr Daniel Curdie, noted his dismay at the contrast of 90,000 sheep grazing on the fine property of an absentee English landlord, while over the fence the Irish tenants scratched for a living. The potato would take no more than three months work, leaving the rest of the year to feed the pig or cow needed to pay the rent, or to cut turf. Eating virtually nothing but potatoes, the bulk of the Irish became "slaves" to easy feeding.

In 1862, the German philosopher Ludwig Feuerbach decided, in a neat pun, "Der Mensch ist was er isst" (Man is what he eats). He applied this theory to the Irish: "You cannot conquer, for your sustenance can only arouse a paralysing despair not a fiery enthusiasm. And only enthusiasm will be able to fight off the giant [the English] in whose veins flow the rich, powerful, deed-producing blood [roast beef]." On the contrary, diet did not so much determine character as reveal social malaise. As Salaman pointed out, the Irish had lost their freedom before they found the potato. "If inertia in human affairs ranks as laziness, then the Irishman was lazy, and with good reason," Salaman commented. In his view, the potato was a perfect instrument of suppression—not because it was a lowly food, but because it was such a good food. When the crop failed, as it did most spectacularly in 1845, the entire society collapsed, a warning against ever losing husbanding skill and independence.

More than one-third of Australians in our formative years were of Irish descent. They came as convicts, sent out for political crimes or sent on from English cities for rebelling in the only ways they knew, and they came as assisted migrants. John Sherer reported in *The Gold-finder in Australia* (1853) meeting a high-spirited Irishwoman on the way to dig for gold. "Digging," said she, "by the powers, I've done nothing but dig all mi life in mi own country . . . Ireland's as good a country as iver was blest with a dacent pisantry, but for the landlords and parlimintin rogues that has been its curse this manny a day. I'm sure a bit of mate, unless it wur pork, never entered my mout from Sonday to Sonday; and if a man gets fat on beef there, sure it's only wi looking at the mate on the bones of the living bullock . . . for a poor woman that's able and willing to work, there's no country in the world to equal this. Is there, Make?" "No, indeed!" said Mike. "It bates Ireland itself, only the 'tatoes are not so good: but the beef and the mutton make up for that."

The Irish peasantry, apart from occasionally adding mashed potato to bread dough, employed but one method of preparing potatoes, boiling, and but one utensil, the cauldron. It was always a circular pot, with two side handles and three legs, and either hung above the open fire, or stood over the hot ashes. Originally made of pottery, the cauldron was used as early as 1500 BC; bronze forms occurred a thousand years later and iron replaced it in the sixteenth century. Such pots were found in colonial America. And a relatively modern version, with smallish handles and three decorative ribs, was common in Australia. It was called a "camp oven". For roughly the first century, Australia's humble home cooked with the same cauldron as the Irish.

As for another sign that the Irish found this a home away from home, visitor after visitor in early years complained about extraordinary drunkenness. John Dunmore Lang, who believed the people should be taken off whisky and shown the pleasures of light wine, conducted a vehement campaign against "swamping" NSW with Irish. He claimed that the first object of the Irishman was to be employed as a constable, which enabled a life of comparative inaction, and the second ambition was to obtain a licence to keep a public house. In early years this had been easily obtained, he said, since visiting magistrates were "not infrequently" wholesale liquor importers.

Such comments reflected the prejudices of middle-class observers and, in Lang's case, unabashed anti-Catholicism. However, I can accept that the Irish helped keep our drinking separate from our eating. Pubs in Ireland, even today, could be models for the typical Australian pub: male, uncivilised by food and compellingly popular. Drunkenness is escape and the Irish long had troubles. They were in a sense practised in the modern helplessness which hit Australia hard, and still does. The Irish, with their enforced neglect of the food arts and resort to alcohol, were ideally suited to uncultivated Australia.

EATING AND DRINKING IN 1839

The "impressive" new Sydney market

ARRIVING in 1839, the bride of a successful squatter, Louisa Anne Meredith recorded *Notes and Sketches of NSW* of her first heady months. Her book gives a new arrival's view of colonial eating and drinking. Although she pretended "no great judgement as a gastronome", she attended to the food, from her well-to-do perspective. Meredith found Sydney's "impressive" new market building "well supplied", the display of fruit in the grape season being very beautiful. She noted abundant, cheap peaches and Van Diemen's Land apples, frequently sold at sixpence each. She discovered loquats, a "pleasant acid berry", and the "detestable" prickly pear. Orange groves and vineyards along the Parramatta supplied the "metropolis" with most of its fruit, and she found a very different type of lemon and a pretty, fragrant fruit called a "mandarin" orange. One approved method of eating the enormous "water-melons", which she thought insipid but which were seen piled up like huge cannon-balls at all fruit-shop doors, was to cut a hole, pour in a bottle of Madeira or sherry, and mix it into a cold pulp.

She was impressed by the fish, particularly the plentiful and cheap rock-oysters, the smaller crayfish and the whiting was perhaps best of all. The schnapper was very nice, "though not esteemed a proper dish for a dinner-party". She never saw any native fish at a Sydney dinner-table, the preserved or cured cod and salmon from England being served instead at a considerable expense, and to her taste, not comparable with the cheap fresh fish. "Being expensive, it has become 'fashionable', and that circumstance reconciles all things," she explained. She learnt of several good inns, much frequented by bachelor settlers, and one to which when married they took their families. "Whilst you are served with 'King's pattern' plate, and by half a dozen waiters, you miss many of the commonest comforts to be found in every wayside hostel at home." When the Merediths moved to their estate, "Homebush", on the Parramatta River, she found that while the gardens might be "small editions of Paradise", the want of water was a curse which no dweller in England could imagine. She suffered dust, hot winds, and ants, which "bury themselves in sugar and drown in jam, cream, custards or tarts".

The worship of Mammon reigned triumphant, status being accorded at once to the rich, she said. "No 'lady' in Sydney (your grocers' and butchers' wives included) believes in the possibility of walking," she wrote. "Most gentlemen have their whole souls so felted up in wools, fleeces, flocks and stock that I have often sat through a weary dinner and evening of incessant talking, without hearing a single syllable on any other subject." The colonial ladies spoke of aught besides dress, domestic events and "bad servants". Single men could not be assigned female convicts, but married people applied for them, free women demanding such exorbitant wages. When you had domestics they were usually drunk. Praise some cookery and your friend would reply: "Ah! yes, she is an excellent cook, but we can so seldom keep her sober". Meredith heard of a Christmas dinner party assembled as long as patience would endure, the bell being rung without reply, and the hostess, proceeding to the kitchen, finding every servant either gone out or rendered incapable of moving.

Like so many travellers, she was struck by the desolate ring-barking. Unlike England's planted groves and woods, here, unless a settler saw a bare, unvaried, shadeless, dusty expanse, he fancied his dwelling remained "wild and uncivilised", she said. As for the habitations of the working-class (for poor there were none), instead of neat clean cottages with vegetable-plot, herbs and sweet flowers, she found wretched hovels of heaped turf or "slabs", and out front heaps of ashes, chips, broken bottles, old casks, rags, bones and shoes . . . "Not a herb, not a cabbage is to be seen". Adjoining one uncomfortable Blue Mountains inn, she found a "small plot of potato-ground, but no attempt at neatness or improvement"; and around the back—in "one vast undistinguished rubbish-heap"—she detected a "large conversazione of pigs" and, finally, several children "lying or lounging about in close companionship with the pigs".

At country pubs, "What can you give us to eat?" brought one universal reply: "''Am an' eggs, Sir". Mutton chops formed the usual accompaniment. "So ham and eggs we had, and mutton-chops too; but from their being fried all together, in the same dark-complexioned fat, the taste of these viands was curiously similar, and both of impenetrable hardness," she said. "The frying pan is in perpetual requisition, and seems to have scarcely time to cool between its performances; that, and a small iron pot in which the tea and coarse sugar are boiled together, form the sole cooking utensils of many a labourer's household." Tea, at every meal, was the colonial kitchen beverage, and the quantity of meat eaten at least thrice a day might well have compensated for the loss of beer. And there was the damper, which she considered "exceeds in closeness and hard heaviness the worst bread or pudding I ever had". It was the "worst way of spoiling flour", an "indigestible food". In the bush, where brewer's yeast could not be procured, and people were too idle or ignorant to manufacture a substitute, this "excellent damper of a good appetite" was the only bread used. When she arrived, flour cost £10 16s per quarter, so that ground maize, boiled rice and other things were added to the bread. Yet, such was the desire for it to be white, that she did not remember one instance of the flour being unsifted, which would have provided more, healthier, but brown bread.

I have complained that Australian food is distinctively detached from the soil. Louisa Anne Meredith reflected upon this after being served by a dissolute young woman at the "Rivulet" resting place just over the Blue Mountains. After the repast, Meredith had strolled down to the banks of the rivulet, where the verdure of the flats showed how excellent a garden might be made. But she feared it never would. "Idleness and drinking are such besetting sins," she observed, "that nothing demanding bodily exertion is attempted. Meat can run about and feed itself on the wild hills, and flour they can buy; fruit and vegetables they 'don't heed', as they would demand some little labour to produce." It was, sure enough, a lazy food, but it was not through sin, it was because people like her grazier husband constructed life that way, keeping a mostly male workforce on rations and ruining cultivating elements like the Dungarees.

3

The Aristologist

Australia's first cookery book, published in 1864, showed the wonderful variety of foods possible, but emphasised the isolation of the gourmet

THE FIRST Australian cookery book was the *English and Australian Cookery Book: Cooking for the Many as well as the 'Upper Ten Thousand'*, published in 1864. It was written by "An Australian Aristologist", the thin disguise of a top dog in Tasmanian society, Edward Abbott. An "aristologist" was a student of the "art of dining", a word devised in London in 1835. The comparatively late publication of such a "first"—books had already appeared on a long catalogue of Australian topics—suggests, besides a relative lack of interest in cooking, that the well-to-do were satisfied with the British books they brought. Emigrants' guides had contained rudimentary recipes and advice, including Caroline Chisholm's two-page "Bush Cookery", but, certainly, Abbott's was the first we recognise as a cookery book.

He plundered from English predecessors, but unlike later authors he acknowledged his debt and compiled an enlightened scrapbook of recipes, hints and background information. Its 300 or so pages were printed rather densely and virtually without illustration, its many quotations and comments could now seem obscure, but it was written with the gusto of the times. In fact, the "Aristologist's" cookery book was not only this country's first, but in both scope and earnestness can still be claimed to be the best. Further, the evidence of the book suggests that no Australian could before or since have eaten better than its author. He could propose a realistic "colonial banquet" of asparagus, turtle soup, trumpeter with butter sauce, lamb *à la poulette*, roast kangaroo, Australian blue cheese and fruit, and suggest a new wine

Edward Abbott

with every course and liqueurs with coffee. Or for a "family meal", he could recommend a rabbit curry, rice and strong beer — the real thing in those days — followed by green apricot pudding, which he endorsed as the "best article in the pastry line that can possibly be made."

If the use of herbs signals sophistication in cooking, then Abbott was familiar with numerous, including thyme, sage, tarragon, elecampane and three varieties of parsley. To him, basil was a "herb in everyday use", and he employed garlic freely, quoting the English publicist of cottage farming, William Cobbett, "Why buy this when you can grow it in your garden? The stuff you buy is half drugs . . ." Then, as now, the bulk of the population ate without gastronomic finesse, but it is worth exploring the peculiar circumstances under which at least one Tasmanian could eat, drink and write so merrily.

Rise of the modern gourmet

While one of the costs of early industrial development was a decline in the general standard of eating, the fortunate in London and Paris dined exceedingly well in the early nineteenth century. Indeed, the very social and technological changes which impoverished mass eating generated endless novelties for the well-placed and ambitious. While the Roman gourmet, Archestratus, had to travel the ancient world, now the pleasures of the palate could be shipped to you. Leaving the countryside, the rich met more often over dinner, shared the secrets of good grocers, became familiar with the delicacies of other lands and swapped recipes and cooks. In solving the riddles of city eating, they became the earliest modern gourmets. Our first cookery book writer, Edward Abbott, was greatly influenced by them.

Similar factors gave rise to the first restaurants, which blossomed in Paris after the French Revolution. The gourmet La Reynière, who published his *Almanach des Gourmands* guidebook between 1803 and 1812, gave three reasons for the multiplication of establishments which didn't merely feed but provided gustatory delights. The first restaurants in Paris in the 1770s resulted from the rage for English fashions, for the English "as is well known, almost always take their meals in taverns", he said. Secondly, the French Revolution in 1789 brought a new ruling elite to Paris, and they needed to eat and relax. The undomiciled legislators "drew by their example all Paris to the *cabaret*". The third reason (the most commonly given) was that the breaking up of aristocratic houses drove cooks to the public for support. The chefs not only landed on Parisian streets but also departed for the rich households in England.

At the same time that Jean Anthelme Brillat-Savarin published his food philosophy, *La Physiologie du Goût* (1825), London's political, literary and medical leaders took an exceedingly educated view of their stomachs. Listing the many doctors who had written excellent cookery books, Dr William Kitchiner wrote in his *Cook's Oracle* (1821): "If *Medicine* be ranked among those Arts which dignify their professors, *Cookery* may lay claim to an equal, if not a superior distinction;—to prevent Diseases,—is surely a more advantageous Art to Mankind, than to *cure* them." In writing his Australian book, Edward Abbott quoted many of these seminal gourmet works and, in particular, two classic essays by Abraham Hayward in the *Quarterly Review* (July, 1835, and February, 1836). The philosophy of dining agreed in spirit, Hayward considered, "with Lord Chesterfield's well-known axiom, that whatever is worth doing at all, is worth doing well: for we presume no one will deny that dining is amongst the things worth doing occasionally." The second essay was ostensibly a review of a weekly magazine, *The Original*, produced by a London police magistrate, Thomas Walker, who combined a health fetish with travel and gourmet wisdom.

Walker considered the ideal number of people at a dinner table was eight.

Solitary dinners ought to be avoided, he said, because "solitude tends to produce thought, and thought tends to the suspension of the digestive powers". Meals ought to begin with champagne, he advised. Not favouring excess, he advocated simplicity and the "happy mean". His ideal menu was, "Turtle, followed by no other fish but whitebait: which is to be followed by no other meat but grouse, which are to be succeeded by apple fritters and jelly." Ahead of his time, he simplified the typical dinner *à la française*, where dishes were arranged on a table before the diners, to *service à la russe*, the modern system of successive courses.

It was Thomas Walker who invented the term Edward Abbott used for his nom-de-plume, "Aristologist". "The Greek for dinner is Ariston," Walker wrote, "and therefore . . . I call the art of dining, aristology, and those who study it, aristologists." The *New English Dictionary* (the Oxford) listed the word, indeed, citing Abbott's use. But "aristologist" never caught on—perhaps because it seemed to derive from "aristos", meaning the best. Besides we already had gourmet (earlier French for winetaster), gourmand (a long-established English adaptation from the French, and meaning a glutton), epicure (after the Athenian philosopher, Epicurus) and gastronome (from the Greek for stomach). Aristology, gastronomy, or whatever we call it, was the appreciation of the positive side of food industrialisation—becoming familiar with exotic delicacies, the ease of congregating in city restaurants, the subtle sauces of the cooking range, the wonders of the cookery book . . .

Abbott's privileged position

Edward Abbott was among the first, "currency" generation, being born in New South Wales in 1801. His father, Major Edward Abbott, had despatched the laconic report in 1808, "The Colony is quiet. There is no money." Major Abbott took his wife and three children to Hobart Town in 1815 to take up an appointment as deputy-judge-advocate. "Despite his small knowledge of law and his large concern for the welfare of his own family," it was said, "Abbott was very successful." As a teenager, Edward tasted Blow My Skull, the favoured drink of an early Governor Davey, and described in the book. With a "stronger head than most of his subordinates", Davey would set up a wattle hut outside Hobart, would barbecue a pig and challenge allcomers to decline a pannikin of his mixture, of what must have been about every available alcoholic beverage. It was a tough society, busily killing off the indigenous race of extraordinary meat eaters.

Young Edward was appointed his father's clerk in 1818 and shortly after took up grazing land, worked by convicts. In 1839, he founded the *Hobart Town Advertiser*, to support the governorship of Sir John and Lady Jane Franklin. The first issue revealed him as something of an Australian nationalist and a radical, who believed the people were the source of legitimate power, although he wouldn't make all people equal. "It is by the rich and labouring classes pulling together that *all* are benefited," his leading article said. "It is the common doom of man that he must eat his bread by the sweat of his brow, that is, by the sweat of his body or of his mind." When Tasmania achieved self-government in 1856, he was elected Member for Clarence, and in 1864, the year of his book, he transferred to the upper house. With the formation of rural municipalities he had been elected Warden of Clarence, a title by which he was known when he died on April 4, 1869, at the robust age of 68, and was buried at St Mark's, Bellerive, where a memorial stands.

In other words, our author got in on the Tasmanian ground-floor. He was considered a "prominent colonist" who was caught up in the turmoil of the times, a self-possessed man who could afford an "interminable" claim for compensation for some of his father's resumed lands. He could be thought of as a Tasmanian squire, patron of field sports and the turf and "noted at all times for his open hospitality and the excellence of his *cuisine*". In a town of 25,000 people, he could obtain the recipe of Colonial Grape Wine, a simple ferment of grapes, sugar and brandy, from a member of the Tasmanian bar. He borrowed the recipe for Tasmanette, a liqueur obtained during jam-making and the creation of Mr Allport of Aldridge Lodge. Overall, he was comfortably placed to write what the *Tasmanian Times* called a "very readable book indeed, and eminently characteristic of the author's peculiar studies, favourite pursuits and natural humour".

Agreeable agriculture

By all accounts, within months of the colony's foundation in 1804, Van Diemen's Land was already eating better than NSW, with apparently a greater willingness to consume emu, swan and kangaroo, and with English village horticulture, dairying and brewing better adapted anyway. While squatting was a bit of a flop, the colony was exporting wheat to Sydney by 1816, when the area under cultivation already was outstripping that in NSW. On the first day of 1820, the weekly market for settlers' produce offered wheat at 8s a bushel, cheese 2s a pound, ham 2s a pound, butter 3s 6d a pound, new potatoes 10s a cwt, fowls 3s a pair and eggs 2s 1d a dozen. On January 1, 1822, colonists formed an Agricultural Society. In 1833, the *Van Diemen's Land Almanac* reported the success of apples and plums was "so astonishing that it needs to be seen to be credited".

Henry Melville, writing in *The Present State of Australia* (1851), went on for pages about the delights of Tasmanian gardens. "Seed that in England would produce a vegetable of two pounds weight will," he said, "frequently give one of seven or eight . . . peaches, nectarines, &c, grow in great plenty, and there being little or no demand for them, the pigs generally come in for a full share." Derwent potatoes were celebrated on the adjoining continent for their superior quality. As for the introduced bees, whose honey was being used in lieu of malt in making very superior ale, "these busy little colonists are fast spreading all over the island," Melville wrote. Horticulture was a favourite study, and there were few persons even in the towns who did not possess gardens of some kind. A high government official supplied Melville's milk. Gentlemen "live by their estates," he said. "Let a man be ever so wealthy . . ., he will still be a farmer, either as an agriculturist, or a sheep-owner, and as such, he will become a butcher, or a baker, selling his mutton or beef to the Government, or converting his grain into flour, and the flour into bread for the convict rations." It would seem, then, that Edward Abbott belonged to a most agricultural community.

Governor Macquarie reported in 1825 that most of the best tracts within the spacious valley from Hobart to Launceston were already held by a few individuals on the easiest terms. A hundred or so immigrant families, who arrived between about 1820 and 1831, came to dominate Tasmania culturally and politically. Among them, a native-born landowner like Edward Abbott would have felt a very senior fish indeed. Their near-feudal estates presented a picture "of nature subdued and trained by art," a visitor wrote. Willows clustered "emerald bright" along the streams, with "No broken fences, no gates without latches" and the cleared land "quite unblemished by stumps". Gardens studded with English flowers "looked and smelt like home", deer grazed in the parks of Panshanger, Clarendon and Quamby, larks, linnets, pheasants and sparrows flitted through the trees. The landowners kept wages down and provided cottages, gardens and runs for cows, pigs and poultry. Some faithful retainers were so long in service that the *Mercury* described them "as much a part of the estate as the most valued trees and as little likely to leave." Ebernezer Shoobridge had 85 cottages, school and library at Bushy Park and presided over his people's mutual improvement and cottage garden societies. The Reibeys of Entally feasted the district children on New Year's Day and most proprietors provided food and beer or cider to enliven harvest festivals.

Abbott reprinted part of a poem which described a ploughing match at Rokeby in 1863. After the tournament, the Governor and Mrs Gore Brown led the company into a tent, which contained a marvellous sight:

> For there was a store of viands good—
>   Beef, mutton, lamb, and veal;
> And tongues, and hams, and sucking-pigs;
>   As far as e'er did squeal.
> There hens and cocks, and bubbly-jocks [turkeys]
>   Were plucked, and stuffed, and trussed;
> And puddings crammed so full of plums,
>   The cook "was sure they'd bust!"

And on a "lordly dish upraised" was a pie baked by the Warden of Clarence, Abbott himself.

In mid-century, Tasmania gained a reputation for the beauty of its women. This was put down to the cooler climate, which didn't bleach complexions, just as it drew rich mainlanders for summer and produced bountiful berry fruits. There was another reason—for the first time in Australian history, with the men gone to the goldfields, here was a whole colony with a predominance of women. An abundance of women, bountiful gardens and orchards and an unhurried economy, what more incentive could a squire need to dedicate a cookery book to "his fair countrywomen"?

He gave a recipe for "Mrs ---'s Pastry", provided by "an elegant Australian lady, whose fair hands could fabricate by this simple mode crust infinitely superior to any professional daubing". And, he went on to say, "its intrinsic goodness was wonderfully enhanced if the eater was acquainted with the maker". His book also reprinted correspondence he had concerning flour with Louisa Anne Meredith, the author who had now moved from NSW to her Tasmanian estate. Upper-crust women had to know how to run the household, most especially because of the difficulty finding good servants. Explaining the plight of the common cook back home, Abbott recommended what she was to do. Why, "pack up her traps, without delay, and slope for the colonies, where she will be better paid, better fed, better treated, have tea three times per diem, and find a husband very soon after she arrives!"

Appropriate food technology

Abbott enjoyed a human scale of food technology, where machine had not yet out-matched nature. Two staples of the British diet, bread and beer, being prepared by relatively tricky fermentations of a basic ingredient, were suited to specialist production. In fact, they were already artisan trades when England despatched its Australian colonies. So, as soon as Tasmania set up, it attracted the basis of a food industry in miller-bakers and brewers. Within 30 years the colony had 40 water and wind and one steam-mill. Within another 30 years, in the year of Abbott's book, there were 107—48 water, 29 horse, 10 wind and 20 steam-mills. So Abbott had access to plenty of stone-ground flour, from wheat grown in its then accustomed cool climate.

In 1820, two breweries commenced in Van Diemen's Land and by 1829 there were nine, five of them in Hobart Town. Peter Degraves erected the Cascade Brewery and Malt House in 1832, to supply beer, ale, porter, and yeast for bakers. In 1850, there were 48 breweries in Tasmania. Abbott praised Mr James Milne Wilson's pale ale, although Mr Walker's bitter was also highly esteemed. Both were exported to Sydney and Melbourne. It wasn't just out of local pride that Abbott preferred his local brew, since hops and barley were at home in Tasmania's cooler climate. It was a different brew in those days, what the English would come to cherish a century later as "real ale". Abbott actually championed the new long-life "lager" beer, not realising how it would lead to the sugary, pasteurised fizzy drink of recent times. Just as Abbott had access to honest flour, he enjoyed the peak of the Tasmanian breweries. Domination by bigger money reduced their numbers to 20 in 1875 and 11 in 1895.

Other Tasmanian industries established during Abbott's time included wine, cider, vinegar, aerated waters, cordials, salted meat, ham and bacon, jam and biscuit-making. Most of them were on an innocuous scale compared with eventually big businesses like the cannery, Henry Jones and Co (IXL), which traces its roots back to a company founded by George Peacock in 1861. This relative unimportance of food processing gave Abbott little concern with food adulteration. Mind you, he did advise grinding your own flour and brewing your own port, especially if you procured Lord Pembroke's recipe. You might also purchase spirits and beer from reputable firms, and avoid bright-coloured peppers, spices, sauces, anchovies and herrings, and green pickles, "ie, pickles artificially coloured," he said. "Avoid coloured confections, especially those green, blue or red," since poisonous salts could be expected. Finally, he said, "weigh and measure your purchases when brought home. You will be then sure of full weight if the articles are good and be more able to detect the bad." The food industry still belonged to the local grocer.

As for home appliances, Abbott enjoyed nearly all the technological advances that good cooking could stand. While gas lighting had arrived in Hobart in 1857, gas stoves had not overcome natural buyer resistance to ranges of any kind. Abbott boldly cooked on an American wood stove, his being "The Golden State" of Johnson and Fuller, Broadway, New York. "Meat baked in their ovens cannot be distinguished by the taste or flavour from that roasted in front of an open fire; provided the joint is basted occasionally," he ventured.

While Abbott considered the Sydney hotels were "first chop", he felt they fell down on having melted butter at breakfast, again a problem of sticking to cool climate habits when Mediterranean olive oil would have suited better. However, he would solve the hazard with a patent butter cooler. He recommended the Simpson portable freezing vase, which was powered with a mixture costing 34s a cwt. He also gave the chemical formula. Where ice was available (probably from mountains, importers and new freezing plants), he suggested a small "refrigerator" or portable ice-safe for keeping wine, butter, etc, and costing £4 10s and consuming only 50 lbs of ice weekly.

Interest in indigenous dishes

Abbott quoted W. C. Wentworth's nationalistic poetry and enthused about indigenous foods, which to him were an alternative "game". He told of roast wombat and roast "porcupine", roast emu, ducks, pigeons, wattle bird, turkey bustard and black swan. With obvious relish, he listed the fish available in each colony. To him, the Tasmanian trumpeter was "without exception the finest flavoured fish in the Southern Hemisphere, and it is said to rival the turbot in delicacy." To taste it, he recommended visiting the Ship, Derwent and Webb's hotels.

He provided several recipes for kangaroo, including stuffed and baked with gravy, kangaroo pasty ("even more palatable" than venison pie), jugged kangaroo, kangaroo hashed and even kangaroo ham, since he fancied his ability in curing hams. His wine sauce for venison, hare or kangaroo was a mixture of port, claret or dark Sydney wine, good gravy and a tablespoon of currant jelly, "warmed and served". His sharp sauce for the same meats was white wine vinegar, white sugar, simmered and served. One of his hare and kangaroo stuffings comprised beef suet, bread crumbs, parsley, shallot, marjoram, thyme, nutmeg, pepper, salt, cayenne, held with egg. He gave most attention to the "kangaroo steamer", with three recipes, one of which was from Mrs Sarah Crouch ("the lady of the respected Under-Sheriff of Tasmania" and probably the previously-mentioned pastry expert), and which, along with the instructions on kangaroo ham, had obtained a medal at the London Exhibition of 1862. He quoted Henry Melville's statement that "of all the dishes ever brought to table, nothing equals that of the steamer". Made by mincing kangaroo flesh, the steamer incorporated pork or bacon (to make up for the animal's particular lack of fat) and left to steam by the fireside in a saucepan. It was commonly bottled for preserving.

He quoted Mrs Meredith's description in *My Home in Tasmania* of "sticker-up cookery", in which pieces of kangaroo were stuck on a clean stick about four feet long and erected vertically to the leeward of a fire. On top was speared a piece of delicately rosy fat bacon. "Then the bacon on the summit of the spit, speedily softening in the genial blaze, drops a lubricating shower of rich and savoury tears upon the leaner kangaroo cutlets below, which forthwith frizzle and steam and sputter." Then Abbott described a couple of local dishes submitted by an "old hand", and perhaps not known to the "new chums". These were "Pan Jam", which was essentially a fry of jointed kangaroo tail, and "Slippery Bob", which consisted of kangaroo brains made into a batter with flour and water and which was fried, a tablespoonful at a time, in emu fat. As Abbott commented, it was "'bush fare', requiring a good appetite and excellent digestion".

Making little more than passing reference to "Colonial Damper", he preferred to discuss yeast at length, quoting correspondents to the London *Times*, to persuade readers of the virtues of some 30 or so types of bread and yeast cake. And while he certainly had great affection for the new land, he defended the "national Christmas pudding," plum pudding. "We like these quaint old customs and ceremonies and hope they will be always kept up in the old country," he wrote.

Abbott was nationalistically impatient, respected the traditions of England, and was also commendably cosmopolitan. He must have travelled widely as a young man. "We have shared the hunting cloak," he wrote in his newspaper, "with the red Indian in the far west wilds of the American forests." His recipes included curry, soy, gazpacho, haggis, pilaw, macaroni, brioche, kebabs, syllabub, mint julep. Eliza Acton's great English cookery book had contained a section of Jewish recipes, and so did the Aristologist's on "Hebrew Refection".

He quoted the view that "Beer and wine met at Waterloo; wine, red with fury, boiling over with enthusiasm, mad with audacity, rose thrice against that hill on which stood a mass of immovable men—the sons of beer. You have read history; beer gained the day." Yet, recognising Australia's greater similarity with the Frenchman's clear sky than the Englishman's damp soil and cold sun, he wrote enthusiastically about various local wines. He shared the excitement at setting up Mediterranean industries which would enrich both the table and the exports. As his book went to press, he had hopes that salmon ova would hatch in Tasmanian rivers. But, like his book, they were to disappear into inhospitable waters.

There was an epicure, Abbott wrote, who, when handed a plate so hot in a Tasmanian hotel that it burnt his fingers, with great coolness gave the "garçon" a crown, saying, "Such an unusual circumstance deserves a recompense". An ill-bred booby, commented Abbott, would not have appreciated the luxury of a hot plate but would have cursed. He was surrounded by ill-bred boobies. In his preface, Abbott relayed the experience of a visiting English "exquisite" at a dinner given by an uncultured Australian Wool King. When asked what he had been given for dinner, the dandy replied languidly: "There was mutthon at th' thwop of the twable, mutthon at ther botham of the twable, and th' west of ther swheep in twandles." That is, sheep was all this brutish squatter provided to eat, and sheep had also been made into the candles. Abbott continued: "I am desirous of some reform of the *cuisine* of some of my countrymen's establishments, and I am vain enough to believe that I shall effect that object by this publication."

Despite his hopes, the book did not reach a second edition, and copies became extremely rare. Much later, in 1970, Paul Hamlyn published a dolled-up but almost textually complete version under the title of *The Colonial Cook-Book*. The "Australian Aristologist's" excellent work reflected the wonderful natural opportunities the country offered, the excitement in setting up a new civilisation, in scouring the world for ideas, the genuine possibilities which being detached from soil offered. These were overwhelmed in the harsh rush to set up an arm of an industrial empire. Yet, while Abbott was especially privileged in a semi-feudal society, there were elements of his comfortable position—the appropriate agriculture, soft technology and proper respect for food—which we can envy.

THE NEXT COOKERY BOOKS

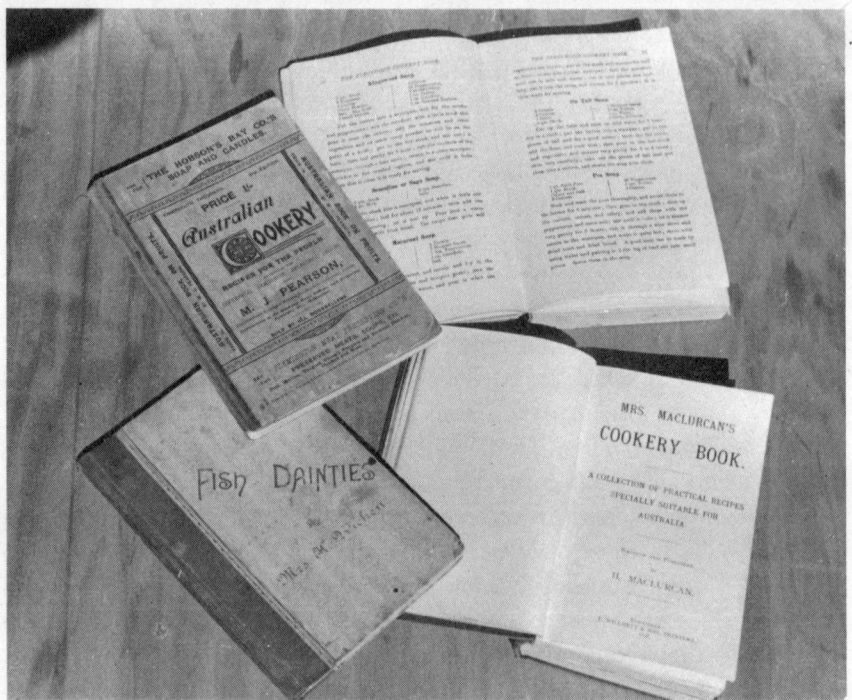

The burst of Australian cookery books came in the 1890s

THROUGHOUT the nineteenth century, most Australians served meals very plainly, avoiding the pretensions of "made dishes", that is those beyond the unadorned fried, roasted and boiled slabs. It didn't leave much demand for cookery books, as Edward Abbott found when his disappeared without much trace in 1864. For the first century, those in need of textual guidance would have imported it from Britain, and Abbott hoped his book would combine the "advantages of Mrs Acton's work with the *crème de la crème* of the cheapest of Soyer's productions". These names would have been familiar to his readers, Eliza Acton having aimed her great *Modern Cookery for Private Families* (1845) at the "indefatigable" middle-class, and the prolific chef Alexis Soyer noted for soup kitchens for the poor and in Ireland.

Abbott made no reference to what was to become the most famous of all English cookery books, *Beeton's Book of Household Management*, which had appeared in 1861. It was named after its publisher, Samuel Beeton, as with similar works from Warne's and Cassell's. It was edited by his wife, Isabella Beeton, when she was only 24. Only after she had died in childbirth in 1865 was it known, along with several hugely-successful companion volumes, as *Mrs Beeton's* . . . It would symbolise the era of the mass cookery book.

As far as I have discovered, the second local cookery book after the

"Aristologist's" was the gas-promoting *Australian Cook* by Alfred J. Wilkinson in 1876. Chef at Melbourne's Athenaeum Club, he provided recipes typical of the straight-forward English book. In 1878, a popular pamphlet appeared in Sydney, called *Russell's Useful Family Receipt Book* and which sought quickly to save its price by revealing how to prepare 30 of the new groceries, like ginger beer, horehound beer, vinegar, jam, raisins, macaroni and pickles.

The rush of recipe books came in the 1890s, a generation after Abbott, when gas and then food companies sold new ideas on dining, when the "middle-class" complained of difficulty finding and training servants, when progressive women sought to uplift themselves and families through the latest English and American ideas on good diet and manners, when domestic science was fitted into now compulsory education, and when most people could read. Two urban writers, Margaret Pearson and Harriet Wicken, were trained in London at the South Kensington School of Domestic Science, giving their books and many lectures a British flavour. Theirs was a proselytising style, as they sought to raise the culinary standards of the masses. Pearson's *Cookery Recipes for the People*, which included several gas stove advertisements, spread the gospel from 1888. Wicken, who commenced editions of her *Kingswood Cookery Book* in England, brought out Australian versions from 1888. She produced a domestic economy textbook, *The Australian Home* (1891), an advertising booklet, *Fish Dainties* (1892), and contributed the recipe section to P. E. Muskett's *Art of Living in Australia* (1893).

During a period of agricultural expansion, writers like Mina Rawson, Hannah Maclurcan and Jean Rutledge addressed themselves to well-to-do country women. Struggling to adapt bourgeois elegance to rough bush life, they entertained with "at homes" (when the select called in their gloves and left visiting cards) and prepared lavish teas and fancy social spreads. As well as stories about bush pioneers, Mina (Mrs Lance) Rawson published a series of cookery books, starting in 1878 at Maryborough, Queensland, and continuing under at least six different titles into the 1890s. She provided instructions for common British recipes—like scrambled eggs, broths, oyster soup, curries, macaroni, roast chicken, stuffing for geese or ducks, potato cakes, oat cakes, short crust pastry, lemon cheese and toffey, as she spelt it. And, as she argued, "Almost every young matron has among her wedding presents a good Cookery Book—either Mrs Beeton, Warne, or some equally good and useful for town use." But these became useless in the bush, owing to the "scant material to work with". So she also encouraged using native products, with such recipes as wallaby soup, baked bandicoot, pigweed salad and boiled thistles.

Mrs Maclurcan's Cookery Book, its first of several editions in about 1897, was much grander. Hailed as one of the best cooks in the country, Hannah and her husband ran the Queen's Hotel, Townsville, which advertised "excellent cuisine and cellar". It was very like an English book of the period, with more French cuisine than later cookery books. Typical of six menus suggested for dinner for six or eight persons was:

> Oysters.
>
> Turtle Soup.
>
> Baked Barramundi.
>
> Beef Olives.
> Chicken Cream.
>
> Roast Fillet of Beef Larded.
>
> Roast Turkey and Bread Sauce.
>
> Asparagus on Toast.
>
> Angels Food.   Cherries in Jelly.
>
> Fruit in Season.
>
> Olives and Devilled Almonds.

She spent many pages on local dishes, with sections on crab and prawn recipes and with much more than usual on fish generally. She also used a lot of tropical fruits like mango, guava, pineapple and pawpaw, as well as providing a section on icecreams, including granadilla and passionfruit ices. In 1901, Hannah Maclurcan took over Sydney's Wentworth hotel.

Jean Rutledge's highly successful *Goulburn Cookery Book*, first appearing in 1899, was designed to meet a "want, especially among the women in the bush, who have often to teach inexperienced maids, and would be glad of accurate recipes". Any dish, she said, must be "mixed with brains". Her soups, meats, puddings, cakes, beverages, confectionery, jams and pickles were "old familiar friends". Indeed, her collection was suspiciously similar to Eliza Acton's in England more than half a century earlier. Out of approximately 1,000 recipes, local additions did not exceed a kangaroo recipe, a couple of new names for simple meat dishes, "Carpet Bag à la Colchester", a few scone, pudding and cake variations and passionfruit icing.

F. Fawcett Story published her *Australian Economic Cookery Book* in 1900, hoping wives might tempt their men away from restaurants and clubs. Along with baked custard, baked quinces and Charlotte Russe, her long list of puddings included the beguiling Mafeking, Baden, Khaki, Shrapnel, Hopetoun and Federation. With such local cookery books deliberately adapting English ways, they tended to suppress a distinct style. In fact, as more books came out, the more predictable became the cooking. It was because we left our diet to the food factories.

PART II
Feeding the city
The age of the railways (1850s–1930s)

S. T. Gill, *Premises of Samuel Henderson, ham and bacon curers,* Footscray, c. 1870

How we entertained a prince

CIVIC LEADERS outstripped each other in lavishness, if not always refinement, to welcome Prince Alfred when he undertook Australia's first royal tour in the last months of 1867 and first of 1868. The nation erupted with picnics, luncheons and banquets with the best French and local wines and public feasts with "groaning tables" of roast beef and plum pudding. Queen Victoria's second son was presented with local delicacies like kangaroo tail soup, turtle soup, Murray cod, wallaby pie and emu-egg omelettes. He interspersed rabbit and kangaroo shoots with inspections of vineyards.

To the west of Geelong he toured the Barrabool Hills, a gem in Victoria's wine industry, and at Louis Pettavel's newly-named Prince Alfred Vineyard a "prolonged halt was made, to the delight of locals". At Newcastle, he refused invitations to descend a coal mine, preferring to add Hunter wineries to the itinerary. "As elsewhere in this vast land," he pronounced, "I am once again struck by the surprising excellence of your local wines." North of Adelaide, a vigneron at Para, Mr Duffield, presented lunch and a case of wine, before the Prince went on to accept a silver casket with a gold replica of Ridley's reaper from the Gawler Total Abstinence League. Although his equerries Lord Newry and the Hon. Elliot Yorke were later labelled "dissipated", the Prince diplomatically told the abstainers that he should "ever strive to follow" their good example.

The leisurely tour did not pass without dissension. At a Sydney picnic—with stout, oysters and buttered brown bread before noon, and champagne, chicken and lobster after—the Prince was wounded by a shot fired by Irish nationalist Henry James O'Farrell. The victim was rushed in a boat to Government House, while 1,544 guests finished off 1,182 magnums of champagne and 798 bottles of beer, not to mention their own precautionary and "copious supplies of even more ardent spirits". While the incident has been accorded historical prominence, perhaps a more revealing celebration had just occurred in Melbourne.

The somewhat radical paper, the Melbourne *Age*, had been intrigued "to find a community like ours, freed from aristocratic restraints and influence, ready to shout and sing with joy, and decorating our streets over the visit of a Prince." The paper became a strong supporter of a "Free Banquet", to be attended by the Prince and the city's poor on the banks of the Yarra River and the idea of Mr L. L. Smith, a prominent business leader. Soon the *Age* was carrying a daily tally of gifts to the banquet: "Mr Degraves, MLC, a ton of flour; Mr Ford, Chemist, a fat pig; Mr Watson, wholesale druggist, a bag of sugar . . . Mr Chapman, music seller, 1 doz. concertinas". A ladies auxiliary, under the Governor's wife, Lady Manners Sutton, organised women wearing white muslin and blue rosettes to wait upon eight squares of tables, which would accommodate 4,000 people at one time, allowing 18 inches of standing room.

The Reverend J. I. Bleasdale—a Catholic clergyman who vigorously supported new industries like wine, silk and later friend James Harrison's meat freezing—agreed that the Prince's health should be toasted in the wine of the country, and selected 1,000 gallons. Bleasdale saw wine as the "natural antidote to spirit drinking, and all its baleful effects in this hot and dry climate". The *Argus*, a much more patrician paper, had called the banquet the "Free Feed" and now said it was to be a "Free Guzzle" as well. The *Church Times* declared itself alarmed by the "growing love of ostentatious extravagance and the growth of sensual gratification" in the colony. In a letter to the *Age*, "Citoyenne" suggested also a breakfast for the bourgeoisie, who would bring hampers to the public gardens. "Imagine," she wrote, "the flavour of a sandwich eaten in the presence of Royalty, to the sound of music and the scent of flowers."

The date set for what the *Age* hoped would be "surely the greatest event in the history of the colony", Thursday, November 28, 1867, turned out to be hot and windy. In their more extravagant moments, the organisers had predicted 10,000; by noon 40,000 had arrived and by one o'clock waited a "great sea of pent-up waters", which was then permitted a dismaying rush through the mile of ropes into the enclosure. By now quite parched, they found water limited to one outlet. They could only eye two zinc-coated wine fountains, which were fed through overhead copper ducts from great butts placed in the trees. But the ladies pleaded with them to behave properly and, while few police attended, there were numbers of clergymen to "impart an elevated atmosphere to the proceedings".

By 2.30, the enormous crowd was thirsty, hungry and impatient. Melbourne's police chief, Captain Miles Standish, galloped back to Government House to warn that he couldn't assure the Prince's safety. When Mr Smith announced from the dais that Alfred declined to attend, the people stampeded for what the *Argus* called a "bacchanalian picture of unbelievable horror" and the *Age* a "disgusting debauch". The crowd of between 70,000 and 100,000—which would have been close to half Melbourne's population—swarmed everywhere looking for food, grabbing cases of champagne reserved for the voluntary workers, cutting hoses from the wine butts, and catching squirts of wine in odd containers. Young men clambered the trees to the barrels, only descending at darkness "like drunken possums". The *Age* condemned the police for not attending in significant numbers and the Prince's advisors for restraining him. Mr Smith called Captain Standish a "chicken-hearted meddler" and declared "if the members of the Ladies Committee were brave enough to attend, the Prince should not have been deterred". But the *Argus* concluded that the event demonstrated the "natural baseness of the masses".

The startling response to the Melbourne "Free Banquet" revealed that Australia, as early as the 1860s, had emerged as a modern mass society, which was to be tagged the "working-man's paradise". This was no longer the society in which Alexander Harris yarned over the pot of tea, nor where Edward Abbott supervised the rustic pleasures of a ploughing match, but a community busy in offices, factories and on construction sites, and in which civic leaders, grappling with popular culture, contemplated a vast and impersonal public. Our superiors then, as often since, had trouble recognising that the colonies, "freed from aristocratic restraints" and at the mercy of the "natural baseness of the masses", were modern metropolises.

The eminent colonist W. C. Wentworth said that the gold rushes had "precipitated Australia into nationhood". The flood of adventurers from 1851 onwards stirred up the economy, erected the Eureka stockade, clamoured for democratic government, demanded land for small settlers, settled into regular jobs and formed the trade union movement. The year 1851 happened not to be just when Hargreaves found gold, but also when Victoria and Albert held their glorious Great Exhibition to bourgeois deities in London. Massive flows of capital, particularly English, shot into colonial railway construction and the expansion of cities, especially into dormitory suburbs, so that Melbourne emerged as if overnight in the golden 1850s. But Sydney had already taken off, with its population reaching 50,000 and its annual growth rate an astounding 10 per cent in the 1840s. The other cities took the same arithmetical leap in succession, Adelaide in the 1870s, Brisbane in the 1880s and Perth with its 1890s goldrush. By 1851, one-third of the population was urban, and by 1901 over one-half. Australia had taken on the look, and taste, of the city.

4

Metropolitan paradise

After toasting the goldrush in champagne, our expanding cities adopted inventions like stoves and icechests, and revelled in the world's cheapest living

WRITER WILLIAM KELLY recorded signs of gold madness when he reached Melbourne in 1853. With farm labourers deserting their plots and extra mouths to feed, common cabbages could command 2s 6d each and eggs 18 shillings a dozen, he said. For a "sooty" lump of meat and a cold potato, some "gritty" bread and a glass of "saccharine" ale, he paid an eating-house 8s 6d. Yet at a performance of "Hamlet", gold-diggers in the audience barracked grave-diggers onstage about the depth of their sinking, popped champagne during the interval and pelted nuggets at the curtain calls. A land sale outside Melbourne was enlivened by a brass band and each bid was toasted in champagne, each block auctioned "in a flood of sparkling eulogy" and each purchaser's fortune "copiously celebrated".

With the goldrush, merchants enjoyed great prosperity. On the diggings, Kelly found an excellent supper of "the beef and mutton of Victoria, the bread of South Australia, the butter of ould Erin, the coffee of Ceylon, the sugar of Mauritius, the tea of China—while the ham of York, the marmalade of Scotland, the sardines of France, the condiments of India, were only waiting for a beckon to jump down our throats from the surrounding shelves". Back in Melbourne, he noted the arrival of Yankee clippers loaded with consumer goods. He wandered the wharves, "speculating on the possible uses to which many strange and fantastic articles could be applied". They probably included the new range of American agricultural and kitchen equipment, which, like many American schemes and influences, followed the gold seekers from the Californian fields. Australian food, produced by an industry spanning nations, was already shaped by American influences.

Among the imports was New England champagne, which Kelly said "went off like all creation in California". He could swear that it also "went off" in Mr L---n's store "like the Malakoff battery in its fiercest mood". Such was the high-pressure of the aerated chemical that the bottles were fully twice as heavy as for the genuine wine, he said, and were fastened with "wires thick enough for an electric telegraph". Softdrinks, which were really flavoured soda water, had been invented a few years earlier in Philadelphia, and so this "champagne" presumably also had its sparkles added.

Another imported American luxury of the 1850s was ice. Mechanical refrigeration was still at the experimental stage and ice cut from Wenham Lake near Boston was shipped worldwide in great quantity. Kelly saw "fevered" crowds besieging the bars of the Criterion and the Union as soon as the three titanic monosyllables "Ice! Ice! Ice!" went up over their doors. "It was not until I came to Victoria, and got half baked in the dry, roasting, hot winds of the country, that I became fully indoctrinated in the virtues of ice," he said. What a transition, he thought, from breathing Australian dust to "sucking the frigid essence of a brandy-spider through a straw".

During 1858, according to another observer, Frank Fowler, 500 tons of ice were sold in Melbourne at fourpence a pound. The ice went into some of the American-style cocktails now popular. "Nothing is done without the nobbler", Frank Fowler wrote. It was the common name given a drink, and conceivably related to the American "cobbler". A "break-down" was another. To pay for a nobbler for another was to "stand", to "sacrifice" or to "shout". Fowler named favourite beverages, again reminiscent of Californian examples, including a Spider (lemonade and brandy), a Smash (ice, brandy and water) and a Lola Montez (Old Tom, ginger, lemon and hot water).

Fowler also summoned up the evening scene in the library of a snug villa on Sydney Harbour in the late 1850s. All the English magazines were on the table, from the "profound" *Quarterly* to the readable *Dublin University*. A gentleman read aloud *Aurora Leigh* to a dozen ladies and gentlemen, who took glasses of a delicious beverage on the table. The beverage? Fowler listed the ingredients: "Let the evening be warm, the guests genial. Get a few large Koh-i-noors of Wenham Lake ice, a bottle of full-bodied claret, a half a pound of white sugar, three lemons, a bottle of champagne, ditto of soda water, a nutmeg, and a large punch-bowl . . ." A koh-i-noor, by the way, was a big diamond, which the ice must have approached in value. The sugar was rubbed yellow on the lemons, placed in the bowl with the lemon peelings, rained with nutmeg, the ice added and the claret stirred in until the sugar was melted. Then, "give one guest the soda water and another the champagne and at the solemn signal, let them pour both into the bowl". Now ladle out, and tell Mr Fowler if he was not justified in calling it delicious.

The "working-man's paradise"

When newcomers settled into urban life, there was still something marvellous about it. They came to call Australia the "working-man's paradise". The phrase was used by writer Henry Kingsley in 1859, and repeated endlessly. Visiting his grazier son, the English novelist Anthony Trollope decided in 1873: "It is a Paradise for a working man as compared with England . . . His diet will always comprise as much animal food as he can consume, and if he be a sober, industrious man he will never find himself long without work." Like the "Lucky Country" a century later, the concept did much to induce complacency. In this chapter, we investigate the taste of this urban Eden, where a family had a steady wage and little fear of hunger.

While the upper-classes kept a kitchen garden, orchard, maybe a cow and even a separate country estate, many city workers had terrace houses with no garden at all. Even when the building-society suburbs stretched out in search of the countryside and the usual block occupied the quarter-acre which might just feed a family, the bourgeois ideal became an ostentatiously ornamental garden, featuring unproductive lawn and a miniscule vegetable plot. Most homes were not centres of production—of eggs, milk, cheese, bacon, bread and beer—but of consumption—of packets, tins and bottles. Feeding was not based on what we grew, but what we could pay for from a wage. We were stranded in suburbia.

Yet the early city still seemed more rural than today's—the gaps were sown with productive gardens. Frank Fowler described vines growing everywhere in Sydney in 1859. "You press out the rich juice as you walk!" he wrote. Healthy agrarian habits could become hazardous in crowded centres. Effluent, which would have enriched a garden, went into open gutters. To ensure reasonably fresh milk, cows were kept crammed in backyards. Butchers slaughtered their own beasts. The city had to be cleaned up and, for instance, the Melbourne City Council prohibited butcher-shop slaughtering when it opened abattoirs at Flemington in 1861. Although backyard killing remained common in East Collingwood and Fitzroy in the 1860s and persisted into the 1890s, it had become illegal with the abattoirs at Clifton Hill. Even in 1912, a Royal Commission found 48 abattoirs in Sydney and suburbs. The work was centralised at Homebush in 1916.

This was but a small example of the necessary metropolitan infrastructure. Sometimes private companies provided gas, electric light and omnibuses. Government instrumentalities borrowed heavily abroad to fill the gaps, from running water to garbage collection. Sewerage and health regulations climaxed a succession of technical and organisational glories, which only reinforced our feeling of triumph over the "idiocy of rural life". But when we condemn the unkempt cows and dirty drinking water, we should not blame "unenlightened" agrarian living. It was city crowding that had created the plagues.

In the solid, five-room house, material well-being seemed to keep improving, a good example being the introduction of the ice-chest. It was a novelty for Edward Abbott in 1864. But by 1893, Dr Philip Muskett could write that both ice and "refrigerator" were within the means of nearly all—"thanks to the rapid development of scientific knowledge". It prevented waste by keeping food sweet for a second meal, he said. A decade later, E. C. Buley could say that the ice-chest was a "necessity rather than a luxury, for in this way only can the drinking water be kept cool and the butter set upon the table in a state of solidity. The ice-cart goes from door to door as regularly as the milk-cart throughout almost the whole of the year."

The house also gained a stove. At the beginning of the nineteenth century, cooking was mostly done on an open fire, with the damper being our most obvious result of hearth-stone heat. The bigger house enjoyed a bigger fireplace, with a spit, grate and perhaps a separate brick bread oven. Late in the previous century, physicist Benjamin Thompson (Count Rumford) produced the first real kitchen range—enclosing the fire made it safer, more efficient, more easily controlled and could combine cooking in pots with an oven. In 1802, an Exeter iron-founder George Bodley patented the closed-top prototype of English bricked-in kitchen ranges. Yet the main stove used in this country until at least the 1880s was a "colonial oven", just a box which was set into a fireplace, with wood burnt both underneath and above. In cities the cooking range offered so many conveniences that it was installed increasingly through the second half of the century. The first English cast-iron models were displaced by free-standing American and French "kitcheners" which, by further containing the fire within bricks, kept the heat in the kitchen bearable.

In 1873, Mr A. R. Walker introduced the gas cooker to Australia. In September, 1875, his and various other stoves competed as part of the Inter-colonial Exhibition in Melbourne. The chef of the Athenaeum Club, Alfred J. Wilkinson, provided an elaborate dinner for 20 persons on a £4 Walker stove. "The dinner was pronounced excellent by all present," the *Age* reported. In a book of gas recipes, the *Australian Cook* (1876), Wilkinson marvelled that: "fuel conveys itself into our houses, requiring nothing but the spark of ignition to instantaneously supply us with the exact amount of heat we require for any given purpose of cookery." In Melbourne in 1880 the young Metropolitan Gas Company offered for hire locally-built "Walker" stoves in three models and gas was in widespread use by the new century.

Utensils were simultaneously transformed. The early settler possessed no kitchen equipment beyond a knife, pannikin, axe and cast-iron pot to be suspended over the fire, the same as the Irish crock and called a "camp oven". Louisa Meredith had noticed a devotion to the frypan. A light tin or two-pint pot was eventually adapted as a "billy" for tea-making. This might sound like the rural kitchen, but was typical in early towns. Describing the Melbourne two-roomed cottage of 1853, John Sherer said the fireplace had: two or three cast-iron saucepans, a frying-pan, a gridiron, the "indispensable" tea-kettle and a camp-oven for baking. "It being the substantialities rather than the delicacies of life which figure on the table of the colonists, a great variety of dishes or kitchen-ware would be rather an encumbrance than otherwise," he wrote. With stoves arrived labyrinthine catalogues of cheap utensils in tinned steel, cast-iron and enamel, which could provide the masses with the conveniences of brass and copper utensils used by the rich. While the refinements made for ease and subtlety, the progress was not without gastronomic loss. There was much to be said for the taste of roasting-spits and brick ovens.

The routines of city life, the dictates of entirely purchased foods and the encouragements of suppliers of gas cookers and cheap utensils kept Australian eating and drinking moving in a predictable direction. Typical meal times were established by 1834 when a Sydney book called the *Mirror of Literature, Amusement and Instruction* gave them as eight, twelve and six o'clock. The basic foods were bread, beef, mutton, pork, milk, eggs, fruit and vegetables, tea and alcohol. This pattern had not changed when outlined by E. C. Buley in 1905. The usual regime for the working-man was breakfast of chops or steak (although Buley said there was a chance of taking the doctor's advice of fruit, toast and coffee). At midday, if unable to go home, he might patronise a sixpenny restaurant (as cafes were called). Finally, at six o'clock the working-man had a "substantial tea, with cold or hot meat", and very wisely dispensed with the English supper. At every meal he drank two or three large cups of tea and appeared "little the worse for it".

It was a plain cookery, with little local stamp. *Mrs Beeton's Everyday Cookery*, published in London in 1907, considered that Australian cookery had become "English in character, while in the hotels the French cuisine plays a prominent part just as it does the world over". Yet the authors found some vegetables unknown to the English—such as soursop, paw-paw and choko (our name for a South American plant)—and some unusual fruits—like loquat, gramma, passionfruit and the similar granadilla. The book's selection of typical recipes reflected the indigenous materials, with an emphasis on flathead, schnapper and kangaroo, and offered Apricots and Rice, Granadilla Cream and Peach and Pineapple Marmalade.

How we ate and drank

"Generally speaking, food in Australia is cheaper and more plentiful than in England, but poorer in quality . . . In short, our food is somewhat coarse, albeit wholesome enough." Insights like that into feeding in our metropolitan paradise were provided by a young journalist, Richard Twopenny, who in 1883 published *Town Life in Australia*. A son of an Adelaide archdeacon, he wrote from Melbourne, which had more "go" at the time than Sydney, was well-lit with gas, but received undrinkable water from the Yarra.

"Of course, meat is the staple of Australian life," Twopenny wrote. Not that we knew how to prepare it in any delicate way, "for to the working and the middle, as well as to most of the wealthy classes, cooking is an unknown art". In everything the colonist liked quantity, he said. He once heard a guest say, "I don't like your nasty little English slices of meat; we want something that we can put our teeth into." Imagine that man's misery when dessert came on the table, and he was asked whether he would take a *slice* of pear! Twopenny exclaimed. The working-man could get mutton "almost for the asking, and up-country almost without it," he said. Better quality could be found up-country too, as the sheep and cattle had otherwise often to be driven long distances for slaughter. Prices varied 1½d to 4d for a pound of mutton, 2½d to 6d for beef, 4d to 8d for veal and 7d to 9d for pork.

All kinds of fruit and vegetables, except brussels sprouts, were cheap and plentiful. But "vegetables are for the most part despised, though the thoroughly old English dish of greens remains in favour, and potatoes are largely eaten," he said. Quoting random prices from a market-book, he gave: artichokes 1½d a lb, tomatoes 2d, beetroot and cabbages 1s 6d a dozen, potatoes 6s a cwt. During the season, fruit was very cheap. Splendid muscatel grapes could be bought in Adelaide for 1d to 2d a lb, peaches 3d a dozen, apricots 2d a dozen, raspberries 5d a lb, cherries 2d a lb, strawberries 4d, plums almost nothing. "But by far the best," he said, "is the passionfruit."

The inferior quality of fruit and vegetables was due, he said, "to the grow-as-you-please manner in which the fruit is cultivated, pruning and even the most ordinary care being neglected." The love of gardening was not at all common—"it is not a sufficiently exciting occupation". Nevertheless, through plundering friends' gardens you could get as fine-flavoured fruit as anywhere "and to taste grapes in perfection you must certainly go to Adelaide". He wrote that the "flour is the best in the world, and the bread wholesome and sweet; but the toothsomeness of German and French bakers is not to be had, and the finest qualities of flour are all shipped to England."

"Tea may fairly claim to be the national beverage," he said. A large majority drank it with every meal, even including those he called the "Metropolitan middle-classes". With them, however, it was more usual to drink beer with their midday meal. Not that a colonist drank much at meals. "He prefers to quench his thirst at every opportunity that may occur between." In Melbourne all drinks were sixpence. The price in Sydney and Adelaide varied from fourpence to eightpence, according to the drink. This was expensive, and Twopenny told the story of two well-known colonists who, upon landing from the P&O steamer at Southampton, immediately ordered two nobblers of English ale. One put down a shilling and was walking off, when the barmaid offered eightpence change. "By G----!" they exclaimed. "Let us drink our shilling's worth."

It required some education to acquire a taste for claret, Twopenny conjectured. The lower-middle and lower classes liked wine sweet and with "body". The uninitiated took sherry and port for their spirituousness. But, like their American cousins, the Australians believed no wine was worth mentioning by the side of "champagne". Everyone was born with a taste for it. Moët or Roëderer's *carte d'or* was the party-goer's criterion of success. Most champagnes, like other imported wines, were "specially prepared for the Australian market". "The quantity of spirits drunk in Australia is appalling," said Twopenny. Not merely the lower classes, but also the wealthiest and most leading citizens got drunk, "though their names do not, of course, appear in the papers or in the police reports." There was no trade at which more fortunes had been made in Australia than the publican's.

While Twopenny considered that the working-class lived "ten times better" than their fellows in England, the middle and upper classes lived ten times worse. "If it be true that, while the French eat, the English only feed, we may fairly add that the Australians grub," he wrote. It was partly the "servant problem". It took a lot of trouble to get and keep a good cook, and "there is nothing the Australian abhors like trouble," he said. It was above all a "money-making place". "How can you expect a man who—for the greater part of his life—has been eating mutton and damper, and drinking parboiled tea three times a day, to understand the art of good living?" he asked. The normal dinner of the wealthy man with a good cook was beef or mutton, roast or boiled, potatoes and greens, bread-and-butter pudding and cheese. While the details might change it was always what the wife called "a good plain English dinner, none of your unwholesome French kickshaws." Without a reasonable cook, the wealthy man might lunch at his club, where the meal was fair, but in the evening his cook's puddings ranged from rice to sago and from sago to rice. Her favourite summer dish would be stewed fruit.

The "servant problem"

One of the shows of financial success in Victorian times was to hire domestic servants—after all, the safest way to distinguish oneself from the workers was to employ labour oneself. No family was considered "middle-class" without at least one maid to clean, wash, make beds, answer the door and cook. Historian Beverley Kingston has pointed out that a successful man had a house full of women—wife, daughters, servants. Until about the First World War, something like one in every ten families had a servant. Earlier supplemented by convicts and then Irish "orphans", there were never enough and they tended not to understand the job. Mistresses wasted days at registry offices finding applicants and explaining how "Biddy" should set the table and roast a joint. "Unfortunately, four-fifths of our servants are Irish—liars and dirty," Richard Twopenny wrote in 1883, no doubt reflecting the general opinion of the comfortable class. She "stares in astonishment to find that you don't keep a pig on your drawing-room sofa."

As the years passed, the servant "problem" worsened. Despite lower pay and frequently terrible conditions, young women preferred the deadly routine of peeling in canneries or dipping for chocolate makers. It would seem that they opted for the crushing temptations of industrial society—progressing, as it was described, from slaves to "wage-slaves"—to demonstrate advancement. Even this liberation was short-lived when marriage welcomed them into totally unpaid labour.

The cooking campaigners

The housewives of the metropolis, removed from a traditional society in which knowledge might be handed down the generations, turned to cookery books, the new women's magazines and to lessons. Some classes were given in NSW public schools in the early 1880s, according to health campaigner, Dr Philip E. Muskett, but without any practical results. Then early in 1886, Mrs Fawcett Story, who taught cookery at the Sydney Technical College, was appointed lecturer to student teachers at Hurlstone Training College. The first cookery class was started at Fort Street Public School in 1889. By the next year, 270 pupils received instruction, and by 1891, numbers had grown to 757. Meanwhile, in Melbourne, Margaret Pearson was giving public lectures and teaching in several Roman Catholic schools. Describing Margaret Pearson's lectures for the gas company at the Centennial Exhibition in Melbourne, the *Argus* (December 4, 1888) said they were attended by "maids and matrons of every degree in the social scale from the general servant, who wishes to qualify for the more important office of cook, to the lady of fashion, who, for the moment, has 'taken up' cookery as her latest and most engrossing fad".

Reforms urged by people like Alexis Soyer in London and pushed by domestic science enthusiasts like Margaret Pearson and Harriet Wicken were taken up by "Rita", the social editress of the Melbourne *Herald* in the 1890s, her writings collected into a modest volume of *Cottage Cookery*. The working-class woman could vary the fare by investing spare pence in a list of extra groceries, she said. She also drew attention to "sorrel, dandelion, dock, etc, as vegetables that cost nothing". Rita understood from charity workers that it was hopeless to expect the needy, who most require it, to manage carefully. Given money, such women had bought a piece of ham, fancy biscuits, expensive jam or some tinned food—their excuse being that they wanted something "tasty". The well-to-do, in her opinion, weren't doing much better. If only they understood as much as French women about the possibility of the cuisine, she sighed . . . "Remarkable simplicity is the note today".

Rita was dismayed that schoolchildren were not provided the soup kitchens of Continental cities, but could spend their money at nearby "lolly shops".

Giving children cake between breakfast and lunch or as the chief part of lunch she considered "vulgar". She urged all mothers to take trouble teaching table etiquette since this was a country where "so many in the humbler walks of life reach, in short periods, prominent positions". Yet it was pleasant to notice the improvement among the "well-read, industrious, progressive women", who had adopted the more delicate cooking methods of the iron stove and mass-produced pots and pans. "These modern utensils make cooking easier, cleaner and healthier. Cookery today is more delicate and conservative," she said. The chefs had shown the way with the rules of this "conservative cookery . . . to bake when possible, to steam such things as vegetable marrows unpeeled, to use the liquid of stews for gravy, to cook by steam instead of boiling things in water, to cook generally as to retain the flavour and nourishment of what is cooked, and so forth."

Rita's hopes seemed to become perverted within a generation. To her, cooking was intellectual work and she cited the names of great cookery writers, Parmentier, Ude, Soyer, Brillat-Savarin, Beauvilliers, Francatelli, who were "men of superior intelligence and taste", as well as Ruskin, Sala, Dickens and Thackeray, who had shown themselves interested in the dishes of the day. And her concluding hope was obviously before its time. "One day," she wrote, "there may be a Chair of Gastronomy, or a Minister of Gastronomy, when 'the first of the sciences' will receive the attention it is worthy of. Just remember that when a Minister for Labour was first mooted, it was thought fantastic too." A little later, there was much agitation for Sydney University to set up a chair of domestic science, although it was never filled.

At the time of Rita's campaigns, two opposing forces could be seen encouraging eating and drinking towards, on the one hand, experimentation and elegance and, on the other, towards conformity and plainness. A sign of puritan denial was the anti-alcohol movement. Some members of the clergy had long urged wine and not spirit-drinking for a more civilised community. But others of them, along with business leaders, preferred punctual workers and blamed individual failings for poverty. They despised the demon alcohol. During the 1880s, such financiers constructed mammoth temperance hotels; for example, in just one city, the Victoria, the Grand, the Melbourne (later the Australian) and, largest of them all, the Federal, which was completed for the centenary exhibition. Women joined the temperance cause, which, since the idea was that wives would vote against alcohol, was often associated with the female suffrage movement.

The world's cheapest living

The run of economic prosperity, verging on madness with Melbourne's land-price boom, collapsed by 1890, curbing some fortunes and reorienting the cocky new labour movement. Yet, almost paradoxically, the economic slump only seemed to encourage good dining. Through until the Edwardian era, restaurants blossomed. Cookery books became ambitious. As seems to happen with economic rupture, some victims turned to self-employment. The author Ada Cambridge described how after the "bursting of the boom", as if somebody had turned off the gas, daughters who had seemed to live entirely for pleasure turned to helping their ruined fathers and to supporting themselves. They became milliners, dressmakers, "typewriters", dentists, kept various little shops and ran tea-rooms, or waited in them or made cakes for them.

Soon, statistician T. A. Coghlan, a poet of the superlative, churned out figures—like those in *The Seven Colonies* (1901)—to show how remarkably cheap living was in our paradise. For instance, of an average annual expenditure per inhabitant of £36 19s 5d, he found that only £15 15s 7d went on food and drink—that is, only 37·5 per cent. In Great Britain, the figure was 42·2 and in Germany 49·1. As for the annual consumption of meat, while the average in Great Britain was 109 lbs and in America 150 lbs, in Australia it was 264 lbs. This was four times as much as in Germany and ten times as much as in Italy.

An inquiry by the Commonwealth statistician in 1910–11 found that the average spent on food had fallen to 29·3 per cent, while percentages in other leading industrial nations were between 54 and 60. "It is not unlikely," the government investigator considered, "that expenditure on food alone furnishes a true indication of the standard of material well-being." And so, Australia, with the world's cheapest food, came to be thought of as enjoying the world's highest "standard of living". The statistics seemed to prove the workers' "paradise" claim. But such indicators, while useful propaganda, didn't tell us how well people lived. They applied only to the market economy, ignoring the self-sufficient content, which might have provided peasant pleasures. They relied on unwarranted assumptions, such as that more meat was beneficial. The diminished proportion spent on food could equally have been interpreted as showing how little value the "working-man's paradise" put on it.

THE CITY MARKETS

Eastern Market, Melbourne, 1880

AS SOON AS farmers had produce to sell, markets were being set up, becoming fashionable, losing custom, burning down and being rebuilt or enlarged. But, while they were a city's secret heart of colour, smell and movement, attracting shoppers, ownerless dogs, courting couples and poets, they tended to be beneath the attention of mainstream observers from Governor Macquarie onwards, and so their history is submerged by neglect.

Governor Bligh apparently opened Sydney's first market in 1806. A "new" market was opened on March 4, 1809. Situated in Market Square in Market Street, it was a paling enclosure around some sheds, open on Tuesdays and Saturdays from sunrise to noon. A little further out, in Hay Street, in 1834 opened the "Hay market". Sydney's markets had impressed Alexander Harris and Louisa Meredith. So, too, the French visitor E. Delessert wrote in 1845 about the good meat and vegetables, lots of oysters, yabbies, lobsters and fish, and the great variety of European and tropical fruits in such abundance they were fed to the pigs—he felt the fruit could have been used as eau-de-vie (brandy) and cider. Delessert also liked the busy markets on Saturday evenings.

Market Street remained important until the Queen Victoria building, which opened in 1893, failed to attract customers and was handed over to other uses. The site had been handy for water-borne produce, but now the Darling Harbour railway yards were busier. So the Haymarket area dominated, until the despatch of the road-based wholesale market to Flemington in 1975. During all that time there were assorted other venues, including fish markets at Woolloomooloo and Redfern, soon forgotten. Also forgotten was the Sydney market delicacy—boiled peas—as much a speciality as chestnuts in Italy, roast potatoes in England and peanuts in America, the *Picturesque Atlas of Australasia* found in 1888. Well, almost forgotten, because Harry's Cafe de Wheels in Sydney's Woolloomooloo and Cowley's pie carts in Adelaide still served peas 100 years later.

The first Melbourne market, the Western, opened in December 1841, under the control of market commissioners elected by householders (there being as yet no town council), in the market square behind the Customs House. About the same time, a hay and corn market was started where St Paul's Cathedral stands. Early in 1842 a cattle market was underway in Elizabeth Street. In 1846 rabbits were reported to have escaped from the original, Western Market in Collins Street and were breeding under the nearby police office. Early in 1849 a market house was erected there, and in the 1850s replaced with "Bowden's Folly", described as "unsightly and useless catacombs" which became reserved as the wholesale market.

The Eastern Market got going at the top end of Bourke Street about the middle of 1847 and for three decades was the main venue, eventually known as "Paddy's" and removed in 1960 for the Southern Cross hotel. It opened Saturday nights, when it was lit by flaming gas pipes, according to the Melbourne *Leader* in 1858. One man proclaimed "brooms for a bob", the paper said, Cheap John (the Chinaman) auctioned a packet of stationery and others shouted "Heating happles, three pounds a shilling" and "Bakers and boilers, four pounds a shilling" or offered Paisley shawls, soap and books. But the feature of the market was the confectioners' stalls, "blazing with light and glittering with wonderful feats in the art of making sugar candy", the paper said.

In 1888, John Freeman wrote that Melbourne was "pretty well off for markets," being able to boast of eight—two for vegetables and dairy produce (the Eastern and Victoria) and one each for meat, fish, fruit, hay, horses and cattle, and pigs. The Queen Victoria market had gone up in 1878 and immediately replaced the Eastern in importance. Imagine the scene, described by Freeman, of the Victoria market, extending along Victoria Street from Queen to Peel Streets. It was formed of a number of avenues, with corrugated iron roofs and the dealers standing on flagged floors, while the horses and carts stood on pitch. By five o'clock of the morning, the market gardeners were at their stands and the early-bird retailers arrived. By six, business had commenced in earnest. Housekeepers appeared, their appetites so much keener at breakfast, and the early rising and a long walk doing them good.

Freeman noticed a newly-married couple winding about the crowd, carrying one or two sticks of celery, a cauliflower, two or three pounds of apples and perhaps a half-dozen eggs tied up in a handkerchief. A boy staggered along under the weight of a pillow-case of vegetables, while his grown-up sister carried a basket of apples, a brother had a watermelon under each arm and another carried a basket containing butter and eggs.

One avenue was devoted to dairy produce, where butter in tubs and in pound and half-pound pats was laid out on clean cloths and wholesome women in white sleeves offered it at a penny a pound less than the shops, along with eggs packed in chaff. A sucking-pig, with an orange in its mouth, stretched out on the tail-board of the cart, along with joints of fresh pork, guaranteed dairy fed. Vociferous merchants drew attention to the unrivalled quality of their cheese, hams, bacon and pickled-pork and sometimes veal, spread out on trestle tables, not to forget their ketchup in wine bottles, tomato sauce in jars, and honey in the comb and pots.

Another avenue was given over to butcher's meat, where a side of mutton varied from "two bob" to half-a-crown, while lamb might reach three and sixpence. Mutton at two shillings a side could hardly be considered a dainty dish, but good, thought Freeman, for the Sunday joint of a poor man with a large family. To enumerate the various vegetables would have been to list the whole edible vegetation of the colony and all stacked there every market morning in such quantity as one wondered where it all went. It proved, he said a century ago, that the people of Melbourne had healthy appetites.

City retail markets lost their dominance as food retailing evolved with the form of city transport. People walked about the early towns, or rode if they could afford the hay. Thus much food was collected personally at the marketplace. But much was also distributed on foot. Among hawkers flocking the streets of the first century, and longer, was Sydney's demented "Flying Pieman" (William King, 1807–1873), who took wagers that he would complete bizarre pedestrian marathons, like 1000 quarter-miles between a tent and a coffin in 1000 quarter-hours. Frank Fowler reported in Melbourne in 1859 "all the classic cries of London, from hot potatoes to iced ginger-beer". In Sydney, he said, Hunter River steamers generally arrived so late with fresh prawns that it was not unusual to be awakened at one or two in the morning by a fellow shouting under your window, "Fine fresh prawns," at sixpence a pint. "If the musquitoes are about it is as well to buy some of these prawns, and sit at the window and eat them for amusement," he advised.

Walter W. Campbell later recalled the old cries of his 1850s Sydney childhood. He heard the muted shout of neatly-dressed "muffin-men", their muffins, crumpets and tea-cakes draped with a white cloth and the basket covered with green baize. Others touted delicacies such as pigs' trotters, saveloys and oysters in bottles. The pie-man was a "conspicuous institution, his meat pies kept warm in a large tin box, supported on thick tin legs and kept warm by a small charcoal stove". At Easter the street cry for hotcross buns was the well-known "One a penny, two for tuppence!" Not only selling the same cheap and savoury dishes for the lower-ranks as in London, the vendors speedily disposed of perishables: fish, milk and bread. Campbell thought the most welcome in his boyhood was the refreshing water-cress man, who carried a large basket on his head and cried "water-cree-sesses", putting emphasis on "cree" and drawing out "sesses". "Milk-ho!" was familiar in the mornings, the cans suspended from yokes on the dairyman's shoulders.

Transport during the gold rushes was still on foot, although witnesses remarked on the exceptional number of horses. As the suburbs spread, successful street sellers also adopted horse and cart, beginning the distinctively Australian delivery of milk and bread. When Thomas Sutcliffe Mort resided at Darling Point in Sydney in mid-century he was amazed at seeing no less than eight or nine baker's carts competing for a few neighbours—"hence the high price of bread," he thought. Carts even dispensed drinking water. One version has it that, gathering at water-carts manufactured in Melbourne by Furphy, people would learn incorrect gossip, which came to be known as a "Furphy". John Freeman noted the appearance about 1870 of the Saveloy Machine, a horse-drawn, coal-fired furnace, with an "abominable nuisance" of a steam whistle to attract customers for hot suppers not just of saveloys but pies and baked potatoes. By the turn of the century, E. C. Buley noticed the ice-cart, milk-cart and the dangling cart of the "rabbit-oh".

Meanwhile, in about the 1870s walking gave way to public transport, at first the horse-drawn omnibus, then the electric tram and finally the railway. City forms evolved accordingly, taking food distribution out to district shops. A Royal Commission on Customs and Excise was told on June 2, 1905, that Italians had captured the fruit trade in their shops. "They make splendid displays in their windows" and if they seemed to charge more than the hawkers then "they pay high rentals and have to make allowance for serious deterioration in the fruit they handle". The fruit hawkers were "harassed at every turn, and are constantly being summonsed and fined", their barrows moved on by municipal authorities and police. Yet fish hawkers survived on foot well into the present century, and the cart-men delivering milk and bread continued to be more distinctive than we usually realised.

5

The Chinese exception

The goldrush Chinese stayed on as market gardeners, an early immigrant group destined to grow and serve the fresh fruit and vegetables that factories could not offer

THE WHITE diggers of the 1850s watched with fascination as the Chinese arrived at the goldfields in files which extended for miles. Their slight figures were dressed in blue "short frocks and voluminous petticoat-trousers" and enormous hats beneath which coiled their pigtails. They bent beneath belongings on each end of a six or eight-foot bamboo, "keeping up a shuffling kind of trot, their very legs seeming to stagger and their bodies to waver under their loads". On the goldfields, the Chinese kept to separate camps with narrow streets of calico tents or bark huts. There were gambling saloons galore, theatres, herbalists, letter-writers, a joss house and eating houses. Several might live in one little room with a few boxes, benches, scanty cooking utensils, jars, teapots and cups of Chinese pattern, chopsticks, gilt emblems, tapers next to the fire and implements for opium smoking.

Describing the 10-foot wide main street at Castlemaine camp in Victoria, E. C. Booth wrote in *Another England* (1869) that cooking was continuous, and the chief ingredient seemed to be underdone dough. Attached to every Chinese restaurant—and every camp had several—was an oven of rough clay, big enough to admit a large pig. The purchase of the pig was a "matter for grave debate and much thought", with the running of soft tapered fingers down the sleek side of the sleeping beauty. A Chinaman never drove a pig and so, according to Booth, "There is no more ludicrous sight in the world than a long piece of rope, with a pig at one end and a Chinaman at the other".

The way the visitors ate actually came to appeal to some, like one

THE CHINESE EXCEPTION

Queenslander, A. J. Boyd, who wrote in the 1870s: "In my humble opinion it is a far more agreeable sight to see a Chinaman eating rice with chopsticks from a neat wicker-cased bowl than to see a man with a lump of greasy beef under his thumb on a piece of bread, sawing away with a sheath knife at his lips". And he appreciated their stir-fry cooking: "They will serve up an excellent repast with the most meagre materials," he commented. But most people despised the alien gold-seekers, who specialised in the endless washing of dirt left by others, and who, instead of the "honest working-man's smoko", paused for a few minutes "chow-chow" of rice.

The Chinese became the model of the immigrant group who, drawn by the hope of riches, filled a gap in our horticulture and our diet. The Chinese invasion had begun with an early English dream—promulgated over the years by James Matra, E. G. Wakefield and others—to populate Australia, under white money and masters, with coolies. British traders turned to such a traffic after their nation abolished the African slave trade in 1833. Squatters imported 1,200 or so Indian and Chinese coolies into NSW in 1838, often to do the "women's work" on stations. Then, in the First Opium War (1840–2), British gunboats annexed Hong Kong and secured five other ports for the entry of cheap cottons and opium and the export of tea, sugar and labourers. So, with the cessation of transportation to NSW in 1840, the scheme quickened and thousands of indentured labourers arrived. However, the Colonial Office in London frowned on the project, because assisted migration already worked well enough, so it was gold, Free Trade's lubricant, which finally brought the Chinese flood. By early 1852, shipping companies advertised the gold discoveries widely in southern China, so that Chinese still refer to California as Chiu Chin Shan (Old Gold Mountain) and Australia as Hsin Chin Shan (New Gold Mountain).

The suddenness and magnitude of the invasion frightened white diggers. The first census in 1854 counted 2,341 Chinese in Victoria. Early the next year, the number passed 10,000 and by the middle of the year 17,000. The 1861 census showed 24,724 Chinese men and eight women in Victoria and 12,986 men and two women in NSW—close to the probable total over the next three decades of around 40,000. The Chinese were continually robbed, assaulted, burnt out, had their pigtails cut off and were mocked and stoned by children. One by one the colonies closed their ports to them. But, when bullied off the goldfields or eventually leaving them to the company mines, the large proportion turned to a task for which our great-grandparents should have thanked them.

Chinese on the goldfields were supplied by a chain of compatriot merchants, storekeepers, gardeners and fishermen, who dried their catch to send inland. This trade steadily broadened and by about 1880 they virtually fed every settlement in Australia. The Chinese had long been used by the squatters as cooks and gardeners. "The poor despised John Chinaman has—with unceasing toil, with infinite manoeuvring, by means of prehistoric wind-wheels and pumps as old as Egypt in design—made a little oasis blossom for them," observed E. M. Clowes in her *On the Wallaby*. They then also became the cooks for eating-places and hotels. E. Marin la Meslée, who wrote in 1883 that no other nation had such "elementary, not to say abominable cooking", reported when travelling with the French consul, that the "yellow cook at Fry's Hotel in Gundagai treated us wonderfully". The 1895 edition of *Mrs Beeton's* commented that many Australian hotels found it easier to hire Chinese cooks in place of Frenchmen. The Chinese cafe and takeaway would not be accepted until the middle of the next century. They cooked in European style—just as they grew familiar fruit and vegetables, their major contribution.

As horticulturists, they rented or fenced off land with some sort of water supply and undercut the prices of existing growers. When she arrived in rural Victoria, Ada Cambridge pronounced that "with a poultry yard and a cow, and John Chinaman's vegetables, even a poor parson could live like a prince." Two or three times a week, regular as clockwork, "John" came to the back door with his vegetable basket. Every little community depended on the most despised, and most reliable, man, she wrote. With their "marvellous patience," *Mrs Beeton's* recognised they were the "best gardeners in the Colony, their mode of irrigation being superior to any other". They had found new use for the beautiful wooden pumps they had brought for gold-washing.

While they first fed rural expansion, the main contribution was to civilise the tremendous city growth, boosting the dreary meat, flour, tea and sugar with good, cheap greens. Just as emancipists provided fresh food to early Sydney and German settlers tramped into Adelaide's market, Chinese particularly nurtured Melbourne's surge of the 1880s. Market gardening became their main occupation, employing one in every three working Chinese men. Two out of every three were involved in some way with the food supply. La Meslée observed in 1883: "Today on the outskirts of every Australian town, great or small, one comes across those beings who look as though they are suffering from chronic jaundice. They are vegetable purveyors, and without them these delicious necessities for European tables would be beyond the reach of most people." A contribution, however phrased, to be grateful for.

What sent them

The majority of the Chinese immigrants came from Kwangtung province, the southernmost of China, and nearly all of them from the fertile Canton Delta. Although with a warm climate and roughly 18,000 square kilometres producing two rice crops and a dry crop annually, the total Kwangtung population had reached 30 million in 1860 and densities were often 8 or 12 per hectare. While it has been estimated that three "mows" of cultivated land (roughly one-fifth of a hectare) were necessary to sustain one person, the allocation was often half this. With rising rents, taxes, banditry and foreign exploitation, the peasants turned from rice to more valuable cash crops like tobacco and opium poppies and came to look forward to remittances from migrant workers. Putting the well-being of his clan above his own comfort and ambitions, a man would set out on the hazardous search for foreign fortune. He would work hard and long at unwanted jobs and, if going into business, choose something like import-export which didn't require long-term committment, for relatively few settled overseas.

Marriages were arranged, and a migrant worker would return periodically to his wife. Only occasionally did he take her, or marry abroad (and then occasionally to a second wife), which kept the number of women in the overseas community very low until a permanently expatriated group multiplied. The Chinese government disapproved of overseas work, which explains why it did not make strong protests against discriminatory laws in the USA, Canada and Australia.

Of the peoples of the world, the Chinese have been probably the most preoccupied with food, an element in their civilisation outlasting others. China's population explosion, a rise from about 150 million in the early 1700s to about 450 million by mid-nineteenth century, was triggered by the availability of food, particularly new crop varieties from the west—maize, sweet potatoes, potatoes, peanuts, followed later by tomatoes and peppers. The Chinese peasant had already mastered the richly varied environment, knowing every edible particle of it, which helped withstand famine. The stir-fry cooking technique conserved precious firewood. With it, the cooks were exceedingly adaptable, which again made for survival, and so too did their tremendous collection of preservation methods, and their insistence on balance, between *fan* and *ts'ai*, between *yin* and *yang*.

Reinforcing this was the strong tradition of moderation. Overindulgence was so sinful that dynasties could fall on its account. Chinese parents told their children to eat till they were "seventy percent full". A great deal about all this was at last collected for the English-speaking world by K. C. Chang in *Food in Chinese Culture: Anthropological and Historical Perspectives* (1977). And in it, E. N. and Marja L. Anderson said that the high population densities and surprising lack of famines, other than those associated with social breakdown, confirmed that: "the southern Chinese diet feeds more people, better, on less land, than any other diet on earth."

Their great adaptability, frugality and experience—the opposite of the Australian characteristics—filled our horticultural gap. The Chinese, like the Irish, were a highly visible group in the mid-nineteenth century. While the Irish reinforced our crude attitudes to eating and drinking, the Chinese, although dominating our urban vegetable supply for several decades, failed to influence us. The reason for these opposite impacts can be seen in the appalling contrast in their home food supplies—while the Irish arrived in cultural tatters, the Chinese came too richly-laden.

The market gardeners

The census of 1891 showed there were 3,841 Chinese market gardeners in NSW, 2,104 in Victoria and 2,564 in Queensland. On the outskirts of almost every town, E. C. Buley wrote in 1905, the ramshackle hut was unmistakable, the roof patched with strips of rusty tin, and the broken windows obscured by sheets of dingy paper. While a half-dozen or more crowded together in this "hovel", in the tumble-down stable might be found a sleek, well-cared for horse, luxuriating in comfort. "Fat as a Chinaman's horse" was a simile of significance, he said. The garden itself was a picture of neatness and good management, the little square beds of cabbage and onions free from weeds and flourishing as a result of constant diligence and "a system of liquid manuring it would not be advisable to investigate too closely, if the vegetables are to be eaten".

Historian Weston Bate has investigated the Chinese gardeners at Melbourne's seaside Brighton, where by 1887, eleven Chinese ratepayers rented 107 acres, mainly from European market gardeners. There had always been complaints about the way nightsoil was dumped on the "Chinaman's garden", but antagonism increased in the depression of the 1890s, when they proved well insulated against falling prices. They were victimised by nightsoil carters, fined for working on Sunday, assailed by missionaries, but stoutly defended by the Brighton council's health officer, Dr Macnash. When the council acted in 1902 against various Chinese residents for keeping dirty premises, the doctor reported that their accommodation was no more crowded than the first-class cabins of a passenger steamer.

And in 1907 he rebutted what he described as sensational statements from the Board of Health. In his 20 years at Brighton he had known no disease among the Chinese which could be attributed to insanitary surroundings. They kept urine in stone jars until it generated ammonia, it is true, but they poured it carefully, when diluted, between the rows of plants. They used excrement also, but inoffensively, and they cleaned their vegetables better than any Europeans. They were anxious to please, he explained, yet like other market gardeners they could not be expected to cover 40 or 50 tons of stable manure. About their inadequate drainage (and he was not one to wink at an offence, as the Brighton dairymen well knew), they were like nightmen and workers in sewerage, quite immune to typhoid and diphtheria. They could not be called "monuments of insanitation and municipal complaisance" in Brighton, whatever the situation elsewhere.

Another defender of the Chinese was journalist E. M. Clowes, whose book *On the Wallaby* contained arguments about the valuable food lessons the

Chinese could have provided. "You see a lot of white men working in the market gardens round Oakleigh and Garden Vale," she wrote in 1911. "They stop to talk with each other, to look round at the sky and distant landscape, to enjoy a few quiet puffs at their pipes; above all, to spit on their hands. The Chinaman never looks up, never stops from dawn to dark. He divides his ground into little oblong patches, with channels between to conserve every drop of moisture; he pampers the young weak plants, shading them from wind and sun with bits of sacking, boards, or slates; he loosens the ground unceasingly round them, and waters untiringly."

Nevertheless, "I do not for a moment advocate Australians working in this manner," she said, "a man must sometimes straighten his back and look around him, must have something of a soul beyond early tomatoes and green peas; but still there is very much that he could be taught from the alien in his midst; and it is a schoolboy's poorest excuse not to learn from a master because he is personally distasteful to him." Australia needed more vegetables most terribly, if it were to escape from the scourge of cancer, she said. And it needed more flower gardens for its spiritual needs, as a humanizing, home-making influence. Nothing struck a new chum more forcibly than the utter lack of any attempt at beautifying the outside of up-country cottages, save with empty condensed milk and jam tins.

She was told by the principal of a Melbourne horticultural college: "I would give anything to have a Chinaman to teach my boys vegetable growing . . . But the Minister would never allow it, and if he did I should have the whole country about my ears." Weren't we wrong? E. M. Clowes asked. "After all, as wise men of all ages have realised, it is from our enemies, not from our friends, that we learn most, and the Chinese native is after all perhaps a trifle older than the Australian—though you in my dear foster-country must really forgive me mentioning it."

The principal centres of Chinese congregation even a century ago were the Haymarket-Dixon Street area in Sydney and the east end of Melbourne's Little Bourke Street. E. M. Clowes frequented "Lilly Bulke Street" early in the new century and would "sup on savoury ragout of duck, served in a porcelain bowl, flanked by lesser bowls, each filled with some mysterious odoriferous condiment, or venture daringly on eggs of an infinite age and most potent flavour". When she pried into the kitchen, "clean as a new pin fragrant with all the mysterious scents of the East", she saw great cauldrons in which brass-bound cooking vessels steamed and simmered. She lifted the green jade teapot out of its wadded case and sipped tea from fragile little bowls, kept ever at hand in a basin of clear cold water.

Clowes marvelled how the "cooks in the eating houses—stout high-priests, Buddhas of gastronomy—slice the infinitesimal shreds of pastry, for garnishing soup, with the most monstrous knives". To her, "all the men in the china, the provision, and the herb-stores, the cook-shops, and gaming-houses, have existed since the beginning of time—till at last their souls have become indifferent alike to good and ill; life appearing, to each, but a task to be finished with, one bead in the necklace of eternity, an oft-repeated routine, where philosophy has ousted pleasure."

Chinese market gardeners—often operating in partnership, four or five sharing the planting, weeding, watering, harvesting and hawking, and often associated with Chinese greengrocers—joined the nightly converging on the central markets. No customer would think of giving 'John' the price he asked. "An offer of about half is made," noted John Freeman in 1888, "and if the smiling Celestial thinks that is not sufficient, the haggling is continued." Freeman found many "chattering" Chinese hawkers at the Melbourne fishmarket. He told of the horseplay, including "bonneting," hurling a small fish or ball of wet fishy paper into someone's face, usually a Chinaman. "If John protests against such treatment, his protestations are received with a yell of delight". Another trick was to slip the back basket off the hawker's pole, so that the front also fell down. The Chinaman would let loose all the vulgar English he had mastered. One morning when this happened, the Chinaman turned and struck the nearest bystander, who happened to be innocent. This delighted the crowd, especially the real culprit, who "patted John on the back and told him not to be afraid, but to go in and win". The working-class had grounds to fear cheap and "subservient" Chinese labour, which showed itself happy to collaborate with the bosses.

Eviction

At a mass meeting in 1881 to protest against Chinese on stations, a speaker moved that: "every squatter and farmer who employed Chinese labour should be burned out. A box of matches would work a cure". The larrikins who hung about street-corner hotels were described in 1883, "accosting unaccompanied women or—what they regard as the acme of delight—kicking insensible and plundering some wretched Chinaman". On May 1, 1890, the *Bulletin* said: "We know the Chinaman better than most people . . . He produces two things—vice and vegetables". Among its first acts in 1901, the national government decreed that immigrants had to pass a 50-word dictation test delivered in a European language, later "any prescribed language". This nasty British trick—since an unknown language could be picked—was the basis of the White Australia policy.

In Queensland, racial exclusion worked for the Chinese, since white growers lost their black labour and, although a bounty was given to sugar growers who employed white workers, Chinese clans soon dominated especially the banana business. With White Australia, Chinese residents could remain, others could still enter as merchants, students and ministers of religion. In 1934 came official recognition of the entry of assistant and replacement traders, gardeners and cooks. However, the numbers here declined steadily

THE CHINESE EXCEPTION

from 29,627 in 1901 to 9,040 in 1947, the proportion of Australian-born rising from 6 to 41 per cent. Reflecting a wider tendency, the Chinese became more urban, 32 per cent in 1911 and 60 per cent in 1947. Their market gardening declined as capital substituted for labour, as technology substituted for patience.

As early as 1893, it was reported that a Mr Plumber, with 40 acres on the Murray near Albury, had erected a turbine to irrigate "larger and better stuff" at lower prices, and had "beaten the Chinese clean out of the field". In 1920, a NSW Department of Agriculture publication suggested that larger areas than the Chinese one-acre-per-man could usually be more profitable with less intensive crops and some horse cultivation. The local approach to tillage was exemplified by Cliff Howard's invention at Gilgandra, NSW, in 1920. His devastating idea was that an engine should turn hoe blades, whether on a tractor "rotavator" or the faithful walk-behind rotary hoe. As the suburbs encroached on good horticultural land, rail and truck transport made possible more distant, specialised farms relying on heavy doses of chemicals. With canning, cool storage and then freezing, big capital could enter where only the meek had fared. By 1979, a flurry of Sydney newspaper articles announced the eviction—from plots behind the Matraville drive-in theatre and nearby La Perouse—of four of the city's last six Chinese market gardens.

More and more, the Chinese had taken their skills to running cafes, often with "English" dishes but also, increasingly, with a version of Chinese food. In the 1950s, white Australians were at last found eating in the Chinese restaurants which spread through the suburbs and provided oases in country towns. With some exceptions, the ever-adaptable Chinese cooks compromised tradition by embracing frozen, prepared ingredients. Much was said about how well they were "assimilating" into our ways. Their children moved into the professions (books by two scholars, C. Y. Choi and C. F. Yong, providing leads for this chapter). In the Whitlam years, restaurants like the Taiping in Sydney, gained fashionable status. Debate between the Cantonese versus the Peking styles extended to appreciation of "yum cha breakfasts", the plucking of passing delicacies from the waiters' trays permitting variable-length business luncheons. Then, between 1978 and 1981, boats of mainly Chinese refugees from Vietnam gave another boost to the Chinese cafe business.

The Chinese community could be accepted since it was no longer a threat—with immigration controls to keep it tiny and still seen to be taking laborious jobs avoided by the ordinary Australian. But why had we finally accepted their cuisine, however much compromised? The novel ingredients, combinations and rituals with chopsticks intrigued us, during a period when further massive inroads by the food industry would shake our expectations about eating.

THE TEA AND SCONES OF QUONG TART

Quong Tart

NINETEENTH-century Chinese arrivals divided into two classes. One was referred to most crudely as the "sweepings of the Canton River" and the other was the merchant elite. While the former were mainly peasant farmers, the latter often made a deal of money, wore smart European clothes and, although they would have been accorded low status in China, were held in an extraordinarily high regard in materialist Australia. Lowe Kong Meng was the recognised leader of the Chinese in Victoria, having commenced as a tea-importer in Little Bourke Street in 1854, and with another prosperous merchant, Louis Ah Louy, he was instrumental in establishing the Commercial Bank of Australia. A similar, even more public figure in Sydney, was Quong

Tart. His wife, Margaret Scarlett of Liverpool, England (who married him in 1886 and bore six children), collected together a short biography, a fascinating picture of tea-rooms of the Victorian era.

Mei Quong Tart was born in the Canton district in 1850 and when only nine apparently pleaded to accompany an uncle who was taking a shipload of labourers to the Braidwood fields in NSW. He fell in with the family of Percy Simpson, who employed many hundred miners, principally Chinese. While Alice Simpson educated him and converted him to Christianity, Mr Simpson gave a share in a rich claim, "which the fortunate young protégé turned to the best advantage". He employed about 200 Chinese and Europeans, built a villa at Bell's Creek, erected a school and church, was patron of the manly sports, became naturalised, learnt Scottish songs, joined Manchester Unity Lodge and the Freemasons. In 1874, he was farewelled at a public banquet— Quong Tart singing "Auld Lang Syne"—because he had made up his mind to establish himself as an importer of tea and silk in Sydney.

In 1881, he sold tea in the Sydney Arcade and, as an advertisement, handed out sample cups. He had so many takers that he had to find larger premises and charge for tea and scones. In 1885, when he had already opened no less than four places, he extended to the Royal Arcade in King Street— where one lady asked him for a "cup of tea and a Quong Tart"—and to the bamboo pavilion at the Zoological Gardens, called the "Han Pan", and a year later to refreshment rooms at 777 George Street. On Saturday, December 21, 1889, after a second trip to China, he added King Street tea rooms on a magnificent scale, the total cost being £6,000. Sir John Robertson proposed the toast, "Fill your teacups, gentlemen all." He triumphed again with occupancy by 1899 of the failed Queen Victoria markets with his Elite Dining Hall and Tea Rooms.

Quong Tart considered it far pleasanter to have a chop well cooked, daintily served by a well-apparelled waitress, than to have it thrust upon one in a discourteous manner. Accordingly, his rooms were artistically arranged with trickling ferneries, marble reservoirs in which golden carp swam, hand-painted mirrors, massive Chinese wood-carvings in green and gold and hundreds of fans, which "tempted the wayfarer". There were a plentiful supply of lavatories, with hot and cold water, writing rooms, luxuriantly furnished smoking rooms, and separate rooms for ladies.

He ordered his employees to treat all alike, whether they wore silk dresses or cheap prints. He did not apply the iron hand, "Such a method fosters antagonism for each other, and produces class hatred and industrial revolt," he thought, according to his widow's biography. His employees were not mere machines, and to keep in touch he held a harbour excursion or a musical evening. His wife was impressed with how he "combined the astuteness of the man of the world with the high principledness of the Christian and so left an example that business men might profitably follow."

He moved easily about Sydney society. When warned that he was infringing the heart-shaped trademark of a rival tea merchant, Clifford Love, he took the problem to a benefactor, Mr J. H. Want, KC. Want asked, "Hullo, in trouble? Woman, eh?" "No," said Tart. "But I've lost my heart and all through Love. But when you lose one heart you should gain another, should you not?" Then, Tart took a piece of paper on which he had drawn a double heart, and said, "There, sire; in future my trademark shall be two hearts instead of one, and closely interwoven." Sparkling with fun, at a Sydney banquet Quong was pressed to take more "fizz". "No, thanks. If I took more of that stuff, I shouldn't be a tart, but a roly-poly." He told a church bazaar that a lady had no reason to boast about her eggs, "Here's Mr Hawthorne, MP. I was with him at Leichhardt last week and his good wife—why, I saw her lay a foundation stone two-ton weight!"

The young gentlemen attached to a "certain Governor's retinue" were entertaining young ladies and engaged Quong Tart to do the catering. Quong, not wishing to trifle with his reputation, brewed from leaves which cost 7/6 a pound. After a little muttering one of them told Tart, "Look here, old chap, what the dickens do you mean by giving us slop water for tea? Be good enough to have the damned stuff removed, and have something drinkable substituted." More in sorrow than in anger, he ordered his staff use some "one and threepenny tea". The Government House "connoisseurs" pronounced it, "excellent, old chappie".

Quong Tart invested his total energies in the public philosophies of his new country, even to the extent of belittling his own birthright. His enthusiasm for self-made men extended to "always having a kindly word for the newsboys of Sydney". So, one Saturday afternoon in December, 1893, he arranged to treat 250 at his tea rooms. The youngsters first paraded the streets of the city, headed by the Croydon School Cadet Band, and carrying bannerettes indicating the names of their newspapers. They ended up seated at five long tables, and as fast as the good things vanished, the waitresses replaced them, until the boys had to confess that their efforts to clear the tables had failed. Afterwards, leading men of the city gave instructive addresses, the boys leaving better for the tea and advice tendered.

While our history refused to learn from Quong Tart's peasant compatriots, we showered public affection on the middleman. Spending much time opening fairs, bazaars, flower shows and Highland gatherings, he loved being thought of as "MacTart". Quong Tart was as "well known as the Governor himself, and is quite as popular among all classes," the *Daily Telegraph* noted on October 10, 1897. The *Goulburn Cookery Book* in 1899 contained a recipe for Quong Tart Scones, with sugar, butter and extra baking powder. On August 19, 1902, a robber wounded Mr Tart at his Queen Victoria office. Although it was not fatal, he died of subsequent pleurisy on July 26, 1903.

6

The tyranny of transport

Some Australian farms might have been the havens of children's storybooks, but most were producers of durable foods to be rushed by train to the cities and the world

AUSTRALIAN cities had been established at the ports where flour, sugar and tea were unloaded. A little fresh food came either from town gardens, dairies and butcheries or from the fertile outskirts. The land beyond a half-day's tramp lay with the graziers. But this changed with the railways, which reached far out for food. The railways investment was not simply to feed our emergent workforce. In 1838, Benjamin Disraeli had seen England as the "workshop of the world" and, since the workforce had to be healthy, the world had to be England's farm.

British investors spent vast sums on iron tracks throughout the empire and private companies commenced work in NSW, Victoria and SA around 1850. Hardly had the first sod been turned, when labour and other costs soared through the distraction of the goldrush. Governments had to take over and raise even bigger money in London. By 1870, a thousand miles of track were open in eastern Australia, each link celebrated with a grand banquet. By 1890, the length was 11,000 miles, accounting for an enormous debt to Britain. The ridiculed differences in the States' railway gauges scarcely mattered, because the colonies were connected by ship—the lines merely sought to bring the hinterland into the world.

Between 1870 and 1896, British meat consumption rose by a third, with the proportion of imported meat trebling. Starved Britons began to eat fruit again, initially as jam, later also fresh fruit like bananas. The consumer goods market was transformed by the rise of the shop, with stocks from food factories and the colonies. Although the British rural industry was further dismantled, cheap imports from around 1870 led to a better-fed society there.

The railways thus signalled a new era in Australian agriculture, opening up monotonous broad-acres for wheat, dairying and irrigated horticulture. Shipping food around the world, we did not dot our landscape with self-sufficient farming villages. Instead, we erected corrugated-iron communities investing large sums of borrowed money in machinery and fences. Half way through our history, the railway brought Australians closer to the land than ever before or since. It provided a gloss of cultivation in an uncultivated land. It gave us an illusion that we were rural. But we weren't. We were a developed nation.

The novel style of primary industry shaped our eating. While more people could enjoy fresher fruit and milk, more varied vegetables, less weary beef and cheaper mutton, the convenience of rail tended to keep even bush kitchens dependent on factory supplies and city recipes. Producing for transport, the farms grew the sturdier vegetables like potatoes and carrots and provided the raw materials for the utterly typical "Aussie" white bread, camp pie, condensed milk, tinned apricots, bottles of tomato sauce and lollies.

The railways tamed the bush in all sorts of ways. When the young French writer, E. Marin La Meslée, and the French consul dined on fowl at the Mittagong railway station in 1876, they hit on the idea of tasting the wine of the area. However, the waiter announced they were not licensed to sell any kind of alcoholic drink. "What!" exclaimed the consul, Monsieur de Castelnau, "What can people drink here then, when they are thirsty?" The waiter offered tea, coffee, lemonade, seltzer water (soda-water) . . . "That stuff," said the consul. "Do you want to make yourself the laughing-stock of the whole world?" "No, sir," the waiter offered, "it is the same in every railway refreshment room in NSW—they are all run on strict temperance principles. It's a government rule."

An attempt at peasant agriculture

Agitation for "closer settlement" came to a crescendo with the railways. There was "such an aspect of dreary desolation" in the interior that the traveller would be painfully impressed how little progress was made by the "arts of civilisation", the NSW Land League's manifesto claimed in 1859. Patches of agriculture were "so few and far between" that the great bulk of the people were still fed with imported breadstuffs, it said. With pressure to feed booming populations, the new colonial governments joined the push for land reform, to "unlock" grazing land for more intensive production. The most famous legislation was John Robertson's NSW Act of 1861, by which selectors could purchase as much as 320 acres of cheap Crown land so long as they subscribed to certain conditions of cultivation and residence. The creation of these family farms aimed, according to contemporary writer Richard Twopenny, to "compel large owners to sell, and establish something answering to a peasant proprietary, or, more strictly speaking, a yeomanry tilling its own soil." The impetus was opposed legally and illegally by squatters, who belittled the small farmers as "cockatoos", or "cow cockies", kept contented with their golden syrup, or "cocky's joy".

The Victorian Land Act of 1862 included a quite Arcadian "novel industries" clause, under which favourable leases were offered to farmers attempting some new crop. By the end of the year 62 people had applied for leases within the Port Phillip region, 21 of the applicants intending to establish vineyards. Many others sought a mixture of vines with olives, oranges, lemons and so forth. But few of the 30-acre leases succeeded—their more delicate table wines did not transport like robust hotter-climate brews—and soon after Prince Alfred's visit in 1868 vineyards collapsed all around the Barrabool Hills and Sunbury. Undeterred, the legislators appointed a royal commission in 1871 to "report how far it may be practicable to introduce into this country branches of industry which are known to be common and profitable among the farming population of Continental Europe . . ." A century later Victorians could resurrect the vineyards, but back then we needed to churn out city rations.

With the dismantling of agrarian Britain, farm labourers had been dragged, rioting, from the countryside and sent to Australia. Now many of them were set up, to the ring-barking of eucalypts and mounting of horse-drawn machines, in an entirely new concept in agriculture. With new workers, preservation techniques, money, land, rapid railways and clippers and steamers, Australian agriculture developed beyond wool to food, with beef, wheat and butter. This second stage, the incorporation of our soil into the global food trade, was most intense between 1870 and the 1914–18 war. Some commentators have scoffed that Henry Lawson and Banjo Paterson's pastoral romance was already out-dated when the *Bulletin* was launched in 1880. But it served to create a legend, when the time of the farm had arrived and "The mighty Bush with iron rails is tethered to the world."

Statistician Timothy Coghlan considered Australia and New Zealand by the end of the century the richest countries in the world. He calculated Australian primary production to be worth about £22 per inhabitant annually. This compared with Canadian of £16 5s 6d, US £14 14s, French £11 11s and British £7 18s 6d. In the *Seven Colonies* he stated: "From primary industries Australasia produces more per inhabitant than is produced by the combined industries of any other country." Yet his figures neglected the enormous non-market production of still largely peasant economies. And our productivity of wheat averaged 8½ bushels to the acre (in SA 4·69 and Tasmania 19·05), where French productivity was 18½ and English 31. Our transport-based agriculture had entered the international food business with plenty of land, awash with funds and with unlimited technical ambitions.

New agricultural techniques

The farm of our imagination, the farm of children's picture books, is a self-contained unit reaping the sun's energy, with fowls picking up spilled grain, pigs welcoming skim-milk from cows, manure enriching the garden, trees providing fruit successively through the year, willows by the stream used for baskets, flax stripped to tie vines and vegetables. And so on. Railways disconnected internal links and plugged factory farmyards into cities. Efficient farms required special machinery and factory-made feeds and fertilisers. They tended to specialise in a single commodity, which made work boring and opened the overcrowded crop to plagues, which meant more chemicals with every season. Loose connections led to environmental degradation—and the irony of the pig factory dumping manure into creeks while the fertiliser factory poisoned the air. And the new links made the farm dependent on markets and the providers of equipment, feeds, fertiliser, chemicals and capital, which centralised control.

Some crops like grains could be carried around the world without much deterioration. But most foods required preservation—like the traditional salting of butter, drying of fruit and fermentation of cheeses and wine. New techniques were devised in Europe, the United States, Argentina and Australia. For instance, meat could be carried canned, chilled, frozen and reduced to an "extract". Fruit was tinned, chilled and dried. Milk was dried into powder and "condensed". And butter and cheese were salted, tinned, chilled and dosed with preservatives. The nineteenth century was quickly cluttered with a myriad schemes and inventions, as enthusiasts and entrepreneurs sought bonanza. Keith Farrer in 1980 detailed many in *A Settlement Amply Supplied: Food Technology in Nineteenth-Century Australia*. He claimed mechanical refrigeration as "very largely an Australian innovation", a Geelong journalist James Harrison having devised a machine for manufacturing ice on a commercial scale in 1851.

Bolstering this production push, government bureaucracies expanded, and set up departments of agriculture and agricultural colleges. To take an instance: in 1888, the new Victorian Railways Commissioners reduced freight charges for dairy produce, placed special rolling stock to carry butter and proposed £50,000 to equip 170 country stations with goods sheds to receive dairy produce. At the same time, Premier Duncan Gillies supported a plan to spend the budget surplus on bonuses for the best produce, the best packing methods, the invention of agricultural machinery, subsidies for the establishment of butter factories, fruit canneries and drying plants, agricultural education and prizes for imports of new seeds.

Industrial farming so shaped our food that we should run through some of the highlights, commodity by commodity.

Wheat

Before the railways, the production of wheat was largely manual—perhaps an animal dragging a single plough—but often the family shared the hoeing, hand broadcasting and harvesting with sickle and scythe. The nineteenth-century factory's cast-iron implements steadily replaced the village blacksmith's sturdy tools. Early machines were cumbersome, but by the end of the century, one man and a mighty horse-team could sow, harvest and cart the bags of a cheaper commodity to the railway siding. South Australia industrialised wheat almost from the colony's foundation, partly because land policies encouraged fair-sized plots, as opposed to either the squatter's endless rangelands or cottager's garden. Clearing was easy and the lands were within reach of the sea. The want of seasonal labour led to attempts at mechanisation and in 1843 John Wrathall Bull's stripper—a contraption taken up by John Ridley—combined stripping the heads of wheat with threshing. The SA farmers made a killing by shipping flour off to the goldfields where high prices could be asked, and when the population settled down, wheat became attractive in Victoria.

In 1884, Hugh Victor McKay, then only 18, constructed a machine which stripped, threshed, winnowed and bagged the grain in one run. Even though Justus von Liebig's report to the British Association on biochemistry for agriculture had laid the foundation in 1840 for "artificial manure" (chemical fertilisers), Australia's abundant land did not require superphosphate until the 1890s. Then, the breeding by William Farrer and others of short-stalked soft wheats adapted grain to dry-weather farming. We were on the way to the "f.a.q." ("fair average quality") standard.

Beef and mutton

The original primary industry, grazing, had supplied wool to Europe, but beef and mutton were only consumed locally. One way to use carcasses was discovered during the 1843 slump—"boiling down" to tallow for candles, soap and industrial grease. Success stimulated experiments with canning. In France at the end of the eighteenth century Nicolas Appert had preserved foods by bottling, a novelty which delighted Parisian chefs, who could present delicacies out of season. Tinplate had just begun to be made in England and the first meat was canned in London early in the new century for seafarers. In 1845, a Sydney grocer and ships' chandler, Sizar Elliott, became probably the first person to can meat in Australia. The biggest early enterprise was launched near Newcastle, NSW, in 1848 by brothers Henry, William and Richard Dangar to supply the British Admiralty. Having to import tinplate was only one of their burdens, which multiplied with higher labour and cattle costs after the goldrushes, and so they disbanded in 1855. It was not until 1866 that further attempts opened the British market, 10,000 tons being sent there during the peak year of 1871.

The third edition of *Mrs Beeton's* in 1880 described the Australian meats as "wholesome and cheap, two great points in their favour". The price ranged from 4d to 9d per pound and it could be got in almost any sized tin, from 1 lb to 6 lbs. But, as Beeton said, "an objection has been raised by some as to the appearance of Australian and other tinned meats when turned out of their tin holders; but there are sold pretty dishes for the very purpose of lessening the ugliness . . . and garnishing now much and properly in vogue as an ornamentation to nearly all of our dishes, very much aids us in the matter." With a reserve tin or so of foreign meat in her cupboard, the English mistress "need never feel her heart sinking in her shoes when unexpected visitors arrive". In a less gentle climate, canned meat came to be termed "tinned dog" and gave rise to "camp pie".

There was a lot of meat to get rid of. A classic substitution of capital for labour had taken place when graziers replaced shepherds with fences. In 1860 there were four million cattle and 20 million sheep, but by 1880 the numbers had risen to 7½ million cattle and 62 million sheep. In 1890, there were more than 10 million cattle and nearly 100 million sheep. And that's not to mention the unfenced rabbits, canned in enormous numbers. Meanwhile, a committee of the British Society of Arts deliberated from 1866 to 1881 on how a meat supply might be assured from the colonies, apart from that in tins. The answer was refrigeration.

In July, 1873, the Geelong inventor, James Harrison, consigned 20 tons of frozen mutton and beef to England, but the meat deteriorated. Four years later the first frozen meat was shipped from Buenos Aires to Marseilles in the *Paraguay*. In early 1880, the first successful shipment of Australian frozen meat arrived in London on the *Strathleven*. Since ice crystals damaged the cells, frozen flesh lost colour when thawed, looked sodden and tended to be stringy and flavourless. Sheep getting the better pasture, beef was the inferior product of the hard outback and distant north. Its supply was irregular and in the wrong season, and grading was lax. The industry then, as later, suffered fraudulent practices. For such reasons, those countries nearer Britain which merely chilled beef for shipment squeezed us out of the market, until successful Australian chilling in the 1930s and the Meat Board in 1936 brought order to the industry.

Dairying

Thomas Sutcliffe Mort, the "man of vision", introduced orderly wool auctioning and became involved in sugar, the AMP Society and a dry dock at Balmain, Sydney. In 1860, Mort bought Bodalla, rich land south of Sydney, to develop a healthy country estate with tenant farmers. Characteristically, he turned it into a big, modern dairy. The first installation of a cream separator is claimed for Mort's company at Mittagong, NSW, in 1881. About that time, perhaps originating in Kiama, NSW, in 1884, other farmers organised cooperative butter factories. But what the dairying industry really needed was refrigeration, which, from 1866 until his death in 1878, Mort worked on with engineer E. D. Nicolle.

As an owner of large workshops, Mort saw he could profit by building refrigeration equipment. As a pastoral financier, he could use it to develop new meat markets—a venture which sent the frozen meat to London on the *Strathleven.* And as a milk and butter producer, he could improve access to the Sydney market using refrigerated transport. He founded the NSW Fresh Food & Ice Co, whose chilling works, cold stores, milk depots and refrigerated railway vans became the basis of Sydney's Darling Harbour dairy distribution network. By 1893, the Fresh Food & Ice Co advertised it would "deliver, daily, to all parts of the City, Suburbs, and Country, milk, ice, cream, butter, poultry, fish, game, pastry, &c". The company proudly offered fresh fish to residents of every country town of NSW and Brisbane. "A telegraph order from any country town, despatched before 1 pm (provided the Telegraph Department do their part), is certain of execution by mail train the same day," the advertisement claimed. Their refrigerating works at Harbour Street were, "without doubt, the most extensive and expansive of their kind in the world". Pasteurisation, which had already lengthened beer's life, was first used for milk in 1889, but only slowly introduced and not as a health measure so much as another transport tool.

Fruit

Fruit growing leapt forward with the goldrush, many fruit districts owing their origin to adjacent goldfields, among them Bendigo, Ballarat, Young, Batlow and Charters Towers. It expanded after the 1880s as a result of irrigation, canning and drying, cool storage and refrigerated transport. The canning of both jam and fruit had been first carried out in Tasmania. George Peacock commenced jam-making in a factory in 1861 in Hobart and went on within a few years to conserve whole fruits, the firm taken over by his employee, Henry Jones, in 1891. Dozens of competitors canned jam and fruit for export and home.

Irrigation had got underway in many areas of Victoria, the "cabbage patch", before Canadian brothers George and William Chaffey were persuaded, following their Californian successes, to invest in pumping from the Murray River. They arrived in 1886, created amazement by choosing the rundown cattle station at Mildura, where by 1890, there were 3,000 settlers with wine, citrus and dried fruits. Australians became devoted to peaches, apricots and pears of Victoria's Goulburn Valley, home of SPC and Ardmona.

Sugar

White sugar has status among urban workers, but highly-refined sugar also keeps better, to the benefit of producers. The Colonial Sugar Refining

Company (CSR) was formed in 1855 to take over a refinery established in Sydney in 1840 to process imported material from the cheap-labour tropics. After early experiments, the cultivation of sugar-cane re-emerged in the 1860s in northern NSW and Queensland. The year 1885 saw the maximum number of 102 mills in NSW but, as steam power replaced animals, this was down to 24 in 10 years. Queensland growing was developed on a plantation system with large estates, often absentee owners and Kanaka labour. Federation was not popular among planters, given that the other States were against non-European workers. The high labour costs, too easily interpreted racially as "white men in black men's country", then meant that Australia led in the mechanisation of cane cultivation. One family with machinery replaced a plantation of slaves.

Rural "hardship"

The farmers who finally turned Australia from a net importer to exporter of food in the decades around Federation are really the people we've thought of as our "pioneers". They were not convicts, not single adventurers, but married couples—the basic small business partnership—sent to develop an industry. The farm families tended not to inherit their wisdom, but learned from annual agricultural shows and from the *Bulletin*, the *Land*, *Australian Town and Country Journal*, *Australian Home Journal* and *New Idea* and department of agriculture gazettes. They practised an agriculture and way of life novel in world history, living in relative isolation and coming together in another innovation, the country town. It accumulated a railway station, Royal and Commercial hotels, bank, police station, primary school, circulating library, mechanics' institute, stock and station agent, newspaper office, telephone exchange, soft-drink bottler, and, failing all else, general store.

In his *Old Colonials*, A. J. Boyd described the rise of one rural identity, the "Bush Butcher", in the Queensland of the 1870s. Someone generally started butchering, Boyd said, as soon as there was a population in an outside district to warrant the killing of three or four beasts a week. He started boiling down at his kitchen fire, in a kerosene tin, and devoted his parlour to the salting of unsold beef. Under his bed might be found salted tongues and a few hams in preparation. But tallow, hides, horns and bones also made ready money. "He then sets up a spring cart and horse to run his beef around to his customers, and erects a smoking house, and a boiling down battery," Boyd said. The butcher then retained a boy to go around for orders.

If he had a glut of salt meat, he informed citizens that his cattle had broken free and there would be no fresh meat for three days. Was there any salt meat? Well, yes, the butcher thought there was a little left. He rapidly became one of the most important men in the district, invariably chairman of race meetings and seeming to have command of money. By the time he was being suspected of stealing cattle, he had large killing yards, known by an odour of decayed offal and a great resort for crows, hawks and dingoes. The pigs, wallowing in the mire and fighting for garbage, were another great source of profit for our butcher. Costing him nothing to keep, they got coarse and fat. But the butcher never partook of his own pigs, having a weakness for the farmer's bacon, Boyd concluded.

Although derided as such, the farmers were not peasants. They took pride in forcing forward civilisation, in beating back nature's frontier, in standing alone, in doing back-breaking work, in accumulating capital, in mastering transport. They were concerned with daily bread merely as a commodity price. They ate to live and they lived to improve their material and social position. Many collapsed into poverty or back to factory-work. Yet some crashed through. While they set out to produce perhaps a single commodity like wheat or butter, they nevertheless—with their kitchen garden, a few fruit trees and hens and a pig—established what we think of as the rural way of life. Half-way through our history, many of them even undertook mixed farming, demonstrating its protection against weather and commodity price fluctuations.

An article in the *Argus* on January 13, 1902, described the "Hard Lot of Farmers' Wives" in Gippsland. Mother began work before the sun rose, the reporter found. She milked, fed calves, pigs, fowls and then got breakfast—of cold salt beef, porridge and tea. She cleaned, and made bread. Then came dinner—of mutton, potatoes, rice and tea. She helped plant potatoes and find the pigs. Then after milking, it was tea time—of cold beef, bread and butter, tea—but if times were bad, merely bread, dripping and tea. After tea, she had clothes to make, maize to shell, or potatoes to cut for the morrow's planting.

The reporter talked to a woman established 20 years, with a field of splendid oats, a paddock of sprouting maize, five acres of potatoes, an orchard by the homestead, a barn full of hay and sheds for cows, horses and pigs. Yet, she complained, it cost what the peaches and apples were worth to put them on the market. "You town people are the State's babies. You get coddled and fussed over," she said. "We in the country are just stepchildren . . . You say, 'But you've got railways'. Have we, though? It's you that have the railways; we pay for them. We send away our milk, cream, butter, fruit, eggs, potatoes. We pay the carriage, mind you! We go to the stores, and buy groceries, calicoes, flannels, blankets, and again we pay, not only cost, but carriage!"

The article described a new property, where the man turned up dark red soil with a single-furrow plough, the woman had a hut with a big flat fireplace occupying all one end of the room, and which held a camp oven, a kettle and a pot. The woman said, "We're just white slaves" and the man, "Look here, they're building this country on the farmers' bones." Such passions led to collective action through cooperatives, State intervention and, from the 1920s, the Country Party; although each step seemed only to lead to more centralisation and more farmers forced off the land. Chronicles of endless hardship (many collected in Eve Pownall's *Mary of Maranoa: Tales of Australian Pioneer Women* in 1959) served several political interests—from those opposed to closer settlement to the settlers themselves.

No doubt it was a tough life—especially for those opening up unsuitable country. Yet other evidence can be called to demonstrate the romance in it, certainly from a distance, as when novelist Rosa Campbell-Praed looked back at her Queensland bush childhood in the 1850s and 60s. It was a wonderful, active childhood, in spite of periodic scarcity of rations when drays were flood-bound for months on end and pumpkin appeared day after day, she said. The native women showed the children how to plait "dilly bags", a word which passed into the language, and make drinking vessels out of gourds. Her father moved about, working a banana plantation on the Brisbane River and then trying to raise sugar and cotton. "For pure joy, nothing comes up to a canefield," she wrote, "for a child it is paradise . . . the shoots of sugar cane are most toothsome, and sweeter than store goodies."

Gone bush again, she recalled frying birds' eggs in the sun on a sheet of zinc, water in the casks that "tasted as though it had been boiled" and the legs of the dining table standing in billies of water to discourage ants. She recalled picking grapes to place in large basins on the verandah, setting figs and melons for jam, scouring milkpans for the dairy, cleaning bins of weevily flour, preparing prickly pears for jelly and putting corn through the cutter, with the crackling sound of the orange grain rolling out the machine's red mouth. She described the bush version of a *pot-au-feu*, a sort of fishpot from which you might land half a wild duck, a whole parrot, a lump of kangaroo tail, a slice of salt junk or a bit of salt pork.

Rosa Campbell-Praed described the homestead store as a weird sort of place, with a great dark space above the rafters, and filled with cockroaches and white-ant nests and strange iron implements, drums of tobacco, bottles of concoctions. One side was piled to the rafters (if the drays had come in lately) with bags of flour and mats of sugar, which exuded syrup and attracted ants. Below the shelf of groceries was a big flour-bin and compartments for black ration sugar, a lighter sort and white sugar for the head station. And, of course, there was an immense tea-chest.

Country cooking often became something of an inspiration, encouraged by relative closeness to the soil, busy community entertaining and few distractions. There were home-grown fruit and vegetables, fresh cream, home-cured bacon . . . With ready cash and weak traditions, and with less need for warmth, country women were quick to adopt the clean and controllable cast-iron stove. It excelled at gently scalding cream, boiling jams and preserves, and baking roasts and cakes. The men took fruit cake into the paddocks and the women competed at social events with lamingtons. But notice how the ingredients of the homestead store—flour, sugar, sago, rice, cocoa, coconut, etc—were portable commodities brought by train.

The Tyranny of Transport

In 1966, Geoffrey Blainey entitled his interpretation of Australian history *The Tyranny of Distance*. To him, our early years were shaped by isolation, later conquered by fast clippers and railways. That Blainey saw transport as liberating Australia is perhaps not surprising, given that he wrote during an era of unprecedented faith in mobility. But he also over-estimated distance's hold on the country. In fact, I find it more satisfying to look at the whole of Australian history as suffering a tyranny not of distance, but of transport.

Aborigines, who covered a fair bit of ground themselves, might not have regretted isolation's protection. But then came the schoolbook conquerors of distance, the sea voyagers and outback explorers, expanding the glorious empire. Even the pioneers complaining of loneliness were actually put there—like the convicts—by transportation. From the start, the inhabitants commuted to and from Britain, tramped, plodded with bullocks and then hastened with Cobb & Co between towns and stations, and within a few decades had cluttered the streets and paddocks with almost as many horses as we have cars.

In a country like Italy you can still find tremendous regional variety in eating and drinking habits. Until a few years ago people in one valley might be quite unfamiliar with the dishes cooked in the next. Across the Alps, French cooking is quite different, although there's a subtler shift of cuisine along the Mediterranean because of the ease of shipping. In Australia, cooking has distinctively lacked any such regional variation. Country fare has scarcely differed from city. In fact, the food is remarkable for being directly derived from styles half-way around the globe.

From the day the First Fleet unloaded its stores, there has been no greater evidence of transport's tyranny than our food, which has had to be portable, often ruling out variety and freshness. The early colonists survived on rations of sugar, flour and tea, as if members of some mobile army, and even their children and grandchildren were reared on provisions lumped from other continents. Our foremost industry, grazing, was notable for its peripatetic practitioners, who merely "squatted". As we have now seen, sedentary styles of farming were not established seriously until a century after restless Captain Cook.

The new style of primary production was not self-sufficient, but set up along railway lines to feed populations in distant metropolises and even on the other side of the world. The very farming techniques tended to be extractive, on the assumption that you could either move on or import fertiliser. Even when the move to the country finally swung the balance of the food trade from imports to exports, provisions were commonly carted from other centres—apples from Tasmania, flour from South Australia and sugar from Queensland. Whether the evidence is scurvy, monotonous rations, or utilitarian agriculture—our food has suffered a tyranny of transport.

GRANNY SMITH

Claimed to be the only photograph of Maria Ann "Granny" Smith

MARIA ANN SMITH died long before her apple came to prominence, so that much of her story is lost. However, the "Granny Smith" who cultivated one of the world's most successful varieties was born with the surname of Sherwood at Pearsmouth, Sussex, in 1800. She married Thomas Smith from a nearby town and the couple grew hops, before setting off aboard the *Lady Nugent*, arriving in NSW in 1838. They and their five children eventually settled on land fronting the Great Northern Road in the Ryde district. With sons farming in the area and two daughters marrying local orchardists, she became by her late sixties widely known as "Granny".

Her husband an invalid, she took the produce of their small orchard to the city markets. One local story was that she brought back from market some cases containing rotting Tasmanian apples, probably French Crabs. She tipped them among the ferns beside her creek. A few years later—it was now probably 1868—she discovered in place of the rubbish a seedling bearing a few fine apples. Grown from a seed, it was a cross-breed, and interesting. Among the visitors she showed the apples to were Mr E. H. Small and his 12-year-old son (who recalled the story in 1924). Mr Small decided they made good cooking apples, even though Mobbs' Royal and others seemed to fill the need at the time. The boy found the green-skinned apples good for eating.

Another version (recorded in 1956 by her grandson, Benjamin Spurway) was that a fruit agent, Thomas Lawless, gave her the French Crabs to test their cooking quality. Granny made apple pies, throwing the peelings and cores out the kitchen window, and a seedling grew close to the wall. She died soon after—on March 9, 1870—and the variety was taken up by orchardists around Parramatta, including Edward Gallard and her sons-in-law, James Spurway and Henry Johnston.

In the NSW Department of Agriculture's *Gazette* in 1895, Albert H. Benson recommended "Granny Smith's seedling" as a late cooking apple suitable for export. He also obtained the variety for the department's Bathurst farm, which was a big step towards its widespread use. In 1904, the *Gazette* published a colour plate of two varieties, including Granny Smith's, incorrectly suggesting it had come from Bathurst or Penrith. On retiring from the government farm, Mr G. K. Wolstenholme planted out a very large acreage at his Montavella orchard, a few miles from Bathurst. He promoted the variety with free cases to leading business and professional men, clubs and hotels in Sydney. The fruit merchant, Fred Chilton, handled the Montavella crop and, experimenting with cool storage, imported oiled wrapping tissues from America to solve cool-store "scald". Picked from March, the Granny Smith could be stored until November, a tremendous attribute.

The original tree was soon cleaned out and, although a small nearby park in modern Eastwood was named after her in 1950, Maria Ann Smith's gift to good eating can be added to the list of insufficiently recognised legacies of our pioneering women. We should rejoice in the eating and cooking qualities of the apple, but we should not forget that its real secret was that it kept, which made it readily transportable. "Granny" developed her apple on the eve of food's massive mobilisation for shipment across the oceans. It was exported significantly after the First World War and, by 1975, about 40 per cent of the national apple crop was of Granny Smith's, and 50 per cent of apple exports. By then, it was also grown extensively by competing southern-hemisphere exporters, South Africa, New Zealand, Argentina and Chile and in France and the USA.

Its success was parallelled by the pear, Packham's Triumph. Bred in 1896 by Charles Henry Packham at his property "Clifton" in the Molong district of NSW, it was a cross of Uvedale St Germain (also known as the Bell) and William pears. Also a "very good keeper", it amounted to 60 per cent of our pear exports by the 1980s. While nineteenth-century orchardists and nursery breeders produced countless varieties—offering a succession of tastes, textures and qualities through summer, autumn and winter—twentieth-century merchants preferred predictability.

7
The first food factories

The packaging and advertising of processed foods—epitomised by the refined white flour of giant roller mills—created household names like Arnott's, Rosella and Foster's

THE MOST SYMBOLIC of all the chimney-capped food factories which arose in Australian cities from the 1870s was the roller mill for cheap production of white flour. Traditionally, a pair of horizontal stones had ground wholemeal, then sifted, or "bolted", to give white flour. Porcelain rollers, developed for the wheat plains of Hungary by Ganz & Co, separated grain into "fractions" of any desired hue. Rollers were quicker, required no time-consuming regrooving of stones, separated the nutritious bran for stockfeed and, without the wheat-germ oil to go rancid, produced longer-keeping flour.

Like other technological developments, rollers reached here quickly. W. Duffield & Co tested them in their Union Mill at Gawler, South Australia, in 1879. Early the next year, their nearby Victoria Mills had, in addition to 27 pairs of stones, 12 sets of porcelain rollers. The Ganz mills were now exhibited and installed in Sydney. David Gibson of the Carlton Flour Mills became the first Victorian to adopt them in 1881. Two years later, the big Melbourne miller, Thomas Brunton, related the strange tale of two dogs in Germany, one fed on white flour and the other on pollard. The dog fed on pollard grew stronger, while the other hungered and died. Brunton rightly feared that the wheat germ, which was attached to the husk and removed by the roller mill, constituted the real nutrient. But with Gibson's flour bringing higher prices, Brunton and the other millers were forced to change.

Two decades earlier, *Heaton's Australian Dictionary of Dates* counted

151 steam mills, eight water and one windmill in Victoria, representing 2,619 horse-power and driving 487 pairs of stones. Many were in country areas, where they could select choice wheat. But with more sophisticated technology, readier access to city finance and the railways to bring in the grain, the city mills prospered and amalgamated. During the 1880s, milling in Australia became a centralised, urban industry. The working-class had plenty of white bread, biscuits, cheap cakes and puddings, but since white flour was nutritionally inferior, it was a hollow advance.

For centuries in Europe, white bread had enjoyed extra status, presumably not through any magic in the colour, nor just because of its higher price, but because, staying longer in the digestive system, it was wrongly assumed to provide more goodness. While both germ and bran were appreciated nutritionally by a minority, purer and more refined whiteness appealed to author E. J. Brady in *Australia Unlimited* (1918), when he lauded the breed that had just stormed Gallipoli. "There will be white Australian loaves and good Australian beef and butter to give them stamina," he eulogised.

Mr E. J. Birbeck, the baker whose enthusiasm had earlier brought about the federal master bakers' association, "glorified" white bread in a speech to its conference in 1925. Attired in traditional white cap and apron, he called scripture to witness that "the bread which God rained down from heaven was white." He blazed: "White bread is a badge of modern life. It belongs to the world of today, to freedom, to constitutional government, to all cleanliness of living, to all that is worthwhile. Black bread is the bread of serfs, ground on coarse stones and baked in a hovel. The white loaf of bread is born on the sunny wheatfields of Australia (no sunshine like Australia's), milled in a sunlighted mill, and baked in a hygienic bakery." Epitomised by white flour and white sugar, processed food now had ideological purity.

Tin can cornucopia

From about 1870, Australian workers—like those in Britain, the US and Germany—began to enjoy a cornucopia of biscuits, jams, confectionery, cordials and pickles. Condiments and snacks, which had hitherto been handmade and imported largely for the rich, became working-class rewards. The floury, sugary, salty and acidic fabrications tended to be gastronomically loud, but they gave life a sparkle and—like the bushman's flour, sugar, tea and spirits—were readily storable and transportable. Shelves were not just filled any more from gardens, from the home-preserved pantry, or even by neighbourhood baker-millers and publican-brewers, but by factories, which incorporated steam-powered, iron contraptions, mass production techniques and ideas of food science and "scientific management".

The rapid rise of urban conglomerations, and the working-class army, was accompanied by, in effect, the industrialisation of the grocer. No longer were a grocer and family expert in purchasing, in blending, in curing and in weighing and bagging, competing less on price than skill and reputation. Now a dedicated retailer purchased from factories, invited mail-order sales and opened impersonal chains of stores operated by relatively unskilled labour. Not only expanding horizontally in this way, some shopkeepers grew into manufacturers. Again, they employed unskilled labour to bring cheaper and more durable products to the much bigger market.

One example of the emerging manufacturer was William Arnott, born in Scotland in 1827, apprenticed to a baker and migrated to NSW at the age of 20. It was in 1870 that he expanded his biscuit shop to a factory in Newcastle, with 12 rotary ovens turned by a steam engine and fired by coke from the basement. The Arnott's company was on the way to taking over many other biscuit men of the time—names like Guest, Motteram, Menz, Brockhoff, Miles, Ware, Morrow and Swallow. Their new market was captured in a Swallow & Ariell advertisement for not merely "Ship, Cabin and Dog's Biscuits" but, additionally, "all kinds of Machine, Fancy and Dessert Biscuits". By 1885, the fully-mechanised Swallow & Ariell factory at Port Melbourne kept butter under refrigeration and employed 370 people. In the same city, Evan Rowlands employed almost as many making soft-drinks and soda-water. The Red Cross Preserving Co in Chapel Street, South Yarra, employed about 150 in jams, pickles and sauces.

Abel Hoadley, who had immigrated in 1865, had founded his jam and pickles factory at South Melbourne in 1881. Dismayed by seasonal supplies, he would in a few years turn to confectionery and his son create the Violet Crumble bar in 1923. In all, in 1885, more than 6000 people worked in Melbourne's more than 700 food and drink establishments, although these were still mostly bakeries and butcheries with only one or two hands. There were still many take-overs and some important names to come—like the Rosella Preserving and Manufacturing Co, which Mr H. R. McCracken and Mr T. J. Press started in a Carlton backyard in 1894. Running straight into financial trouble, they were taken over by a group led by Mr F. J. Cato, from the Moran & Cato grocery chain, which had grown from two shops in 1881 to 40 in 1889. Rosella would make its first tomato sauce in July, 1899.

No longer always sold in anonymous sacks and boxes, the products were packaged in small quantities and a brandname advertised tirelessly. No longer was it just a chest of China tea, now it was a packet of Bushell's, it was not just any old ship's biscuit, it was advertised with a drawing of "Albert Haydon, Champion Juvenile Cyclist of Australia, aged 7 years . . . Fed from birth on Arnott's Milk Arrowroot Biscuits". No longer were we invited to taste fruit at a market barrow, now we were to enter the grocer's shop and ask for Rosella Tomato Sauce by name. It was during that era that we were taught to treasure the attribute of "cheapness". We were encouraged to expect "reliability" in our food, not varying between biscuits, packets or seasons. We were persuaded to value "convenience", being advised to leave

THE FIRST FOOD FACTORIES

the preparation of food to the hygienic cogs of factories. We were to look for "quality"—in the factory sense of consistency and long shelf-life. We learned to trust brandnames.

Registered trademarks grew in importance, and the nature of advertising changed. Take those in Harriet Wicken's treatise on domestic economy in 1891, *The Australian Home.* There were the traditional ads for J. G. Hanks & Co, Family Grocers of 514 George Street, Sydney, who always had on hand a good supply of French gelatine, angelica, crystallised cherries, parmesan cheese, and so forth . . . and for C. J. Christie, Tea Merchant, who stocked finest Ceylon, Indian and China teas in half chests, quarter chests, canisters and packets . . . But then, there were also the newer ads for manufacturers' trade names, what came to be known, as opposed to "retail", as "national" advertising. There were Robert Harper & Co's table requisites ("Genuine High-Class Goods") like: "Star" oatmeal in 7 lb packets, "Pearl" rice in 7 lb bags and "Pioneer" table jellies in pint and half-pint squares. Harpers urged: "N.B.—See that they bear the firm's label, as in that case they have left the factory under a guarantee of being in exact accordance with their labelled descriptions"; and again at the bottom was printed: "If you desire to practise true economy, ask for the above when giving your order to your grocer, and accept no substitutes".

The Imperial Manufacturing Company took up an entire page to display its registered trade mark, a sailing ship. This was a "guarantee that none but the VERY BEST INGREDIENTS are used". On other pages Imperial advertised—with ship proudly sailing—their coffee with chicory, baking powder and "Portable Table Jellies . . . any lady can prepare them without trouble in a few minutes . . . Full particulars for the manipulation of the Imperial Jellies are on each packet, which also bears the Company's Registered Trade Mark". The advertisement even explained a "very pleasing and artistic mode of serving the Imperial Jellies" in half oranges, an early example of what Australian cooking was to become.

We may laugh at these quaint claims, but they managed to establish that there was no need for you to rely on freshness, habit, the experience of shopkeepers, or your green fingers. The last advertisement in Wicken's book was for R. A. Melsom, Telephone No 607 in Sydney, who was an "Advertising Contractor". As well as preparing books, pamphlets and catalogues containing ads, Melsom offered: "Advertisements Designed, and Estimates Given for all Colonial Papers." Literally out of the techniques of the American quack medicine men—the sellers of patent cures—had arisen the advertising industry.

Food additives

The "invisible hand" of the marketplace pushed manufacturers to find ways to make and distribute food more cheaply, usually through preservation, but also by introducing counterfeits like margarine. Invented in France in 1869 by Hippolyte Mège-Mouriès as the result of a competition organised by Napoleon III to find a cheap substitute for butter, the process was not taken up commercially by the French. But his patent was bought by a Dutch firm which was exporting "butterine" by 1880. The first Australian factory was commissioned for proprietor F. J. E. Phillips by an American, E. A. Clark, in February, 1885, on 2½ acres of river frontage at Yarraville. Fat collected from butchers was churned with skim milk and "Danish Butter Colouring" and sold as butterine. Production in March, 1886, was 6½ tons a week and it was eagerly sought by biscuit makers, but resisted by the dairy industry. In Britain the name was banned in 1887, margarine being substituted. Victoria's Margarine Act of 1893 prevented retailers substituting it for butter.

Sometimes the manufacturers' eagerness endangered health. In England in 1820, Frederick Accum outlined the dangerous ways in which the food industry improved on nature in a *Treatise on the Adulterations of Food and Culinary Poisons*. The crimes included the addition of alum to whiten bread, poisonous methods of brewing and pernicious colourings for sweets. He showed how chemical methods could detect impurities. The eminent Royal Institution was persuaded to hound Accum out of England and the campaign was not really taken up again until the medical journal *The Lancet* commissioned investigations in 1851. The work led in 1860 to "An Act for the Preventing of the Adulteration of Articles of Food and Drink" and influenced Australian thinking.

Edward Abbott advised readers in 1864 to beware of bright colours, but wasn't particularly perturbed. "Adulteration", explained Richard Twopenny in 1883, "is as yet unknown, or but very little known, for the simple reason that it costs more to adulterate than to provide the genuine article." Yet in March, 1876, the Melbourne *Argus* published scientific analyses of 25 milk samples, which indicated watering down and skimming off of cream, and in July followed up with an exposé of poisonous colours in sugar confectionery. Newspapers also showed that tea was being adulterated, probably before it entered Australia, since spent tea leaves were recycled to China for "facing", using Prussian blue and turmeric. In 1883, a newspaper campaign against tea imported by Clifford Love & Co was resolved when samples were sent to London and two analyses showed them to be adulterated.

Four bakers were prosecuted in 1885 for adding alum to bread. Other adulterated commodities included butter, "butterine", aerated waters, ales and porters, spirits, biscuits, cocoa, chocolate, coffee, preserves, sauces, mustard and vinegar. The campaigns led to tighter legislation, the Victorian Pure Food Act of 1905 being hailed as some kind of first in world terms. (Upton Sinclair's sensational exposure of the Chicago meat packers, *The Jungle*, led to the first US Pure Food and Drug laws in 1906.) In the end, such regulation tended to favour big manufacturers, which could afford to work with and manipulate health controls—some dangerous additives like nitrites in bacon curing just had to be allowed. Fears too about hazards tended to obscure graver questions about artificiality and the more alienated relationship people now had to their food—both as consumers and as factory workers.

Factory work

An idea of work in a food factory was supplied to the Victorian Shops Commission in 1883 by Thomas Guest, who said he was "astonished" to learn that boys of 10 and 11 worked in his biscuit factory. To the same hearings, a truant officer testified that 20 children that young worked at Swallow & Ariell. Women especially were brought in to carry out the menial tasks—Doreen in C. J. Dennis's *Sentimental Bloke* sticking labels on pickles jars—as if to continue part of their housework. Florence Gordon wrote in the *Australian Economist* in August, 1894, that women in Sydney commenced in confectionery, biscuit and jam-making at about age 14. They laboured about 48 hours a week, usually from 8 am to 6 pm, with 45 minutes for dinner, taken where they stood. Since confectionery and biscuits needed clean, ventilated workplaces, the conditions for the women there were generally good, although for jam often deplorable. The unions prevented women performing key jobs, so they prepared, packed and labelled on a weekly wage from about six to twelve shillings. Workers in the food-related industries of paper-box and paper-bag making complained, Gordon wrote, "that the paste hardens on their fingers and cuts the skin, and they are only allowed to wash their hands once a day . . ."

Joseph Parry, pickler, knew that his Sydney factory was damp and salty. Even though he had a well-drained cement floor, he claimed at a public inquiry in 1911–12 that he had provided his girls with clogs to protect their feet. However, he said, they preferred their own high-heeled boots. According to a union secretary, Alfred Carter, conditions were so bad that the girls had no choice but to bring blücher boots. The onions were soaked in brine before peeling so that, according to Parry, there was "none of that crying over them or watering of the eyes at all . . . It is just as pleasant and easy to peel an onion as to peel an apple." The women earned, depending on their speed, from six to 11 shillings weekly. Alfred Carter said there was one exception: "I think Parry's have got the fastest woman in Australia at onion peeling, whose name is Dawes. She may earn a shade over 12 shillings."

Beatrix Tracey asked in the *Lone Hand* in October, 1908: "Are women to be permitted to descend towards a condition of life which, disguise it as we may, is practically a return to their ancient plight, and, becoming wage-slaves, forget how to be worthy mothers? . . . The woman in industry is there, usually, because she is cheap labour . . . an economical alternative to machinery."

How Americans started Australia's most famous beer

Beer came to be regarded as the national beverage, but it was not drunk in quantity for the first half of our history. Brewers had great difficulty since the raw materials and techniques belonged to cooler climates. Too high temperatures produced poisonous and foul fermentation. Back in 1834, a Sydney book *The Mirror of Literature, Amusement and Instruction* said that the brewers' use of substitutes for hops "produces the heaviest sleep, excessive pain in the head and irregularity of the bowels". The wealthier classes never touched colonial brews, preferring imported ale.

Gradually brewers came to terms with the conditions. They improved the brew with cleanliness, by adding cane sugar up to 40 and 50 per cent, and eventually with refrigeration and pasteurisation. Louis Pasteur's studies of fermentation from the 1850s became the foundation of microbiology, but, contrary to myth, he was not solving medical problems but those of winemakers and brewers. Pasteurisation could kill unwanted yeasts and so stop unwanted fermentations. Taking up Pasteur's *Etudes sur la Bière* of 1876, a scientist with the Carlsberg brewery in Copenhagen, Emil Christian Hansen, revolutionised the industry with pure strains of yeast. A visiting beer judge at the world exhibition in Melbourne in 1888, Dr Carl Rach, thought that there could be "no country in which more severe demands are made on the durability of beer". Yet by then, he said, some of the large breweries recognised a solution lay in pure yeast.

Until that time, colonial beers were English-style strong ales, with a definite local "twang" to them. In his *Organic Chemistry* (1842), Baron Liebig had noted that, while English, French and most German beers became sour on contact with air, this defect was absent in Bavarian beer. It was called "lager-bier", or "beer for keeping"—*lager* being German for "store". The secret was the so-called "bottom fermentation" yeast, working at cooler temperatures. The beer was matured, which increased the carbonation and which is why it was called "lager". Here was a keeping beer, when keeping qualities were most desirable in our food history.

About 1882, the Cohn brothers of Bendigo began brewing lager on a small scale. In 1885, some Germans failed in an attempt in Collingwood, Melbourne. The firm of A. W. & T. L. Ware succeeded in Adelaide. It was now that W. M. Foster arrived from New York and started business, with his brother as a junior partner, in Rokeby Street, Collingwood. That an American could succeed was not surprising since "lager-bier" had swept the US in the 1860s. Local brewers were impressed by William Foster's plant, which separated "dirty" and "clean" processes into separate buildings. Another feature was a 60 horse-power "Corless" steam engine to power ice-making machinery and cool the fermenting room and cellars. It was installed by an engineer specially brought from New York.

Foster's "practical and scientific brewer", Mr Sieber, came with both

German and American experience. He commenced brewing in the first week of November, 1888, and the public were supplied from February 1, 1889. Most of the beer was bottled, the labels declaring "warranted to keep in any climate" and "much improved if kept cool". When William Foster complained that importers of German and American lagers were cutting prices by one-third to run him out of business, the government granted additional protection. The company supplied hotelkeepers with ice, free of cost, during summer months.

Soon, other firms offered lager—the Victoria Brewery advertising: "Lager-Bier in bulk and bottle, Brewed by an Expert Brought specially from America for the purpose". At the end of the century there were, along with Foster's, still 39 breweries in Victoria. But in 1907, during "rationalisation", six companies, including Foster's, combined as Carlton and United Breweries Ltd, which soon had a monopoly, as did lager.

An important figure behind the superiority of Melbourne brewing was Auguste de Bavay, a Belgian disciple of Pasteur and who arrived at the Victoria Parade brewery in 1884. In four years he had isolated "Australian No 2", the first pure top-fermentation yeast used commercially in Australia and possibly in the world. In 1894, he switched to Foster's as head brewer and a few years later he engaged in an odd newspaper dispute with Emil Resch in which he defended the traditional "malt and hops" beer against "sugar" beer, which he helped produce and which had laid the foundations of a powerful brewery fortune. De Bavay became the technical brains behind the Cohen and Baillieu family businesses—notably Carlton & United Brewery, Broken Hill zinc extraction, and paper-making.

In Sydney, brewing became a battle between two giants, representing the clash of the English and the Irish. With connections in the hop business in Cranbrook, Kent, the Tooth dynasty opened the Kent brewery in George Street in September 1835—but they were involved in much more, as merchants, pastoralists, makers of Kameruka cheese, in the Bank of NSW and CSR and so on. The founders of Tooheys were two brothers whose family raised cattle in Victoria and prospered in the gold days. In the 1860s, they bought into Sydney breweries, the Albion tracing its history back to 1827. Tooths and Tooheys, entering on grazing money, were just the breweries out of dozens that were "fittest", with recourse to capital to meet any challenge.

The first real shake-up came in the 1880s with new technology, and with the economic difficulties of the 1890s the numbers plummeted from 80 to 40. There was a recovery around 1896, the year that lager apparently arrived in NSW. Sydney had four big brewers—Marshalls, Reschs, Tooths and Tooheys—and a number of minor ones, which were swept away with the Federal Beer Excise Act of 1901. Further centralisation under pressure for efficiency, laboratory control and rational marketing, and there were two.

MR MacROBERTSON

One of the "Old Gold" dipping departments, 1921

THE FASTEST "rags to riches" story of our food industry, or so a promotional biography in the 1920s would have us believe, was that of Macpherson Robertson, founder of the confectionery firm which put his signature *MacRobertson* to "Old Gold" chocolate assortments, "Cherry Ripe" bars, "Freddo Frogs", "Columbine" caramels, and very many others. On July 20, 1922, the Melbourne *Herald*, under the headline "From Newsboy to Millionaire—a Romance of Industry", commented: "For sheer unflagging industry and grim devotion to a single cause, Mac. Robertson's record is probably unique in all the annals of commerce."

He was born in Ballarat in 1860. While his Scottish father was in Fiji, his Irish mother took Mac, at the age of eight, along with his brothers, to Scotland, where they lived six years at Leith, the port of Edinburgh. Robertson "persuaded" his mother that he should earn a living in return for agreeing to attend school, and this was his regime:

3 am.	Rose, walked to Edinburgh, picked up newspapers and delivered them on way back to Leith
7.30 am.	Lathered faces for a barber
9 am.	School
6 pm.	Lathered more faces
10 pm.	The day was my own

"It was no hardship for me to have to rise at 3 o'clock in the morning and tramp through the snow," he said later. "All this seemed quite natural in industrious Scotland, where one was surrounded on every hand by thrift and hard work." His scanty schooling ceased at the age of 10 and he tried 10 different trades before one of his friends told him, "I'm working at Miller's, sitting down all day long making 'sweeties'." When his mother took the boys back to Victoria, he quickly found more jobs in confectionery works.

In 1880, at the age of 19, he decided to go into business on his own. He began in their bathroom in Fitzroy. His basic equipment was a pannikin which he heated over a later much-featured "nail can", an iron drum which had finished its days carrying nails and was now an improvised furnace. "Aladdin's lamp", we were to learn, "accounted for no greater wonders than those originating from this can, for from its humbleness has developed a stupendous and truly Australian industry."

He melted sugar syrup, using 20 plaster-of-Paris moulds to make sugar dolls, mice and horses. He manufactured Mondays to Thursdays and carried them on his head from shop to shop on Fridays and Saturdays. Within five years, he could be photographed with three dozen employees and a delivery cart outside his mother's house, now a Fitzroy factory. An early product was Cough Drops, with a slogan "Sonny, what yer crying for?" In 1893, he undertook a tour of England and America for ideas and by the turn of the century his staff exceeded 300. He had begun hiring women to undertake the repetitive tasks of the high-volume confectioner. Even then, he and accomplices were installing automatic machinery to replace human labour. This was given a great fillip in the Great War, when he invested £250,000 to build unprocurable machinery.

In 1920, he employed 2,000 people, on an average wage of just over £3 weekly. They turned out 700 varieties of sweets. The factory was vertically integrated, so that it or subsidiaries supplied machinery, condensed milk, maize oil, starch, casks and all packaging materials. Remaining sole proprietor, the expansion entirely financed out of profits, he had built a "great white city" of more than a dozen factory buildings. The site of his mother's original bathroom could be found amid tons of cough drops, toffees, barley sugars and fruit drops in the boiled lolly section. In 40 years, he had become the "highest taxpayer in the Commonwealth of Australia."

In the early 1920s, Robertson commissioned a luxurious book to commemorate his "colossal industrial achievements". *A Young Man and a Nail Can* shows him always erect in a white suit, arms folded across the chest. The photographs of his factories—their backgrounds simplified and even redrawn—indicate efficiency, proud modernity. Seventy or so women, in nurse-like uniforms, can be counted labouring on identical stools in just one of the "Old Gold" dipping departments, where "purified cold air is brought to play on every chocolate coated by these experts". In another part of the factory, new machinery had already taken over some expert chocolate coating.

Putting assorted chocolates into boxes was not so easily mechanised and the main "Old Gold" packing department was "light, airy and scrupulously clean—one of the finest workrooms in Australia". Then there was "Aladdin's Palace", so named because of the brilliance of the satin-finish confections, such as "Cinderella", "Valentines" and "Silkee" Bon Bons. The phenomenal success of "Columbine" Caramels had dictated extensions to automatic machinery.

The dozens of white-coated women in the French and Marzipan Confectionery Department occupied "one of the largest workrooms in Australia", while the "Milk Kiss" department, although small, mechanically wrapped many tons weekly. Below all these workrooms was the heavy machinery roasting, grinding, sifting, mixing and refining the cacao kernels into cocoa and chocolate. The cooling chambers of two chocolate "depositors" could mould 200,000 tablets each working day. Robertson's book showed the stables of the vast horse transport section and many "celebrated greys" on parade. And the first motors were installed in the garage. Towering above these achievements was an advertising signature of 1,100 brilliant electric lamps, installed by the firm's Electrical, Plumbing and Building staffs, its 123 ft-wide scrawl considered the "largest and most attractive Electric Sign in the Country".

One of the main impressions of a gallery of colour photographs of products is excessive Englishness. Robertson appears to have hit upon an escapist marketing formula based on a British Isles as some long-lost paradise, peopled by "Lady Gay", "Dolly Varden", "Beau Brummell" ("inexpressibly delightful"), Gainsborough "Masterpieces" or "Tally-Ho" Nougat tins. The book stirred great admiration, particularly in the breast of the director of the embryonic CSIRO. Sir George Knibbs wrote to Robertson on April 21, 1923, denouncing the popular doctrine that "mere physical labour produces all that comes from effort." Clearly, the mind and the will were the secrets of Mac's success. "I have great admiration for the pioneers, who," he wrote, ". . virtually carry the multitude forward in reasonable comfort . . . (they) are the 'friends of the workers', even if, in the course of so doing, they amass great wealth."

As well as preparing the book, "Mac" Robertson took to showing around celebrities, like on January 31, 1924, Lord Leverhulme, the English founder of the detergent and margarine multinational, Unilever. "At 61 years of age, and white of hair, Mr Robertson is one of the most surprisingly energetic young men I have encountered," claimed a Melbourne *Herald* reporter on July 20, 1923. Leading the way up two stairs at a time, Robertson would arrive at a group of old hands, whom he knew by nick-name. "This man and I used to work at the same bench in the old days," he would say, "Many a kick and cuff you gave me, too, didn't you?" and the veteran smiled and nodded. The *Herald*'s "G.C.D." could not but fail to be reminded of the stories by

Samuel Smiles (1812–1904), Scottish "bard of the self-made engineer". "Certainly," said the journalist, "no captain of industry written up by Dr Smiles, no self-made hero of fiction, began more humbly or rose more surely than Mr Macpherson Robertson . . ."

The outburst of self-promotion by Robertson in the early 1920s had a simple explanation—that Cadbury's was setting up at Claremont, Tasmania, and Nestlé was launching into chocolate-making in Sydney. The book explained, "The true Australian will find pleasure in the knowledge that not only are these confections made in an Australian factory by Australian labor, but all the artistic boxes, cartons, and labels are produced in the same Works." And so it is ironic to bring the story forward. After founding an airline and having part of Antarctica gratefully named after him, Robertson died in 1945. His successors disposed of his "rambling" Fitzroy buildings in 1965 and built a modern plant at the outer Melbourne suburb of Ringwood. Then, in 1967, after a takeover battle with Mars, Cadbury's bought MacRobertson's. No longer was the giant "Australian from hair to heel!", but had been swallowed by its English competitor. Gone were the nineteenth-century chocolate millionaires, now Samuel Smiles' heroes were replaced by serious-minded bureaucrats, in foreign corporations.

But that is to leap ahead. All that energy thrown into transforming food loosened some of our appetites for experimentation. The rise of food processing also saw, not altogether paradoxically, a time for the gourmet. The estate-less and privileged urban taste-seeker could enjoy novelties cooked in delightful shapes and forms. Each milestone in Queen Victoria's long reign, each stride towards Federation, each linking of railway lines, was celebrated with toasts in French champagne and long menus of turkey and truffles, Charlotte Russe and Gelée à l'Australienne. It was the time of elegant picnics—for which bottled and packet food was ideal. And the decades up to the Great War were a time for some excellent dining out, when Australia enjoyed some surprisingly fancy restaurants.

Robertson and Lord Leverhulme

8

Bohemian restaurants

Rapid innovation in food processing in the late nineteenth century also brought interesting times for the gourmet. Some restaurants would stand up well against today's best

ANY DAY between noon and two in the principal streets of Melbourne in the 1870s, handbills were thrust at you, "the wonders of which will strike an English labourer or mechanic dumb". So stated the journalist, "The Vagabond", as J. S. James called himself. Imagine poor Hodge, he wrote in his collected *Vagabond Papers* of 1877–8, who lived on bread, bacon and ale, reading that a breakfast with a choice of 10 hot meat dishes, bread and butter and "two or three cups of tea or coffee" might be had for 6d. Or a dinner with a choice of six soups, 12 kinds of meat, including beefsteak pudding or stuffed ox-heart, and six puddings or pies, also with tea, coffee and bread and butter and also for 6d. Supper, both before and after the theatres, was even more bewildering: stewed rabbit, haricot mutton curries and some 15 other dishes, with salad, beetroot and tomatoes. "A land which can furnish such delights for 6d," declared the Vagabond, "must, surely, be the working man's paradise."

These sixpenny, and fourpenny, restaurants were said to have been started in Melbourne in the 1850s by an English immigrant, David T. Way. And along with their posh cousins, the shilling restaurants, they survived at the same prices for more than 50 years. In his book on Melbourne life in 1888, John Freeman wrote that in a shilling restaurant, which provided alcohol and often a separate room for business ladies, you couldn't hear your order called out to the men in the kitchen, while in the cheap ones, no sooner had you told the waiter, than everyone in the room knew. One waiter could take a half-a-dozen orders at once and shout: "Roast beef one, outside cut, plenty gravy . . . Boiled mutton two, one, no sauce . . . Corned beef one, potatoes only . . ." And E. C. Buley still sang their praises in 1905. By then, however, the shilling restaurants outnumbered the sixpenny, and many had become 1s 3d, he said.

Not that the sixpenny restaurant was ever any gastronomic heaven. Most men, thought the Vagabond, suffered a perpetual combat between their tastes and their exchequer. "Where one has a soul for turtle and ortolan, it is hard to descend to sausages . . . it is a mere question of supporting nature . . ." This evaluation was shared in 1883 by Edmond Marin La Meslée, who wrote for a French audience of our public dining: "Everywhere the menus are identical and, what is worse, they never change throughout the three hundred and sixty-five days of the year. Invariably beef, mutton and poultry, boiled and roasted, roasted and boiled; the everlasting dish of potatoes and sometimes some soggy boiled vegetables; the meal ends with a kind of hash, an incredible concoction rejoicing in the title of *pudding*."

The Vagabond said that, especially in summer, there were more flies in the dishes than refined prejudices might fancy. The sausages were "bags of mystery", the enormous consumption proof that "faith was strong" in the colonies. The stews, mostly served for supper, were not equal to the *pot au feu* of the French peasant, although the ingredients were as miscellaneous. He wondered how the multiplicity of dishes could be served at supper when not available in the middle of the day. Then he discovered that "stewed lamb", with a little curry stirred on the plate, became "curried mutton", or with a few slices of carrot was "haricot mutton", or with a few boiled potatoes mashed in was "Irish stew". Rabbit pie and fish were considered luxuries, and were announced by placards in the windows. He was struck by the dearness of eggs, boiled or poached being 9d. Chicken, if available, was a shilling.

Some sixpenny spots on the principal thoroughfares shone "with plate-glass, white linen and pretty waiter girls", the Vagabond said. But this extra display, and the cost of handbills, caused a perceptible diminution of the viands. The best feed was at the smaller restaurants, kept by hard-working married couples. At one o'clock there was a tremendous rush, every seat at the little tables being occupied. Someone sitting out near the door might order "corned beef and cabbage" a dozen times, on each occasion it being captured en route as "my order". One or two establishments employed girls enticing you to order beer from an adjacent bar. But mainly the waiters were men, "not a class—They are refugees from all classes." The cooks had mostly begun with damper, the Vagabond said. He also knew one cook who was thoroughly educated, had passed years in Parisian society, and was heir to £15,000 a year.

E. C. Booth wrote in *Another England* (1869): "Sixpence exercises a somewhat singular and powerful influence over the liquid department of the Melbourne commissariat." It was the price of any drink at a public house. Many of the best hotels had what was known in San Francisco as a "free lunch" for all who purchased a sixpenny glass of beer—chiefly a plate of corned beef and potatoes, about half the food of a sixpenny dinner. John Freeman in 1888 knew hotels where you could get a glass of ale for threepence—and between 11 and one o'clock their counters carried plates piled with oblong pieces of sausage meat between layers of pastry. The Vagabond mentioned that counter lunches, as we later knew them, were taken advantage of by people who would consider it beneath their dignity to be seen in a sixpenny cookshop. He considered the hard-up clerks should "put their dignity to one side, and take a dinner in a sixpenny restaurant, which, up to this time, I consider to be the most wonderful example of Victorian progress and prosperity which I have met with."

The earliest restaurants

Every generation of Australians has believed that it has enjoyed the country's first decent dining out. The preceding account of Melbourne's sixpenny restaurants in the second half of last century may have surprised some readers, but Australians were dining out with much more style much earlier than that.

The first licensed hotel in New South Wales, established at the end of the eighteenth century, had a considerable reputation for its French chef. The hotel belonged to James Larra, who was transported for stealing a silver tankard from a coffee-house in King's Cross, London. He settled at Parramatta in 1796, built a single-room wattle-and-daub hut and soon gained the colony's first licence. In 1800, he re-built his Freemasons' Arms in brick, with bedrooms, and had the best French food prepared by a cook from Paris. In July, 1802, the visiting naturalist, François Péron, noted:

> During the six days we remained at Parramatta, we were served with an elegance, and even a luxury, which we could not suppose obtainable on these shores. The best wines, such as Madeira, Port, Xeres, Cape, and Bordeaux, always covered our tables; we were served on plate, and the decanters and glasses were of purest flint; nor were the eatables inferior to the liquors. Always anxious to anticipate the taste or wishes of his guests, Mr Larra caused us to be served in the French style; and this act of politeness was the more easy to him, because amongst the convicts who acted as his domestics, was an excellent French cook, a native of Paris, as well as two others of our countrymen.

A presumably more typical meal was described in an advertisement in the Sydney *Gazette* of July 3, 1803:

BOHEMIAN RESTAURANTS
NEW EATING-HOUSE
Victuals Dressed in the English Way

Rosetta Stabler respectfully acquaints the Public that she prepares Boiled Mutton and Broths every day at 12 o'clock, and a Joint of Meat Roasted always ready at One, which, from its quality and mode of serving, she flatters herself will attract the Notice of the Public.

Visitors from Remote Settlements, Mariners, &c, will find a convenient Accommodation at a moderate expense . . .

Rosetta Stabler had arrived on the *Glatton* in March. Her husband William was transported on the same ship and by 1806 was a ticket of leave man, cook for his wife.

Such eating houses, taverns and street vendors greeted early Sydney arrivals and wayside huts sprang up on the bullock-tracks. The goldfields were quickly catered from tents and cheap restaurants sprouted for the urban workforce. Frank Fowler in 1859 wrote about "scores" of oyster saloons in Melbourne, several in Sydney. "As in London," he said, "they are to be found, with private boxes, red-curtained—in the neighbourhood of the theatres." Although ordinary families rarely "dined out", they did travel a lot and go to the markets, then to pleasure gardens, where there was food. From the start, eating-out, the natural activity of a mobile, consumer society, was intrinsic to Australia. In fact, the colonies can be assumed to have had an extraordinarily high ratio of eating places relative to almost any other population. The discerning traveller rarely found great restaurants, but a number of places rightly gained reputations.

An early contender for Melbourne's first fashionable dining place must be the restaurant at the Union hotel at 38–40 Great Bourke Street, between Elizabeth and Swanston Streets. It was built about 1849, probably for Thomas D. Hodges, who certainly held the licence very soon after and who was said to have been a British politician. According to William Kelly's *Life in Victoria*, which mysteriously disguises Hodges as Mr T---d---n H---d---s, he had brought out with him from Paris the chef who had worked for one of the greatest gourmands of the day, Lord Henry S---y---r, and who was now paid the exorbitant sum of three guineas a day. Kelly considered that Hodges brought French cuisine to Australia, and also introduced all the luxurious articles of modern upholstery. He described the scene in 1853:

> The spacious *salle à manger* was thronged in its centre, and crammed in all its corners, at breakfast, luncheon, dinner, and supper. Every seat at the *table d'hôte* was engaged dozens deep in advance, and every private room and cabinet had its party or its vis-à-vis. Vulgar viands were eschewed by common consent. Julienne soup and *potage à la reine* superseded ox-tail and mutton broth; *fricassées*, *vols-au-vent*, and *salmis de perdreaux* cut out legs of mutton, sirloins of beef, and overgrown hams; while plum-pudding,

together with apple-pie and cheese-cake, ignominiously retreated before the irresistible advances of *omelette soufflée* and *truffes au vin de champagne*. The fluid revolution was no less extraordinary; the familiar foam of Guinness's stout or Bass's pale ale was regarded as an abomination, and the man would be little short of a hero who possessed a sufficient moral courage to initiate his potations with anything short of champagne or sparkling Moselle.

An important point is that Thomas Hodges, who sold out in March, 1854, like James Larra before him, ran a hotel. The main presenters of good food in those days were the substitute homes, the hotels. William Kelly also praised the Criterion, where British cookery was "expelled to make way for the gustatory novelties and sophistries of the Soyer school" (Alexis Soyer being the best-known French chef in England.) In the 70s, Goyder's Hotel in Collins Street, Garton's and Tattersall's were recommended for good eating. But wealthier men preferred to lunch at the Melbourne Club, the good chef being, in fact, a feature of the real homes away from home, the gentlemen's clubs. It came to be said in Sydney there was no other club where the "wine and wit are so old" as the Australian Club.

Versions of the true Parisian restaurant, elevating dining to an art, arrived here, as in California, in the early 1850s. G. H. Wathen wrote in 1855 that the first years of gold brought to Melbourne "numerous handsome restaurants, so common all over the continent of Europe, though they have never succeeded in England". Many were kept by foreigners—French, German and American—and they had almost superseded the old-fashioned "chop-house" and "coffee-room", he said. Garryowen's *Chronicles of Early Melbourne* claimed the first restaurant had been Richard Graham's tea, coffee and dining room, advertised in March, 1840, at the corner of Flinders Lane and Elizabeth Street. However, that probably fell into the category of a "coffee-room", or "cafe". By the 1850s, and following the Union hotel's lead, some of the restaurants were as fine as anything we have ever had in this country.

The first in Sydney was the Café Restaurant in George Street, advertised by the Messrs Cheval and Poehlman in 1854. It was both a cafe, where *café-au-lait* and *café noir* might be had up to midnight, and an adjoining restaurant, with dinners in the "best style of French and English cookery" ready at all hours. The *carte* was too varied to be enumerated, the advertisement declared, but it indicated a selection from the impressive wine list, including Rhenish wines and French clarets, sauternes and champagnes. The *Illustrated Sydney News* on February 11, 1854, welcomed this "attractive temple dedicated to the genius of French Cookery", which had lifted the "thickest darkness" then immersing Sydney in culinary matters. It would, the paper thought, gratify the palates of those with a taste for something better than "scorched legs of too-recently-killed mutton or sodden beef redolent of brine". Within days, there was a nearby competitor, Aux Frères Provençaux-Café Restaurant de

Paris, at which the Messrs Budin and Mellon publicised dinners at 3s 6d, 5s and 8s. Like so many of our restaurants, it took its name from a Parisian exemplar.

Mixed up in this development of restaurants was the coffee-house. Coffee, which arrived in England in the seventeenth century, was regarded as the drink of intellectual stimulation, as can be seen from Frank Fowler's description of Sydney social spots in 1859. While the wealthy enjoyed the "usual club-house attractions of libraries, billiard-rooms and good cooks", the middle class had cafes and concert rooms, and the working population had "the theatre, the literature institute and the lecture-hall". The Mechanics' School of Arts in Sydney, he said, was a "noble institution", entirely free of debts, sending some hundreds of pounds to England yearly for newspapers, magazines and the newest literature, with an efficient roll of teachers and featuring a "commodious reading-room with coffee-room attached". While in London the coffee-house evolved into gentlemen's clubs, and from Paris to Vienna the *café* would remain a lively meeting-place and spot to read newspapers, the Australian cafe would develop an entirely different level of intellectual fervour.

Belle Epoque

Australia enjoyed a boom of restaurant dining around 1890–1910—the "late-Victorian and Edwardian" era of the English and "La Belle Epoque" of the French. Social historian John Burnett found in England that dining out had become a fashionable entertainment of the upper-classes. "Society" women at last dined in public, he said, partly as a result of their growing emancipation, a desire for conspicuous consumption, the building of fabulous dining rooms and the cuisine of the great chef, Auguste Escoffier. Perhaps in Australia we simply followed London fashion. However, it seems to me that there was a deeper cause behind the parallel rise in dining-out in several countries (and probably behind food fads like vegetarianism). The boom followed a period of considerable upheaval in the food supply. It was in the interest of the new processing industry to free us from culinary orthodoxy, so that we would experiment with unfamiliar products. And fast railways, food technology, advertising, refrigeration and gas stoves sometimes provided exciting foods. So the very forces which so easily standardised food also produced novelty and stimulated the appetite.

In Sydney in 1895, according to one of the directories of the time, we might have visited Adam's Cafe, 482 and 484 George Street, opposite where the new markets were being erected. Open from 8 am to 8 pm, it was cool, well-ventilated, well-lit and catered for some of the town's leading merchants and representatives. Mr W. Adams made a point of procuring the season's delicacies—including Scotch Finnon haddock, Vancouver salmon, New Zealand whitebait and Tasmanian trumpeter—and featured top Australian clarets and hocks. For lunch in the central city, you could procure at Mr Theo Lang's Café Monaco a single course with drink for 1s; two courses 1s 3d; three courses, 1s 6d. At the Dîner Parisien, 24 Hunter Street, Monsieur Adolphe, ex-chef of the Hotel Métropole, offered an excellent breakfast or dinner for 1s 6d (wine included).

And the Paris House had opened at 173 Phillip Street. Soon under Gaston Lievain, it would be a long-lived restaurant where menus came inscribed with the words, "cuisine artistique". William Moore included in his little book, *City Sketches* (1905), a "Diary of a Day", parts of which read like an advertisement for Lievain's establishment:

1 pm—Lunched à la carte at the PARIS CAFE. The cooking here is excellent. After soup some fried whiting, and branched off to roast snipe. Had some strawberries and cream. Delicious!
3.30—Met Gertrude; "I want to try the South African craze, Russian tea," she murmured. Entered the PARIS CAFE. "Like something with it?" we asked. "A toasted crumpet please," she responded, sweetly.
6.30—Dined at the PARIS CAFE. The 3/- menu is perfect. The Ragout of Duckling was extramenta. We slowed up with Vanilla Ice Cream. Delightful! Must come here early and come often.
10.30—Supper at the PARIS CAFE. Devilled oysters tip-top. Fried flounder ditto. I trembled at the way Gertrude attacked the Quail. Then nothing would suffice but that we should have an "Omelette Soufflée".

The Paris cafe was popular among Sydney artists and writers. In his short essay, "Ghosts of Gastronomia", G. F. Everett in 1928 recalled rotund and genial Gaston Lievain welcoming him into one of the intimate rooms for Saturday lunch with figures like the Lindsays, "Lionel with camera and tripod and Norman so frail, pale, dynamic". Otto, the head waiter, deft and discreet, organised soup served steaming in silver tureens, lobster Newburg, poulet en casserole, turtle-steak (the shell displayed in the hall, as a guarantee of good faith) . . .

Another restaurant recalled by Everett was the Trocadero. A seven-course dinner, with wine, for two and sixpence! What gay dogs they felt when they took some "charmer" to the Paris House or "Troc". For those places were then on the *Index Expurgatorius* of Suburbia, he said. Everett also listed Baumann's, where newspaper editor John Norton, the "Napoleon of King Street", would send a scared copyboy to order his daily "Bull-meat and violets", steak and onions. At Watson's fish cafe, Chinneries, for a few shillings your table would resemble a whaling station. Bill Walker's two floors on Park Street had a menu of 50 cooked dishes for busdrivers and cabbies. The "whole of Sydney" met for morning tea at the ABC Rooms in Pitt Street. Pfahlert's Grill had its be-napkined rounds of stilton cheese, crystal bowls of crisp celery, porterhouse steaks, pewters of foaming ale. The host at the Metropolitan, Ushers, hung an appetising display of game from the rafters—hares, black ducks, kangaroo tails, venison, pigeons, quail, wild turkeys. That little place in the Strand Arcade specialised in strawberries smothered in rich yellow cream, not the anaemic watery stuff of a few years later. At Rainaud's, a tiny room in Castlereagh Street, Madame would spit a chicken that would make even the M. Dalley, last of the gourmets, smack his lips. Such is what impressed G. F. Everett when he recollected the Sydney of the first years of the new century.

However, for Australian reminiscences of the Belle Epoque you could not beat George Meudell, who in 1929 left us an endearing record of 50 years of the high life, *The Pleasant Career of a Spendthrift*. A stockbroker and well-travelled man of affairs, Meudell must enjoy claims to having been Australia's most flamboyant gourmet.

George Dick Meudell

Pleasant career of a spendthrift

When George Meudell, the rich son of the Bank of Victoria's general-manager, came down from Bendigo with six bank clerks to see Briseis win the Cup (it was 1876), Melbourne was then roughish, wide open and frankly immoral, he found. Bars did not close until 11.30, "wowsers" hadn't yet been invented and the police force was below strength. So the Exchange Hotel in Swanston Street was filled with well-dressed "hetirae", gay, laughing and chatty, everyone drinking bubbly and nobody tipsy. Diagonally across at the Blue Posts Hotel, later unnervingly the Temperance and General Life building, about six bars were filled with a hundred "filles de joie", the kerosene lamps shone brightly and the barmen (barmaids had not been discovered) busily opened Moët & Chandon, Pommery & Greno and Krug by the dozen. At the Earl of Zetland, our seven young men saw more "Cyprians" gathered in a crowd of fifty. And so on, right up Bourke Street, they stopped at all the bars, and also Ned Britton's for oysters and Jack

Heard's for dressed crab. To Meudell, until the "Puritans annexed the money and power of the community", there were three things in life: wine, women and good food. The night before Briseis won the Cup, he was inducted into a hedonist adulthood. From then, he was an unrepentant epicure, who spent a fortune all over earth in hotels, clubs, private houses, trains, steamships and restaurants.

In the Paris of the Belle Epoque, Meudell was taken to a supper at the Café Américain, perfectly decorous and quiet, at which the gentlemen were dressed in evening clothes of the finest make and the four lady guests wore nothing. When Maxim's first opened, he went with a violin-playing Melbourne MP, who conducted the orchestra. In London, he and a mate listed 110 dining places, and ticked them all off. He went to the Café Royal (haunt of Oscar Wilde and Aubrey Beardsley), but the best of that lot was the Café Verrey, Regent Street. "We tried them all and liked 'em all, including the dozens of fair and frail ladies we met . . . Life then was one delirious *plaisance*, supported by rude health and lots of money," he said.

At the Hotel des Indes in Batavia, 17 little Javanese house-boys brought him 38 dishes in slow succession, and upon a foundation of boiled rice rose a pyramid of shark fins, bêche de mer, birds' nests, guinea fowl, lychees, pork, jams, edible puppy, turtle, ginger, lobster, turkey, salted almonds, etc. They called it "riz-tafel". Meudell wrote that when he and Dan Lazarus, MP for Bendigo, did a trip round the earth, via Samoa, they saw R. L. Stevenson's house, and made friends with two Samoan Princesses, who "looked like Vestal Virgins and were not". Coupled with the girls, they slid down a smooth rock into a cold deep pool, till they didn't know "whether we were frozen or on fire". They were treated hospitably by the chief, then everybody got tipsy on kava.

Meudell claimed to be among the first guests at the great Palace Hotel, opened in San Francisco in 1875, and the best eating place in the United States because the cooking was international and the food infinitely varied, he said. "And Mother Gum and I have lived in five hundred hotels together in all the four corners of the world, so we ought to know a good hotel when we live in it." Making gastronomic excursions in that "savage" city, New York, one morning early his mate and he called at the already legendary Delmonico's and consulted the *maître d'hôtel* about a special dinner *carte blanche* with wines *en suite* for every course. Then they returned to the Waldorf Astoria Hotel and slept until the elegant dinner was ready. Even Apicius, the Epicure, who lived in Rome and spent £800,000 upon delicacies for his table, would have liked that meal, he thought. "In my youth I've done a bit of kangaroo hunting, pig-sticking, going down mines, and climbing high mountains, but for pure placid enjoyment give me as a pastime the sport of searching for fresh foreign restaurants," he declared. Meudell ticked off cities like he ticked off restaurants and women in London. So he was in a position to judge Australian dining.

According to him, entrepreneurs Spiers and Pond had "pioneered" Melbourne's catering trade. Felix Spiers and George Hennelle had run the Theatre Royal Hotel in Bourke Street East in the 1850s and Spiers and Pond added the Café de Paris restaurant about 1859. The pair brought out an English cricket team for a tour in 1862, before retiring with their fortune to London. Meudell said that an early pastry cook, J. F. Gunsler, wanted to move his cafe to the centre of the Melbourne Block, the recognised promenade of the *haut ton*, "similar to the Board Walk of Atlantic City". He advertised for a partner with £5,000, found a gold buyer named H. G. Iles, who had made a "rise" suddenly out of some gold shares, and they opened the Vienna Café. It was a real European café-restaurant, well furnished and conducted on Parisian lines, he said. Gunsler and Iles invited Meudell to join them at their first dinner and meet their chef and, after that, he became an habitué.

The Vienna Café later became the Australian Café, which he said became a club for clever men and the near-clever. As a young man, Meudell had a mania for founding leagues and associations and belonging to clubs. He joined about a dozen. He was elected to the Authors' Club in London as a contributor to the Sydney *Bulletin* for 40 years. Elected to the Athenaeum Club in Melbourne in July, 1889, he believed it was well-managed, comfortable, and "excepting at the French Club, there was no better dinner in Melbourne." The French Club had been founded in the 1870s by Dr James George Beaney, a surgeon who wore diamonds all over his clothes where there was a peg to hang them and whose dinners, Meudell said, were rare and recherché, "precious as the apple of the eye". Charlie Gates, of Taylor, Buckland and Gates, arranged dinners at the Australian Club, which "were too ethereal almost to eat. Yet were they duly eaten."

Meudell reported that nobody knew how to order a dinner in Melbourne until the 1880s, when Lacaton at the Maison Dorée and Halasy and Denat at the Café Anglais, next to the old *Argus* office, taught the land boomers which was the right end of the asparagus to nibble, and that *poulet en casserole* was the summit of deliciousness. Incidentally, his views were backed up by a visiting Frenchman, O. Comettant, who wrote in his book *Au Pays des Kangourous* in 1890 that he found a "lack of the true art of cooking" and "abominable" shilling meals, although he appreciated staying at the French Club, and found three good restaurants, the Maison Dorée, Crystal Café and La Mascotte. Meudell explained the neglect: "Nearly all the rich Australians had labourers for grandpapas and shop-girls for grandmammas. We are, in fact, we Australians, a nation of crude raw people, the very antithesis of sybarites." Meudell also pointed out that few wealthy men had mistresses, "well-born, well-educated ladies who are well paid to make rich men happy," and essential in France and Italy for epicurean advice and companionship. Meudell was Australia's prodigal son.

LET'S GO TO FASOLI'S

Fasoli's, Melbourne, 1905

IN OTHER LANDS, the quest for fine food could lead to the provincial cuisine of farms and inns. In our industrial nation, good dining has invariably belonged to the cosmopolitan chefs and cheap ethnic spots of the city centre. So let's hunt out a forgotten example of the immigrant cafe which became fashionable for a left-wing, literary "cafe society". Let's go to Lonsdale Street, Melbourne, at the turn of the century.

It is a wide and rather undesirable street. Between Exhibition Street and Jones Lane, and sided by monumental masons and a fancy goods and underclothing shop, we see a low, straggling building. Over a door is a faded attempt at blazonry, "Pension Suisse". Opened under that name by F. Forceau in 1861, it has been a combined boarding rooms, wine "hall" and restaurant under at least eight owners, the earliest Swiss. This is not surprising, given their part in Victoria's early flourishing wine industry. More recently, the names became more obviously Italian. The projecting lamp gives the name of the owner since 1898 and by which the place is now familiarly known, "Fasoli".

It is the "only bit of the Continent in Melbourne," observes William Moore in 1905. E. M. Clowes, the writer, thinks that the "great-and-good in family masses" do not know of the small cafe's existence—most strangers carve out a future by identifying as much as possible with the country and people, she says. Looking back in 1947, another writer E. J. Brady would go so far as to decide: "It was, in its intellectual relations, probably the most important temple ever dedicated to the worship of the Eternal Values in Australia." The memoirs of yet another literary habitué, Robert H. Croll, would list some of the poets, artists and dreamers who eat here and the rollcall will take two pages. Fasoli's, a modest, inner-Melbourne trattoria, is a fashionable haunt of the Bohemians.

There are two private rooms at the front, where the family live. Between these, a narrow passage leads to a large room, with one long table running down the centre. Then, the kitchen, where we might linger to have a word to the hostess, an Irishwoman from County Clare. We enter the dim dining room soon after six o'clock, to make sure of our seat at the table, with its vases of artificial flowers. It is a plain, homely place, with the simplicity of an old-time inn. The two daughters are busy over the long table, at which never more than thirty are served each evening. And then out for a moment onto the bench in the courtyard, pleasantly cool under the willow in the hottest evening, to sip a vermouth and chat to the Italian-Swiss host, Vincent Fasoli, who speaks a slow, difficult English—only answering, volunteering no remarks. Also, in the yard are great dark casks of wine straight from Italy, or so Fasoli says, and about which the old host is forever busy with a funnel and many bottles, for white or red is free of extra charge to all customers.

Dinner commences at 6.30, the usual time in these days. Custom forbids guests starting until Dave Wright—a local solicitor who "visibly practises no law"—sits at the head of the table and fills his glass with red. The meal is very much what you might expect in a trattoria. The appetiser is home-made salami. Then you have a choice of a half-dozen salads. Next is soup or a large plate of spaghetti—the proprietors make their own pasta—with the "necessary" parmesan cheese. Only one main course—it might be osso buco, spezzatino di vitello or something stewed in the heavy copper pots. To follow are perhaps sweets, fruit and cheese, including gruyère and gorgonzola. There is "dark or white" wine *ad lib*, as one reporter puts it. With black coffee, the "whole banquet costs you a trifling one and three". But the food hardly seems to count compared with the ambience: the nondescript building, the enclosed yard, the cosmopolitan comradeship "for the merely intellectual man or woman".

There is the "Man of Memory"—the aforementioned Dave Wright—who dextrously manipulates his macaroni while discussing Maeterlinck and George Bernard Shaw. He speaks Italian like a native, his French is that of a Parisian, he has an encyclopaedic grasp of philosophy and can quote poetry by the furlong. There is "Monsieur Volubilité", bubbling over with information, who wants the world to stop revolving while he ejaculates. Who is the lady at the end of the table? That's "Mademoiselle Bon Bon". Fasoli's wouldn't be complete without her. She is peeping at a book, turning her searchlight eyes on D'Annunzio. She must be the acknowledged Queen of Bohemia, with the wit and sparkle of a Frenchwoman, the friendliness of a matey Australian, the vocabulary of a dictionary and the curiosity of an emu. Who could guess she is destined to marry a deacon and become prominent in ecclesiastical society?

Then there is a Senator, a *Punch* artist, a member of the Comic Opera company, a poet, an Italian, the first violinist from a theatre, a sub-editor of one of the dailies, a big German who might bring from his garden some tarragon for your vinegar, a Frenchman who owns a vineyard a little way out of Melbourne, a German merchant, a Greek youth. Among the art students is one with inordinately long hair, smoothed back from his forehead and cut all the same length. There are as usual a few young women, mostly of the quiet, rather wan, student type—saving one vivid creature, of immature years and marvellous maturity of intellect, whose self-possession makes one feel like a crude child. The students regale each other with choice morsels from the week's *Bulletin*, the bible of Bohemia.

The coffee is brought, the table cleared. The Frenchman on our right delicately burns his spoonful of eau-de-vie over his coffee, and then sets our neighbour on the left aflame with some argument or other. The old Irish hostess, her night's work done, sits knitting and looks at E. M. Clowes and her eyes say as plainly as any words, "What children those men are! what blaguers!" They are lighting up their cigarettes around the room, filling the air with the "incense of modernity". It is now that talk is at its best, when our Italian friends, exhausting their vocabularies, enforce their arguments with severe blows on the table.

So we retire to the outer region, known as "The Yard", the moon behind the solitary willow. Here we finish our smoke, conscious of the dome that shelters us all. Alongside, a quartet get a trifle excited over a game of dominoes. Inside they begin singing, a well-known Italian song. "Bravo!" It is a popular song. Now "Il Trovatore". "Respect for Verdi!" calls a signor. "This is no coon song," he intimates and the company succumb to silence. A Boulanger march, with thrilling refrain. An American woman warbles about Dixie or some other town in music-hall land. There is a comic song about Piccadilly, which completes the cycle of national melodies. Dave Wright may be a hippopotamus of a man but can whistle like a canary. It is pleasant to have some melody tonight at the Fasoli piano, for the traffic of the world will jar on the morrow, and the rhythmic murmur of the universe will be hushed.

In about 1905, Fasoli will move to ampler premises in King Street, the present place to be taken over by their eldest daughter, Kate, and her husband Lorenzo Camusso, and renamed the Café Bohemia. Patronised by members of the Victorian Socialist Society, the Café Bohemia will advertise regularly in the society's weekly organ, an advertisement in 1909 reading: "The only place in Melbourne where you can enjoy a good meal and feel at home with the many good folk that frequent the cafe. And if you like to amuse yourself, come along on Wednesday night—you have a chance to see the Melbourne bohemians enjoy themselves à la Continentale." But, tragically, Victoria's fine vineyards are about to collapse—and along with them the old Pension Suisse—as Australians turn to an unparallelled period of puritanism, milk and orange juice.

It almost seems as if they held the 1914–18 war to kill good restaurants. When George D. Meudell published his memoirs in 1929, he damned our food. While America was made up of nearly one hundred nationalities, he said: "Australia, having only one people, 96 per cent British, has only one diet: steak, chops, beef, mutton, potatoes and gravy (don't forget the gravy), with suet pudding and slabs of cheese. Every Australian home dinner is so amusing and so very English. Our women can't cook and our men do not know the art of good eating. There is no epicurism in Australia, no fine sense of gastronomy as the prop of happiness. There is not one first-class restaurant in the Commonwealth so far." Characteristically, Meudell blamed the demise of the good life on the motor-car and the Puritans taking control of the money. Indeed, bureaucratic industrialism created a clutter of Kraft cheese, Kellogg's cornflakes and six o'clock closing, lean times for the epicure during a period of nation-building wholesomeness.

9

Family goodness

The austerities of the Great War killed off restaurant society, leaving the workers of tomorrow to be built up with fads for orange juice, milk, cornflakes and processed cheese

IN THE MELBOURNE winter of 1925 this cheery banner appeared over the clocks at the main entrance to Flinders Street station:

> Spark up! Get on the good health route,
> Each day take home some citrus fruit.

Above the Elizabeth Street entrance spread the prescription:

> Heed what wise physicians say,
> Citrus fruits are Nature's way.

And Spencer Street station greeted with:

> Take home some citrus fruit tonight;
> It's good for health and appetite.

These and posters up in stations throughout Victoria were the work of railways chairman, Harold Clapp, in his latest "eat more" campaign. He later introduced the all-steel, airconditioned, streamlined *Spirit of Progress.* But in the early 1920s, he not only "electrified the Melbourne suburban lines but 'electrified' the whole State with original ideas and high-pressure methods," as the railways later put it. Indeed, he altered our eating habits . . . And in ways entirely typical of the regimented, temperate 1920s.

 Within months of taking control of the railways on September 17, 1920, Harold Clapp prepared his first "Eat More Fruit" campaign. "If the demand for fruit can be stimulated," he explained to staff, "more will be required, consequently more will be grown, and so more transportation will be demanded." We later became used to road safety, bush-fire and litter sloganeering, but Harold Clapp's energetic urging aroused incredulity and some opposition.

In 1922 the chairman despatched wagons of fruit, with salesmen aboard, into all parts of the State. The next year at Flinders Street he opened the first of a chain of kiosks selling fresh fruit, dried fruit and nuts. During Peach Week in January, 1925, these stalls sold an extra 70 tons of Elberta peaches. Two years later, when the "Week" became "Peach Fortnight", the railways sold close to two million peaches, "equivalent to two peaches for every man, woman and child in Melbourne". Starting with 100,000 books of raisin recipes, over the years he distributed recipes for apples, black currants, loganberries, grapes. During gluts, his station-masters accepted orders for cases of fruit.

In the summer of 1924-5, he began the first of many campaigns for dairy produce, the railway refreshment rooms selling "pasteurised milk in sealed bottles". Simultaneously, stewards hawked sixpenny icecreams down the corridors of express trains. The railways icecream recipe: "1 pint cream, 1 pint milk, 2 egg yolks, about 2 teaspoons vanilla, 1 coffee cup castor sugar. Mix and freeze." Icecreams in little buckets remained a feature of train travel, as they did for an outing to the movies. But there were two even more important items which Clapp popularised, and which also became specialities associated with railway stations.

In October, 1923, the Victorian Railways opened a bakery, not just to supply pies and scones to its refreshment rooms, but more importantly to launch a novelty, raisin bread. Clapp's bakery was large and modern and in 1925 the railways used the first wrapped bread in Australia, its 600 raisin loaves daily consuming two tons of raisins a month. "At the outset of the raisin bread campaign," Clapp's 1926 report stated, "only three bakers in Melbourne were manufacturing this commodity, whereas more than 100 are now undertaking its production. From this may be gauged some idea of the effect of this propaganda on the raisin consumption of the State."

If you bought a drink at a cafe in the 1920s, according to the railways magazine, you were often given a "dubious draft flavoured with some chemical concoction that tasted as though it had been brewed by a laboratory assistant in a fertiliser plant". Pure fruit juice was scarcely thought of. This changed in November 2, 1926, when Clapp opened a fruit juice stall at Flinders Street station. Behind the counter of white vitrolite, with black edging, stood a line of 10 uniformed attendants, each at her Sunkist fruit juice extractor, the first in the country. Customers purchased fourpenny tickets at a cabinet, presented them at the counter and selected orange or lemon. The attendant cut the fruit, squeezed the juice and added sugar, syrup and soda from an American-looking fountain. "There is no admixture of chemical mysteries," the superintendent of Refreshment Services, Mr W. D. Bracher, recorded. "The drink produced is pure and wholesome, and being full of vitamines [as it was still sometimes spelt] is both a healthful restorative and a thirst quencher." During the first 12 days, 44,000 drinks were squeezed and before 12 months one million. Within five years the railways operated 27 fruit juice stalls on its platforms and had become the biggest customer of Victorian citrus growers.

The depression did not immediately affect pies, fruit cake, raisin bread, fresh fruit or juice, since passengers turned from "sit-down" meals to these cheaper snacks. However, with faster trains cutting journey times, with expresses switching since 1908 from hampers to dining and buffet cars, and with people going by road anyhow, the need for platform refreshments declined. The railways became penny-pinching, stopped building new lines, and sought outside money for agricultural publicity campaigns. What was worse, with the depression, the Clapp style of government propaganda suffered a terrible setback.

In February, 1930, the new Prime Minister, Mr Scullin, appealed to farmers to grow more wheat. This was echoed in the States, with the Victorian Premier, Mr Hogan, calling for a "million more acres". It was a desperate effort to boost export income. Clapp responded "wholeheartedly" with a Grow More Wheat campaign. The Victorian farmers, as invited, grew the extra million acres—1,034,065 acres, to be precise. The national harvest of 213·6 million bushels was the highest ever reached. However, instead of the promised 4 shillings a bushel, farmers received approximately 1s 8d. World prices had dropped to an historic low. The Australian wheat historian Dr Edgars Dunsdorfs called it "one of the great disasters in Australian economic history". The Clapp approach was caught up in the calamity. This does not detract from the achievements in the 1920s of Clapp, and railway administrators in other States who followed his lead, to persuade Australians of the healthy qualities of fresh orange juice, a glass of milk, a packet of raisins and an apple. Why had Harold Clapp done it? The explanations expose powerful forces shaping our eating and drinking in the 1920s, promoting products with a secret quality we could call "family goodness".

Regimented eating

Railway lines, extending into even the most inhospitable land and taking settlers with them, were by far the biggest investment of State governments. With American motorcars and trucks coming off post-war production lines, railways began to "lose money", as if they were meant to be profit-making enterprises. The railways had to be justified. In 1930, historian Keith Hancock spent several pages of his classic, *Australia*, mocking the demands of politicians that Clapp's railways should create jobs, promote decentralisation and thus in Hancock's terms, "inaugurate the new social order". He wrote: "Since the State spreads its networks of railways and water-channels to encourage production from the land, it has been tempted to go one step further . . . it has settled yeomen on their farms and planted peasants on their plots."

State Departments of Agriculture urged the family farmers to greater productivity. In 1924–5, Clapp despatched his first "Better Farming" train of 15 carriages. One truck carried grass specimens illustrating the before-and-after effects of top-dressing pastures with "artificial manures". Not merely was the train "an Agricultural College on Wheels but a Domestic Science College as well", with instruction in cookery, needlework, child-care and domestic hygiene. "A stroke of genius," declared the visiting Reverend Dr Lauchlan MacLean Watt in 1932. "The train is one of the greatest things in the world—an apostle of prosperity and enlightenment." These were the years in which growers' cooperatives flourished and the Country Party emerged, exerting political punch. Over-production, which brought "orderly" marketing through government-supported commodity boards, led to Clapp's "eat more" propaganda.

The era of mass literacy and mass newspapers had arrived around the turn of the century. Then the Great War had shown governments the value of exhorting populations through advertising. Lagging behind the United States by a matter of months, Australia's first commercial radio licences were issued in 1923. In Europe this medium brought dictators to power; in Australia it brought salesmen right into the living room, where they stayed. It was another opening for Clapp, and the railways started weekly broadcasts on 3LO in 1925–6. From 1927, the British government's Empire Marketing Board spent £1 million each year advertising imperial imports. Clapp described a "generous aspect" to his propaganda, "a sacred duty to devote time and money to the patriotic cause", and "a debt of honour to a land which abounds in riches".

Housewives became a self-conscious group at this time, the Housewives' Associations and various Country Women's Associations being formed in the early 1920s. When these women came on electrified lines to shop, they rested at Buckley and Nunn's tea rooms, lunched in the department store cafeterias, and left children at a crêche Clapp introduced at Flinders Street.

At home, while most had iceboxes, the luckiest housewives now looked forward to fridges—kerosene, gas and electric, now that electricity had reached most suburbs. A big local maker, Edward Hallstrom, commenced making kerosene fridges in 1923. Named after British physicist Lord Kelvin and claimed to be the first electric models in the US in 1914, Kelvinators were imported in 1926. Founders of the local Email company began selling them in 1927. Refrigerators also went into shops, selling Clapp's milk, fruit juice and icecream.

Clapp's campaigns reflected the new concern with vitamins, the discovery of which had been precipitated by the appearance of beri-beri in rice-eating countries. The cause was shown in 1912 to be the removal of the vitamin-rich germ by the modern mills turning out white rice. After scientists exposed the nutritional incompetence of war-time governments, marketers of oranges, raisins, milk, yeast extracts and other products extolled vitamin virtues. Accompanying the concept of healthy food came the idea that children needed special treatment. Previously, they had usually eaten what the parents ate. Now commerce devised entirely new "needs". Baby foods were developed by Gerber in the US. Breakfast cereals, processed cheddar and baked beans were childish foods accepted also by adults, whose taste joined the littlest common denominator. For Clapp's first juice stall, he contrived the slogan, "Children, Yes, and Grown-Ups, Too—!'

Little typifies the 1920s, however, like the temperance movement's attempts to prohibit alcohol. An early success had been Sunday closing in Tasmania in 1858. In 1881, NSW hotels were forced to close at 11 pm. In various States, a system of "local option" then gave "wowsers", as we now called them, the power to vote out nearby licences. In Victoria, one such local option poll in 1920 closed 105 hotels. In NSW, the Liquor Amendment Act cut the number of licences from 3,063 in 1905 to 2,037 in 1940. (Even in the 1980s the NSW licensing authority was still called the Licences Reduction Board.)

Most notorious of all Great War restrictions was six-o'clock closing— hotels shutting early in South Australia from 1915 and in NSW, Victoria and Tasmania from 1916. From the 1920s, anti-liquor crusaders also persuaded governments to hold referendums into the outright prohibition of alcohol, some votes coming close, but all of them lost. In those years the annual beer consumption averaged only 50 litres, falling in the early 1930s to around 30, making the inter-war period the most sober in our history, compared with 100 litres again by the 1950s. In California, Prohibition had knocked down the wine industry, growers turning to oranges and raisins, providing Clapp's inspiration. The railway refreshment rooms, long "run on strict temperance lines", found their era.

Clapp was at the top of a powerful public service elite, consciously manipulating an entire population. He arose when the crisis of world war had welded the modern State apparatus—as much electoral as electrical—for keeping the troops in line. The new "mass society" flocking twice daily beneath Clapp's Flinders Street clocks was to be moulded into a nation of consumers. The industrial army, which had set out on convict rations, now marched on vitamins. It was an era of faith in "Australia Unlimited", in the persuasive powers of mass media and in the scientific study of "national diet", to borrow the title of a statistical survey by D. T. Sawkins.

Clapp also represented the influx of American ideas and products in the

1920s, forerunners of considerable Americanisation in a parallel post-war decade of the 1950s. His American father had arrived in the goldfields in 1853 and became an entrepreneur of Victorian coaches, buses and trams, schemes he borrowed from across the Pacific. Born in Australia in 1875, Harold Clapp left for his father's country in 1901, rising in the railways there, until invited to return, at the age of 45, to take over the electrification of the Victorian railways. And so, just as the Chaffey brothers had brought irrigation from California, Clapp had seen how the ensuing glut had been relieved there by publicity. He knew the secret of "inner sunshine" in oranges and "iron" in raisin bread. Harold Clapp was admired for his "American pep and hustle". He preached American ideas of "service", telling his stationmasters they were "salesmen", who had to find why business had been lost to motor transport and *get it back*. He issued a staff memo on Developing a Pleasing Personality—"worth more than money in the bank".

The 1920s saw increased American influence on food. In 1920, a Leeton Cannery official, John Brady, toured the US and returned with the idea of the Murrumbidgee Irrigation Area rice industry. A Californian, S. M. McKimmin, opened the Golden Gate Sundae Shop, said to be Australia's first soda fountain, in Sydney in 1921. In 1923, the Wattle Path Palais de Dance at St Kilda, Melbourne, claimed the biggest soda fountain in the southern hemisphere, 29 ft long with 16 syrup pumps gushing a dazzling variety of drinks. The first of the big American food companies moved in. Philip K. Wrigley, the founder's son from Chicago, had set up chewing gum operations back in the war. Life Savers, the candies invented in Cleveland, Ohio, in 1913 and successful with the wartime blockade of German mints, arrived in 1921, the company selling out to local interests in 1925. H. J. Heinz was importing its canned products, although it didn't set up a cannery until 1935. And there were two further revealing American names.

Destined to dominate our eating and drinking, the first giant food corporations came to the fore in the 1920s. The main names were: Kellogg's and Kraft (from the US), Nestlé (Switzerland), Cadbury's (England) and Peters (Australia). With hindsight, we can see that these corporations pushed early "convenience" foods, most simply defined as those needing no cooking outside the factory. Even in those days, it was realised that the new products simplified breakfast and provided after-school and bedtime snacks. The products were advertised as providing extra energy and added body-building for growing children. Clapp's work fitted in with all of this. Further than that, the typical products of those nation-building days were designed to relieve an agricultural glut. In fact, the products shared a single source of "family goodness". The secret was a potent four-letter word: Milk.

Each of these businesses was set up, with government encouragement, to sell more milk. More milk, meant to be carried by Clapp's trains, meant to keep the emerging Country Party contented as British post-war butter demand fell drastically, meant to bring profits to these big corporations, and meant to produce a race of youngsters not lacking essential vitamins. Let's look at milk's revolutionary new forms.

Condensed milk

One of the ways to deal with a milk surplus was to seal it in cans, making it handily transportable. Gail Borden invented sweetened condensed milk in the middle of the previous century in America and milk condensors were installed in Melbourne in 1882. The Swiss firm of Nestlé set up its first plant at Toogoolawah in southern Queensland in 1908, arguing in its *Milky Way Housewife's Book* of 1914 that condensed milk was "the best substitute for the mother's milk". In the 1920s publicity boosted the company's "model condenseries", supplied by considerably over 7,000 cows . . . "imagine them in their ideal setting of wooded hills and river-watered pastures . . . sleek, healthy cows, selected for the rich creaminess of their milk, the purity and quality . . ." Nestlé produced "Sunshine" powdered milk from 1937.

Milk chocolate and cocoa

Nestlé opened its chocolate factory at Abbotsford in Sydney in 1918, "surrounded by beautiful lawns and gardens in twenty-two acres of picturesque grounds", its workers doing daily exercises, and producing tablet chocolate the next year and chocolate "mixtures" in 1920. The English version of the enlightened employer, Cadbury-Fry-Pascall, followed on at a Hobart site selected by a technical commission sent from England in 1920. As the Cadbury's slogan explained, a full "glass and a half" of milk went into "Dairy Milk" chocolate blocks. The Cadbury cocoa drink, being imported at the end of the Victorian era, changed from "Bournville" to "Bournvita" in Australia to remind us of its newly-confirmed life-giving properties. Nestlé won young hearts with the introduction in 1934 of Milo Tonic Food.

Icecream

Peters used "the health food of a nation" as an icecream slogan. Mr F. A. B. Peters, an American from Michigan, started his Peters American Delicacy in 1907. He established his Melbourne operation, destined to become the principal force, on June 20, 1929. The family businesses which would later form the Streets Ice Cream subsidiary of Unilever were also all set up around this time: J. P. Sennitt & Sons (which commenced ice and icecream making in Melbourne about 1910), Streets (Edwin Street started in Corrimal, NSW, in 1920), Lynams (Parramatta, NSW, 1934) and McNiven Bros (Sydney, 1936). While icecream was often sold directly from dairy factories, and adjacent iceworks, it needed refrigeration in corner stores before it could create a mass market. Icecream was big in the US at the turn of the century, and, as in Britain, it took off in Australia in the 1920s. In 1923, the Eskimo

Pie—icecream in chocolate—was sold in Sydney under licence and with foil wrappers imported from the USA. The date given for the first milk bar in Australia is 1933.

Breakfast cereals

Dr John Harvey Kellogg transformed a Seventh-Day Adventist sanitorium at Battle Creek, Michigan, in the last decades of last century into a "veritable fountainhead of faddism". He *manufactured* foods, especially Kellogg's Toasted Corn Flakes, the artificiality considered somehow purer. At one time no less than 40 competing breakfast food companies all listed their addresses as Battle Creek, and the odd "Elijah's Manna" of Dr Charles Post grew into the enormous General Foods corporation (Maxwell House, Birds Eye, Burger Chef, etc). Dr Kellogg gave increasing attention to the not insignificant technical challenge of producing uniform and long-keeping flakes out of "corn-pone", or maize hash. The advantages of the cereals became apparent for small families taking their breakfast on the run and, while not outstandingly nutritious, they were a delicious dressing for milk. Kellogg's began making Australian cornflakes in rented premises in Chippendale, Sydney, in 1924, and set up the Botany factory in 1928.

Processed cheese

James L. Kraft got into cheese in Chicago in 1903, buying it at the markets and reselling it to retailers. Discovering how perishable some types could be, especially without refrigeration, he developed "processed cheese", preserved by heating and adding chemicals called emulsifiers, making distribution much easier. His company sold transportable cheese to the US forces during the Great War. The blue and yellow packets of Kraft processed cheddar were brought to Melbourne in 1926 by a local food processor, Fred Walker, whose best wartime effort was "potted" or "club" cheese, mixed with sodium metabisulphite preservative and sealed in a pot. With the post-war dairy surplus, the Victorian government encouraged various manufacturers to find some form of cheese preserving for export. Walker's bringing of Kraft to Melbourne is claimed by the company to have taken cheese consumption from 3 lb to 11 lb per head over the next 50 years. But Walker had already done something even more monumental than introduce Kraft—he had promoted the most beloved of our proprietary foods, the greatest fount of family goodness of them all, Vegemite.

VEGEMITE

Vegemite advertisement in the 1920s

THE NATION-BUILDING 1920s entrenched the industrial family and the commercial food supply. We discovered cornflakes at breakfast—eroding our claim to "meat three times a day". We discovered snacks like processed cheddar and icecream and drank orange juice and cocoa. We sobered up, with six-o'clock closing, hotel shut-downs and attempts at prohibition. So nutritious Vegemite was entirely typical of the period. Except for one irony—the spread which epitomised "family goodness" was made from brewery waste.

Fred Walker had started in business in Melbourne in 1908, developing lines like "Red Feather" canned butter, canned dripping, potted cheese, camp pies and liver pastes—for export, for wartime rations and for the outback. In 1919, Walker found another way to preserve nourishment, a beef extract like British Bovril, which was supplied from ranches in South America and Australia and was being sold here with an ad: "A 'Little Bovril' Keeps the Doctor Away". Walker's version was launched as Bonox, a keen seller for decades.

The Carlton & United Brewery also tried an extract from its spent yeast, called "Cubex". It failed and by February, 1923, Fred Walker & Co negotiated to buy the brewery's spent yeast, from which to make a version of English Marmite. Fred Walker also appointed a 30-year-old chemist named C. P. Callister to the project. The country's leading food technologist in the inter-war period started in a small room in a corner of Walker's Albert Park factory, with a desk, a sink, an Oertling balance, some glassware and a few bottles of chemicals. In the centre of the room was a very thin workbench, at which he developed what was known by the end of the year as . . . Vegemite. It is said the company first considered calling it "Parwill", in response to Marmite ("Ma might").

It was not a run-away success. However, Callister came across the Kraft patent for processed cheese, which Walker tied up in a visit to the US in August, 1925. With the bowdlerised cheddar, the company's total sales doubled in a year. More importantly, Walker's local sales began to exceed exports, which had implications for the sales effort of other products. It is worth seeing how the company went about addicting us to Vegemite.

An early press advertisement described Vegemite as: "The Vitamin vegetable paste for use in sandwiches, soups, stews and gravies. It is full of vitamins and very nourishing." To emphasise its scientific benefits for growing children, the drawing depicted a boy in academic dress standing on a ladder and peering through a magnifying glass into a huge jar of the "World's Wonder Food", as it was sub-titled. A girl, neither wearing gown nor standing on a ladder, admired her man. Back in 1925 Callister had sent samples to London for testing for vitamins. Vitamins were popular knowledge, but still vitamin B had not been differentiated into B_1, B_2, etc. It was another eight years before the isolation of thiamine (B_1), in which brown bread and Vegemite excel. It was also long before nutritionists became concerned at the over-use of salt—ten per cent of Vegemite was salt, *Choice* reported in October, 1981.

In 1931, the Kraft Walker Cheese Co engaged American advertising agency, J. Walter Thompson, which had arrived in 1929 mainly to handle the General Motors account. In one early campaign, it enclosed with the other Kraft products free gift coupons for Vegemite, the standard technique to get people to sample a still unfamiliar product and indicating the way in which Vegemite rode to success on cheese marketing. In 1937, a limerick contest awarded prizes of Pontiac cars. Just before the war the company gained authorisation to advertise in the *Australian Medical Journal*, which became, according to a 1978 company document, "in effect, official endorsement of the product to medical practitioners throughout Australia". While the services were purchasing Vegemite in 7 lb and 8 oz tins and ½ oz ration packs, the company took advertising space to explain its civilian rationing policy and to keep the consumer "aware of the product and its virtues".

The post-war baby boom created a "huge new market" for which, in 1954, an agency employee composed the well-known "Happy Little Vegemites" jingle. During the fifties the advertising "heavily under-scored the medical and health authorities' recognition and acceptance of Vegemite, positioning the product as a family health food". One theme was "Put Vegemite next to the pepper and salt whenever you set the table". Another device was short essays about talented children, which became in 1957 a magazine and television campaign featuring the Sara Quads and Lucke Quads.

After the National Health and Medical Research Council then allegedly found a vitamin B_1 deficiency in the Australian diet, the agency took up a tough, "Me starving my Family" stance: "even the best diets provided by the most conscientious mother could be lacking in vitamin B_1". In fact, the NHMRC concluded in 1959 that "excluding alcoholics", the great majority of Australians received sufficient thiamine and many people consumed "unnecessarily large amounts" in the form of medicinal preparations. So alcoholics, rather than children would have been more likely to gain from the advertising of this brewery waste product.

Demographic studies showed that in the 1960s the below-fives were not going to be as big a market as the 15–24s, and so the strategy became, "you had Vegemite when you were young, continue to have it during your teen years and into your adult years". But such direct appeals proved ineffective, and sales only lifted substantially in 1969 when the agency decided to return to the "strategy that helped make Vegemite a household name and helped put the product into 90 per cent of all Australian homes"—showing the value of Vegemite for young children. Apparently the advertising for children got the adults. From 1972 until 1977 the campaign was "Pass the Vegemite please, Mum." In 1978, "Happy Little Vegemites" nostalgia was tried, to "remind today's mother of how good Vegemite was for them when they were children." And so, processed and flavoured brewing waste nourished another generation.

With the product's popularity, the company turned over the years to using waste also from molasses distillation and to growing its own yeast, but it still relied on spent brewer's yeast. The company's coyness about this was such that a pamphlet "What is Vegemite?" available in the late 1970s said no more than it derived from "yeast", and a wall-chart for science classes concealed its raw material as "Saccharomyces yeast". In an age of ecological awareness, the use of an otherwise industrial pollutant should have been regarded as a credit for the beloved brown spread.

Fred Walker's death in 1935 paved the way for the total acquisition by the American Kraftco of the local operation and, with it, Vegemite. So the most Australian-seeming proprietary product, which once proudly bore the name Fred Walker & Co, was American. Fred Walker might be forgotten except that his name continued on certain Kraft cheeses. His and Dr Callister's item had become a near addiction, something expatriates hungered for. It seemed so Australian that, despite several attempts, Kraft have never been able to launch it properly in any other country. It just happened to be introduced at the right "family goodness" moment. Such a yeast extract would have been impossible in the United States between 1918 and 1933 because Prohibition made breweries illegal.

10

Dainty cooks and sudden drinkers

Between the world wars, men took rations to work and drank quickly till 6 o'clock closing, while women were encouraged to "civilise" the society with sweet fantasies

"IS THIS all men can do with a new country? Look at those tin cans!" D. H. Lawrence's clever image of Australia was rusty cans chucked on every bit of dirt. In his novel, *Kangaroo*, he presented the country in 1923 as "towns— and corrugated iron—and millions of little fences—and empty tins". He wrote that our very ground seemed "weary and drabbled, almost asking for tin cans". Behind the bungalows "lay a whole aura of rusty tin cans chucked over the back fence," he said. That impression exposed the cluttered, but uncultivated heart of Australia. We fed not from the soil, but from tin cans.

Lawrence experienced what we could regard as Australia's most typical eating and drinking—that between the world wars. Our memories don't go back much earlier. And, in relative isolation from Europe, our culture had probably grown its most "Aussie"—with the wattle and *On Our Selection* still not quite lost to the American invasion. Food shaped by convict rations was taken over by the makers of tinned foods. But that didn't stop us embellishing breakfast, lunch and tea in ways about which we can become nostalgic. Let's continue with D. H. Lawrence's perceptions.

Within the "millions of little fences" of the sprawling settlements, Lawrence noticed the scattering of corrugated iron shanties with their rainwater tank, verandah for the woman's kitchen, odd bits of garden, "very white fowls clustering for bedtime", and a "rubbish heap of ashes and tins slipping into the brambles". The biggest zinc roof would be the hotel's. The "stores", where the people drank sticky aerated water, were just "flyblown shops with corrugated iron roofs". And delivery carts and the baker's boy on his pony flew around the wilderness.

It seemed to Lawrence a curiously proletarian society, which real men should revolt against, and which frightened him into flirting with fascism. Business went on at full speed, but only because it was the other end of English and American business, and it left Sydney as "just a substitute for the real thing—as margarine is a substitute for butter," he wrote. Yet it was tempting to settle here. "We could have a cow, and chickens—and then the Pacific and this marvellous new country," his hero hoped. But his wife's good sense prevailed: "The farms don't really belong to the land. They only scratch it and irritate it, and are never at one with it . . . Australia feels as if it had never been loved, and never come out into the open. As if a man had never loved it, and made it a happy country, a bride country—or a mother country".

About the eating and drinking, Lawrence noted the cheap meat, coffee with a lot of chicory in it, good butter and milk and "brownish honey, that also, like the landscape, tasted queer, as if touched with unkindled smoke". The people had four o'clock tea, then proper tea at six or half past, with meat and pies and fruit salad. One meal comprised "cold roast pork with first-class brown crackling on it, and potato salad, beetroot, and lettuce, and apple chutney; then a dressed lobster—or crayfish, very good, pink and white; and then apple pie and custard-tarts and cakes and a dish of apples and passionfruits and oranges, a pineapple and some bananas; and of course big cups of tea, breakfast cups". A neighbourly gift arrived of persimmons and passionfruits.

When the novel's hero was entertained by a powerful Sydney figure, they were waited upon by a Chinaman, offering a silver dish of hors d'oeuvres and a handsome crayfish with mayonnaise. The host asked: "Let's talk about Peach Melba. Where have you had the very best Peach Melba you ever tasted?" Our strange society forced Lawrence to ponder the battle of the sexes—between the feminine gentility of Peach Melbas and the male stolidity first represented in Sydney by workmen lying on the grass "eating food from paper packages".

Meat pies and tomato sauce
Through his yarn-spinning hero, Billy Borker, the writer Frank Hardy revealed something of male attitudes in a story, "How the Melbourne–Sydney Argument was Settled". Two representatives arguing in a border hotel at Albury harped on such matters as the harbour bridge (an oversized coathanger) and the Yarra (the only river in the world that flows upside-down). When Melbourne Mick would say that Australian Rules football drew bigger crowds, Sydney Sam would call it "aerial ping pong". They'd turn to climate, Sam knocking the rain, and Mick responding that Melbourne enjoyed more sunny days a year. Of course, the border pub served both beers. If Mick said

there was more alcohol in Melbourne beer, Sam would say that was why there were more alcoholics. Billy Borker tried settling the dispute by switching beers. But they'd take one sip of the foreign beer and spit it out. Finally, Borker decided they'd send a sample of the best Melbourne and Sydney brews—marked A and B—for CSIRO analysis. Back came the telegram: "Thorough test made—Stop—regret inform you both horses have yellow jaundice".

That captured the male stereotype. The men were urban workers, but with a hankering after the bush, revealed by their fascination in horse-racing. Even their Sydney–Melbourne rivalry was based on the clash of different origins, competition for gold, uneven land booms, conflict over free trade and tariffs. Their uncritical acceptance of the CSIRO symbolised the rise of the expert and the state. And the whole thing floated from the 1890s on factory beer—beer which, if Frank Hardy's observation was correct, secretly disgusted us.

According to the stereotype, the men had basic eating habits, which flowed from bush origins. Back in the 1850s, William Kelly had noted a "dead down" among gold-diggers on all "made dishes" (our modern idea of complementary foods arranged on a plate), the men wanting a slab of what they knew to be meat, simply cooked. Visiting in the 1880s, Percy Clarke wrote about the "universal habit of bolting of his meals", colonials boasting of this fast feeding and saying that a "slow feeder is a slow worker". It was an attitude to food which devised such nick-names for a camp cook as the "doctor", "greasy" and "poisoner" and his mate as the "slushy", to take examples in G. A. Wilkes' *Dictionary of Australian Colloquialisms*. The same approach continued in the mixed grill served in what became known between the wars as the "Greeks", the cafe remembered in country towns. You dined even worse at pub counter-lunches. It was the tradition of the grace: "bog in, don't wait". Or an uncle who put his breakfast chop in his porridge, with the grunt, "What's the difference, it all goes down the same way". Or in more modern times, ABC journalists I knew who formed a Dirty Eaters' Club to dine appallingly in public. Its gastronomic height was believed to be reached in the Carpetbag Steak, beef stuffed with oysters, a combination also occurring in the United States, although I have not confirmed where it originated. Men also cooked over the fire at barbecues. And for the worker's lunch and after the football match, it became the meat pie and tomato sauce, although this was as truly Australian as the Holden car.

Not until the Second World War, or perhaps a little earlier, was the meat pie and tomato sauce mentioned as a "national dish". However, pies had arrived with the British, the Flying Pieman one of many street vendors in our first towns. British cookery books in the early years of our settlement contained several variations. In his 1864 cookery book, our "Australian Aristologist" quoted a medical opinion on the "Danger of the Meat Pie" (not leaving a hole in the crust to let out poisonous gases). Writing about the top of Melbourne's Bourke Street in 1869, journalist Marcus Clarke described the coffee barrows, with urn kept hot by charcoal, and the stalls at which a pieman poked a hole in the crust with his finger and poured from a long-spouted can a "gravy" of salt and water. A fellow customer reassured Clarke, "Mutton's cheaper than cat".

In the 1890s, Melbourne journalist "Rita" recommended the meat pie for the packed lunch for men and schoolchildren. Here it replaced the big agrarian midday meal, destroyed as a family get-together by the separation of workplace, and classroom, from home. Tomato sauce was being bottled from the beginning of preserving factories, and at least by 1868. With the advent of automatic machinery, the strictures of the depression and the need for street comfort in the war, the meat pie and tomato sauce was accepted as a characteristic "fast-food". In Adelaide, the pie rolled over in pea soup became a "floater".

Pressures to conform were strong between the wars, but it would be wrong ever to consider men marching totally in step to coarse meals. Many genuinely loved Sydney rock oysters, yabbies or "crays" boiled in a drum by the river, the weekend fisherman's catch, as well as a good T-bone steak. And it would be negligent to disregard among the men numbers of cultivators, quietly building their own houses, filling the backyard with cabbages and settling down, as Lawrence saw it, with a wife, cow, chickens and the Pacific. Many were strict abstainers. But the dominant model of male behaviour was aggressively uncultivated. We made lazy eaters and sudden drinkers.

Against the rough male attitudes to food, formed in our early years, was increasingly pitted the adorning approach of a woman, expected—as childbearer, cook and shopper—to make the society decent. She represented gentility, parsley by the back path, little cakes, pots of tea and teetotalism. If the damper symbolised our first, male century, then now succeeded the pavlova. If the male stereotype was to emerge as Frank Hardy's Billy Borker and as Bazza MacKenzie, then the female counterpart was Barry Humphreys' Edna Everage, whose attitudes were moulded in times when a most desirable quality was "daintiness".

Daintiness

Through recipes and water-colour impressions of translucent jellies and chocolate crackles, the booklets distributed by food manufacturers in the 1920s showed how to adorn sideboard doilies, tea plates and silver serving baskets. *Dainty Recipes: A Book of Selected Recipes by Nestlé* demonstrated for the "discriminating housewife" easy, economical and attractive dishes of "purity and daintiness". In the Robur Tea company's 6d booklet of *100 Tested Recipes—Afternoon Tea Dainties*, a make-believe genius of the modern culinary arts, "Robiere" (Miss Nell Rapley of Melbourne's Emily

McPherson College of Domestic Economy), offered: "Luxury—at a farthing a pot", and dainties including lamingtons, cornflake nutties, cream puffs, butterflies, rainbow cake, brandy snaps, ginger nuts and drop scones.

Daintiness often took the colour pink. Our culinary genius, Robiere, suggested afternoon tea menus—each of no less than six or seven plates—for a "Bridge Tea", "Celebration Tea", "Marigold Tea" and "Pink Tea". In this case, pinkness came from salmon, tomato, rosewater, cochineal, carmine and crystallised cherries, not to neglect the strawberries and cream sandwiches. In his novel *Riders in the Chariot* (1961), Patrick White evoked this pink world when, in need of comforting, Mrs Jolley rushed to the oven to bake a pink cake. While she baked she even sang her favourite "pinker hymns" and had a vision of "the Jesus Christ of the long pink face and languid curls". All was sanctified by cake . . .

You could see the forces at work late last century—in Mrs Wicken's small *Fish Dainties*, distributed freely in 1892 by the short-lived Mutual Provedoring Company to promote its refrigerated fish supplies to Melbourne. In a series of worthy articles in the 1890s, the social editress of the Melbourne *Herald*, "Rita", concerned herself with what we might think of as the "quality of life" and, as she interpreted it, "taste", although she also slipped in the word, "daintiness". "Many people think," she wrote, "that wealth is necessary to make the distinction between 'feeding', 'eating' or 'dining'. It is not . . . After a very reasonable amount of money, the chief requisites are knowledge and taste." You could show your refinement by simple things such as oysters *au naturel*, some fish daintily prepared, a fine cheese, crisp celery, a perfect salad, the choice and arrangement of dishes. A dainty dinner could be done for half a crown, when the average woman thought "daintiness costs half to one guinea," she said.

Not surprisingly, the great promoters of daintiness, which turned mere "feeding" into "dining", were the modern food companies. They could not make much sales progress with the rough tastes of workmen. However, they could coax housewives to adopt profitable frills. They could persuade shoppers to ask for highly-advertised embellishments like chocolate, desiccated coconut, custard powder and jelly. They could convince women to accept a new role as consumers. Daintiness—which embodied "feminine" qualities like lightness, prettiness and gentility—was part of a long campaign to pervert the traditional caring concerns of women into petty materialist preoccupations.

The concerted effort of the emerging food companies, State bureaucracy and well-meaning collaborators like Rita to mould a sober society of workers and consumers, chasing a simplified style of bourgeois culture, was probably the sort of impulse which led to the foundation in NSW in 1922 of the Country Women's Association. Its carefully "non-sectarian and non-political" activities included bringing comforts to the outback, helping the less fortunate in other lands, and raising money with recipe books.

The popular cookery books of the inter-war period tended to come from the CWA, the fund-raising committees of private schools, domestic science teachers, home economists with gas companies and newspapers. Reliable housekeeping advice thus arrived from well-placed farm wives, the anglophile middle-class, official educators, progressive industrialists and the new mass media. The *Australian Home Journal* had been launched in 1894. The *New Idea* was founded in 1902. In 1926 came the *Australian Woman's Mirror*. And the *Australian Women's Weekly*, established in 1933, became the most successful. From those days, each State featured its own standard cookery books — like *Miss Schauer's* in Queensland, the school teachers' *Commonsense* in NSW and the *Green and Gold* in South Australia (fund-raising for a private school). While the textbooks tended to reinforce plain, English-style cookery, the magazines were hungrier for novelty. They drew on the manufacturers' recipes pushing particular food ingredients, and also asked readers to send in ideas. This encouraged recipes which added fiddly bits to tea-party fare, with special emphasis on cakes.

Cakes which our women can lay claim to, even if based on borrowed principles, included lamingtons, Anzac biscuits and the pavlova. Lamingtons, the chocolate and coconut coated cubes of cake which appeared in recipe books about the First World War, would seem to be named after Baron Lamington, who was governor of Queensland from 1895 to 1901. A nice embellishment to the theory is that the word refers to a "lamina" of gold, apricot jam filling to provide moisture to left-over cake. Anzac biscuits, of coconut, rolled oats and golden syrup, were in the recipe books by 1925. And there were numerous other local specialities, like Jubilee cake, which seems restricted to South and West Australia and which has remained a category in the cooking section of our local annual show.

Determining which cakes are uniquely Australian would be a major research project. I had gone along with gem scones being indigenous until I discovered them in a nineteenth-century Canadian book, which renders them suspect. The English are familiar with the marble cake, which divides the mixture in three parts, flavoured and coloured with vanilla, cochineal and cocoa and which are placed in the cake tin in piles. The recipe was contained, among other places, in the NSW cookery teachers' *Commonsense Cookery Book* of the 1920s. A few pages later was rainbow cake, which required identical ingredients but put into three sandwich tins so that layers went on top of each other, with jam between. It is possible that rainbow cake is an Austral extravagance, but who could be sure?

It has frequently been asserted that the Peach Melba was ours. While Dame Nellie was, and the dish became very popular in tinned peach form, it was devised in the singer's honour by the French chef, Auguste Escoffier, in 1893. He worked at the Savoy in London and, with manager César Ritz wishing to encourage women to be seen at the hotel, he was expected to name creations—like this peach-half and icecream—after well-known women.

Childishness

If damper and the rest of the "muttonous" diet can be allocated to the men, and pretty things to the women, then the commercial favourites went to the children. In fact, much of our food became increasingly childish. Between the wars, Vegemite became the kiddies' spread, Milo and a host of softdrinks and cordials their beverages, and they enjoyed a long list of "lollies" (an Australian word): Violet Crumble bars, Minties, Cherry Ripes, Columbines, Polly Waffles, Jaffas and Fantales. Food manufacturers picked out the profitable children's market, ensuring that they needed special food. It was part of nation-building. Also, I think the low gastronomic expectations and the defensive humour of the working man could be reconciled with women's "dainties" by making food a childish fantasy. Seeking the lowest common denominator, the food business appealed to juvenile tastes. One exceedingly typical product—which, shall we say, set solid in the 1930s—gives a good illustration of this: jelly crystals.

Nineteenth-century cooks simmered calves' feet to make the aspic for all kinds of moulds, shapes and jellies. They dangled them down wells to set in the unremitting heat, such was the pioneering drive to achieve the fragile forms which epitomised daintiness, Englishness and the imposition of machine-made shape. Then, and until the late 1920s, the recipe books generally advised using gelatine, where the food factory boiled the calves' feet for you. The Davis Gelatine factory at Botany in Sydney claimed to be the world's biggest.

Such was the direction in which the industry was moving that manufacturers sweetened, flavoured and coloured gelatine, put it in a packet and promoted it like a new toy. Bert Appleroth started his Aeroplane Jelly company in 1928 and was soon "delivering" jelly crystals in Tiger Moth planes and persuading the new radio audience to sing "I Like Aeroplane Jelly". What did its chemical composition matter when a food could become such a brightly-coloured plaything for the whole family? So the reasonably sophisticated shapes and moulds of the last century became the gastronomically trivial delight of capitalism's family. Jelly was crude, dainty and childish.

Eating between the wars

From a sheaf of old recipe books and recollections we can visualise the typical kitchen, provisions and meals between the wars. The stream-lined kitchen with built-in cupboards was already advocated, but in most houses the sink, the wood or perhaps gas stove and the dresser stood around the walls. In the centre, encircled by chairs, was the large kitchen table. Some places were lucky enough to have a pantry and sensible cellar and most enjoyed an ice-chest, probably in the laundry to be accessible to the iceman. The dining room was a separate, dauntingly formal, photographic shrine to the family, and only used when entertaining.

The *Commonsense* book (my edition is about 1925), representing pretty standard ideas, provided a list of Kitchen Requisites. As well as obvious equipment like a "good stove", "1 cook's knife" and "1 rolling pin", there were also more telling items such as "set of skewers", "1 gravy strainer", "1 boiler and steamer", "1 potato masher", "pie dishes", "blanc mange mould", "pudding basins", "patty tins", "1 pair sandwich tins", "1 swiss roll tin" and "1 tin opener".

Standing along a shelf were canisters labelled, in descending order of size: flour, sugar, rice, sago, tea and, if there were a sixth, coffee. The Pick-Me-Up Condiment Co Ltd advertised a representative list of groceries: tins of tomato soup, cooked spaghetti and baked beans, bottles of Worcestershire, anchovy, tomato and Father's Favourite sauce, and jars of lemon butter and cherries. As well as that PMU selection, the pantry cupboard might contain almonds, anchovies, dried apricots, baking powder, gelatine, barley, chutney, cocoa, curry powder, coffee essence, dessert fruits in syrup, flavouring and colouring essences, gelatine, and tins of sardines. Pickles were recommended as a "spur to jaded appetites". Probably the housewife did her own preserves, including jams and chutneys. Dripping was collected for cooking.

As well as being visited by the milkman, grocer, greengrocer and butcher, some people went to the baker to collect their bread hot for breakfast and for the cut lunch. You could go around the corner to the grocer. A visit to the dairy was an even bigger thrill, since it had naturally thick cream, dairy butter and probably fresh eggs and bacon, since chickens and pigs were still offshoots of dairying. Many people's backyards contained rows of carrots, a lemon tree and maybe a loquat or quince or a passionfruit vine and mint growing by the rainwater tank. Scraps went to the "chooks".

Breakfast was a hearty meal, with oatmeal porridge or the latest American breakfast cereals, doused in milk and white sugar. This was followed by a hot course of bacon and eggs or grilled or fried chops, steak, sausages or liver and bacon, or a combination of these with eggs. There was a rack for the toast, scraped with butter and jam. This was all taken with cups of tea, milk for the children.

Morning tea, like afternoon tea, was universal. As a cookery book said, "there is nothing so convenient to have in the kitchen as a well-filled biscuit tin". The workmen and schoolchildren took a "cut lunch" of sandwiches, cake or biscuits and a piece of fruit, and the lunch box would also have separate grease-proof packets of cake and biscuits for the "smoke-oh" or morning recess. Like other recipe collections, the *Commonsense* devoted a section to sandwich fillings, which included almond and celery, anchovy, apple and celery, cheese and nut, cucumber, egg, ham, salmon and lettuce, sardine, sweet (dried and candied fruit) and tomato. Each of these warranted a step-by-step recipe and at the end was a list of other suggestions: spaghetti, sweetcorn, baked beans, marmite, cheese, gherkin and chicken.

People who worked in town might sit down at a nearby cafe, or take away fish and chips or a pie with sauce. Children might patronise the corner store, which offered pies and pasties, cream buns and softdrinks. "I didn't have lunch at school very often," my mother recalled of her Adelaide childhood, "but if I did I would buy a penny bowl of pea soup from the little tuckshop. Later, I can remember buying a Violet Crumble with my 3d instead of a pasty". When women went to the city to do the shopping they might arrange to meet at tea-rooms or to lunch at a department store. For a lonely lunch at home, they might have leftover corned beef with tomatoes, an omelette, or something on toast like tomato and egg, and an apple or banana.

"Whether the main meal of the day is eaten at midday or after the day's work is done is a matter of convenience and personal habit," the *Woman's Mirror* cookery book still wrote in 1937. While on the farms, people tended to make the midday meal the main "dinner", in towns, the evening meal was more likely to be the hot one. It was more often than not called "tea", and taken, as Lawrence found, at six o'clock. Whenever it was held, dinner was of three courses, commencing with pea soup or broth. Next came a meat dish of beef or mutton, with potatoes and at least two other vegetables, mint sauce or horseradish sauce and possibly Yorkshire pudding. Boiled mutton appeared with carrots, turnips and caper, onion or parsley sauce. The *Commonsense* also listed salted or corned beef with carrots, turnips and suet dumplings. One cookery book recommended that fish was "one of the most easily digested articles of diet". The *Woman's Mirror* book noted a tendency "to eliminate the characteristic flavours of rabbits, hares, and game by soaking them in salt water for hours". The *Commonsense* had sections on Green Vegetables, Root Vegetables and Dressed Vegetables. The greens made quite a list: asparagus, broad beans, French beans, boiled celery, cabbage, cauliflower, chokoes, globe artichokes, green peas, spinach or silverbeet, vegetable marrow, pumpkin—and all of them boiled. The alternative was "baked vegetables", its recipe calling for "1 lb of pumpkin, potatoes, parsnips, onions or chokoes".

Then, a pudding, sweets or dessert—like sago pudding, tapioca pudding, bread and butter pudding, roly poly pudding, apricot charlotte, fruit pie and baked custard, and stewed prunes with custard. The *Worker Cook Book* (edited by poet Mary Gilmore from the woman's page of a union newspaper) gave some idea of the then preoccupations. There were 41 pages for meat, 8 for fish, 6 for vegetables, 14 for breakfast and luncheon dishes, and 26 on preserving. Against that, flour-based cooking gained enormous weight—with 8 pages on bread, 9 on pastry, 35 on cakes and no less than 23 pages on puddings.

The *Commonsense* divided them into Boiled Puddings, Steamed Puddings,

Milk Puddings, Summer Puddings, Sweet Pastry and also Stewed Fruits, which meant apples, gooseberries, peaches, pears, plums, prunes, quinces and rhubarb. That book actually had two specifically pink items here—Pink Rice and Sago, which was one of the summer puddings, and Pink Sugar, whose cochineal sweetness could decorate browned white of egg on puddings. The ingredients for its fruit salad were: 3 bananas, 6 passionfruit, 1 small pineapple, 2 pears, 3 peaches, a few strawberries, 2 oz of sugar, cream or custard and icing sugar. Mind you, the aim was to reduce the fruit to unrecognisably tiny pieces (grating the pineapple and cutting finely peaches and pears), which then stood for an hour so that a "nice syrup may be formed and the flavours blended together". The recipe was placed in the salads section—between cold beetroot salad and lettuce salad, in which lettuce leaves were carefully examined, washed and then "sliced very thinly or torn into small pieces with the fingers". Such was the demand for daintiness.

The routine was neatly interrupted by the weekend, which might in good weather have brought a picnic of lamb chops and the national beverage, billy tea—with perhaps a crate of apples, good honey or cream being brought back to town. Saturday afternoon was dominated by sport, with the men going off to the football ground in winter and perhaps returning for crumpets and a light evening meal of beans on toast, sausages and mashed potatoes. Sunday lunch was a big day for a roast, ideally a chicken. The evening meal was perhaps a real "high tea", using up cold meat, salads, scones, cakes, cheese, fruit and so on. The leftover joint would probably survive until Monday evening when it was made into patties or shepherd's pie. Heinz came up with the idea of a salad on Mondays, along with their mayonnaise. Few of us don't feel Monday-ish on Mondays, a company booklet observed. It's back to work day. It's washing-day. It's "cold meat day". Now dull food is depressing. It's wonderful how a gay, unexpected dish can cheer you up. "Get into the habit of serving salads on Mondays. Take your Heinz Mayonnaise out of the cupboard. Get out this recipe book. Consider the possibilities of the larder—and get to work . . ." And so through the week again until Friday, when many families replaced butcher's meat with fish. Religious significance had not been removed from food, and many people started a meal by saying grace.

In those days, recipe books contained a section on invalid cookery, an indication that the elderly and incapacitated weren't packed off to an institution so quickly. The *Commonsense* approach to "Convalescent and Children's" included barley water, beef tea, brain cakes, stewed chop and rice, steamed custard, junket, a sweet omelette, and "toast water", which was literally water suffused with toast.

Tea was the principal drink, taken throughout all meals, at elegant "at homes" and in a billy boiled by workmen. Coffee was often in the form of essence, sweetened and frequently mixed with chicory, the original adulterant. Despite near-prohibition, beer was the main alcoholic beverage, with some spirits and fortified wines such as sherry. Wine was relegated to either export or derelicts at wine saloons. Parties might demand fruit cup, lemon squash, ginger-beer cordials, and just perhaps a cautious glass of champagne. Children's parties had cocktail frankfurts, bread covered with hundreds and thousands, angel cakes and raspberry balm.

If a family were socially ambitious and really bunging it on, they might have provided extra courses so that dinner went: soup, fish or entrée, meat dish, salad, pudding, savoury and coffee. The fish might have been steamed whiting, crumbed oysters or kedgeree, which was salmon, rice and hard-boiled egg. The entrée might have been curry and rice or beef olives. The savoury, a "small piquant titbit to remove the sweetness from the mouth", included angels on horseback (usually oysters on bacon), cheese straws, macaroni cheese or Welsh rarebit. In her early 30s book, Miss Drake thought that: "Men, especially, consider a meal quite incomplete without a savoury, and naturally, it always forms an important part of the menu".

Cookery books had noticeably declined in Anglo-French pretensions (partly owing to the widening audience, and also because food had become drearier). Hors d'oeuvres, if they existed, now tended to fall under the heading "appetisers", hollandaise had given way to Sauce Mornay, the gelatine shapes were losing out to jelly and icecream. A meal seemed to have become more shameful and private (hedonistic pleasure irrelevant to national goals), leaving guests to be invited to afternoon tea and supper. The possible range of "teas" extended to a "kitchen tea", which was a local invention for pre-marital gift-getting. As a tip to hostesses, the *Woman's Mirror* book said the recognised allowance for each person at afternoon tea or supper was "two sandwiches, one piece of cake and one serving of sweet". The elaborate spreads came with a twenty-first, engagement, wedding or anniversary. If you were catering for a wedding, you might be advised to allow cold meats, sandwiches, small cakes, biscuits, jelly, trifle, tinned fruit or fruit salad with cream, coffee and tea.

After D. H. Lawrence, Australia seemed isolated and short on visitors whose insights put our eating and drinking into an international context. However, after visits in 1936 and 1938, the eminent London ballet critic, Arnold Haskell, published *Waltzing Matilda*, which indicated that he dined well at gentlemen's clubs, found the "perfect gastronome" in Adelaide's professor of law, Arthur Campbell, thought the inaugural meeting of the Victorian Wine and Food Society a little "over-ambitious" and considered the "best meal in Australia" was at Usher's hotel in Sydney. Haven of well-to-do country visitors, Usher's prepared piping hot vegetables for the individual, oysters Mornay and Kilpatrick, and grilled garfish.

Travelling widely, Haskell congratulated the zealous Harold Clapp for the standard-setting meals of the Victorian railways—the roast beef "worthy of Simpson's" and the milk of the "Grade A quality usually reserved for babies".

At a small country hotel, he would be served—in "portions generous, sometimes aggressively so"—vegetable soup (not tinned); fried fish (usually schnapper); choice of roast beef, mutton, lamb or turkey; salad of lettuce, tomatoes, spring onions; boiled and baked potatoes; fruit salad with lashings of cream or apple pie; and tea or coffee. Haskell said that the cheese was "very poor", even in dairying districts, but "magnificent butter" was put on every table. Save a few in Adelaide, Australians did not drink dry wine, producing a bottle of something sparkling at a jollification, he said.

Depression

With the depression, the slowdown of the industrial cogs—when bread prices tumbled chaotically—encouraged neat kitchen gardens and sent "travellers" on the "wallaby track", to be fed from ration cards which could be cashed at declared dole stations. Other depression recollections included bread and dripping; drinking out of Marmite jars; buying reject fruit, or bones and fish heads for soup; extending eggs with water; borrowing an egg and parting bad friends because you couldn't return it; receiving a charity hand-out of plum jam, condensed milk, golden syrup, three or four loaves and a big hunk of meat. Yet, while the depression left rotten memories, it had surprisingly little effect on recipe books.

In 1931, Dr Morse's Indian Root Pills published a brief, quickly yellowing booklet on *How to Save and What to Cook*, including recipes for cold custard tart, curried sardines, curried beans, mock tripe (from mutton flaps), loquat jelly, brain cakes and marrow cream (a jam of marrow and sugar). Dr Morse's 1934 pamphlet included "Pink Cream", which was boiled rice coloured with cochineal and spread on raspberry jam and covered with desiccated coconut. In 1939 the pamphlet provided a page of uses for stale bread. "Constipation is the root of nine-tenths of the sickness of man, and a large proportion of the sickness of women," it proclaimed one year, ignoring the influence of fibre. Such sordid oddities as being stuffed with stop-go white bread and laxatives contributed to our culinary history as just another disciplinary force towards centralised monotony, part of an unbalanced diet of baked beans, condensed milk and processed cheese.

In 1936–38 and 1944, the National Health and Medical Research Council conducted the nation's first and last major dietary surveys. From such figures it is possible to estimate the inter-war consumption of various basic foods. For instance, the average Australian ate about 200 lbs of flour per annum. The weight of meat was about the same, the larger proportion being of beef. We consumed about 100 lbs of sugar, tea at the rate of about 7 lbs, milk 200 lbs, butter 30 lbs and cheese 4 lbs a year. To put that into perspective, in comparison with the bush rations of "10, 10, 2 & ¼", the flour, meat and tea were halved, while sugar maintained its inordinate level. It went into dainties like the pavlova.

THE PAVLOVA

Herbert Sachse and pavlova

"A SYMPHONY of silence! So Pavlova has been described," began the report in the *West Australian* on Tuesday, July 9, 1929. "But who, seeing the famous ballerina for the first time as she stood on the deck of the mail steamer *Maloja* at Fremantle yesterday, could apply the description? It was Babel itself!" Speaking Russian, French and English, she demanded to know if there were any "een-deeg-in-ous" birds, as the newspaper spelt it, she could add to her collection. The reporter managed to share her cab into Perth, with husband-manager Victor Dandre, several bouquets and already three cages of birds. "They are funny, these Australians," she pronounced in the cab. "They like art, and many, many of them understand it, but they do not help it . . . Their artists must go abroad to become great. No, you have your gramophones and your dance parties—ugly jazz—and you seem satisfied." As the cab drew up at the Hotel Esplanade, she concluded: "Great art needs to be built up on fine ideals". The next night she gave the first of 11 evening and four afternoon performances at His Majesty's Theatre. "Exquisite Pavlova! . . ." began the *West Australian*. It was her only Perth season, on her second Australian tour. She died two years later. Yet her memory survived at her hotel, the Esplanade, because there six years later the chef whipped up the meringue and cream cake which perpetuates her name.

The story of the pavlova's rise to popularity is worth telling because, besides being a dainty contribution to culinary art and regarded by many as our "national dish", it illustrates how history and cooking intermingle. Its arrival is a tale of boom versus bust, the luxury life versus back-breaking poverty, and Australia versus New Zealand. It involves two converging stories: that of a grand hotel and that of a small settler who turned into a cook.

The discovery of gold in Western Australia in the 1890s was a bright star amid economic gloom. It drew thousands of eastern staters, who quadrupled the West's population in a decade and who bucked the local establishment by voting to join the Federation. To one such couple, drawn west from the Barossa Valley to Boulder City in the goldfields, was born on May 12, 1898, a son, Herbert Sachse. In the same year, another of the flash hotels sprang up in Perth, to be known as the Esplanade. It was lit electrically, and cooled by the breezes from the Swan River. It had a bowling green, tennis courts and boats for hire. And in 1921, the Esplanade became the centre of industrial conflict. A maid refused to take the management its afternoon tea tray, saying "come and get the bloody thing yourself". The management sacked her, the staff walked out, and the owners employed strike-breaking Chinese labour, despite mass union protests.

In the same year, 1921, Bert Sachse and his bride, Mary, borrowed from the new Agricultural Bank, awash with money from the British government trying to guarantee overseas food supplies and a market for manufactured goods. They started to grow wheat at a place called Kwelkin. But the great scheme collapsed. A Royal Commission into the activities of the "Ag" Bank later concluded that its trustees were wrong to push wheat into worse than marginal land. Bert Sachse, with four daughters and a son to support, found the cost of "super and seed" was more than he was getting and so fell further into debt. In 1926, when he could see no way ahead, and also because his wife was suffering a terminal disease, he simply walked off the farm, the family early victims of the depression. Overseas capital dried up from 1928, but not, of course, debt repayments. Overseas wheat prices dropped. And thus came 1929, the year of the Wall Street collapse and Pavlova's visit.

Like so many people in a depression, Bert and Mary entered the catering industry, starting a restaurant and pie shop at Mullewa, 300 miles north-east of Perth. "Mary taught me to cook and one day a shearers' team passed through the town," he recalled. "They needed a cook, so I went with them on the station run." Between shearing seasons, he began taking jobs in hotels. "I wouldn't work anywhere the chef was no good. I was still learning and I wanted to learn from the best." Through the steadiness of his disposition, with his eye for arrangement, he became a reliable hotel chef and applied to the Esplanade for a job. It was thus that, each of them in their mid-thirties, the fortunes of Bert Sachse, the Hotel Esplanade and the Commonwealth of Australia coalesced to produce the pavlova.

THE PAVLOVA

In 1934, Mrs Elizabeth Paxton succeeded her husband as licensee of the Esplanade and under her invigorated guidance the afternoon teas became very desirable occasions for the wives of Perth's fortune-makers. One day she called in her manager, Harry Nairn, and they approached their chef to devise something special. Tall, upright and what his second wife described as "a very ordinary chef", Bert Sachse experimented for a month. "I had always regretted that the meringue cake was invariably too hard and crusty, so I set out to create something that could have a crunchy top and would cut like marshmallow," he recalled for a reporter. He lit on the secret of adding cornflour and vinegar to the whipped egg whites. These were his ingredients, slightly more complicated than usual: Six egg whites, six ounces of sugar, ounce of cornflour, just under a dessertspoon of vinegar, few drops of vanilla essence, good pinch of cream of tartar, one-third pint of cream, three or four passionfruit.

According to Paxton family tradition, the pavlova was named at a meeting at which Sachse presented the now familiar cake. The family say that either the licensee, Elizabeth, or the manager, Harry Nairn (as Sachse also said), remarked, "It is as light as Pavlova".

The lightness, sweetness, richness and comfortable luxury of the pavlova may seem to make it an unlikely depression dish against powdered milk, Milo and mince. It is, however, in the nature of a fantasy, with all the froth and bubble of a Busby Berkley movie. It was when "daintiness" was a great virtue in food. It arrived, too, when Western Australia, the first State to contract economically, was also the fastest to revive, largely due to the return of gold-mining. While the pavlova was created by a "battler", it was for afternoon teas where women were no doubt celebrating the return of their good fortune. According to memories, Sachse came up with the pavlova in 1935, when things certainly were looking up. The percentage of WA trade unionists who were unemployed was 6·2 when Sachse walked off his property in 1926, reached 28·7 at its worst in 1931 and was 15·7 when he introduced the pavlova. The "structural readjustment" of the economy had thrown him into another career entirely. "People have always got to eat," was his rationalisation. Then, with recovery, he provided a tribute to optimism.

The ingredients belong to the times. The foundation of whipped egg-whites and the whipped cream came from the rapidly expanding dairy industry in WA, the milk output of which rose from 18·3 to 33·6 million gallons between 1928 and 1932. The large dose of refined sugar came from CSR's new-found over-production. Australia did not export sugar until 1925. In fact, wartime import difficulties had encouraged "Billy" Hughes to make Australia self-supporting by guaranteeing producers a good price.

The passionfruit was an obvious fruit with which to dress up the pavlova. For at least 50 years it had been mentioned as a popular, characteristically Australian ingredient, used a lot for cake icing and flavouring of sweets. The

Goulburn cookery book at the beginning of the century gave recipes for passionfruit glaze (icing), jam, jelly (in the sense of strained jam) and Passionfruit and Sago Shape (a moulded cold pudding). A couple of decades later the *Commonsense* recipe book had Passionfruit Cream, Shape and Sponge (all "summer" puddings) and a cake filling, as well as a sandwich cake flavoured, filled and iced with the fruit. Its fruit salad contained no less than six passionfruit. In the 1920s, too, the Davis Gelatine company promoted an Austral Trifle, featuring cake, whipped cream, jelly and passionfruit. In 1925 Spencer Milton Cottee of Lismore in NSW registered his label for a drink called Passiona. It was considered a reasonably sophisticated embellishment, and when E. C. Buley expounded upon town and country life in 1905, he wrote: "Wine-flavoured passionfruit may be had at threepence a dozen".

The Kiwi claim

In *A Taste of New Zealand in Food and Pictures*, N. A. Munro stated in 1977: "It is often claimed, and perhaps justly, that the 'Pav' of affectionate parlance is New Zealand's first and only contribution to international cuisine — that is, excluding foodstuffs native only to this country". Munro credited the idea to a nameless "benefactress" and fancied a date of "probably 1926, when the great ballerina toured this country, or shortly afterwards". To help check this for me, librarians of the National Library of New Zealand kindly consulted their collection of cookery books. In fact, they found a recipe for "Pavlova Cakes" in Mrs McKay's *Practical Home Cookery, Chats and Recipes*, published in 1929. The ingredients were roughly those of a pavlova, but it was not the pavlova as we know it, because the mixture was baked into three dozen little meringues. It seems a coincidence that the New Zealand cook was impressed by the ballerina's lightness and whiteness.

But there is more to the New Zealand claim than this. Even earlier, in *Terrace Tested Recipes*, collected by the ladies of Terrace Congregational Church, the second edition published in Wellington in 1927, there was a recipe submitted by a Mrs McRae for Meringue Cake. This was three whipped egg-whites, eight ounces of sugar and a dessertspoon of cornflour (the pavlova ingredients less vinegar), put into two well-greased sandwich tins "in a fairly hot oven on a low shelf and leave until the fire is almost out". The two halves were filled with whipped cream and cherries or strawberries, or served as two cakes. From similar recipes published in 1933 and 1934, I think it fair to say that the Meringue Cake was common in New Zealand in the early 1930s. Its form varied, but it was to all intents and purposes what we know as a "Pavlova", sometimes even complete with passionfruit on top.

Bert Sachse said in a magazine interview in 1973 that he sought to improve the Meringue Cake. There was a prize-winning recipe for Meringue Cake in the *Women's Mirror* on April 2, 1935. It contained vinegar, but no cornflour and was of two parts filled with whipped cream. The recipe was contributed by "Rewa", who happened to be of Rongotai, New Zealand. If Sachse read the *Women's Mirror* and other magazines for ideas, as his widow told me, he might have seen this recipe. We can concede that New Zealanders discovered the secret delights of the large meringue with the "marshmallow centre", the heart of the pavlova. But it seems reasonable to assume that someone in Perth attached the name of the ballerina. As Bert Sachse implied, he distilled, or codified, a widespread New Zealand idea, to which was added a catchy name, and all of this was legitimate, common and like the crystallising of genius. In those days of sea travel, New Zealand was closer than Perth to Australia's main centres, and had almost joined the Federation. For us to be confident the pavlova is a truly Australian dish, it's a pity it didn't.

I have not discovered how the pavlova spread beyond the Esplanade. Remember that only in 1930 was Perth at last connected by telephone across a "sea of solid ground" with the eastern States. In 1933, the State voted in a referendum two-to-one to secede from the Commonwealth, although this petition was over-ruled by the British parliament. The first appearance of the pavlova in recipe books that I've found was in the second edition of *Calling All Cooks*, published by the SA Gas Company in 1941. It had not been included in the original edition only a year earlier. It seems it was already known throughout south-east Australian rural districts. Possibly the most common tale before the Sachse story became widespread was that the pavlova was invented by a "Melbourne society hostess". I have traced chains of passed-on recipes to Victoria. That the dairy districts of Victoria were long prepared for the pavlova is indicated by an anecdote of novelist, Ada Cambridge. Shocked at the luxurious fare at church "tea meetings" at Warrnambool in the 1870s, she recalled: "One year, when the 'treat' food was provided, as usual, by the ladies of the congregation, each cooking to outvie the rest, I took upon myself to remonstrate with them for their cruelty—in stuffing the poor children with unlimited cream-cakes and meringues. Yes, actually meringues, on my word of honour".

Australians overseas, discovering how nationalistic they can become, tend to rush into pavlova production at the slightest provocation, smuggling in passionfruit seeds to plant. In this way, the pavlova has been introduced to the United States, United Kingdom, South Africa, etc. In 1958, Elizabeth Campbell gave recipes for Fruit Salad Pavlova in her *Encyclopedia of World Cookery*. During the 1970s a number of pavlova shops opened in Australian cities and also in the US.

In the *Good Food Guide* to British Isles restaurants in 1977, a glossary of food terms referred to the pavlova as a New Zealand offering, which changed the next year to Australian. Hilary Fawcett, who compiled the glossary, wrote to me about the change: "There does seem to be controversy as to whether the wretched thing originated in NZ or Australia and I was reduced to doing a straw-vote count. However, during the following year I read what sounded like the authoritative account of what seems to have been its first appearance . . . and phoned the Australian High Commission for confirmation. It was included, by the way, when there seemed to be a rash of Pavlovas in English restaurants, and it seemed useful to distinguish it from meringue (with which it was constantly confused with the pejorative description 'undercooked' or 'sticky') and the more sophisticated *vacherin*". The glossary defined the pavlova as "a soft meringue case filled with fruit and cream" and the vacherin as "rounds of meringue layered with cream, fruit, and sometimes liqueur and ice-cream".

The march of progress

In 1962–63, the Hotel Esplanade battled the Perth City Council to retain its verandah posts, disappearing elsewhere to ease car parking. But it was only a skirmish before the final reverse. In 1968, the hotel was bought by L. J. Hooker, a developer who wanted demolition. The National Trust gave the building its A-rating, making it one of the State's most vital structures. The *Bulletin* commented: "The three-storey brick building breathes colonial opulence and the grand days of gold . . . Now the brash days of nickel are here and the Esplanade must yield to steel and concrete". The hotel came down in 1972.

Three years later, when for the thousandth time he saw just a hole in the ground, newspaper columnist Kirwan Ward had reversed his opinion: "For years it had lent character, dignity and charm to a city that can do with all three . . . But then came the developers with dazzling visions of soaring towers and thunderous clichés about the inevitable march of progress . . ." What replaced it? There was the "New Esplanade" next door, but incredibly, a decade later, the site itself was still just a hole in the ground. You never know, Perth's "city fathers" might yet be sorry they let some strange economic logic pull down a lively old monument where the pavlova was named.

Meanwhile, chef Bert Sachse had left the Esplanade in the early months of the Second World War. He joined the RAAF and they made him a sergeant cooking instructor. During the war, he met and married his second wife, Ellen. In 1955 he joined the Palace Hotel, where a Swan Lake Pavlova Co sales person tried selling some to him. "I invented the pavlova," he responded, "and I can make them with my eyes closed. But good luck to you if you can make them commercially." Waiting for the Palace to be demolished not long after the Esplanade, he died on April 1, 1974.

It is possible, if ungenerous, to deride the pavlova for culinary innocence. It was adopted from New Zealand. Yet Herbert Sachse made a genuine, crystallising contribution. The pavlova served its original purpose admirably. It then caught the popular imagination. Distilling the Australian concept of sweet living, it is the single great discovery thus far of our cooking.

PART III
Fresh from the freezer
The automobile ascendancy (1940s–1970s)

Coles New World supermarket, Dandenong, 1963

Sliced white

IN AUSTRALIA'S first towns, bakers sold the fresh, crusty, delightfully inconstant loaves which had symbolised daily renewal since ancient times. Innovations like roller-flour, factory yeast and outside-fired ovens culminated at the beginning of this century in the so-called "automatic" bakeries, providing tinned loaves which had less character and crust and were blander in texture and taste. In 1938, bakers accepted the inevitable and re-named their Master Bakers' Association the "Bread Manufacturers' Association". It would not be long before a few large companies mass-produced sliced white, which was hastily-baked, chemical, tasteless, crustless and wrapped like soap.

Even more mysterious than why we tolerated such deterioration was why bakers saw their salvation in the very standardisation, automation and mass marketing which ensured their own extinction. At annual conferences, bakers aired recurring grumbles against declining consumption, government controls, under-cutting, rising labour demands, crippling delivery costs and brown bread advocates. Yet, year after year, the meetings tried to decide whether the answers really lay in extra machinery, more scientific baking, fewer competitors and advertising, all of which would ease out the small baker. The tragedy of twentieth-century baking is worth telling in a little detail because it summarises what we have already seen happening to Australian food, and it introduces the story from the Second World War until recent times. Economists have generally gauged success by the "size of the cake"; it might have been more appropriate to worry about the quality of the loaf.

At the end of last century, the baking of bread went from a handcraft to machinery. When Mr J. T. Kelly entered the trade in 1880 baking had not changed much from the first settlers. Bakers still purchased stone-ground flour, Kelly later recalled at a bakers' conference. They still made their own yeast and comparatively little was needed to make the progressively larger masses of "ferment", then "sponge" and finally dough. It added up to eight or ten hours of quite sophisticated rising. Loaves were referred to as "crusty", since they weren't baked in tins, he said. There were some cottage loaves and twists with a three-piece plait, but our bakers chiefly produced loaves called "turnovers" (also apparently termed Scotch French loaves), in which the dough was rolled out in a rectangle and then folded in and then over. The batches of turnovers, touching on the backs and ends like large rolls, were then baked on the floor of a brick oven. It was a traditional "inside" oven— "inside" because wood in five-foot lengths had been burnt beforehand inside the oven. Provided the yeast was in good condition, no better bread, in Kelly's later judgement, could be wished for.

However, Kelly happened to join the industry at the beginning of considerable change. For one thing, to reduce handling, bakers were successfully eliminating the sponge step, making dough from ferment, he said. Bakers already produced some long 4 lb upright loaves in tins. Traditional ovens were also being replaced by furnace ovens, where the wood kept burning outside during baking. And the major innovation was roller flour. Kelly considered the quality dropped with the finer grains, but little could stop the introduction of roller-mills.

By the time compressed yeast made in outside factories arrived about 1906, eliminating the need for both ferments and sponges, bakers foresaw a "future harvest of intelligent mechanical ingenuity and chemical knowledge". Since the 1850s, engineers in England had designed a succession of machines which could take over various steps in bread-making. By 1908, the NSW Arbitration Court considered a triangular dispute between the operative bakers (the workers), the master bakers and the so-called machine bakers (Abel & Co Ltd, Hunter and Sons, A. McKee, Michael Moran, Frederick E. Pilcher and James Granger). The essential question was whether the same labour conditions should apply to both "hand" and these new "machine" shops, with such devices as the sifter, blender, mixer, divider, rounder, final prover, final moulder and the draw-plate oven. A machine bakery, doing about 3,000 loaves nightly, could be equipped for £1,200, plus ovens.

The operatives favoured keeping baking in the hands of skilled tradesmen, the supply kept up by a system of apprenticeship. With machinery a great deal could be performed by "men or youths who required little or no skill and little or no knowledge". Mr Justice Street observed that the dispute raised issues seen frequently before and likely in the future: "I mean the question of machinery versus men". But machines could not be stopped, and the Brisbane

Automatic Bakery, opened in July, 1914, was claimed as the country's first wholly mechanised bakehouse, in that no hand needed to touch the dough. Expensive automatic machinery was the only safety for the "most harrassed trader of all times—the baker," one of them, Mr F. B. Withers, told a conference in 1915. Yet the big bakers were "sucking", as Mr G. S. Blair put it, "the lifeblood from the masses for the benefit of the few."

Another of the constant pressures irritating bakers was their operatives' demand for "day-baking". Bread had traditionally come out of ovens at dawn. But the union claimed it could provide fresher bread if members worked through the day. Joseph Pey, an operative of 25 years standing, told a court in 1914 of his misery, working through the night, and that his wife was on drugs on account of her nervous condition. The skirmishes continued for years, much day-old bread being sold to reach agreement.

Australian bakers had been tempted into providing bread to grocers. By the turn of the century, the re-seller under-cut the delivery carts, and bakers proposed that, in the interests of "public health", bread should again only be sold in bakers' shops. The *Australasian Baker* wrote in October, 1916, that the custom of supplying shops was probably of too long standing to be discontinued, but surely the baker had the right to stipulate a "price consistent with the possibilities of solvent trading". When baker William White asked a meeting what the curse of the trade was throughout Australia in 1916, a chorus replied, "the re-seller". But bakers also competed against each other. A Victorian inquiry into bread prices in 1919 asserted that bakers had formed their associations in the hope of fixing prices and ruled against a price-fixing cartel which bakers had just formed with flour millers.

In 1925, master bakers became irate about competition from a "certain proprietary commodity belittling bread" and the "prolonged propaganda by patent food vendors". We can take it that this nameless evil was cornflakes. Average annual bread consumption fell steadily from 100 kg per person in 1926. Bakers ascribed the decline to the "improved standard of living, the introduction of breakfast foods, and the decline in the palatability of bread". Baker Mr R. Robbins noticed that wealthier workers were discarding their cut lunch for a hot pastry and cake, although he disagreed that the introduction of machinery had caused the standard to deteriorate. Frank B. Withers said that, while bread competed on price, the breakfast food manufacturers boosted food values with publicity. He tried to urge bakers, rather than be "buffeted into the backwash", to contribute to a publicity fund in favour of the old staff of life.

Australian bakers were not keen to wrap their bread, a common habit in the United States since the 1890s, with brandname clearly stated. Following legislation for day baking, bread hadn't time to cool before wrapping. Yet health authorities were urging "hygienic" wrappers, a particularly perverse demand since a good crust does not harbour germs like the clammy wrapped loaf. When Clapp's Victorian Railways introduced wrapping to Australia in 1925, the master bakers became "unanimously opposed to bread wrapping on the grounds of cost, uncertainty of hygienic benefit, total lack of public demand and the prospect of its forcing trade into the hands of monopolies." But by 1928, three Sydney bakers were wrapping.

As early as 1909, a baker at Yass, NSW, Mr T. P. Williamson, had built his own motorised van, averaging nine miles an hour, for outlying deliveries. In 1925, Mr A. Bassett from the Maugham-Thiem Motor Co discussed with bakers the European development of the tiny, high-efficiency engine. Light motors had so reduced running costs that they should be given further consideration for house-to-house delivery, he urged. Several bakers expressed dissatisfaction with the running costs of their heavy-cylindered vehicles and most bakers were not yet prepared to sacrifice Dobbin. "You can't educate a motor-car to follow the driver along the street," was the feeling. It was a vexed question since, as the Gepp Commission found in 1936, bread cost more to deliver than to bake. The economic attrition of motor against horse lasted more than half a century before the carts gave way without a clear benefit to bakers.

With a reputation as the trade's expert on costing, William White had claimed in 1928 that expensive machinery had not lowered production costs. When the Gepp Commission looked at the figures in 1936, it too suggested that hand bakeries were much more efficient than machine bakeries. But the re-named "bread manufacturers" decided at conferences that competition from "one-man", "partnership" and "backyard" bakeries was "unfair", since they could work outside industrial regulations. We shall soon see that the Second World War had a tremendous effect on food production. The intense pressures towards the efficient use of labour—like the governments' reintroduction of price control on bread and zoned delivery rounds—halved the number of bakeries in Australia. Even if "chaotic cut-price competition" would soon return, the "irresponsible" baker getting inferior bread into the street earlier, bakers praised the savings in "manpower, petrol, tyres, shoeing, etc", and the price of bread was reduced in some States by the promised halfpenny.

The industry was harried by campaigns to enrich bread with vitamins as done in allied countries. Science came to the aid of the manufacturers, following an "historic" meeting in 1941 in the offices of the *Australasian Baker* between the editor, the association secretary, a representative of flour millers and the prominent nutritionist, Dr F. W. Clements. The discussions "precipitated" research by Clements, which was undertaken with the "generous" aid of millers. The result, a "monumental" paper in the *Medical Journal of Australia* (May 24, 1941), found no real need to add vitamins. Yet, reading the paper after the years, I wonder if the argument—enriching white bread with vitamin B would pointlessly put back what milling had removed—rather begged the question of what should be removed.

During the war, too, NSW manufacturers formed a committee and fund to "influence food authorities, educate the bakers themselves and correctly inform the public mind" on the nutritional benefits of bread. They financed a Bread Research Institute, which commenced under Mr E. E. Bond on July 1, 1947. The severity of the criticism of the industry would soon be "tempered thanks to the influence and standing of the BRI", baker William Sloan put it. One of the institute's successes would be to persuade farmers to plant harder wheat than the traditional English soft grain, which our bakers said was appropriate for biscuit-making, but which has made the best French and Italian loaves. Hard, or high-protein, wheat had superior "baking quality", which made it rise better with less responsive machine baking.

An advertisement in the *Australasian Baker* in early 1938 had claimed: "SLICED BREAD made fortunes in England for those who were first in the field —Slice Masters are your great opportunity!" Apparently no-one took the bait immediately because when Harry Gough introduced sliced bread in 1939 at his Sunshine Bakeries in Newtown, Sydney, it was hand-sliced. Melbourne bakers agreed to "prohibit" slicing and wrapping in 1942. But from 1950 the Procera company imported a number of Hayssen slicing machines into all State capitals and by 1960 about one-third of all bread was sold sliced.

In 1949, William Sloan said, "More and more the trade needs the engineering mind for bread production." The boys in the bread classes at East Sydney Technical College knew less and less about dough-handling, because they had no chance to touch it at their factory. Fermentation times kept coming down and the rising of dough was being banished in highly capitalised countries like the USA and USSR. High yeast quantities, chemical additives and violent mixing were pushing dough-making into a continuous process, machines churning it out at the flick of a switch. Between 1957 and 1961, there was a craze for American continuous-mix plants—compact, fully-automated and producing finished bread in 1½ hours—but it was soft, cake-like and unpopular. The Bread Research Institute worked on "no-time" doughs, although Australian bakers often stopped short, with "rapid" doughs. The changeover was stealthy enough to "avoid any significant consumer reaction to the slightly different bread characteristics," food technologist W. Lewis Jones noted in 1970.

Bread manufacturers introduced the 1 lb starch-reduced loaf in the 1950s to compete with crispbreads and a startling leap in now packeted biscuits. But they were still disunited and vainly trying to drum up enthusiasm for national advertising. The managing director of Procera, James H. Tucker, said that the bread industry lacked advertising and public relations experts— in short, the trade lacked "know-how", he said. But if master bakers had failed, the emergent giant bread companies got their marketing act together. In 1963, the marketing manager of Buttercup, David Metcalfe, pointed out that great technological advances into mass production were now to be repeated in selling. Bread merchandising was being "revolutionised by the supermarket". Private cars were transforming cities, and, with many Australians driving to the shops, about half the bread was already sold over the counter. Only in Queensland was home delivery still entrenched, and one representative, Mr J. P. Ryan, predicted that the trade would be dragged down "if chain stores are allowed to degrade bread to the level of a cut-price, catch line."

However, it was too late. Most towns and suburbs had lost the old style of baker. In the 1950s, big millers raced to buy each other out and to tie up the shrinking market by buying up bakeries. Bread manufacture came to be dominated by two firms, Allied Mills (Buttercup, Home Pride, Siebers) and George Weston (Tip Top and Sunblest). What was more disturbing, the few companies were divisions or subsidiaries of flour millers. Allied was an Australian company, which also produced our top-selling margarine, while George Weston was a Canadian-British miller which owned such other products as Big Ben pies, Ry-Vita biscuits and Twinings tea. The notable addition in Melbourne was Bunge, the world's largest private company, which produced Sunicrust. As well as bakeries, the millers owned the stockfeed business. In 1945, pigs were still primarily a sideline to dairy farms, and poultry farmers mixed their own mashes. But the discard from white flour was nutritious and millers moved into battery chicken production. Bunge started a mammoth piggery near Albury, its Fidelity Feeds supporting "some 20,000 pigs, bred under highly scientific and hygienic conditions".

Probably no industry in NSW had been the subject of more investigation and control, Mr Justice Kelleher stated when making yet another report on the bread industry in 1976. He inquired into the by now ritual arguments. While he favoured the maintenance of day-baking, for example, he saw insufficient need for zoning. The industry had always been highly competitive, intensified by declining markets, he said. There was evidence that the large manufacturers offered "substantial discounts" to secure a share of country markets. They also offered "unlimited returns of unsold bread" (the modern "baker's dozen") because supermarkets desired their shelves to be kept stocked throughout the day, the leftovers being taken back by the suppliers. A metropolitan bakery might take back 20 per cent of its production, the returns sold to stockfeed, poultry and piggery subsidiaries. Kelleher noted that the number of licensed manufacturers in NSW had substantially declined from 1129 in 1955 to 497 in 1975. But generally his criticisms were few.

It was an "ancient craft" not greatly altered, he said, and yet he did make mention of some changes in the past 30 years. The need for the traditional aging of flour had been eliminated with the use of oxidising agents. Due to chemical inhibitors the bacterial scourge of "rope" was virtually eliminated. Similarly, better control had been achieved over mould growth, which had been accentuated by wrapping. Yeasts were now faster than before, milk powder was specially treated and new fats and other additives were giving improved loaf volume, crumb and keeping quality. The "traditional" method was now sometimes fully automated, up to the final slicing and wrapping. Because of the wrapping, the manufacturers had to resort to fast cooling in tunnels or by open fans, "not the best way of producing a good quality bread but it is the only one available in the circumstances," Kelleher said. The softer loaf with the lighter crust lost flavour through less caramelisation of crust sugars. Some manufacturers considered that bread made from "no-time dough" was not as good as that under the old system, but the majority of witnesses disagreed.

Mr Justice Kelleher found it difficult to understand the dissatisfaction with the quality of bread. He cited the evidence of Mr Bond, the director of the Bread Research Institute and whom the judge listed as an "independent expert", although, as we know, Bond was appointed with the original idea of influencing public opinion towards bread. Dr F. W. Clements, a "world authority in the nutritional field", as Kelleher saw it, trotted out evidence yet again that our bread did not need enriching with lost vitamins, an opinion which millers had sponsored in 1941. Clements said that the bland flavour of the bread was one of its attractions, as it blended with other foods.

Before looking further into other areas where the war hastened the entry of bigger production units, quality compromises and mass market manipulation, we must consider one enigmatic loaf, which seemed simultaneously to counteract and foreshadow bread's worst tendencies, a national marketing miracle for brown bread. It was Vogel bread, a small, wrapped "mixed-grain" loaf. It was introduced to Sydney about 1960 by a Danish immigrant, Niel Stevns, who was, pointedly, not a baker but a salesman. He had bought world rights to the recipe and name of Alfred Vogel, a Swiss healthfood retailer with an honorary California doctorate. Baked under contract by Siebers, its success was "semi-miraculous", Niel Stevns said later.

Sold in increasingly busy "healthfood" stores, Vogel bread became a symbol of trendy eating. By April 16, 1976, the *Nation Review's* entertaining food writer, "Sam Orr" (Richard Beckett), warned: "Watch for the appearance of Vogel bread; it's a sure sign that the neighbourhood is going to the dogs and that your local publican is about to start serving red wine in the public bar instead of decent schooners and turn his honest beer garden into a bistro." In 1981, Vogel's new marketing chief, Ray McHugh, said the typical Vogel customer was a "middle-income family housewife who buys it for her children because it is good for them, and for herself because she is trendy and stylish". But he was pulling Vogel bread off its pedestal, he announced. It would be sold through supermarkets in Sydney's western suburbs. Stevns had retired to Paris, retaining his "delightful cottage" in Paddington, and had begun to license the trademark of this Australian success-story overseas.

11

The first munition

With World War II, American agricultural and processing experts arrived to show how to mass produce more varied but still portable rations

IT LATER SEEMED odd that historian Keith Hancock could decide in 1930 that we intended to remain "ninety-eight percent" British. "It is absurd to imagine that Australia, because she buys American motor-cars and submits to the deluge of Hollywood culture, is drifting vaguely towards some new political combination," he wrote. And still on the evening of September 3, 1939, Prime Minister Menzies declared: "There is unity in the Empire ranks —one King, one flag, one cause. We stand with Britain". But by the end of the war, America had moved in.

With the Pacific war, Australia was mobilised as a giant US base. The American authorities didn't want mutton and tea for their troops, but beef, pork, sweetcorn, orange juice, tomatoes and chili con carne. They brought out technologists to renovate the food industry with machines and "know-how". By 1945, K. R. Cramp, a first-hand witness of the American food invasion, considered that "almost every phase of Australia's food industry has been profoundly affected by the activities of the remarkable team of specialists brought out from the US to guide and advise us".

Meanwhile, the US troops were "ambassadors" for American food and manners, leaving a taste for cocktails and Coca-Cola. Mrs Maclurcan's 1898 cookery book had contained a recipe for Hamburg steak, but now we grabbed hamburgers at every corner. Dr Muskett in 1893 had mentioned imported tins of American sweetcorn, but now Rosella had a sweetcorn plant, obtained under Lend Lease. The formidable influence of American films and music was joined by persuasive US food marketing. With World War II, American leaders anticipated they could wean Australia off London's commercial influence and, at least from the aspect of food, they succeeded. Here is how it happened.

Preparations for war

Among its preparations for war in the late 1930s, the Australian government assumed more control of food. With fears of profiteering, it cleared the way for price control. With invasion conceivable, it adopted an Emergency Supplies Plan, by which approximately three months stocks were to be held in grocery stores and more in government depots. And it ensured that essential supplies could move quickly to Britain. The possibility of war had been one justification for the boards which controlled the export of dairy produce and dried fruits since 1924, canned fruits since 1926, wine since 1929 and meat since 1936. Now the government finalised the apple and pear board, wheat board, barley board and a committee for eggs.

However, under gunfire, Britain deserted its most distant suppliers and preferred Canada and the US. This "interruption of shipping" plagued our agriculture for two years. Fresh fruit exports to the UK halted. Refrigerated meat was cut in favour of limited shipping in cans. Britain sought diversion of butter to cheese production. So, farmers reduced acreages and let their sons and labourers escape to the glory of the war. But, after two years—soon after Menzies relinquished power to John Curtin's Labor government—a dramatic change re-oriented Australian politics, economics and, of course, food.

The Australian and American governments had agreed to exchange diplomatic missions—it helped our chances of bringing the US into the war and their chances of prising us away from imperial-preference, which hindered trade. The Japanese bombing of Pearl Harbour brought America into a Pacific war. The enemy bombed Darwin in February, 1942. General Douglas MacArthur arrived in March as the "Supreme Commander" of the South-West Pacific area. American troops and Australians pouring home became a great market for food producers. The military demand for canned fruits, for instance, prevented commercial exports and restricted quantities available for civilians.

Furthermore, America diverted food supplies to Russia, so that Britain now demanded urgent help. It was a similar belated change of mind as in the previous war, when Australia's bumper 1915 harvest had gone to waste— leading Prime Minister Billy Hughes to visit England and purchase 15 tramp steamers, the basis of the Commonwealth Shipping Line. By the end of both wars, British deals kept our primary industry prosperous.

The food mobilisation had a multitude of repercussions. It wasn't unusual for the Victorian Railways refreshment services to be informed at 6 pm that hundreds of men would require breakfast at some remote station during the night. McNiven's in Sydney took advantage of a ban on interstate confectionery shipments to expand competition to Hoadley's, while, typical of hastened mechanisation, the Violet Crumble went from hand to machine-wrapping. Almost the entire output of Nestlé's condensed and powdered milk was diverted to the services, and the company opened a special factory in Sydney to manufacture, pack and despatch army rations—at four days' notice, preparing air-drops for the Kokoda Trail in New Guinea.

After March, 1942, every citizen over 16 had to have an "identity card", and women were urged to accept war work, especially in canning, meat processing and on the land. In May, 1942, the government stopped calling up now much-needed rural workers and in October, 1943, the army released 20,000 troops for rural work. Meanwhile, to win the war on the factory floor, government nutritionists coordinated what was known as "factory feeding". With about 400 canteens serving well over 100,000 people, queuing with tray in hand became an established feature of factory work. At the Williamstown Naval Dockyard in Melbourne, patrons could buy a full three-course meal with a cup of tea and three half-slices of bread and butter for 1s 3d. Purchased separately, soup cost 3d, entrée or roast with vegetables 9d, salad 9d, sweets 3d and tea 1d. Multiplied across the nation, the mobilisation of agriculture and the food industry transformed our food.

Rationing

Whatever else might be said about the tragedy of war, the industrial machine beat with excitement. The Second World War soaked up Australia's 10 per cent unemployment and women and others usually outside the wage economy were pressed into service. Therefore, many people actually had more money. With the production of luxuries diverted, more money became available for necessities like food, releasing price inflation. Also, with the prospect of people making uneven sacrifices or unfair profits during the war, the government was expected to control prices in the marketplace, along with wages.

The short-lived Menzies government had promulgated "principles" by which traders could regulate prices according to costs. With the Curtin government, interest rates, rents and wages were pegged to cost-of-living changes. The Prices Branch also fixed maximum prices for hundreds of grocery lines, for many fruits and vegetables and for meat. Yet the retail price index rose 9·5 per cent in the first twelve months of the Pacific war compared with 5·4 per cent in 1941. From July 21, 1943, the price of tea—which had risen 50 per cent—was reduced to its pre-war level and the maximum retail price of potatoes restricted to 6d for 5 lbs. The government came to spend £2 to £3 million annually stabilising each of tea, potatoes and milk with subsidies to growers and importers.

THE FIRST MUNITION

Advertising that food was a "mighty weapon of war" and the "highway to victory", Commonwealth Food Control urged citizens not to waste food and to accept sacrifices for the "boys". "There are foods in plenty to replace those that are scarce, particularly when supplemented from our own vegetable garden and our fowl-yard," an ad stated in the *Women's Weekly* (April 8, 1944). Companies placed advertisements making up for the absence of their brandnames in shops. "Vegemite fights for the men up north!" one exclaimed. "If you are one of those who don't need Vegemite medicinally, then thousands of invalids and babies are asking you to deny yourself of it for the time being." By 1944, the restricted output of Wrigley's chewing-gum all went to help "our fighting men in easing tension and as a morale builder". With the demand for cheese, another casualty was cream—none available until well after the war. The civilian population not only suffered scarcity of potatoes for months, practically the entire supply of pork, canned meat, vegetables and citrus fruits were directed to the US forces. On top of this, the government introduced rationing for tea, sugar, butter and meat.

The Japanese occupation of Java hampered the imports of tea and so the Rationing Commission, appointed on May 14, 1942, distributed an annual ration book, handed out through the electoral organisation over two days. The coupons selected for tea rationed a person to ½ lb per five weeks. Nauru and Ocean Island were lost in 1942, interrupting superphosphate supplies. The Combined Food Board in America allocated 480,000 tons of phosphates to Australia, against normal consumption of around one million tons. The drop of fertiliser hit sugar production. With it also needed for the services and export to the UK, sugar was rationed from August 31, 1942.

Butter was rationed from June 7, 1943, and meat from January 17, 1944. The meat ration originally averaged 2¼ lbs per week. It was reduced 8¾ per cent and then 12½ per cent. Rationing never included sausages, offal, canned meats, pork, poultry, rabbits, fish, bacon and ham, either because supplies remained reasonable, or because none was available anyway. In 1944, different coloured ration books were issued to children under five years and from five to nine; for instance, to give children under nine no tea ration and only half the adult meat ration, while under-fives participated in the Egg Priority scheme. Presumably as a concession to the need for cups of tea in conquering this dry land, residents in specified remote areas were permitted 50 per cent more than the normal ration of tea and sugar. Expectant mothers received extra butter. Extra sugar was available from time to time for jam-making.

Rationing itself made little change to food consumption. Rather, it achieved a reasonably fair distribution of scarce items, virtually the same as our founding rations—meat, flour, sugar and tea—proving the historic portability of our diet. Nutritionists have often noted the wartime improvement in European diets—less sugar and more brown bread—and a parallel but less marked gain was made in Australia. The consumption of milk, eggs, potatoes, fruit and cereals increased, while the consumption of meat dropped considerably, as did oil and fats, sugar and citrus. Most of these trends (except the drop in citrus through the services' demand) were supported by nutritionists, who were having the time of their lives. Following experiences in the Great War, governments believed in ensuring the health of their populations and sought the advice of experts, like members of the nutrition committee of the National Health and Medical Research Council, who published a stodgy booklet of *Diet and Nutrition for the Australian People*. The ABC broadcast "The Kitchen Front", a series of radio talks by the spokesman of its nutrition advisory committee.

Wartime scarcity drained the colour out of recipe books. The *Good Health Cookery Book and Food Manual*, edited by Gerda Harris for the Women's Defence Service in Adelaide, urged that food be chosen with a knowledge of nourishment. What about the waste of throwing aside potato and other vegetable peelings? The loss here was not less than a shilling weekly in an ordinary family, which meant a loss to the nation of some £625,000 a year. "What the book will do is teach how it is possible to spend 10d or 9d instead of a shilling, and yet be better fed." The *Truth* cookery book of 1943, which listed our traditional lamingtons under "Cookies", immediately above it gave Wartime Cream Buns, which used egg powder and margarine and "cream" whipped up out of cornflour, milk, margarine, sugar and vanilla. Printed on newsprint, the book contained a large section of Austerity Menus, with recipes for liver, kidney, mince, Surprise Patties (made with three sets of brains and ½ lb of mince), "meatless dishes" like Vegetable Roast, Austerity Potatoes (half the usual quantity, plus soaked breadcrumbs) and Austerity Fruit Cake (without eggs and with dripping instead of butter).

Empty farms

With farmers and others with war contracts besieging the government with demands for labour, one solution was the Australian Women's Land Army formed in early 1942. The stimulus was the expansion of the flax industry for linen thread for coats, boots, parachute harnesses and firehoses. As well, the women worked on vegetables for drying, crops for canning, dairying and poultry. The women's land army was not large—about 3,500 were enrolled nationally. About 1,500 were in Victoria, which had the biggest flax and dairy production. Twenty women worked at a big poultry farm where 10,000 chickens were hatched every Monday and Thursday morning over a six-week breeding season. From the Griffith irrigation area and the Atherton Tableland they flew thousands of lettuces to New Guinea. In recording this history, Kitty McEwen, Victorian superintendent of the army, reported that farmers were somewhat "disdainful" that a girl could take the place of their son, or usual male help. "Although these girls readily did a man's job," she recorded, "they received no gratuity from the Commonwealth Government, nor any rehabilitation benefits". Many of the women married in the country, she said, often wishing there was a Land Army girl left to help them.

The authorities found a much larger labouring force in the 25,000 prisoners of war and 16,000 interned aliens held in camps in relatively isolated parts of Australia. While the Japanese were unwilling workers and the Germans preferred school classes, the Italians, who formed by far the largest national group, were keen to take up horticulture to avoid "barbed-wire happiness". Dressed in clothing dyed claret colour, many of them were sent out, without guards, as farm labourers. Lt-Col E. T. Dean, veteran of the First World War and a pastoralist, was commandant of Loveday Camp, near Barmera in South Australia. When he cleared two acres for vegetables in July, 1941, he experienced "political disinterest which amounted almost to opposition". But, with food shortages, he was able to plant 440 acres of vegetables, lucerne and research crops, and earn more than £100,000. His people built a piggery for 760 animals and a vast poultry run. With seed imports blocked from America, Loveday grew tomato, bean, beetroot, lettuce and cabbage seeds, valued at £15,000, for distribution by the Commonwealth Seed Committee. At the Loveday camp, like others, an escape tunnel was discovered, with an ingenious ventilation line of milk and jam tins, and various caches of fermenting grape juice and distilled spirits.

Lt-Col C. S. Thane did much the same at the Hay camp in NSW, picking 10 acres of peas in 1943, plus over the season another million pounds of vegetables, 41,000 gallons of milk, 10,000 dozen eggs, poppies and pyrethrum. Repatriation of the prisoners did not commence until the end of 1946 and the last batch left on January 21, 1947. While the Red Cross found that Australian authorities "scrupulously applied the 1929 Geneva Conventions" and conditions were very good, the prisoners made numerous complaints about the allied troop ships, where rations were standard for prisoners in Great Britain, estimated by the Red Cross delegate at between 1600 and 1800 calories, and about half what they had received in Australia.

Before the war, the number engaged in agricultural labour had been 514,000. By March, 1943, this was down to 438,000, despite men in rural industries no longer being called up and the authorities boosting the workforce with women and prisoners. The literal manpower had fallen by 27 per cent. The empty farms had to keep producing, and the Americans brought with them the "knowhow".

"Bloody fine barstuds"

North American visitor Archibald E. Shaw, of Mayne Island, British Columbia, confided to US military intelligence in May, 1942, that: "The great system among the Australians is beer, beer, and more beer. I think it is an organised thing from the higher-ups. It is directed toward keeping the working classes down—by getting them to spend their money recklessly and not allowing them to be educated outside their work". In comparison, American soldiers were carefully selected, better educated, better dressed and better fed. They consumed fancy cigarettes, GI editions of new novels, Kleenex, whisky and, most symbolically, Coca-Cola. Australian troops complained that the Americans, who charmed the womenfolk, were "over-paid, over-sexed and over here".

When Sydney newspaper editorials professed astonishment that liquor production had not been restricted with other commodities, on March 8, 1942, the government ordered a cut of one-third. Although this was soon lightened, with more money around, and more soldiers seeking solace and diversion, the restrictions produced price rises and a vigorous black market. Several nightclubs opened in Sydney especially for Americans, and were supplied by sly-grog shops. US personnel also had four clubrooms in Sydney where they could purchase beer between 3 pm and 10 pm. One politician said that hundreds of Australian soldiers on leave spent Easter Monday, 1944, fruitlessly tramping in search of a glass of beer, yet allied servicemen and drunken women strolled the city flourishing bottles.

You get a picture of the interaction from the 1944 edition of a *Pocket Guide to Australia* prepared for GIs by the US War and Navy Departments. It explained that grateful local newspapers used up scarce newsprint with not only baseball scores but also American recipes for housewives to entertain the visitors. The Digger was apparently nonplussed by the "manners" of Americans in camp and even more so in mixed company, it said. To him those many "bloody thank you's" and "pleases" of the Yanks were a "bit sissified". The Australian soldier said that when an American got on a friendly footing with an Australian family he was usually found in the kitchen, teaching the Mrs how to make coffee, or washing the dishes.

The Australian had just about the slangiest of all the brands of English, the guide explained. The threepenny piece was called a "tray", the sixpence a "zac", the shilling a "bob" or "deener" and the pound a "quid", "frogskin" and "fiddleedee". When the "Yank" went to a "shivoo", he might expect someone to drink "plonk" or a "shandy", or at the "rubbadedub" to "shout" drinks. Australians said "dinner" for lunch, "tea" for supper and "supper" for a late snack. They said "cocky's delight" for molasses, "pudding" for dessert and went to a "lolly" shop for candy. And the best thing any Australian could say was that you were, with classic mis-spelling, a "bloody fine barstud".

A table showed just "How U.S.A. and Australian eating habits differ". Australians were great meat eaters—consuming many times as much beef, mutton and lamb, and a lot more flour, butter, and tea. But they didn't go in for green vegetables and salads and fruits as much as Americans, the guide-book reported. Some of the best fruits in the world grew along the tropical coasts of Queensland, but the Australian, nevertheless, was strictly a "meat and potatoes guy". That housewives "down under" made coffee with a pinch of salt and a dash of mustard was "probably just another Axis propaganda story". That the two vegetables with your "outback" dinner of beef or lamb were fried potatoes and roasted potatoes probably wasn't true either. However, it wasn't a gag that you got a kangaroo steak or kangaroo tail soup in the "outback", especially if you went hunting yourself.

Meat pies were the Australian version of the hot dog and in Melbourne the substitute for a hamburger was a "dim sin" [sic], chopped meat rolled in cabbage leaves. But because of the demand, hot dog and hamburger stands were springing up in large numbers, the American booklet said. So you'd probably see signs like: "500 yards ahead. Digger Danny's Toasted Dachshunds". But you wouldn't find drug stores selling sodas or banana splits.

The "blue laws" made Australian cities "pretty dull places" on Sundays. Maybe the bars, the movies and the dance halls weren't open, but there were a lot of places in America where that was true too. "There's no use beefing about it — it's their country", the pocket guide said. The main drinking was in hotel bars "during the few hours they're allowed to open" and the main drink was beer — "stronger than ours and not as cold". Hard liquor was more expensive and much less commonly drunk. They also made some good light wines. But the national drink was still tea, which you'd find a good drink when you got used to it. Along the roads you'd see "hot water" signs from when Australian motorists would take along their own tea and for a few pence could get hot water and a small billy can in which they brewed their tea. But since the war, there wasn't any motoring.

US lessons in food technology

When the Americans arrived, they went on the Australian rations, which was on a scale of 24 items: 12 oz bread or biscuit, 12 oz flour, 12–16 oz meat, and ham, bacon, fish, eggs, cheese, dried peas, vegetables, potatoes, macaroni or spaghetti, onions, jams, milk, tea, coffee, sugar, salt, rice, oatmeal, butter and dried fruits. But the American leaders had higher nutritional expectations. The vitamins and calories of their 39-item diet were important. The American quartermaster wanted, according to one of its magazines, "to render our American Army the best fed and most bountifully supplied at all times". The Americans repeated Napoleon's dictum that an army marches on its stomach, but in their modern way justified food as the "first munition of war". They said, "For the first time in history, the subsistence effort has been placed on a thoroughly scientific basis".

The US team wanted less mutton and more fruit and vegetables. In February, 1943, General MacArthur informed the Prime Minister that the American food officers desired to procure food directly instead of through the local forces. Accordingly, a subsistence depot, with headquarters and sub-depots in Melbourne and Brisbane, was established under General Hugh B. Hester. The total value of foodstuffs handed to the US forces under Reverse Lend Lease between January 1, 1942 and September 30, 1944, was close to £50 million.

With a shrinking labour force, the blocking of various imports like phosphate fertiliser and vegetable seeds, the Australian government had to increase food production and satisfy American tastes. The Potato Committee pushed the potato acreage from 99,324 to 241,803 acres in three years. More land was sown to vegetables by 1945 than any year before or since, the total more than doubling during the war to 500,000 acres. Before the war, Tasmanian berry-fruit was fairly stable at about 3,000 acres, but by 1945–46, a record 5,390 was reached. Other industries had to be started. Loss of supplies of ginger from Hong Kong and Canton gave impetus to the small Queensland industry at Buderim, production reaching 740 tons in 1946. Within years Australia produced half the world's confectionery ginger. But the ultimate key was mechanisation of farming along American lines.

On a field day in December, 1943, at Pakenham, Victoria, twelve major new agricultural machines were demonstrated. There were still more being manufactured and another dozen under design. The Melbourne *Herald* commented: "Many of the machines demonstrated are likely to revolutionise Australian farming methods. Most of them were developed in Australia, sometimes from American prototypes, with the assistance of Australian agricultural experts and the US Army food production technicians". The machines left the contemporary historian of the food effort, K. R. Cramp, "open-mouthed with astonishment". One tractor-powered implement prepared the soil, sowed several rows of seed, deposited fertiliser, covered up the seed and all in one operation. A mower harvested ripe pea vines and then a viner separated and then shelled the peas, providing 10,000 lbs daily. Major Belford L. Seabrook's family owned America's largest vegetable farm, of 20,000 acres plus 15,000 acres worked by 650 other farmers. It fed the family canneries and dehydrators and was so huge that it could only be worked with thoroughly mechanised equipment, with aeroplanes spraying fertiliser, fungicide and pesticide. "His extraordinary knowledge of agricultural mechanisation and his persuasive influence among Australian farmers have effected an agricultural revolution in this land," Cramp declared.

In terms of food preservation, while the First World War had boosted canned fruits, little had been done with vegetables, "for naturally a people able to procure fresh vegetables with ease would not be concerned with canning them," Cramp wrote. With canning convenient for feeding armies, the 10 million pounds a year before the war rose in 1942 to 50 million and in 1943 to 112 million. The canning companies expanded rapidly, given government help in purchasing land and finding workers. One firm (presumably Edgell's) supplied no fewer than 404,000 cases of vegetables in

1943–44, for which it grew 1,000 miles of asparagus. Reporting these figures, Cramp exclaimed: "War gave a pronounced fillip to the canning industry". Major Maynard A. Joslyn was brought from the University of California to establish the dried vegetable industry. By the end of the war, 35 dehydration plants were at work. Even freezing was introduced, again under Major Joslyn's tuition, and a small beginning made with a Sydney firm in 1944.

The Australian meat processing industry was compelled to upgrade its standards and put out new canned meats. "Some of these I can, from first-hand experience, pronounce as being of superior standard," Cramp said, "Chili Con Carne, Luncheon meat and Vienna sausage are canned delicacies". Two American officers, Majors Kahn and Hallman, introduced the de-boning of meat, which permitted economy in freezer space and a more equitable issue to troops. The new product was a revelation to the Australian Army, as were tropical cured or salt-pack ham and bacon to Australian producers.

The laboratory at Tooth's brewery in Sydney was turned over to American food inspection. Massachusetts food technologist Major Fellers was in charge, with incubators to simulate tropical conditions. The lab not only tested samples for purity and honesty, but was a clearing house of technical information. Fellers and staff held influential schools to familiarise local graduates with American food methods.

The repercussions

The war had multiple repercussions on the food chain, leaving much more than cold stores, wheat silos, sweetcorn factories, quick-freezing experiments and the inspiration of fresh lettuces flown to troops in New Guinea. Milk and bread delivery rounds were now zoned. Potato growers appreciated the benefits of central control and retained Potato Committee measures to "stabilise" the industry. In 1939, 15 per cent of NSW dairy farms had milking machines and in 1949, 60 per cent. The director of the Australian Institute of Anatomy in Canberra, after touring England and America in 1944, introduced Australia's first course in nutrition on April 9, 1945. At Sydney Technical College, F. H. Reuter commenced the first food technology course in 1947.

The big boost to manufacturing—to iron and steel, machine tools, aircraft, motor bodies and the like, as well as munitions proper—had immense consequences. The factories turned to producing consumer goods like motor-cars and refrigerators, which together spawned the supermarket. The government's post-war immigration splurge provided BHP factory-"fodder", some of whom left to become chefs, waiters, restaurateurs, backyard food manufacturers, greengrocers and delicatessen proprietors.

As the war ended, a body called the Overseas Corporation was formed, with a board of a dozen Australian and American business leaders, to sell American know-how and licences to Australian industry. It appointed J. Stuart Lucy managing director of a subsidiary called Market and Consumer Research Pty Ltd, which researched the market for the American version of the pressure-cooker. Lucy concluded there was a potential market for 10,000 pressure-cookers per week. "This was a seemingly extravagant estimate," he recalled later, "particularly for a company with at that time only £100,000 capital". But when Namco pressure-cookers could be mass-produced, sales exceeded that estimate. Meanwhile, through the farm-gate came the Ferguson light tractor, spelling the end to horse-teams. Rather than cumbersomely towing, it actually carried the implement. The tractor was another subject of market research, which indicated that certain "opinion leaders" adopted products and were followed by neighbours. Market research had been stimulated during the war, including a survey of eating habits in NSW. So, too, had the importance of getting the message across, the Australian Association of Advertising Agencies being formed in 1946.

Throughout the combatant world, wartime investment in scientific research stimulated post-war affluence. Processes such as quick-freezing, continuous-process bread-making, chemical extraction of oil from oilseeds and controlled atmospheric storage were to transform food, as would the application of older technologies, such as self-service retailing, canning and warehousing. The food industry would borrow fancy plastics and papers, improved refrigeration and electronic computers.

Invaders sometimes distribute the seeds of useful foods and food ideas. Otherwise, war glorifies warrior virtues, uproots agrarian societies, blockades civilian populations, spoonfeeds armies, mechanises food processes, improves food's portability, invents substitutes like margarine, centralises food policy, reinforces dietary conformity and outlaws fine foods, as with feelings, as "inessential". If food is war's "first munition", it is also its first casualty. The 1914–18 war ended a period of relatively proud dining in Australia. The 1939–45 war again toughened the food chain, alienating eaters further from the source. It again showed the essence of our eating to be rations—of the ocean expedition, penal settlement, out-station, commuter suburb, mobilised nation and next the supermarket world.

COCA-COLONISATION

An early Coke ad in the *Women's Weekly*

TO COCA-COLA, the war offered a tremendous business opportunity. In 1926, the firm's new president, Robert W. Woodruff—endeavouring to "put motivation and organised business effort behind the idea that people everywhere are thirsty"—set up a Foreign Department. Early promotional effort went into putting a special bottle aboard luxury liners bound for distant ports. In March 1930, although Coca-Cola sometimes encountered a "strange and even hostile market environment", he created the Coca-Cola Export Corporation.

Although a Perth accountant, Mr M. E. Pye, had sought rights to produce Coca-Cola as early as 1917, not until early 1937 did Coke send a survey team to Australia, followed later in the year by five Americans and two Canadians to set up business. They were led by Mr J. C. Staton (later a vice-president) and included four salesmen who later became company managers in Adelaide, Melbourne, Sydney and Brisbane. Bottling was done by Long and Barden in North Sydney while the company's own plant was built in Dowling Street, Waterloo, with a staff of 10 and four delivery trucks. Bottling began in South Melbourne, Woolloongabba (Brisbane) and Adelaide on the eve of the war.

Shopkeepers proved wary, so that the early salesmen sold, literally, by the bottle. According to the company, Australia proved "unusual and difficult" through the small, widely-separated markets. Everywhere else, the company has sold franchises to bottle its concentrate, but here it set up the businesses itself, the Sydney bottling plant remaining with the company. With the war, the Army commandeered Coke's trucks; sugar, petrol and other supplies were rationed; and staff joined the services. So, all in all, sales were not what they should have been.

Then in 1943 came president R. W. Woodruff's master-stroke: "We will see that every man in [American] uniform gets a bottle of Coca-Cola for five cents wherever he is and whatever it costs". The company shipped bottling plants throughout the world, as close as possible to combat areas. Ice-makers and beverage dispensers, combined into "Jungle Units", fitted even Jeeps. Company personnel were attached to the forces and designated Technical Observers, known colloquially as "Coca-Cola colonels". Three of them died in the performance of their mission. "We are proud of the job we did," said an executive, H. B. Nicholson, "And so were the GIs. They conducted the greatest word-of-mouth campaign ever afforded any product in history . . . It was like Main Street suddenly stretched around the world".

Towards the end of 1946, more than 155 new Coca-Cola bottling plants operated in six former theatres of war. The Perth plant was salvaged from a Brisbane wharf after being bombed on the way to an island base. The small Brisbane plant had often operated 24 hours a day to supply US South Pacific headquarters under General Douglas MacArthur. Coke's post-war strategy was to aim at the heart. It offered franchises to key people in the local financial establishments. It bought prime sites for its neon signs—like the top of Kings Cross. It sought the approval of future generations by getting projects, films and prizes into schools. It sponsored surf-lifesaving boats and junior rugby league and placed the distinctive red dispenser alongside the tennis umpire. It promoted "teenage hops" and its ads used youthful sex.

Meanwhile, Coke sought to further markets worldwide. Even during war years, Max Keith, in charge of European operations, had "somehow managed to travel" throughout enemy territory to maintain company business. When the German operation ran out of concentrate and developed a new softdrink, it adopted the trademark "Fanta", later to be used everywhere. A common advertising symbol in the 1940s showed the distinctive bottle beside a red planet, along with the curious slogan, "—the global high-sign". A painting widely-used in advertising in the 1950s, called the "Symbol of Friendship", showed Atlas now holding up a bottle, while behind dangled the earth the corporation sought to conquer. A film called "Wonderful World" showed "how naturally Coca-Cola fits into hospitality patterns around the world", three camera crews travelling 190,000 miles in 31 countries to make it. Coca-Cola missionaries took the drink into developing countries, persuading peasants swept into city slums to forsake their traditional diets.

Coca-Cola entered Bulgaria in 1966 and Yugoslavia in 1968. In the 1970s, more than 1,000 million people had access to Coke through four million shops. World sales were estimated in 1974 as 165 million drinks daily. This achievement was due to the "dedication and single-mindedness" of many people, said Coke in its first company history, not the least the bottlers in more than 130 countries. The Export Corporation, "as a world management and sales team, they have so positioned Coca-Cola in the international market that, for a single product, it enjoys a unique and unrivalled recognition and acceptance around the globe". It was the corporation's way of saying that Coke had become widely regarded as the public face of American economic imperialism.

Coca is a South American shrub (*Erythroxylon coca*), the dried leaves of which traditionally are chewed as a stimulant and from which is also manufactured cocaine. Cola is a West African tree (*Cola acuminata*), the seed of which has served for countless years as a condiment and tonic. By a remarkable stroke of fate, "coca" and "cola"—the names of two ancient drugs—just happened to enter the head of an American bookkeeper, Frank Robinson, in May 1886 as the name of the new cordial brewed by his colleague, John S. Pemberton, a seller of what have been called "quack cures". By the turn of the century Coca-Cola—at first a headache tonic but increasingly an invigorating softdrink—was popular at soda fountains and had competition even in Australia. The NSW Aerated Water & Co of Newcastle registered the trademark of "Kolazone"—"made from the kola nut". The Melbourne *Argus* of January 13, 1902, carried the following advertisement:

> The most beneficial drink in the world, mighty 'ALOK' (registered trade-mark of Fisher and Co.'s Famous Tonic), freshly prepared from the celebrated KOLA NUTS. Unintoxicating, but containing more sustaining power than alcohol or spirits.

After the arrival of Coca-Cola, a Department of Health newsletter in Canberra reported that the flavouring was primarily an extract of the cola nut, whose physiological and pharmacological importance was dependent on its caffeine and, to a lesser extent, theobromine content. Yet when I wrote to the company in Sydney in 1979, the manager for consumer affairs, Yvonne Howie, replied: "The formula for 'Coca-Cola' is indeed still confidential". Pepsi-Cola is advertised as virtually indistinguishable, so what have the Coca-Cola company to hide from whom?

A table pinned up at the local dentist's revealed Coke's sugar content to be 10 per cent, or a disturbing four or five teaspoons per glass. These otherwise unpublicised contents illustrate the faith we gained in the "good name" of a food manufacturer. As our ancestors trusted an apple, we believed in Coke. It was artificial in the sense that we did not recognise it from nature, culturally synthetic in that no-one had ever made it at home, false in the sense that it was really just tricked-up water. But worse than that, Coke also symbolised the cargo-cult faith in American ways which we clung to through the 1950s and 1960s. "America" was the model of the future.

We shared a similar history to California and, from our first years, trans-Pacific waves influenced us. The Dungaree settlers wore the equivalent of jeans, kept pigs, grew maize and ate Johnny cakes, hominy, pumpkins and water-melons, all very American. Yankee whalers were common in our ports, clippers brought wheat, kitchen gadgets, ice, cocktails, "free lunches" and restaurateurs. Dairying, cattle, wheat and rice techniques came from there. The Foster brothers brought their lager, Peters brought his icecream and Harold Clapp found his "eat more fruit" inspiration. The first US food firms—Kraft, Kellogg's and Heinz—arrived in the 1920s. American tastes and know-how invaded in the war. Now would come supermarkets, cars, fridges, television, frozen food and junk-food. Recipe books and hotel menus would borrow from America, with "French fries" and "Idaho potatoes". When food seemed sophisticated, the chances were it was an American interpretation. Even "vichyssoise", "chili con carne" and "chop suey", seemingly so ethnic, were American.

12

Carpark shopping

With an obsession for cheapness, plus a new love of cars and refrigerators, Australians embraced the nationally-distributed and standardised foods of the supermarket

IN THE EARLY 1950s, our milkman still leapt the fence before dawn to fill the billy, and top up the cat's saucer. Halfway through the morning, the baker arrived with a big wicker basket and was followed obediently down the street by horse and decorated cart. The greengrocer would always interrupt lunch, whenever we had it, and after hiding away in his tall green van, crunch down the gravel drive with his filled deal box. The grocer took the order one day and his brother brought it the next. Other men brought blocks of ice, carried dripping in huge pincers to the icechest opposite the laundry tubs and copper. Recollections of such tradespeople were smashed to bits, like the prices, by the supermarket.

It was said that the "supermarket killed the corner store". We certainly lost the general store's wooden counter, glass jars of lollies, gloomy bins, carefully stacked shelves and a couple who would weigh out a large slice of muslin-covered tasty cheese, which they had matured for 18 months in their cellar. But in our sprawling cities the big victim was the deliverer door-to-door. Except for some milk and bread rounds, the food and ice carter was all but wiped out.

In the United States, self-service was introduced in 1916 and supermarkets in 1932. As far back as 1926, self-service had been attempted in Victoria. During the depression, "cash and carry" grocers became familiar, the retailers not wishing to extend credit freely nor to provide home delivery. The wartime labour shortage and rationing encouraged "stringbag" shopping.

By the 1954 retail census, there were 766 self-service stores in Australia (3·3 per cent of grocers). At the end of 1957, 1700 stores were self-service. They were also turning into supermarkets, because these 7 per cent of stores already conducted 20 per cent of grocery sales. Since the previous century, the chain store, with its greater buying power, had edged out independent corner shops and now chains upped the size of their outlets. The proportion of groceries sold through supermarkets in Australia rose from one-third in 1968–9 to one-half in 1973–4.

Cars and fridges

Australian eating has been shaped as much as anything by transport, and the world in which supermarkets flourished was created by the car. The big American manufacturers, like General Motors, Ford and Chrysler, already built car bodies here in the 1930s. Before the war, there were 77 cars per 1000 Australians. The war speeded industrialisation, a corporation like General Motors supplying armaments to both sides before it launched "Australia's Own Car", the Holden, in 1949. On June 30, 1961, there were 2,064,871 cars registered—200 per 1000 people, or virtually one per family. Comparing statistics with other countries shows that supermarkets arrived when there were about 100 cars per 1000 inhabitants. It's easy to see the reasons. The average family's weekly food purchases, excluding beverages, weigh about 50 kilograms. This could be carried in a car. Not only that, the car could take the shopper some distance to seek out novelty, bigger shelves and lower prices.

When we had walked about our early towns we purchased our "butter, fresh or salted" from the central market. The expansion of public transport from the 1880s clustered retailing into the central business district and also into shopping centres dotted along the suburban tram and train lines. The mass production of private cars created city sprawl and regional shopping centres surrounded by carparks.

The second necessary adjunct to the supermarket was the refrigerator. Refrigeration had been central in efforts to fit unsuitable eating and drinking to this hot country. Its invention last century had assisted meat-exporting, beer-making and milk distribution. Home icechests had reduced the hazards of melting butter and keeping left-overs. In the 1920s, electric fridges in shops sold icecream. After the war, the fridge became "no longer a luxury, now a necessity" in the labour-saving kitchen. Post-war production lines put a refrigerator into 73 per cent of metropolitan homes by 1955, according to Kelvinator's figures. In contrast with all previous societies, our homes no longer needed to be supplied daily with fresh food, but could do with the main purchases once a week (although milk, bread, meat, fruit and vegetables were only slowly taken over by supermarkets). The recipe-instruction booklet for the early Pate fridge said it would help tremendously with marketing—

"You can buy in reasonable quantities without the urgent need to dispose of food as soon as it is bought . . . buy when convenient, not as you need."

The services of a refrigerator extended far beyond preserving the purity of food and protecting health, the makers of the Electrolux said in a booklet in 1951, "it is a means of greatly increasing the variety of meals, bringing to the table iced drinks, delicious cold entrées, crisp tempting salads and chilled or frozen desserts." Its American-style recipe collection introduced the "Shrimp Cocktail", "Chicken Mousse", "Cole Slaw", "Bavarian Cream" and "Frozen Strawberry Whip". The booklet also claimed: "Drinking plain water becomes monotonous, so we've made some delicious drinks to entice you and your family to drink more water—the Electrolux way. Let's be open-minded to these new suggestions—let's try these cold drinks, which have been tested and approved . . ."

From the advertising of the automobile companies, which also produced a large proportion of the fridges, the Australian "way of life" became characterised by the family car and cold drinks from the fridge or, better still, from the Esky. The car and cooling coincided in the 1950s in what the manufacturer, Malley's, first called its "Auto Box". It was an insulated metal container to keep food and drink cool in the boot of the car. From the logo of an Eskimo and harpoon, the trade name, "Esky", was registered in November, 1961.

The car and refrigerator made us profligate users of fossil fuels. Ideally, we would end up obtaining more energy from food than we expended in getting it. But two senior CSIRO scientists, Dr Roger Gifford and Dr Dick Millington, worked out in 1974 that it took 5·4 joules of energy to put 1 joule on the table, making the modern food business incredibly wasteful. They found that Australian agriculture, relying on plenty of grazing, was comparatively energy-efficient. About 11 per cent of the energy put the food on the farm truck. Then 38 per cent went processing and transporting it to the store. Finally, transport from store to home took up 14 per cent, the home refrigerator 19 per cent (in the days before freezers were common) and domestic cooking 17 per cent. That meant that the car, the refrigerator and the stove each consumed about the same energy as the people. Gifford and Millington predicted that if energy shortages ever forced people to reduce greatly the energy subsidy on food, "return to a much-simplified rural life may be the only way of coming out in front". Certainly, if we did away with the private car and fridge, there would immediately return a troupe of delivery people and horse-carts bringing fresh milk and bread to our door.

Tom the Cheap

To understand how in the 1950s we were persuaded to give up our traditional shopping habits and accept the supermarket, we can examine the case of Perth path-breaker, Tom the Cheap. Mr T. E. Wardle set up as a grocer in Perth using deferred pay from the war. By 1955, he owned the shop, could install a manager and take his family for a holiday to Europe. The voyage gave him a chance to think and he arrived back with a scheme. At the time, the usual mark-up on the wholesale price of groceries was 25 per cent. By keeping it to 10, Wardle could allocate 4 per cent to wages, 1 per cent to rent, 1 per cent to advertising, 2 or 3 per cent to other expenses and keep the rest. He knew price-cutting would have its difficulties, particularly since other grocers strongly supported resale price maintenance, that is, sticking to agreed prices under the threat of having supplies cut off. An article in the *Grocers' and Storekeepers' Journal* of WA explained the "fallacy" of price-cutting: "It is a sign of weakness, it renders quality suspect, it is infectious, it creates bargain-hunters, it brings only temporary advantages, it is a poor means of educating the public, it could force someone out of business, it creates disloyalty and erroneous impressions and it is the first step to financial difficulties." Sensible advice, with which "Tom the Cheap" disagreed.

Wardle decided to risk only £200 discovering what would happen. He rented premises, borrowed a check-out machine and refrigerated cabinets and stocked the store on credit. The public response so exceeded expectations that his problem was obtaining sufficient supplies. As expected, some of the biggest manufacturers refused to sell. He hesitated not, but expanded, because it would be easier to circumvent boycotts by purchasing in large rather than small lots. According to press reports, Wardle flew regularly to the eastern States to obtain supplies. Later, he appointed "five secret brokers in the eastern States who sent him about £6,000 worth of goods each week . . . ." He said: "I strongly suspect a private detective is watching goods arrive at my bulk store and then trying to track them back to their source." The "cloak and dagger" activities provided publicity. In 1959, the turnover of his 15 stores was £1 million. By 1962, when he expanded to South Australia, there were 50 stores turning over £5 million.

He slashed costs, and service. He preferred married women as store managers, since without equal pay for equal work, he saved on wages, and they were less interested in promotion and were equipped to manage the girls, the cheapest of all labour. To keep administration down, managers had to "obey orders and not think for themselves"—following such directions as to give poor display to uncooperative manufacturers. In the first decade, Wardle's office was in a warehouse, without carpets, waiting rooms or receptionists. It had a map of Perth with many red pins, a jumble of abandoned sales samples, price tickets, letters, plans and newspaper cuttings of Sir Winston Churchill and President Kennedy.

The opening of one store was attended by police, marching girls, football heroes, a radio announcer, a piper, jazz bands and a belly dancer. But most of all, Tom radiated cheapness. He exploited in his advertising a caricature of a convict clad in prison garb and labelled "Australia's worst price cutter". He dished up slogans like "competitors say he'll ruin us", "customers love him" and "Tom has 2,500 specials all the time". He created the hysteria of the summer sale with his outrageous business name, garish shops, inexpensive labour and trashy advertising. The deliberate jumble of shoddiness and "specials" maintained an aura of "cheapness" at all costs.

The great god Cheap

Australians have long treasured cheapness and its companions, the cut-price, the bargain and the discount. We have been taught to cherish cheapness because it is the battering-ram against consumer resistance, the means by which the factory forces out cottage industry. The pity is that we have come to understand cheapness above almost all other qualities, whether home deliveries, the joy of the well-designed shop, the social mingling at the counter, superior merchandise, or the grocer's smile.

"This is now the cheapest colony in the world in which English society... can be enjoyed," exclaimed the *NSW Magazine* in July, 1843. Edward Abbott hoped his 1864 cookery book could be kept down in price, "as we live in cheap times". D. H. Lawrence was struck 60 years later by a sale sign, "Prices smashed to bits". Fortunately, we sometimes realised that cheapness brought uniformity, artificiality, poor quality and often only illusory savings. In 1914, the Nestlé company urged people wanting good condensed milk to avoid inferior brands that were cheap. The poorer classes "cannot resist the bait of apparent cheapness", an ad for Foster Clark soon claimed. "Cheap custard powder is expensive."

Arguably, when the supermarket arrived, the poor paid more than others for their food. Lower-income shoppers often did not have a first, let alone a second car. They tended, as a result, to use smaller supermarkets and "delis" and these could cost more. Further, stringent budgets limited the amount that could be devoted to stocking up on "specials" and larger packs. Lacking self-reliant knowledge, they also bought less wisely, the first to succumb to junk-food.

In general, Australians expected their food to be cheaper and they spent less on it. In 1959–60, 19·6 per cent of household income went on food, and five years later only 12·2 per cent. The amount of the retail dollar being taken on food dropped from 33·9 per cent in 1953 to 27·1 per cent in 1977. The small proportion of income spent on food indicates how little we cared for it. It also indicates that some costs had been transferred—for instance, to the expense of picking up goods instead of having them delivered. Yet cost-cutting made big money. Since the volume of sales was high, given quick turnover, then profits to the company should be considered in terms of capital investment. This brought profits within the 10 to 20 per cent range. But even against sales it could look good. "Two per cent on £10 million is £200,000 and he probably earns much more than that each year," wrote two Perth economists, D. H. Briggs and R. L. Smyth, in 1965. "To be Tom the

Cheap is like being the winner of a Sydney Opera House Lottery, only it happens every day." Tom Wardle's sums added up to the cheapest common denominator.

Coles and Woolworths

The two supermarket giants, Coles and Woolworths, entered the grocery business after competing for decades as mass merchandisers of variety goods. Born in Victoria in 1885 to a line of shopkeepers named George Coles, the founding G. J. Coles had been inspired by American business magazine *System* and an overseas visit in 1913, when he was fascinated by American 5 and 10-cent stores and, in England, by Woolworth 3d and 6d stores and Marks and Spencer 1d stores. Adapting its name from the English firm, the original Woolworths Stupendous Bargain Basement opened in Sydney on December 5, 1924. The previous night's papers had promised a "handy place where good things are cheap. Really cheap. The cheapest possible. Come and see. You'll want to live at Woolworths. From 9 in the morning till 9 at night. Woolworths will sell what you want and sell it cheap." It seemed like Christmas. And it was—Harold Percival Christmas, a commercial traveller, and his partners had become retailers of cheapness.

Both companies moved into food in 1958, spending enormous sums to buy up grocery chains, which were busily converting to self-service and expanding into supermarkets. On May 1, Woolworths acquired 32 BCC food markets in Queensland. Coles matched this by purchasing 54 self-service grocery stores in Victoria from John Connell Dickins & Co. Then the next year it bought the Adelaide chain of 17 Beilby stores. During 1960, Woolworths bought nine John Wills supermarkets in WA, 11 Fair Fares in NSW, six Sydney Safeway groceries, 55 Fleming food stores and 57 McIlraiths and opened its first fully-fledged free-standing supermarket, at Warrawong in NSW. And also in 1960, Coles opened its first large, free-standing store at North Balwyn, Victoria, providing customer parking. Soon after, it bought for £9 million the giant Matthews-Thompson chain with more than 250 grocery stores in NSW.

The arrival of big supermarkets was associated with television, and in 1960, the Coles "£3,000 Question" began, by which time a fourth Coles boy received his knighthood. While Tom the Cheap might have chosen unambitious managers, a shoe-string administration and only a small warehouse, Coles and Woolworths were giant bureaucracies, with promises of "only internal promotion to top positions", quality control laboratories, executives in charge of statistics and research and 16 and 18-acre warehouses. Woolworths claimed to be the first retailer whose sales exceeded $1,000 million "in one financial year", occurring in 1976, while Coles claimed the same for the "12-month period" to September, 1976. "Coles," according to the directors in 1978, "has become one of the real forces in the role of improving the quality and style of life throughout Australia".

Coles and Woolworths had ready access to the enormous amounts of capital to invest in bitumen. By building the biggest supermarkets on the best sites, and by heavy advertising of cut-price "specials" and "loss leaders" (articles sold at an apparent loss to attract customers), Coles and Woolworths came to dominate grocery sales like no other traders before. Their neck-and-neck race could be interpreted as fierce competition—or as the identical acts of two giants sharing what economists label an "oligopoly". According to figures in *Retail World* (December 13, 1978), Woolworths held 20·0 per cent and Coles 17·3 per cent of the national grocery market. They shared it with chains important mainly in one State. "A mere two dozen key accounts influence the vast majority of buying arrangements in the Australian grocery trade today," the newspaper commented. In NSW, the top five grocers controlled 85·2 per cent of the business. Victoria's top five held 71·5. The oligopoly was more pronounced in Queensland, where the top three (Coles, Woolworths and TWD) held 85·0 per cent, and worst in South Australia, where a mere three accounts (Coles, Woolworths and Associated) handled 93·6 per cent of the grocery trade.

Coles and Woolworths joined the large "one-stop" shopping complexes, with which city traders pursued their increasingly distant customers. Some centres reached a grandiose scale in the mid-1960s, with Sydney's Roselands and Bankstown Square genuine "one-stop" giants built around one or more major department stores and one million square feet including supermarkets, not to forget the carparks. Centres were "scientifically" located and architecturally and commercially "planned for profits"—with deliberately inaccessible exits and "rigid" formulas for the mix of shops to provide "protected trading rights". The one-stop complex was an artificial village centre, but with the traditional free marketplace replaced by central planning.

The automation of selling

While the big chains assumed illiterate signatures—K-mart (Coles), Big W (Woolworths) and Red S (Safeway)—the smaller triers adopted deliberately cheap and nasty spelling—Minit, Supa Save, Shoprite, Kwik 'n Thrifty, Riteway, Mity Mart, Supa Valu, Serv-Wel and Bi-lo. Retailing took on the faceless energy of an American protestant work brigade, erupting among the aisles and gondalas. "Small and large retailers alike can still 'make a quid' with aggressive trading, instead of complaining" (about issues like late-night shopping, price control and inflation), Jim Fielding of Jewel Food Stores told the industry in 1972. Roelf Vos of the Tasmanian chain chided: "If the going gets tough, the tough gets going." And retail industry columnist Stan Ruller advised: "Heads down, asses up and get into this game boots and all this year, or get out. The survivors of 1973 will be the millionaires of 1983." Sims' SSW supermarket at Sunshine in Victoria stacked 20,000 packets of Kraft cheddar in one pile. Then Woolworths Southlands Shopping Centre, Melbourne, built a mountain of 75,804. Finally, Woolworths found room for 84,160 packets (25 tons), an entire mountain range across their "Family Centre" at Inala, a housing commission satellite town, 13 miles south-west of Brisbane. And people kept buying.

"The industry demanded it—Metro produced it", went an advertisement in *Retail World* (December 1978). "The New Metro M150 Trolley is a whopping 15,000 cubic inches. It's the biggest in Australia, in fact it's double the capacity of 1975's average size trolley. And think what that means in terms of good turnover. Your customer won't be able to resist filling it up."

Aesthetically, supermarkets became calculated landscapes of brash packages, cardboard, plastic, primary-painted prices, the freezers' hum and the chemical perfume of detergent. All the bustle and colour of the fresh market was boxed in a sterilised, standardised and fluorescent cornucopia. Shops surrounded by arid carscapes and deliberately oozing cheapness hardly lent dignity to our society, and like most results of the automobile, cut up communities into isolated alienated pockets. Only Andy Warhol was amused.

Self-service had been, in a simple way, automation. Low prices led to fewer jobs and less attractive ones at that. The percentage of women in retailing grew—55·7 per cent in 1968–9 and 60·2 in 1973–4. Increasingly, too, the companies relied on younger and part-time workers. Symptomatic was the advent of "one-trip" or "non-returnable" beverage containers to cut out supermarket collection of empties. In 1963, ACI introduced throw-away bottles in Melbourne and Coca-Cola installed its first canning line—in Perth to litter the long WA roads.

Supermarkets eliminated skilled assistance and yet with the confusing range—shelves carried about 1500 items in 1950, 8000 in 1970 and 12,000 in 1975—the skill passed to the shopper. In a supermarket, you stood alone against the nation's biggest industry, using every display contrivance. It was usual policy to give greater space to best-selling lines, the bottom shelf to cheaper ones. Supermarkets required heavy packaging not only to have labour-saving portions "pre-packaged" but also to attract the customer's eye with bright plastic bottles, metal foil and "giant economy size" (much more visible) packs.

With the supermarket's emphasis on cheapness rather than quality, food tended to be grown, blended and manufactured down "to a price". Retail giants had trouble handling the fragile, fresh article. They scarcely tolerated the capricious supply of seasonal food. They did not like dealing with the individual cheese-maker, craft chocolate-maker or high-quality market gardener, since the small producer could not ensure sufficient, controlled volume at rock-bottom prices. Supermarkets preferred the long "shelf-life" of tinned, dried and frozen food and those sources which could guarantee regular supply, constant quality and even prices.

Centralisation of selling suited bigger manufacturers, which could deal with a handful of outlets. Since supermarkets took a deliberately impersonal role in selling, food companies could contact consumers more directly. They saw themselves less and less as manufacturers and more as sellers. They adopted the so-called "marketing" approach of skilful product conception, heavy national advertising and clever packaging.

Ironically, of course, affluence made us want the very high-quality, hand-made articles which were now less available. So certain specialist shops prospered to fill the gaps, and then supermarkets replied with "gourmet" sections. This mixture of the efficient and the exotic encouraged experimentation and novelty in cooking. But the overall effect of supermarkets was to replace taste with packaging.

The successful grocer thus offered several dubious advantages. One was "self-service", where customers had to locate and select products without expert guidance. Another was "cash and carry", which meant customers had to pay on the spot, the delivery person and corner shopkeeper traditionally allowing hefty debts. Supermarkets also shifted the burden of distribution costs onto the family car, refrigerator and throwaway package. A third was "variety", which meant pre-determined quantities and the same in every store, the same across the nation, the same all year round. And a fourth was "consistent quality", which tended to be a levelling down. "Before the self-service revolution, food was less homogeneous, more textured, more highly flavoured, less sugary and somewhat more palatable," Perth economists Briggs and Smyth concluded. "Consumers, too, have tended to become homogenised!"

How we shopped

In March, 1978, students of marketing at the Caulfield Institute of Technology in Melbourne watched "closely but unobtrusively" as shoppers moved among the shelves of various Coles, Foodland, Safeway and Woolworths stores. Knowledge of how shoppers went about the task would help them in their professional sales careers. Two of the Caulfield lecturers published the findings. They noticed, for instance, "simple locating behaviour", that is, when a person appeared to know what product, brand and size he or she wanted and simply picked it off the shelf. A typical description went: "Female (about 30) pushed trolley along the aisle and while still looking at products on the other side of the aisle reached out and picked up a litre bottle of Coke—without actually stopping and with hardly a glance." Simple locating was observed in 54 per cent of cases. As the supermarket became busier, towards the end of the week and in peak hours, the proportion went up. Also, mothers with children tended to scurry through. For some reason, people were quicker with cereals—only 11 per cent were seen to browse in the cereal section without buying, yet 16 per cent did so in the detergents and

21 per cent were seen to browse in the confectionery section.

When a person deliberated, it could be a "best buy" choice between brands, the students of marketing found. "An adult male in the confectionery section held two different chocolate blocks, one in each hand for approximately two minutes. He weighed the two in his hands by raising and lowering each hand." Other times it could be comparison within a brand. One woman turned bottles of bitter lemon upside-down and watched perhaps the fruit "solids". Some consumers seemed bewildered by the array of choices. A middle-aged woman returned three times to exchange her selection of breakfast cereal. The presence of more than one shopper brought some of the turmoil into the open. One couple argued seven minutes along the detergents aisle before the woman said they had enough until next week and they walked off without a purchase.

A child said: "Hey, Dad, look at these." Father looked at the softdrink bottles, the child at cans. "We don't want those, they're too expensive," the father asserted. "Only 23 cents each," the child said. "That's right, we'd better get some of those." And the father picked anything from the shelf. The child said: "Mum said we have to get them ring tops. No, not that stuff, get some Pub Soda Squash, Mum likes that." "OK, and we'll get some Cola too," replied the father, who went back to the bottles and selected large Cokes. Only 22 per cent were seen to refer to a shopping list, but to some the shelves acted as reminders. Sometimes they pondered, stared into space, perhaps mentally running over the cupboard stocks or menu plans. At other times, particularly with detergents, "special" prices instigated purchase.

As well as spying on customers, the Caulfield students interviewed 489 shoppers at Coles New World, Brandon Park (34,000 square feet supermarket with 18 checkouts) and at Safeway, Waverley Gardens (40,000 square feet and 18 checkouts). Most shoppers—93 per cent—said they came by car, six per cent had walked and one per cent had arrived by public transport. Exactly one-half came from home and were going straight back, making supermarket shopping an excursion in its own right. Another 15 per cent were doing other shopping. Another 15 per cent were on the way home from work. Only four per cent came from work and were returning, the lunch-hour shoppers. The average tour around the supermarket took 21½ minutes. There was a fair spread, however, with 22 per cent taking less than 10 minutes and three per cent over 50 minutes. The brief trips were obviously topping-up. Half the people said they shopped at a supermarket once a week, 26 per cent shopped twice and 16 per cent three times or more.

Almost half the shopping "parties" were women alone, two out of ten were women with children, and only one in ten did not include a woman. The presence of the male was related to the wife having a fulltime job. The woman who worked fulltime became "an entirely different shopper". She was no longer an innovator or early adopter of new products. Contrary to frequent assertions, the woman who worked was not even quick to take up new "convenience" foods. Instead, she became more organised, visiting the supermarket once a week or less, spending at a faster rate and buying bigger packs.

The amount spent—the "tape" as it was known in the trade—by the once-a-week shoppers was $14 if one person was shopped for, $26.52 for two, $27.46 for three, $29.39 for four and $28.47 for five or more. This supported the adage that two could live more cheaply than one. The spending-rates of once-weekly shoppers were lowest for a woman with children, 87 cents per minute, and highest for a man with children, $1.21.

Asked their attitude to supermarket shopping, five per cent found it very unpleasant, 10 per cent unpleasant, 31 per cent were neutral, 46 found it pleasant and eight very pleasant. Those finding it unpleasant disliked the noise, the crowds and children. The narrow majority who found it pleasant liked the variety in one place, the layout and displays and the "chance to get out of the house". The older the shopper, the more likely he or she was to enjoy it. Women who didn't work tended to like it, also those shopping before rather than after 4 pm.

I can't help feeling that more of us would have enjoyed shopping as a socially and gastronomically exciting excursion if bread weren't stacked away in anonymous aisles, peas frozen in plastic and pineapples, as we shall now see, entombed in cans. I feel that if we had been less preoccupied with cheapness and more with food quality, shopping could have been much more rewarding, and so would eating. That the supermarket was impersonal, unpleasant and even unreal was due as much as anything to its deadly parent, the automobile. No wonder the increasing percentage of Australians who were travelling abroad were so fascinated by street markets, proudly fitted-out shops and elegant food halls—which had been available last century in our "walking", and genuinely free-market, cities.

GOLDEN CIRCLE PINEAPPLE

Golden Circle promotional recipes

SUPERMARKET food had to leap at you off the shelf, and few brandnames leapt like Golden Circle. From the 1950s, its pineapple segments tumbled into sweet and sour sauces and its rings landed on icecream. By November, 1977, a door-to-door survey found that 68 per cent of households kept a can of pineapple in the cupboard—against 61 per cent for peaches, 43 for pears and 38 for apricots. Twenty years earlier, we only really knew fresh pineapples.

The tremendous success was founded partly on the fruit's magic appeal to Anglo-Saxons—slightly exotic and yet safe with all manner of dishes. With tariff protection, Golden Circle had a virtual monopoly of the "tropical" section of the shelves. But not the least the breakthrough came from planning, discipline and an investment in marketing. The pineapple ring provided a highly pictorial item for the advertising explosion of cheap colour printing. Cut geometrically by a machine—called a "Ginaca" after its Hawaiian inventor, Henry Ginaca—the photogenic ring became the gold crown of Australian cooking. When, after two decades, Edna Everage unveiled her satirical "Pacific Grill", it consisted of sausages stuck through pineapple rings.

The Golden Circle factory in Brisbane had been set up in 1947 by a cooperative of pineapple growers, who had responded to a demand created by American personnel stranded in Australia without Hawaiian supplies. It quickly negotiated "highly lucrative" British Ministry of Food contracts. For six years, growers, their sons back from the war and other returned servicemen expanded the industry. Each summer and winter (for there are two crops a year), they despatched fresh pineapples, with tops on, to Australian markets and they sent the bulk, with tops kept for re-planting, to the cannery for export.

There, the line of "Ginacas", each peeling and coring 80 fruit a minute, sent golden cylinders shimmering to a line of female workers for trimming. Further machines cut the pineapples into 1·25 centimetre slices. Workers stacked the best slices into tins, sent others to the "segmenters" for pineapple pieces and the worst to be smashed as crush. From the peel, core and off-cuts (containing more than two-thirds of the flesh) came juice. So, while the ring was the showpiece of the collection, the residue was not all thrown away. In fact, matching the production with the sales of rings, pieces, crush and juice would remain a continual challenge—involving the manipulation of both raw materials and market. For instance, Golden Circle early on invented tropical fruit salad to sell mountains of crush. For this, it pioneered the processing of pawpaw and banana, and chief chemist Mr P. E. Seale's pumping process for automated mixing and filling "slashed" labour costs.

The British contracts ended in 1953–4, with export hazards mounting. Favourable marketing conditions had also encouraged producers in other countries to expand. Heavy competition brought juice prices down in New Zealand and Canada, and so, when cannery manager J. F. S. Brown toured pineapple-producing countries, he predicted total world over-supply by 1959 and a grim price war. Golden Circle couldn't match the cheap labour costs of Taiwan, Malaya and South Africa, and it was at a geographical disadvantage as well. Pineapples are tropical fruit and, once introduced, grow wild along the equator. Southern Queensland is, unfortunately, sub-tropical. Technology could grow pineapples at the South Pole and so it had around Brisbane. All that was needed was careful selection of sites to avoid frost and "very heavy" lashings of fertiliser. If the Golden Circle fruit were slower growing, the winter crop smaller, and more expensive, the simple explanation for a factory at Northgate, only 13 km from the Brisbane GPO, was that this had been closer to the original fresh markets.

While export prospects looked bleak, except as a premium line, the local market was inviting. It was protected by tariffs. What's more, Australian consumption of less than 1 lb of canned pineapple per head per year was one-third the American, by now the standard target. It was, in Seale's excited italics, the "logical *captive market*". So, in 1954, under John Brown's influence, the cannery reversed the policy accepted by so many primary producers. It decided to look after home markets first and only to export the surplus. Australians would pay higher prices to subsidise overseas "dumping".

The cannery raised extra capital, set up sales offices in Sydney and Melbourne and, since overseas markets were already saturated with juice, it decided to push juice first locally. Australia was not a "juice-conscious" market, it needed "educating". The sticky pineapple flavour was best cold, suggesting the softdrink channel. Calculations showed that a 7 oz bottle could be sold in Brisbane for a competitive 6d. Seale received a management edict: We need to begin bottling within three months for summer. "Second-hand bottling equipment was exceedingly scarce in the mid-50s and new equipment quite out of the question", he recalled. "In addition, early samples of bottled pineapple juice had the disconcerting habit of settling into a murky layer of sediment surmounted by a more or less clear and colourless liquid." Yet he met the deadline. The settling, due to natural pectic enzymes, was solved by heating and control of viscosity. He made do with an antiquated bottle washer and a vintage ginger-beer filler. In that first year they sold a million dozen bottles of pineapple juice.

The cannery began price-cutting its canned juice and the country's early supermarket chains, apparently sniffing success, began promoting pineapple juice as "specials". In 1955 juice sales trebled to 4·5 million cans and yet a million gallons went to waste. By dropping the price another shilling a dozen, sales the next year went to 7·5 million, and soon the cannery had to improve technology to wring out every last drop. Drinks had taken the brandname into houses, people liked the juice and "goodwill flowed over to the solid pineapple packs". With this success, the marketing people took to the board a proposal to begin advertising pineapple nationally. They justified this in the need to back up the small, but growing sales team, and to instill "greater brand familiarity" in preparation for the world over-supply expected before 1959. The board provided £10,000 for regular half-pages in the *Women's Weekly* and *Woman's Day*.

Local sales—by 1957 up to 7,700 tons—still could by no means absorb the total crop of around 45,000 tons. Partly because of pineapple competition, canners of peaches and apricots began cutting prices. So the pineapple people devised a plan. Golden Circle selling would become more coordinated, centrally-planned and more manipulative. It moved, in a word, into marketing. According to legend, this approach—where the firm's focus becomes not producing but selling—had just been developed by Proctor & Gamble in the US. It filled a gap left by the less personal supermarket. The essentials of marketing, which has come to dominate Australian eating, can be seen in Golden Circle's schemes for 1958.

To start with, the marketing people needed more information about what happened to their products. So they hired A. S. Neilsen Pty Ltd, the US market researchers who had established in Australia on Unilever's request in 1948. Their first report indicated, for instance, that Golden Circle sold better in the country than the city and also that there was very uneven stocking in stores, often with only one product on the self-service shelves. A survey showed that the multiplicity of brands gave peaches an average "exposure" of

14 ft of supermarket shelves, pears 9 ft and pineapples only 4½ ft. "There were too few brands to get the facings up and wider," researcher Vic Nicholson explained. The way to take up more room was to increase the cannery's own range, so that it in a sense would compete with itself.

Then, the marketing approach led to three interesting tactics. The first was called the policy of "singularity", a plan to disassociate pineapple from other canned fruits so as not to drag the protected, virtual monopoly down in price wars. They advertised an uncomplicated little character called "Pineapple Pete", but a more sophisticated answer would soon emerge. The second policy was "regular promotions", tied to the processing periods of the fruit. They would be: January–February, when summer harvesting was at a peak and buying most enthusiastic; June–July, when the winter crop was processed but when buying was slow; and October–November, to clear warehouses ready for summer again. The chains and groups, now dominating retailing, organised annual store programs, into which Golden Circle would fit. The basis of the promotions would be distributing recipes. Golden Circle's "Test Kitchen" came up with a clever idea for the first winter promotion. It was the "Pineapple Pie". Apple pies might be more traditional, but pineapple was palatable. "Winter is Pineapple Pie Time" was a tremendous success and sales figures for winter, 1958, suggested that we ate between one and two million pineapple pies.

The third policy, later to be known as "extended uses", aimed to educate the housewife to serve pineapple in other ways than just "sweets". Customers persuaded to use pineapple at breakfast, lunch and tea would clearly purchase more. The need for "volume sales" meant that "care must be taken to ensure that the consumer was not put to great trouble, or obliged to strain her budget . . . We must avoid exotic dishes including ingredients not readily available; and special occasion dishes requiring expensive ingredients . . . It meant creating versions of familiar, everyday dishes that included pineapple and could be presented in the most attractive way, pictorially."

The first step was to ask the consumer for ideas. The May 7, 1958, issue of the *Women's Weekly* announced a "splendid new cookery contest with big cash prizes" for recipes containing pineapples. Although the Golden Circle name was never mentioned throughout the weeks of the promotion, it backed the £1,235 award. By May 21, the magazine was hinting that American methods of incorporating pineapple might suggest ideas. "Newcomers might have some recipes of their homeland in which pineapple is used in a method not generally known in Australia," it said. No less than 10,000 recipes arrived, according to the cannery, or 40,000, according to the *Weekly*. Prize-winners were announced on August 27.

Mrs M. Finnis, a member of the Adelaide University Wives' Club (her husband was a philosophy lecturer), won the £100 first prize in the meat section, with "Braised Veal with Pineapple Nut Stuffing." The magazine said that, working in her charming Leabrook home with the help of teenage daughters, she had concocted the recipe from one in the London *Times*. The cake section was won by the "Spun-sugar Sponge" of 72-year-old Mrs Charlotte Walker of Mount Hawthorn, WA. Her love of luxury cooking came from the European blood in her veins, the magazine said. "My mother was born in Alsace-Lorraine, and her recipes were on the lines of Mrs Dione Lucas' and Mrs Beeton's." (American TV cook Dione Lucas had just toured the country, the *Weekly* publishing her 64-page Lift-Out Cook Book.) Mrs B. Haddock, who still used a fuel stove in a worker's cottage on "Golden Arrow" station at Hannaford, West Queensland, won the dessert section with "Pineapple Rhubarb Tart". And, believe it or not, the Grand Champion Prize went, as the *Weekly* blazed, to a "glamorous 21-year-old model from Victoria".

Pat Glover had visited Hawaii two years earlier as "Miss Teenage" and had collected lots of pineapple and other fruit recipes. A former domestic science teacher, she was now a fashion and television model. "I'm being married on August 28, and there are so many things I could do with the prize," she said. "We've been having Sunday parties painting the flat, and while our friends helped Graeme to paint I cooked for them, and it has been great fun." The £5 progress prize she won for "Russian Fruit Gingerbread" had gone on paint for the flat. The £500 was for her recipe for "Pineapple Gourmet Dessert", displayed a few issues later in colour. It was a construction of pineapple icecream, covered with chopped pineapple, banana and ginger and then smothered with pineapple marshmallow. Whipped cream was piped on top and then it was all trickled with melted nut-milk chocolate.

It was now 1959, smart to cook with pineapple, and, as expected, the world market collapsed, pineapple prices dropping from $80 to $40 a ton. With Seale's attention, the factory was operating more efficiently, its output reaching one million cans daily, handled with less overtime. The Neilsen report showed some powerful chains resisted promoting and even, in some cases, stocking Golden Circle. So extra sales representatives were appointed and, to sell record production, £60,000 was devoted to advertising, although at 1·6 per cent of the previous year's sales, this seemed inadequate to the marketing people.

The cannery had been encouraging inspections by southern tourists. The first year the Pioneer bus company put the plant on its list of showplaces, 20,000 visitors came to see "The King of Fruits, By Nature Crowned". Publicity for the Gold Coast and the Barrier Reef encouraged the belief that these were tropical paradises. Golden Circle found its Tropical Fruit Salad far outsold competing tinned fruit salads. "In fact," the cannery decided, "there was sufficient evidence to suggest that the word 'tropical' had some magic powers and that these powers could be used to distinguish our pineapple." In February, 1959, the word "tropical" was added to all labels—so it became "Golden Circle Tropical Pineapple", decorated with coconut palms. Not that the cans contained coconut, or, for that matter, that the pineapple was even grown in the tropics. The labels were not changed too dramatically and little by little more space was given to the tropical background. Cut-out coconut palms for displays were so magic that stores purloined them even for making fresh fruit more attractive.

To emphasise the singular "tropical" appeal, the cannery sent photographers to cooperating resort islands like South Molle and Hayman to take shots of "named scenes" for colour magazines and television. For summer, it advocated "Serve Salads Tropic Style" (a "volume dish and a simple one"). Slices remained the best product for advertising purposes, since "slices allowed the best visual display for pineapple, favouring clear product identification." But stores now promoted every Golden Circle line and customers recognised a Golden Circle product at a glance. In March and November, 1960, it joined Kia-ora to push Baked Beans and Pineapple. A similar deal with Tongala for Fruit Salad and Cream brought "mutually good results". Golden Circle gave up distributing printed recipe leaflets—its labels could carry recipes. By the end of 1961, it had, in effect, distributed 30 million recipes at negligible cost.

There were now "many indications of the brand's strength". A big chain store "specialled" another brand with the claim that it had "Golden Circle quality". Women's magazines included more and more pineapple recipes unpaid. Ideas for new dishes arrived unsolicited from housewives. In a long-term campaign to increase the ways pineapples were served, it promoted its first lift-out recipe book in *Woman's Day* in June, 1961. The best advertising might be "word-of-mouth", but this diffusion had to start somewhere, and the cannery's continuation of this expensive approach must indicate its confidence. Golden Circle had now got up its momentum, but . . . "As Newton observed, it takes less force to maintain momentum than to initiate it . . ." so the publicity continued. Week in week out about two million cans of Golden Circle pineapple toppled off Australia's supermarket shelves.

The experience represents much of what happened to food in the second half of the twentieth century. The company expanded its product range through research, by which it also cut labour costs. Its decision to concentrate its easily distributed canned article on lucrative local markets coincided with the rise of national supermarketing and single-minded and sophisticated selling techniques. This competition between brands and foods profoundly changed eating in the "affluent society", as J. K. Galbraith termed it in 1958. One way, brought out by the pineapple's history, has been the exploitation of a bewildering variety of recipes and colour photographs. Dishes, once in the tender hands of tradition and the natural dictates of crop and season, were now professionally devised to meet sales needs. The recipe sections of the *Weekly* and *Woman's Day* crowned Australian cuisine with the pineapple ring.

13

The industrial kitchen

Identifying gaps on the supermarket shelves, large food corporations shaped, coloured, flavoured and marketed food to fit

IN THE 1970s economists hailed the "integrated research-product-packaging-promotion-distribution operation". With sophisticated production methods, large food corporations, frequently overseas-owned, reached supermarket customers through aggressive marketing techniques. With labels stressing attributes like "instant", "no fuss" and "30-second", new products included entirely prepared foods like dried soups, tinned meat balls, tube mayonnaise, packet cake mix and even frozen complete dinners. "Fastfood" outlets proliferated. Even when not providing the finished article, the food business intruded into the kitchen with recipes showing how to use its products. We had gained "convenience" foods.

The onslaught of "convenience" foods—defined in the dictionary as "needing very little preparation and used whenever one wishes"—finished off our long history of "meat three times a day". A common breakfast became sugary packet muesli and reconstituted orange juice. The abbreviated lunch was a frozen pizza with crinkle-cut chips and salad out of a can. Afternoon-tea was a clear-wrapped cake with tea-bags or a between-meal snack of chocolate bar and artificially-flavoured milk. At work, the making of a cup of coffee was entrusted to the Café-Bar, invented by an Australian cigarette vending machine company in 1964 to dispense coffee powder, milk powder and sugar. And dinner—no longer always called "tea", and often taken before the television set—was a mish-mash of styles and seasons, with frozen ravioli, dried chow-mein, icecream and topping, "international gourmet sensations" taken from "cordon bleu" cookery cards, or a Big Mac.

Looking at what had happened historically, we could see that, after the basic rations of the seafaring age and the manufactured commodities of the railways, the machine now made everything. Our two-century retreat from agrarian eating had industrialised the garden, the pantry and now the kitchen. Big food companies, already in charge of growing, preservation and distribution, took over cooking.

It was all a predictable economic outcome given that stomachs are reasonably inelastic, so that profits could not be boosted by selling greater quantity. Instead, firms had to sell food in more expensive forms, or, in economic language, with extra "value added". A company could charge more for the frozen cake than the flour. In other words, much of the cooking previously done in homes was now shifted to the factory.

Australia's 3,500 food factories employed about 200,000 people in sometimes repetitive or dangerous work. To the traditional culinary repertoire, the factory kitchens added new continuous-process techniques, novel forms of ingredients like "pumpable plastic shortenings" and an extensive list of chemical additives. All so that the home cook would forget how to make pastry, custard, salad dressing, gravy and even mashed potatoes. It was just a matter of opening the Deb, Rice-a-Riso and White Wings or reheating frozen food as if we were stranded on an international jetflight. Entirely abandoning the chopping board, we could dine out with the "foodservice" industry, including an unprecedented number of restaurants. Convenience products made for caterers were called "pre-prepared" foods.

With supermarket selling, the processors manipulated both food and us. Market researchers identified gaps, food scientists devised new styles of foods, packaging companies created fetching guises, home economists found recipes to sell them, and advertising agencies presented us with persuasive social models. Magazines alternated pages promoting gluttony with weight-reduction diets. Television advertising of foods—amounting to around $2 million a day in 1980—was almost exclusively for prepared snacks, icecreams, softdrinks and takeaway meals. Cadbury's boasted in full-page ads for the retail trade that: "We're on the screen so often you'd think we own the stations."

The takeover by the industrial kitchen, virtually complete in the 1970s, was scarcely noticed and yet it trivialised nutrition, freshness and cooking. In 1982, the Broadcasting Tribunal reported that heavily-viewing children ate more advertised foods and had less nutritional knowledge. More than half the eight and nine-year-olds watched television during dinner and believed that advertising character, Ronald McDonald, "knows what's good for kids to eat". A Melbourne survey by Professor Arvi Sali found that one-third of schoolchildren ate no fruit and one-quarter ate no vegetables.

Employing the crude taste sensations of sugar, fat and salt, highly-advertised food added to bowel problems, heart disease, cancer, dental caries and obesity. Yet, with diet causing alarm, the most outrageous product would be advertised with the labels "health", "natural", "energy" and "low-fat". The food industry deliberately endowed the processed article with all the opposite virtues. Battery eggs were promoted as "Country Farm" eggs. Kelloggs adopted the brandname "Papa Giuseppe", Coles used "Farmland" and Petersville "Nanna's" to steal agrarian and homely values. In the late 1970s, the giant US corporation Heinz purchased the Weight Watchers name.

Frozen food was represented as "fresh". Birds Eye stressed that "freshness is not simply requested, it's insisted upon. It's a subject we take very seriously." On television, Papa Giuseppe said its quiche lorraine was snap-frozen so that you could enjoy it "fresh from your own oven". Reporting on television ads to the Anzaas congress in 1975, Margaret Tebbutt commented: "The theme of the healthy, happy family often including three generations suggests the retention of traditions of wise nutritional behaviour."

Labour-saving

To persuade us to abandon old customs had taken a long campaign in favour of "labour-saving" or "convenience" foods. In the 1930s, Foster Clark had recommended substituting its custard powder for eggs. "The hand of progress is nowhere more apparent than in the kitchen," the ad declared. "The manufactured food products have eliminated many of the laborious and expensive cooking procedures which were formerly an indispensable part of the housewife's labours." In the *Women's Weekly* in the 1940s, Kellogg's advertised cornflakes as the "30 second breakfast". Kraft said Oslo lunches with its cheese required, "No cooking. Ready in a jiffy." Meanwhile, asserting "3 meals *not* enough", Cadbury's offered milk chocolate as the "convenient and sensible extra meal". By 1980, a recipe from "Jan Oldham's Kitchen" in the *Woman's Day* could actually use tinned pumpkin for pumpkin soup. "We've made this soup ever-so-easy to make by turning to the store cupboard and whipping open a can of pumpkin," Oldham explained. "Of course, you could make it from scratch using 500 g (1 lb) fresh chopped pumpkin, but it will take longer to make."

Historian Beverley Kingston, chronicling the changing role of Australian women between about 1860 and 1930, noted the "gradual decline in the status of ordinary housewives as they relinquished their claim to and knowledge of pre-industrial skills". With cooking taken out of the home, the status of ordinary housewives declined further. Much was made by the industry of the "convenience demanded by housewives increasingly working outside the home". However, some women felt the loss of cooking.

Writing about *Women's Work: Men's Work* (1979), English writer Virginia Novarra listed woman's "six tasks" which "pre-date the money economy, and all of them arise from a bedrock of necessity". The tasks were: bearing children, cultivating gardens, clothing people, tending the sick and frail, educating and nurturing children, and looking after the home. To Novarra, this was real work, while men played games, often destructive. "The superstructures of self-aggrandisement, empire-building, industrial conflict, and the sheer wanton waste and misuse of resources cannot all be respectably cloaked by the dignity of the appellation of 'work'," she said. If she were right, then the food industry had played its brutish part in demeaning not just "women's work", but real work. Like potting, spinning and gardening, cooking had become an anachronistic hobby. Eat, drink and be automated.

Designed food

Softdrinks had become much more sophisticated in the century since John S. Pemberton invented Coca-Cola. The report of the Hoover awards for Australian marketing in 1975 provided the case of "Solo". Foreign multinationals had now swallowed up the small softdrink firms once dotting our towns. Coca-Cola held about 38 per cent of the business, Cadbury-Schweppes 32 and Amatil 13. Similarly, the cola flavour accounted for about 35 per cent, lemonade 20, orange 15, mixers 10 and lemon 2. The British Schweppes group feared we might reach the American level of 65 per cent cola consumption and so, in 1973, it launched its prize-winning marketing exercise—to create an image, then make a product to match.

Schweppes decided to aim a new product at the "lone male adventurist", the Hoover judges said. The more adult and male, the more removed from childhood associations. "Any female intrusion would reduce the brand's adultness," they argued. Lemon squash of the pubs had "acceptable nostalgia in male terms". The label had to have beer connotations, and the final design was strongly influenced by the American Budweiser beer brand. And the name which fitted was "Solo". Only when the objectives, packaging and advertising were prepared were the Schweppes chemists and flavouring supplier briefed on the desired drink.

They struck at a trial "bullseye" audience of males of 18 to 25 years in October, 1973, and Solo-drinking developed quickly into "almost a cult", the Hoover prize report said. "Post-launch evaluation" pointed to the need for television commercials stressing a consuming thirst, speed, vitality, masculinity, individualistic action, no machinery, a spice of danger and an anti-social spilling sequence of drink dribbling down the chin. They found a "Solo man" of "outstanding male/female acceptability", sports teacher Michael Ace, who performed strenuous athletic sequences. By the end of the summer of 1975, Solo was second only in softdrink sales to Coke.

That was how the industrial kitchen worked. Food was scientifically formed and flavoured to fit marketing models. It now needed to be labelled with a list of artificial flavours, colours, emulsifiers, antioxidants, etc, and was elaborately packaged, aggressively advertised, often bad for us and horrible.

They even tried to make an old Australian favourite like passionfruit part of the manufacturer's palette. Soon after General Foods of the US took over Cottee's in 1966, the maker of "Passiona" advertised in trade magazines: "Passionfruit Unlimited... Food technologists and marketing have recognised its potential as a fruit flavouring for many years... Now Cottee's announce an unlimited supply of passionfruit available in many forms... Frozen juice. Frozen pulp. Sweetened juice. Sweetened pulp. Preservatised juice. Preservatised pulp. And, for the first time anywhere in the world, concentrated frozen juice... Consider the many ways you can use passionfruit to stimulate sales among your product ranges. Icecreams, liqueurs, fruit salads and drinks, cordials and cake mixes..."

Entirely new products replaced traditional foods, as in the case of margarine. An offshoot last century of the soap and candle industry, margarine's raw materials remained largely beef fat and extras like whaleoil, which were subjected to "fractionation, inter-esterification with special emulsions, chill working and resting and then coloured and flavoured". The dairy industry, representing so many "cow cockies", had responded defensively, enlisting government controls, such as quotas on margarine production. Between the wars, cookery books drummed in simple messages, page after page, "Eat real butter—avoid imitations". However, with an advertising campaign in the 1960s, and featuring housewife "Mrs Jones", the margarine companies burst the quotas. Advertising poly-unsaturated vegetable oils, and thus exploiting the cholesterol scare, they lifted sales until in 1977 margarine outsold butter.

The dairy marketing board decided, if not licking them, to join them in aggressive selling. A special soft butter, to resemble more spreadable margarine, flopped. However, they triumphed with another innovation, long-life milk, which could keep unrefrigerated a good six months, its odd taste disguised with heavy flavouring. This answer to the industry's old enemy, freshness, was christened with suitably synthetic names, Big M and Moov. Now producers could distribute to pop concerts and sporting events and, most importantly, move into marketing.

The flavourist

Ian Wightwick, chief chemist of essence manufacturers Bush Boake Allen Australia, was the sort of person the industry would approach for advice on flavouring milk. You needed an adequate flavour, sufficient sweetener and an attractive colour, he counselled in a paper in 1970. The CSIRO had ascertained that the most palatable level of fat was lower in flavoured milk, somewhere nearer two per cent. So you would need to label it "flavoured skimmed (or non-fat) milk", he said. Chocolate was the most popular flavour for milk and he advised supplementing it with chocolate and vanilla booster flavours, together with a dose of salt. The optimum sugar level varied, but he might have recommended 3½ lbs per 10 gallons for chocolate, coffee, caramel or vanilla, while 3 lbs sufficed for fruit flavours. Then, skimmed milk powder could be added to boost the "body" and "mouth feel" of the drink.

The food industry had to add flavours to food for two basic reasons. Firstly, food processing often removed much natural flavour and texture and so chemicals simulated or boosted the original product. Secondly, flavours were used to produce novel foods. Wightwick described these as "aesthetic" or "luxury" foods, and included beverages, confectionery and icecream. "Many food companies", he wrote in 1973, "are desperately attempting to develop new and unusual types of food, quite unrelated to anything occurring in nature and to use their advertising skills to create a consumer demand for such products."

Flavours could be extracted from natural products—distilled from peel, bark, herbs and so forth, he said. And the development of organic chemistry last century led to an enormous range of synthetic organic chemicals, some identified in natural flavours but some so far undiscovered in nature. Natural vanilla flavour was obtained from the cured fruit of a tropical orchid. Fluctuating prices led to successive copies, the first in 1874 being pretty expensive itself. But "vanillin" became a relatively cheap by-product of the sulphite treatment of wood pulp, Wightwick said. Better copies were then blended of a number of chemicals, like the creamy flavouring modifiers 3-hydroxy-2-methyl-gammapyrone and newer and stronger, 3-hydroxy-2-ethyl-gammapyrone.

Blending made the flavour chemist, or "flavourist", as "much of an artist as a chemist", according to Wightwick. Writing about vanilla history, he was even moved to question the loss of the "superb flavour character of genuine vanilla". Perhaps, he wrote, "the tremendous growth of pre-processed foods is destroying the opportunity for finer vanilla flavours to be appreciated due to both processing methods and to severe cost competition". He hoped one day vanilla might be duplicated in the same manner as strawberry, yet, ironically, the superior copy might be rejected by those familiar with the earlier and cruder synthetic blends.

By modern standards, the flavours before the Second World War seemed fairly simple, he said. Yet their impact had been astounding and the food industry still demanded the crude, "traditional" flavours for many uses. Flavouring synthetics took a dramatic leap after the arrival of gas liquid chromatography in 1952, which had found more than 100 separate chemicals in the aroma of the apple. More than 210 chemicals had been identified in roasted coffee. By 1958, the technique enabled a number of companies to unleash a series of new orange flavours. Later, flavours reproduced tastes formed during preparation: for instance, roast meat flavour and artificial smoked flavour.

Food technology

Not only flavour, but all other attributes of food could be tricked up. Food additives included: flavours, colours, nutrients, bleaching agents, acids, preservatives, leavening agents, antioxidants (preventing rancidity), sequestrants (settling out), emulsifiers and stabilisers (separation), humectants (drying out), lustres, anti-foaming agents, whipping agents, thickeners, fillers, etc. Factories commonly worked with odd forms like powdered milk, dried eggs, pumpable margarine. Using enlarged kitchen gadgets, there were whips, mousses and even "meat" spun out of soya beans for sausages, ravioli and other products. Fruit and vegetables which were too small, blemished or machine-damaged could be mashed and then reformed into nicely uniform pieces. "Additional ingredients" could make these fabricated fruits and vegetables even more acceptable to the consumer, the chief researcher for Letona Foods, Mr J. Schwab, told a food science conference in 1979.

Under Australian law, the use of food additives had to be justified on the basis of "necessity". But that begged the question of how necessary it was for kitchen tasks to be done in the factory. If food suffered in processing, was it "necessary" to attempt to simulate the colour, texture and vitality of fresh food? How "necessary" were icecreams, margarines and confectionery that needed emulsifiers and fake flavours, and frozen desserts that needed thickening agents? How "necessary" was a counterfeit like margarine?

Dr Keith Farrer, chief Kraft food technologist, argued in favour of additives at the Anzaas science congress in 1975. Complaining of the "emotionalism" of opponents, and at the same time indicating how disturbing the problem had become, he asked whether you would prefer:

> loaves of bread which are dark brown in colour, harsh in flavour and heavy in texture, and which spoil rapidly, instead of the range of attractive, good keeping breads currently available? Would you put up with oil products of varying degrees of rancidity? Do you want food items free of colour (eg icecream, jellies, toppings, etc)? Do you want sausages and mincemeat to disappear? Do you want prepared mayonnaise to separate? Do you want mushy canned tomatoes, or trouble with your salt shaker, or cake batters that don't rise properly? If your answer to any or all of the above is no then you must accept food additives.

If we were able to put the questions to Edward Abbott, our "aristologist" who last century revelled in un-Farrered food, then he might happily eat brown bread unassisted chemically, accept lasting olive oil, churn icecream out of fresh cream and fruits, be pleased to use traditional sausage spices, clamp a meat mincer to the kitchen table, actually make fresh mayonnaise, bottle his own tomatoes, bake his own sponge cake and even, if pushed, use a salt-mill. But you see, capital had insinuated itself into the food supply and could make so much more out of prefabricated food than the wholesome, homely article.

Market research

Slaving alongside the "flavourist" and other chemical chefs in the industrial kitchen were professionals dreaming up, selling and monitoring the factory feast. Fundamental to the Orwellian world was market research. One of the pioneers in this country was Sylvia Ashby, who in the late 1940s set up the Ashby Consumer Panel to reveal attitudes and habits to many food manufacturers. After helping with biscuits, Christmas cakes and advertising, she received a letter from the Arnott's company in 1959 to say that "we always feel that your panels represent 'the people' and give us accurate information as to what they are thinking and why they are, or are not, buying certain products . . ." McNair Anderson, which for 17 years from 1959 surveyed which advertisements were read each issue of *Women's Weekly*, also conducted an annual "Soft Drinks Barometer" for Coca-Cola. The ASRB company's panel of 3,000 families answering postal questionnaires sampled five tons of Heinz soup in the first six months of 1965. Mike Larbalestier of Marplan imported an Eye Camera in 1965 to cart around shopping centre laboratories to measure dilation of the pupil to test the interest in television commercials for Carnation milk, Nestlé chocolate, Coca-Cola and the shield symbol which went on Edgell packs. People did not like the taste of commercial yoghurt, so Vic Nicholson recommended emphasising added flavours like Spiced Apple. Prying into all kinds of eating behaviour, Dr Peter Kenny in Sydney found Passiona drink to be consumed mainly by middle-aged women as a private indulgence.

Home economists

The needs of colonial feeding had been satisfied by Caroline Chisholm's "Bush Cookery" of just seven recipes. The store-shelf of processed ingredients in the early twentieth century had demanded the *Commonsense, Miss Schauer's, CWA, Green and Gold* and other equally plain texts. Now the coup in the kitchen unleashed a babel of recipes—countless books, magazine pages and leaflets parading labour-saving "food ideas", which reduced cooking to dinner-party flourishes. Instead of timeless routine, the industry glorified novelty, immediacy and the final product. "Add your own individuality with the finishing touches." Use one small tin for "instant elegance". Sweeten, fatten and boost with sugar, cream and a stockcube. It was difficult to end a meal with an honest piece of fruit or cheese—they were harder to provide than the dressed-up article.

Utterly unembarrassed by commercialism, cooking stars like Margaret Fulton and Bernard King launched dishes to promote a brandname. Research for the NSW Egg Board in 1981 showed that 85 per cent of consumers rated Peter Russell-Clarke as a "good" or "excellent" presenter, being seen as "knowledgeable, believable, a food expert and fun to watch and hear". And behind these showbiz cooks was a crew of "home economists". Since the optimistic launching of their profession late last century, many had been reduced to devising recipes for marketing departments.

"Advertising? It's everywhere," glowed J. Walter Thompson home economist, Pauline M. Holden, when revealing "how advertising changes food habits" at a nutrition conference in Canberra in 1971. "Advertising informs, educates and persuades," she said. Housewives no longer needed to make out shopping lists since advertising had created an awareness and consumers could identify the products at the store. Mothers might purchase special treats "to cement family relationships . . . Requests may have come after dining in a restaurant, eating at a friend's place, seeing a cookery television program, or looking at a food advertisement in a magazine," she said. Visual presentation of food, especially in colour, "shows appetite appeal as well as ease of preparation."

Food fashions changed, "not as frequently as clothes—but nonetheless they change," she said. Compare the photographs of salads with those 10 years earlier. "Salad dressing manufacturers have been quick to realise that the tired old lettuce leaf with an odd assortment of garnishes was not going to encourage anyone to buy and sample their products." Exciting new salad recipes in magazine supplements and store advertising "definitely increased" sales of salad dressings. The endorsement of products by "leading Cookery Experts" further influenced women. Twenty years previously, Australians knew little of cake or pastry mixes. Now thousands of housewives used them, the ingredients conveniently weighed out. But there was a twist: "Manufacturers of these goods still allow the housewives plenty of opportunity to use their imagination by leaving some ingredients out, which the housewives must add." Advertising had also "helped sell the concept of freezer-living", which, in turn, was "slowly but surely changing the housewife's life".

Shelley Smart, home economist at Mauri's grocery products division, explained her role in 1978 with the "Forget the Recipe" range of "cook-in" sauces. She was first asked to replicate in her test kitchen four best-selling British varieties—Red Wine, Tomato & Onion, Curry and Sweet & Sour. Then she altered them to suit the marketing department's "profile" of the average Australian palate (a fascinating insight which she would not enlarge upon for me). The company laboratories formulated factory samples which matched her kitchen batches. Next, Smart devised three recipes for each sauce for market research using "in-home replacement". An advertising agency was called in to help find the name, "Forget the Recipe", to design labels and to plan media strategy. The agency hired Bernard King to do six commercials, and to feature the sauce prominently for five weeks on his

"King's Kitchen" program. She now approached the "toughest part of my brief".

For the six commercials she had to find recipes that were very short, very simple and yet carried "impact". For King's program, she had to develop 30 recipes which used everyday ingredients and yet which, when taken from the oven, looked a "meal fit for a king". She had to produce a promotional recipe book, recipes for *Women's Weekly* and *Family Circle* and dishes for colour photographs. And she had to brief cookery editors of papers and magazines for articles about the cook-in sauce. "Timing was important because the articles could not appear before the scheduled launch by the sales force," she said.

The food editor of *New Idea*, Anne Marshall, explained to a Canberra seminar in 1975 that she had about 90 per cent "carte blanche" in planning her two weekly columns. Apart from requesting at least two articles on "budget" and two on Chinese cookery each year, her male editor left planning to her. The odd exception was when the higher echelons decided to enter a circulation war and she had to think up some topical cookery themes with catchy titles for advertising purposes. Her readers weren't sophisticated, socially-minded *Vogue* or *Epicurean* readers, so she couldn't afford to be too exotic or too expensive.

"You start by planning your seasonal articles," she described. Christmas and New Year took up several weeks. Easter could take up two. Then came the annual features such as packed lunches when children went back to school, kitchen teas during the wedding season, pancakes for pancake day, preserving, jam-making and pickling, food for your Valentine, feeding toddlers, children's parties, recipes for children to cook in holidays, cooking for fêtes, a Melbourne Cup lunch, and so on. Add to this your seasonal articles such as summer fruits, cool salads and barbecues or slimming for summer and soups and casseroles and yeast cookery in winter. That didn't leave many weeks to fill in. But "sometimes you can run out of original ideas and it's simply marvellous to have a trip overseas if you can organise it, in order to get your batteries recharged."

Perhaps the most fascinating of the home economist's jobs was explained to me in Sydney in 1981 by Ann Fayle, highly regarded as a "food stylist". She'd trained at the East Sydney food school with Margaret Fulton and worked 13 years with Unilever, until it bought Rosella and decided to move its test kitchen to Melbourne. She went freelance. "A company would say, we've got all these mashed up peas and carrots, what can we do with them?" she said, explaining the job of product development. "I'd suggest a baby food or soup or something, although by the time they produced for a price and mediocre consumer tastes, it'd be nothing like my recommendation. A lot of mass products tend to be appalling." Through the 1970s, Fayle became a specialist "food stylist", preparing food for colour photography. After years working for Streets, she specialised in getting virtually every icecream advertised looking delicious. "Devondale used to fake it up with mashed potato, because the tungsten lamps bore holes in it. I became the only lady game enough to use the real thing. Now it's all right because the photographers use electronic flash."

For a television shot where a spoon came in, she knew how to scoop icecream right the first time, showing the texture off at its most delectable. "If it needs beautiful fingers it has to be a model, but they usually tend to be dumb and take all day. The same with carving turkey, usually they go through millions of turkeys. I can do it first up, or chicken on the breast." Ann Fayle appeared to look down on her audience, and did not even eat icecream, "only fresh from the factory," she said. "The same with Sara Lee, when they do it in the factory, it tastes great, but after a week in the freezers . . . I don't think Australians understand the subtleties of food, but they're definitely turned on by something in their mouth. When I returned from overseas, I was struck by the number of people in the streets feeding their faces. I think it's a psychological deficiency, or whatever."

Fastfood

We had always enjoyed street snacks, but cars brought American-style "fastfood". Fastfood was highly-standardised, advertised and packaged cooking sold by roadside chains like Kentucky Fried Chicken, Pizza Hut and McDonald's. Maurice and Richard McDonald's prototype opened in 1948 in San Bernardino in southern California. The clean, efficient complex with distinctive twin red arches suited the emerging society of housing tracts, shopping centres, industrial parks and busy freeways. Within six years, the McDonalds had ordered eight "six-shake" machines from Chicago salesman, Ray Kroc. A 52-year-old who had tried various money-making schemes, Kroc visited California to discover what kind of hamburger stand could want to make so many milkshakes at once. He decided this was the opportunity of a lifetime, eventually bought out the McDonalds and replicated the operation into the world's biggest restaurant chain.

The hamburger suited the brief menu since its supply scarcely varied with seasons. And the clearly defined steps in its preparation could be carried out by cheap, malleable teenagers. Kroc insisted that each place run according to a rigid "system". Similarly, Harland Sanders based the second big American takeaway formula, Kentucky Fried Chicken, on the juicy results of the pressure cooker on battery, and thus year-round, fowls. He was appalled that his "secret" gravy was compromised during the rapid expansion after the business was bought in 1964 by two Nashville men.

"Colonel Sanders" reached Australia in 1968, followed in 1970 by McDonald's and Pizza Hut. As forces in the food industry's final capture of the kitchen, such chains grew explosively—which suited them to the franchise system, selling rights to local converts. Like followers of a materialistic sect, the franchise holders learnt mottos like "KISS—Keep It Simple, Stupid" and "If you've got time to lean you've got time to clean."

When a graduate in food technology from the University of NSW, Lawrence Milani, tackled the American giants in 1971, his Pizza Inn had the right ideas. "We don't want waiters or prima donna chefs," he explained to a newspaper. "We want to eliminate everyone from the kitchen"—instead, a microwave oven reheated production-line food. Another local food technologist, trying to set up Mr Chips, Harley Antill, praised the "systems operation". He explained: "We want unskilled labour that can be trained to do it by numbers."

But the biggest operators—themselves being bought up by the large food corporations—could buy the best sites, install the complete décor, research the right equipment, arrange the supply from the most convenient processors, pay for the smartest advertising and attract the most committed franchise holders. Instead of peeling potatoes, consumers now peeled open a clammy cardboard box and tugged the corner off a plastic sachet. Instead of choosing their own recipes, they put their faith in the corporate chef at McDonald's "Hamburger Central" in Chicago, its nearby campus of "Hamburger U" awarding Bachelors of Hamburgerology.

The oligopolies

The flavour chemists, food technologists, market researchers, home economists and hamburgerologists were minions within a diminished number of bigger corporations. The gaudy flavours, toy colours and artificial aromas were produced by local names like CSR, CUB, Adelaide Steamship, Castlemaine-Tooheys, Swan, Petersville, Allied Mills, Arnott, Mauri, Inghams, Elders-IXL and a handful of big grower cooperatives, and by foreign names like George Weston, Reckitt & Colman, Unilever, Amatil, Nestlé, Cadbury-Schweppes, Kraft, Kellogg and Heinz. Between them they manufactured just about every brand-name Australians recognised on supermarket shelves. Allied Mills produced, for instance, Buttercup, Siebers and some Vogel breads and Meadowlea and Daffodil margarine.

With the supermarket, dozens of family food factories—often "household names" within one State—had sold out. They found they could not compete with the nationally-advertised article, from a larger factory, with access to more capital, and with more managerial and technical expertise. This centralised control from smaller capitals to Sydney and Melbourne and to New York and London. We could have been eating anywhere in the advanced world, since even local companies steered by northern stars. In the early 1970s, the Bureau of Statistics found that foreign intervention in food and beverage manufacture accounted for one-quarter of ownership, employment and "value added". In general, UK firms had sought to swallow existing companies, while American firms grew of their own accord.

Think of old favourites like Cherry Ripes and Freddo Frogs. MacRobertson was now taken over by Cadbury-Schweppes of the UK. What about Violet Crumbles and Polly Waffles? These Hoadley treats were produced by UK giant, Rowntree, which also had Sweetacre's Fantales, Jaffas and Minties. Vegemite was gone to US Kraft. As for the meat pie and tomato sauce, British George Weston was our biggest pie maker, with "Big Ben". Bunge, the world's largest private company, had the biggest single pie factory, Herbert Adams in Melbourne. Rosella, Fountain and Heinz tomato sauce were all foreign. Our traditional beverage of tea was also overseas-controlled. When Alfred Thomas Bushell had founded his business in Brisbane in 1883, he was in fact married to a family member of the giant English tea company, Brooke Bond. In 1978, when Bushells and its brands like Inglis, Billy, Lanchoo and Goldenia held well over half the country's tea business, the government, "cognizant of a long-standing commitment of the major family shareholders", permitted the English firm to buy it out.

Many local mergers were designed to pre-empt bids by incoming multinationals. For instance, by the end of the 1950s, the Peters company under Mr E. Christensen saw the need to expand, partly to protect itself from acquisition by Unilever. It bought Four 'n Twenty Pies, then Edgell's (which brought the names Edgell, Triangle, Birds Eye and Farmer Ed). It also purchased Socomin, Presto and in 1969 the Sydney half of F. A. B. Peters' enterprises, which had grown into Consolidated Milk Industries. In 1978, the chairman of Petersville, Sir Charles McGrath, boasted that sales were averaging $1.1 million daily. It sold 500,000 cans of food, 500,000 packets of frozen food, 60,000 pies, pasties and sausage rolls and over 500 kilometres of smallgoods daily. The 5,500 employees worked at its own five farms, 26 factories and more than 50 sales and distribution centres. This combine was then bought by H. C. Sleigh, formerly a petrol company. As this book went to press, Sleigh was under attack from Adelaide Steamship, which already controlled Tooths, Penfolds, etc.

While free market competition might occur between greengrocers and restaurants, it tended to mean nothing when it came to food manufacturers, "competing" brands owned by the same one or two firms. By 1974, Arnott's was reported to possess 70 per cent of the biscuit market, selling Iced VoVos, Adora Cream Wafers, Nice, Saos, Jatz and Yo Yos. It also integrated "vertically", meaning that it bought up its suppliers, which didn't extend as far as sugar refiners, CSR, the country's "oldest monopoly". It was all like a giant game of "Monopoly", which, incidentally, belonged to Parker Brothers, a wholly-owned subsidiary of an American food giant, General Mills.

FROZEN FOOD

DURING THE 1960s, Australians became extraordinarily big pea eaters. Sales multiplied eight-fold in the decade. It was because peas were the grape-shot of the frozen food industry. By 1970, each of us ate around 3.5 kg of frozen peas a year, four times as many as Americans, for example. To understand why peas caught on might explain modern eating. Because it was never obvious that we needed frozen peas—when we enjoyed abundant fresh food.

The quick-freezing business was dreamt up by an American, Clarence Birdseye, on an icy visit to Labrador, Canada, in 1915. Snap freezing of small packets was said to reduce damage to the cells of the food, and quickened the process to conveyor-belt speeds. It was no overnight success, however. By the mid-1920s, Birdseye's first plant in New York had tested the market. Then, in 1930, a much larger company, General Foods, launched the Birds Eye label throughout the US. It was not regarded as an essential industry in wartime Britain, and Unilever emerged as the owner of Birds Eye rights there and in Canada, New Zealand and Australia. There had been limited experiments here and use for crayfish exports and Qantas meals. Now Unilever would attempt to create a national market.

The general manager of Unilever's Birds Eye subsidiary in Australia, E. J. McCarthy, told a meeting of Sydney chemists in 1950 that he expected a slog. He needed top quality ingredients to withstand the rigours of freezing. He had to hold stocks for up to a year at lower than normal temperatures to maintain quality. Next, he had to convince shops to install freezers, preferably also at minus 18 degrees C, something it was to take decades to achieve. It made for "high" capital costs, he said. On top of that, he had to persuade consumers who had little trouble finding fresh food year round that they needed Birds Eye Farm Fresh Frosted Foods—"fresh" being linguistic sleight-of-hand, and "frosted" sounding more edible than "frozen".

Birds Eye started processing at Batlow, in collaboration with the Batlow Packing House Co-op Ltd. To stagger the season, it would take crops from four districts—berry fruits, brussels sprouts and late peas from the typical NSW tableland climate at Batlow and Tumbarumba, and beans, sweet corn and early peas from the warmer south-west slopes at Tumut and Gundagai. It installed two 30-place "multi-plate frosters", the pride and joy of the Birds Eye process, in time for the asparagus harvest of October, 1949. It froze a list of 13 other vegetables and fruits through till the next July. With the imported lines, including fish fillets, the range was surprisingly big.

Selling in tins would have been technically superior, but the danger of consumers storing them at normal temperatures was too great. Instead, it adopted the typical cardboard packet with plastic lining. It sold initially in

Sydney and then Orange, NSW, through two dozen stores using old-style icecream cabinets. It appointed an icecream distributor as Queensland agent in 1953. By the time it reached Victoria in 1956, Birds Eye advertised green peas, green beans, cauliflower, broccoli, sweetcorn, loganberries, pineapple pieces, sliced peaches and fruit salad.

The going proved every inch as slippery as expected, and in June, 1959, Unilever sold the name and facilities to collaborators, Gordon Edgell and Sons, soon to merge with Petersville. Unilever continued selling its frozen fish through Birds Eye, and also moved into the icecream business, buying up companies throughout 1959–61.

The success of frozen food seems to have commenced the year that Unilever sold out. That was presumably associated with the opening of the roll-on and roll-off shipping between Melbourne and northern Tasmania. Now the centre of production shifted from NSW to Tasmania and out poured the peas. Contributing to success, International Canners in Tasmania had introduced the distinctive polythene "free-flowing" packs in the early 1950s. The American pea variety known as Frosty Freezer did well and Tasmania's climate produced slower growth, leading to better maturity. The CSIRO came to the aid with a Maturometer, whose measurements formed the basis for payment to growers and for quality control in processing. Other research showed that the puncturing of the skins, known to be necessary for successful drying, was also useful to eliminate wrinkling when frozen peas were cooked.

After green peas, the product which helped Birds Eye was fish fingers. Prepared from frozen cod, sawn into blocks, battered, breaded and lightly fried before freezing again, they "revolutionised the fish-eating habits of Australians". Fish fingers were fully-imported from Unilever's European fish fleet, with no local fish used from about 1957 for more than two decades. Sending away our frozen crayfish and importing unnamed species in blocks, we lost the pick of the oceans.

Unilever's fish fingers owed an interesting debt to Adolf Hitler. To prosper in pre-war Germany, the corporation had to come to terms with the Nazi government. Unilever had a trump card, its control of raw materials for margarine, as its financial director in Germany, Paul Rijkens, recalled. Arriving at a deal with Hitler personally, Rijkens found himself sitting beside Goebels and Goering on a podium at the Sports Palace in front of 20,000 SS members and giving the Nazi salute. While Hitler did not let hard currency out of Germany, he encouraged Unilever to use its local profits between 1933 and 1939 to build a fleet of whalers (for margarine) and trawlers, which formed the basis of its fishing fleet, Europe's largest. While other company interests had to remain in Germany during the war, its trawlers sailed away to join the British Navy, and later to catch Australia's fish fingers.

FROZEN FOOD

Although Birds Eye has been the best-known name in frozen food, there has been a pageant of other brands. As early as 1949, icecream cabinets in several shops carried Chinese meals. In 1952, Easton's marketed lines like Lambs Fry & Bacon, Spaghetti Bolognaise, Savoury Beef and Madras Curry. The true TV Dinners, which included meat and vegetables in the compartments of a "throwaway aluminium tray", found their place in 1959. Waffles were there in the early days, joined by sausage rolls, puff pastry, patty cases, apple rolls and such. No-one predicted the amazing success of frozen chips—under the American name of French fries—which began in Ulverstone, Tasmania, in 1961. Beefburgers arrived in the 1960s, recording annual doubling of production. The icecream avalanche, by 1969, contributed $26 million of total frozen sales exceeding $100 million.

In 1966 cakes appeared, imported from North America and Europe. The name here was Sara Lee, a Chicago company, which began local production at Gosford, NSW, in 1971, their batter cakes being of the "high-ratio" type, meaning that the amount of sugar in the mix exceeded the amount of flour. As well, Sara Lee's sweets soon included cheesecakes (six varieties), Danish pastries, fruit pies, cream-filled sponges, pound cakes and "international" desserts. They went through much the same "basic production flow—preparation and mixing, depositing, baking (batter cakes only), cooling, depositing of toppings, packing, palletizing and transfer to holding freezer".

The biggest sales of frozen foods were achieved by poultry. Although it had been attempted 20 years earlier in Liverpool, Sydney, the real beginning was in 1963, using glycol immersion freezing. This business depended on large-scale battery chicken production, bringing a "change from consumer use of poultry on festive occasions only to that of an everyday meal". Glycol freezing in turn depended on the heat-shrinking Cry-o-Vac plastic film. The clarity of the original film permitted full view of the frozen chicken, although with the "quality image" well established, there was a change to opaque film. According to *Retail World*, in 1978 the relative retail sales of frozen foods went something like this: poultry $200 million, icecream $140, fish $97, frozen cakes, pies, etc $48, peas $37, potatoes $35, beans $21 and other frozen vegetables $16 million. In the late 1960s, the home freezer arrived. By 1978, one in three households was estimated to have a deep freeze. An estimated 1000 freezer trailers transported food around the country, maintaining the "cold chain" from farm to dinner-table.

But the main use of frozen foods was not in the home at all. It was in the "foodservice" sector—meals outside the home—in institutions, canteens, roadside cafes, hotels and restaurants. Freezing was the key to the Chiko Roll, which became a standard item in fish and chip and hamburger shops. It was devised in Bendigo in 1951 by Francis Gerald McEncroe (1909–1979). Before the war, he and his brother took a caravan around country shows selling pies and pasties. Looking for gimmicks, Frank McEncroe tried spring rolls, which changed into "Chicken Rolls" and then the "Chiko"—an egg-batter dough containing meat, celery, cabbage, barley, rice, carrot and condiments. McEncroe moved to Mt Alexander Road in Melbourne to set up a small factory, which happened to be near the Floyd family iceworks. The Floyds encouraged McEncroe to freeze his products for distribution and together in 1955 they formed Frozen Food Industries to market the Chiko and other frozen fastfoods.

Other congealed offerings of the kitchen-away-from-home were more appetising. Small chickens went to clubs for "Chicken-in-the-Basket", poultry pieces were prepared as "Chicken Maryland". Frozen meat cuts could be bought in a range of sizes, perhaps with tenderising enzymes to provide uniform texture. Through the 1960s, Australians ate on average around 1 lb of frozen fish in supermarket packs of less than 1 lb. However, in larger institutional packs, they ate more than double at the beginning of the decade and nearly treble at the end. Icecream came as Forbidden Apple and cassata (which was not a frozen concoction at all in the Sicilian original). Strawberries were handled frozen. Some restaurants came to serve mainly frozen foods, including cheesecake which would appear to have had the brand-name, "Home Made". By 1972, Sara Lee was producing three distinct lines for the foodservice industry—five varieties of batter cakes, four fruit-topped and one plain variety of "French cream" cheese cakes and three types of "Bavarian cream" pies.

In 1969, Peters developed a new "adult" icecream available for icecream parlours and with flavours like lemon meringue, highland fling, banana wave and Amsterdam chocolate. The large industrial caterers, Nationwide, moved towards a central kitchen for frozen delivery to institutional accounts in the mid-1970s. By 1979, they boasted: "Nationwide pre-prepared meals come in 2 kg frozen packs. There are more than 20 appetising varieties in boil-in-the-bag style or in foil trays ready for reconstitution." A Nationwide brochure summarised the arguments for buying canteen meals from their central kitchen: "The main benefit of pre-prepared meals is that labour savings are already built-in; inexperienced staff can reconstitute them . . . accurately portion-controlled and without wastage." The "space-age" microwave oven quickly reheated the frozen offerings.

The reasons for the eventual success of frozen food are not often admitted, although a lot of phoney explanations have been thrown up. The *Current Affairs Bulletin* hailed deep freezing in January, 1950, with prophecies of "the expectant mother cooking a series of meals and placing them in the deep freeze months before so that when she is in hospital her husband is provided with his usual food." Australia's "best-known Home Economist," Betty King, introduced Birds Eye to Melbourne in a 1957 advertisement. "And they're so easy to cook, too!" she exclaimed. "With no waste and no preparation needed." The advertisement continued: "These are the fabulous foods you've read about in those glossy magazines from overseas. These are the most exquisitely flavoured fruits and vegetables obtainable."

Asked to explain the success of frozen peas, Petersville's frozen food manager, John Black, pointed with hindsight in 1980 to the "sheer convenience". He said: "Over the years, consumers also became aware of the quality of the frozen pea and that it was not variable as with fresh and the price of the frozen product did not suffer the fluctuations of supply and demand." So frozen food had foreign glamour, "fresh" taste, reliability and, allegedly most of all, convenience. By cutting out the bother of podding peas, by eliminating potato peeling, by serving fish in neat chunks, by supplying bottomless buckets of icecream, by providing finished cakes and by making sure that these same foods would wait faithfully in the supermarket cabinets every shopping day, the frozen food industry had replaced freshness with "convenience".

Market researcher Vic Nicholson amended the conventional claim that crinkle-cut frozen chips were a "convenience product". He found they were bought for their shape, not for their speed. "If you think about the plate at home, potato most often occurs on it," he said. "The green vegetables change and the meats vary but the potato stays and the housewife knows only six ways of serving it. Potato is the dull corner of the plate and that is the problem . . . We found that the reason that this particular form of frozen chip potato sold best was because of the crinkles. It was attractive and she couldn't easily do it herself. So we asked the company to look at the possibility of various knifecuts and we tested a few ideas and found that by creating decoration we created a market." So not just convenience hooked Australia, but perhaps also "decoration". To that we should add coldness itself. A century earlier ice had created a sensation in Melbourne hotels. Now our hot summers had icecream, frozen desserts and cold Mars bars.

But just how convenient was frozen food? A pamphlet from the CSIRO consumer service in the mid-1970s advised making sure chilled and frozen packaged foods were wrapped in several layers of butcher's paper or newspaper in the store. Take along an insulated container to keep items cold, they urged, and return home as soon as possible after you have finished shopping. They argued against long-term storage in home freezers because some couldn't hold a sufficiently low temperature. Generally speaking, they said, thawed food should not be re-frozen. It should be thrown away because it may have developed a large population of food poisoning organisms. Finally, the CSIRO recommended to thaw poultry and large joints of meat in the refrigerator. "This could take 24 hours or more," they observed. "Since thawing under running water results in loss of flavour, it is not a good idea except in an emergency." The overall convenience of frozen food for the consumer was dubious, as the original consumer resistance suggests.

On the other hand, frozen food was highly convenient for the corporations. With freezing, the convenience commenced with agriculture, processors offering contracts and advice for precise results. Freezing permitted the use of giant harvesters, since bruising need not be so detrimental if the crop could be whisked off to the processing plant. Similarly with the fish finger, it did not matter what kind of frozen catch was sawn up, since it was disguised in crumbs. One of the under-rated virtues of freezing was solidity—although a deep-freeze owner could fracture a foot with a dropped pint of chicken stock, handlers need not treat rock-hard raspberries too tenderly.

Freezing was convenient during processing. Golden Circle might simply hold stocks of one fruit frozen until others came into season for combination in canned fruit salad. Or the multinational firm of Carba—"giants in carbon dioxide"—might advertise in 1980 how whipped cream and jam could coat monster layers of warm cake cleanly using its gas-freezing surface hardening systems. Another tumble-freeze system would keep virtually any diced, powdered or granulated product free-flowing throughout the production or blending process.

Freezing was also convenient for distribution. Supermarket chains had difficulty handling the seasonal supply and short "shelf-life" of fresh produce. The manager of Petersville's frozen foods, K. R. Conlan, told a conference in 1976 how the fluctuating fresh fish supply didn't meet the supermarkets' requirements: "Once distribution is gained through the supermarket or grocery network, the continuity must be maintained. It is a very expensive exercise to have a product deleted and resubmitted in the distribution system. Consumer attitudes to the in-stock/out-of-stock situation does much damage to brand and retailer image and profitability." Much more convenient to put the seasons on ice.

Our preservation of the traditional English Christmas dinner has usually been condemned for providing a hot feast when it was 100 degrees in the shade. But the real point was that the turkey, chestnut stuffing, ham, brussels sprouts, parsnips, and pumpkin all arrived in winter. The plum pudding—like the "mincemeat" in tarts—was originally a means of preserving meat in fruit sugar. Eating by the seasons brings meaning to the annual cycle, provides the pleasures of anticipation, guarantees foods at their peak and brings combinations that go well together. Instead of adapting our habits to the climate, we used the air-conditioner's blast, refrigerator, the deep freeze, quick transport, quality compromises and the Pandora's Box of agricultural science to adjust our climate to our habits.

Freezing was yet another way to centralise food handling, storage, transport and selling. Unlike fresh food, which was the province of the peasant, small farmer, shopkeeper and home cook and gardener, food held in the solid state could be manipulated by the giant, private bureaucracies. And so when some of us did without frozen food, we were like obstinate rustics, objecting to the theft of our gardens.

PART IV
The coming of the quiche
Where we think we reached (1970s–1980s)

Charles Frater in his restaurant atop Sydney tower, 1981

The great wine dinner

"WAS THIS Australia's greatest wine dinner?" the *Wine and Spirit Buying Guide* asked in 1978. Organised by Len Evans at his Bulletin Place headquarters in Sydney, at $300 a head, it was a function fit for a Prime Minister. Unfortunately a late call came to say Malcolm Fraser, who had attended the year before, had a virus. But 19 places were taken by wine lovers like Rudi Komon, Alan David and Anders Ousback, with four waiters, like the *Buying Guide*'s editor, John Parkinson.

The evening started with a couple of champagnes, with both Veuve Clicquot and Pol Roger selecting 1947 as their greatest available year. And then, for the next three hours a "procession of famous names and great vintages made their way to the table, after having first passed the scrutiny of the wine waiters," reported Parkinson. There was a "literal galaxy" of Bordeaux: '53 Lafite, '49 Mouton, '47 Cheval Blanc, '45 Latour and '29 Lafite. Then the burgundies: '55 Chambertin, '53 Hospices de Beaune (Cuvée Charlotte Dumay) and '21 Clos de la Roche. The highlight of the evening was the trockenbeerenausleses: '76 Bernkastler Doktor, '71 and '59 Wehlener Sonnenuhr. After which, the 1908 Cockburn and 1927 Crofts were but aged ports.

Considerable tradition presumably guaranteed some approach to perfection in most of the wines, even if sharing only one bottle of each made them rare pleasures. Over the centuries, winemakers had patiently discovered the right sites, the right grapes, the right techniques, the right set of superstitions to achieve the utmost from vintage to vintage. Patience had been rewarded with distinctive district styles—like chablis, claret, champagne and sauternes. In the case of the trockenbeerenauslese, for instance, the makers selected shrivelled grapes from bunches suffering the botrytis fungus. The really experienced taster would have recognised the tried and true styles and may have detected the local soils, the aroma of the grapes, the tell-tale mark of the old vats. Some would have picked which vineyard they came from and could even, by knowing something of the seasons and how the wine would age in the bottle, have a good idea of the year. The gentlemen must have poked their noses into tulip glasses at that dinner and fallen on their knees in thanks to the centuries of dedication of European nobility, merchants and peasants.

In 1968, the average Australian, beginning to take an interest in wine, consumed around five litres a year. By 1973, this had doubled and five years later again—in the year of possibly Australia's greatest wine dinner—it had trebled to 15 litres. But the wines at that dinner certainly were not representative of the now predominantly white wines the statistician measured. The average Australian enjoyed the fruits of a profoundly different system.

The increased wine consumption may have been helped along by immigration, affluence and exuberant publicists like Len Evans, but fundamentally it resulted from the efforts of the wine industry to wean us onto new fluids. This push can be traced back to the early 1950s, when firms had to develop a local table wine market to replace the British demand for fortifieds. They found part of the answer in German techniques for making lighter, fruitier white wines. In the Barossa Valley, Colin Gramp was persuaded by two visiting German wine technologists to import a pressure fermentation tank in 1953, with which his firm of Orlando produced an innovative 1955 Barossa Riesling. In 1956, pursuing this thinking, Orlando produced a sweet, sparkling wine, Barossa Pearl, which the industry came to regard as winning over the masses. In that year, Lindemans imported similar technology to the Hunter Valley for its Ben Ean moselle, promoted as a desirable addition to the dinner table. The first wine advertised on television, it became the country's most popular.

The deliverer and preserver of modern eating and drinking, the refrigerator, was again a saviour. Homes now had the ready means to chill white wine. Additionally, a lifetime after refrigeration had rescued the breweries, the wineries, without having to rely on cellars and autumn and winter weather, transported, fermented and matured their beverage in cooled tanks.

A more "civilised" way of life was announced on February 1, 1966, with the ending of the "six o'clock swill" in Victoria, hotels able to stay open until 10 pm for the first time in 50 years. The same year welcomed two sybaritic magazines, the *Epicurean* and *Australian Gourmet*, whose publisher soon promised: "You'll be in on a revolution in food and drink." With the early 1970s came the capital investment and marketing skill of big companies—

overseas giants like Philip Morris (the cigarette firm, which bought Lindemans), Reckitt and Colman (Orlando) and Heinz (Stanley) and local brewers Tooths (Penfolds) and Tooheys (Wynns).

These heavyweights slugged it out with the "wine-cask", a collapsing plastic bag, from which glasses could be drawn. The idea took over from the returnable, half-gallon "flagon", through which quaffing wine had been aggressively pushed in the late 1960s. Patented under the name "Airlesflo" by a Victorian engineer in 1966, the cask was tried by Tolley's in 1967. Dependent on bulk sales, Wynn's secured rights to an improved version in 1971. The marketing aim was to "distance" the cask from the flagon by deliberately pricing the cask higher, and to advertise that it provided a single glass for the light and moderate drinker. Within a decade, the plastic and cardboard "bag in a box", as the industry preferred to call it, contained half the table wine sold, leaving the flagon and bottle roughly a quarter each. The cask became associated in the minds of advertising agencies with our allegedly easy-going, open-air lifestyle—that of cars and coolers. With a copious cask in the fridge, women took to wine. We became the biggest wine drinkers in the "English-speaking world".

Not that the industry provided much of quality and character. The old districts had not been selected because of any particular suitability for grapes. The Hunter Valley was convenient to the first good road north. Great Western just happened to be where a French brother and sister had given up digging for gold. Cooler districts in Victoria suitable for top table wines suffered from phylloxera and lack of local market. So early this century the industry settled for port and sherry. Hot conditions produced grapes with plenty of sugar, which fermented into high alcohol levels. The addition of even more spirit guaranteed rugged portability for shipment to the UK especially in the late 1920s and 1930s. With years of evaporation from wooden casks stored in tin roofs, winemakers in north-eastern Victoria actually developed an individual, world-renowned style, the muscats of Rutherglen. Otherwise, following visits in 1936 and 1938, London gourmet Arnold Haskell had already blamed the local lack of appreciation of good wine on the producers, who were "relying on grocer's shop and mass advertising and neglecting the wine merchant and the wine waiter," he said. It was also a mistake to borrow names like "burgundy" and "sherry", and he questioned the "pathetic attempt to grow every type of wine in one district".

The rise of cask white wine happened also to coincide with a dip in the fortunes of the dried sultana, currant and raisin industry along the River Murray. So the new wine industry was simply improvised out of the hot-climate brandy, sherry, and port and dried sultana businesses. The most common wine grape, although not announced on labels, became sultana. The country's biggest winery, but a name rarely seen on labels, became the cooperative at Berri on the River Murray. Quickly-maturing grapes failed to develop real flavour, lacked acidity and were picked in the inconvenient heat of summer, rather than the autumn which made European fermentation easier to control. That winemakers could turn such hot-climate juice into drinkable wine could be credited to technological intervention, with refrigeration and the artificial addition of acid.

"A traditional winemaker of 20 years ago," a senior scientist at the Wine Research Institute, Dr B. C. Rankine, wrote in the journal *Search* in 1977, "would have difficulty in recognising much of the equipment and processes of the modern winemakers." He said it was claimed that between 60 and 80 per cent of the quality of white wine, and a lesser figure for red, was due to skilful technology. Fermentation in the big stainless tanks was now controlled by refrigeration, perhaps with heating to release red colour or distinctive white tastes. Yeasts living around the vineyards were killed by sulphur dioxide and the right one introduced. Various additives were tried, like the germicides, sorbic acid and diethyl purocarbonate. Nitrogen and carbon dioxide were injected into the wine to prevent oxidation. Sophisticated filters made it clear and clean.

Each winery had a laboratory so that wines might have the right sugar level, acidity, astringency and predictable flavour. Although it was illegal for respectable wine in other nations, we added acid to counteract the ripening effects of the sun. "It can be seen", concluded Rankine, "that modern technology has greatly changed the simple art of winemaking." The winemaker could now come up with the right wine for the marketing people to sell to target groups. Dr Rankine gave the example of a sparkling wine that could be given the right colour, the right sweetness and even flavoured with the right "fruit essences" to "encourage" young people to "acquire a taste for wines generally".

Grapes were no longer picked by hand. Harvesting machines straddled the trellises, picking 16 per cent of the crop in 1976 and the majority the next year. The machine's shaking damaged the vines and grapes. So they were harvested in the cool of night and carted under inert gas to prevent them deteriorating. Then tankers rushed juice not to ancient cellars but refineries dominated by "tank farms". The CSIRO entered the technology race by breeding new varieties of grapes adapted to hot conditions. In 1975, after ten years' work, they launched the first three, "goyura", "tarrango" and "tullilah", each of them sultana crosses, high in acid, suited to cheap drinking soon after vintage.

Not all wine-making was commercially debased. A large company like Orlando also produced a limited range of higher quality wines, although its elite Steingarten vineyard on the hills above the Barossa Valley had been the pet project of the old family owner, Colin Gramp. Numbers of small (with the ungainly title, "boutique") wineries sought the cooler climates of Victoria and Tasmania. The technical sophistication of a new winemaker like Brian

Croser (who studied in California and launched the oenology course at Riverina College) did not blinker him to the need for good grapes, which he set out to grow at his Petaluma winery in the relatively cool Adelaide Hills.

However, while a number of quite reasonable wines were made, by and large, Australian wine was a fiddle. In the late 1970s, an Adelaide winery equipment importer, Robert Hesketh, found a sideline as wine broker. He and assistant Mark Swann acted as "middleman" between wine companies. They might get a phonecall from a Riverland winery offering bulk dry white, or a call from Sydney looking for a quantity of premium, current-vintage shiraz. They arranged deals. On the basis of one sample of an unlabelled bottle tasted from Swann's wicker basket, a tanker might soon disgorge millions of litres. A road transport company like Sheppard United Tankers had 50 tankers at times transporting grape-juice and wine.

Buying from other companies and districts, wineries conjured out of often inappropriate grapes a selection of sweet and dry, still and bubbly, light and heavy, white and red wines, plus fortifieds. While a French vineyard would produce one style, the Stanley Wine company, as a subsidiary of Heinz of the US, would produce a veritable 57 varieties. Stanley put on the label of its Leasingham 1978 Bin 61 Shiraz that it was made predominantly from shiraz grapes from Clare, but with amounts of cabernet sauvignon from Coonawarra and malbec from the Barossa added to produce this "soft and elegant" wine. Reading labels became a task in itself: "vintaged at Clare" probably concealed that chilled juice had been brought from the nearby Riverland, "crisp acidity" might hint that the acid had been added, "riesling" might well mean "sultana". Winemaking became largely a worry about "faults", some of which, in other lands, gave wine character. Here, "consistency" became the hallmark of the corporate approach.

With wines made in refrigerated stainless steel with laboratory accuracy, doctored with acid and other additives, blended from anywhere, the winemaker could not expect to develop a distinctive style in the traditional sense. The connoisseur was in little position to sniff out the old delights, guessing the effect of site, cellar and season. Instead, with the cost-effective, clinical approach to instantly drinkable potions, there was a tendency to appreciate the varieties of grape, and to laud the technical skills of individual winemakers. Otherwise, wine's fascination came to be almost totally with the finished product. This was manifested in an obsession with the "taste" of wine, with little regard as to how it came to be that way. Perhaps it didn't matter how a wine was made so long as it tasted good? To me, the taste should have been inseparable from other values, even political. Even if Lindemans made a perfect copy of a great burgundy, it would still be a counterfeit. It would still be a confectionery wine.

That the French have been concerned about honest labels—that a wine was true to place, to grape and to traditional technique—was embodied in the system of "appellation contrôlée", a government guarantee of authenticity. When a case of fraud came before a French court, Len Evans became annoyed by experts reportedly giving evidence that they couldn't tell the difference between the "rubbish" and the genuine, and expensive, article. "Well, I can tell the difference," Evans declared in the *Epicurean* in 1975, "and so can Seabrook and Lake and Hickinbotham and Crittenden and Schneider and Beeston and Halliday and about a couple of hundred other sharp-palated Australians. Otherwise, there would be no point in the whole business." People like Evans should have been jumping up and down like that in defence of our own wines' integrity.

A former British golf professional who settled here in 1958, Len Evans rose through the beverage hierarchy of the Chevron Hilton hotel in Sydney, and began in 1965 the Wine Bureau's promotional activities, which were credited with the "doubling of table wine sales in three years". In 1968, he moved to his own sales outlet in Bulletin Place, in the business district of Sydney, and launched the Rothbury Estate in the Hunter Valley, the first of his winemaking ventures. As part of his publicity, he founded the "Rothbury Society", which offered wine by mail and coloured ribbons for those passing elaborate tasting tests. If wine buffs had been worried less with tasting and more about the economic direction of the industry, they might have been less intoxicated by Evan's peculiarly self-contained way of life, in which he was conspicuously producer, middle-man, salesman, educator, consumer and commentator. By the time he had bought two small châteaux in France and the Packer media organisation paid him $90,000 a year as a pundit, the *Wine and Spirit Buying Guide*'s light-hearted "most unpredictable advice" award of 1981 went to his including in "the best wines around" a Rothbury Estate Individual Paddock wine.

Aussie men now boozed a little less on beer, sometimes took uncharacteristic pride in their sense of smell, struggled for poetic expression, and sometimes even let women join in drinking. But I can't help wishing we were more concerned that short-term financial logic, combined with technical expertise, had substituted the romance of grape-picking and old stone cellars with mechanical harvesters and refrigerated tanks. And so it was not without significance, despite the new obsession with wine, that Len Evans' contender for Australia's "greatest wine dinner" did not include one Australian wine.

In a paper in 1980, Monash University historian A. E. Dingle showed that Australia's extraordinarily volatile alcohol consumption slumped during the depressions of the early 1840s, 1890s and 1930s and peaked in periods of prosperity like the 1830s, 1850s, 1870s, 1880s, 1950s and 1960s. He suggested that Australians turned to heavy drinking when we had excess cash with little else to spend it on. However, that argument did not explain why we turned from spirit to beer and now to wine-drinking. The massive investment of the food industry turned many of us into wine-loving gourmets.

14

Oh, for a French wife!

Theories for the gourmet boom from the 1960s included immigration, increased overseas travel, bulging household budgets — but the most likely explanation was the food industry's shake-up of cooking

FOR THOSE eating out in the early 1950s, the typical meal was at a cafe, cost 2/6, and comprised steak and chips, bread and butter, tea (white or black, the latter with lemon), and icecream with passionfruit or rockmelon. That was the report of Mary Gallati, the daughter of a London restaurateur (Mario Gallati of the Caprice) and later a cookery writer herself, who visited Australia in 1953. In a Sydney coffee shop she ordered chocolate meringue pie, icecream and coffee.

"Why," said an MP when he took her out to lunch, "they haven't a wine list! Would you believe it!" If alcoholic drinks were served, the licensing laws were absurdly strict, bars (where women were not permitted) closing at 6 pm and eating-places only licensed to serve drinks until 9 pm, she said. Most restaurants had dancing and were night-clubs. She was invited to a night-club by an Englishman and since he had not ordered wine before 9 pm, they could not have any, until he produced an English driving licence. The waiter looked at it, the head-waiter looked at it, and then they served wine. "Don't ask me, but there it is," Gallati wrote. On a showboat in Sydney Harbour — glamorous at night — she was shaken out of her reverie by a waitress: "Wot d'yer want? A milk shyke? Wot flivour?"

In 1958, another English writer, John Douglas Pringle, found that waitresses, like others serving the public, "often seem to acquire a permanently sulky manner, as if they were always trying to prove — to themselves as well as to you — that they are only doing this for money and have no further obligations." As for the food, Pringle recorded that: "The small but excellent oysters and the huge but excellent prawns make a good introduction to the inevitable steak, and the discriminating soon learn that the best red wines from the Hunter River and South Australia are as good as all but the very best in France." Australian wines, Mary Gallati also thought, required careful selection but they were very reasonable. "The average standard of catering is high," she said. "Plenty of food is to be had, and inspectors do regular rounds of restaurants and cafes to ensure cleanliness. The premier restaurants, however, do not compare with our London premier restaurants." Invited to the swanky Sydney restaurants, Prince's and Romano's, Pringle noted their "ugly side", where "smart, hard-faced, wealthy women lunch together and try to attract the attention of the photographers and 'social reporters' sent there by the newspapers".

Both visitors remarked on the good life of the squatters, Pringle believing they approached closest to enjoying real culture. Staying with well-to-do graziers near Yass, Gallati dined on trout from the river, lamb casserole, fruit and cream and a glass of milk, all home products. And then both were attracted back to Kings Cross. Mary Gallati loved its cosmopolitan delicatessens. Pringle reported: "You can dine well in Sydney at half a dozen European restaurants at King's Cross or the city, though for some curious reason it is hard to find one where you can sit outside by the harbour."

But then something happened to liberalise drinking laws, to throw open restaurant doors and to usher in the fancy food boom, where more than a minority took the winecask and pâté out on the patio. Giving away the three plain meals of meat and cups of tea, many homes discovered sweet peppers, eggplants, zucchini, avocado pears, yoghurt and brown bread. After pornography, no subject was now exploited so cynically even by otherwise respectable publishers, presenting endless texts on French and Chinese cuisines and fads like vegetarian cooking. This chapter tries to explain the epicurean outburst, with first the more usual reasons.

Multicultural society

Flavouring what was otherwise pretty dreary fare, it would seem that in the 1950s, in places like King's Cross, it was possible to find something that was regarded as "Continental". It was the harbinger of the 1960s coffee shops, gelato bars, foreign restaurants, European breads, biscuits and chocolates, and Elizabeth David recipe books. Both Gallati and Pringle had implicitly accepted immigration as the antidote to deadly eating. And it came to be a cliché in the next couple of decades that our palates were broadened by the post-war population boost.

It didn't matter if you were SA Premier Don Dunstan, whose cookery book acknowledged: "After the war, the influence of migrant groups, particularly the Baltic, Yugoslav, Italian, German and, to a lesser extent, Greek, influenced Australian food habits for the better. The Hungarian influence, concentrated in the food industry, was enormous." Or whether you were the Petersville corporation which, in a magazine advertisement celebrating its 50 years in business, said that the "influx of European settlers had a greatly beneficial effect on our Australian diets after World War II." Three decades into the nuclear age and Australians believed they had a "multicultural" society—an updated American "melting-pot"—with a diet to match.

While dispossessed peasants being transformed into BHP and car factory workers quickly upheld some values of the industrial society, they were inclined to desire food as mother prepared it. So they frequented their own clubs, restaurants, bars, butchers, bakers and grocers—institutions which could attract curious outsiders. And they did not altogether adopt Pringle's "permanently sulky manner" to pre-industrial skills like fishing, gardening, waiting and cooking and the long hours of the family business. Other migrants, often bourgeois refugees, brought managerial and technical skills, and a taste for the higher pleasures of symphony orchestras and cream sauces.

Among the successful entrepreneurs from post-war migrants, N. Slezak founded his giant Socomin import business within a month of arriving in 1949; Andrew Lederer, a Hungarian arrival in 1957, turned a Sydney butcher's shop into Presto Smallgoods; Hermann Schneider established Melbourne's Two Faces restaurant in 1960, after arriving in 1956 on a whim to cook in the Olympic village; and Salvatore Della Bruna claimed to have set up "Australia's first pizza house", Toto's, in the "little Italy" of Lygon Street in Melbourne on July 7, 1966.

But the immigrants really only provided long hours, skills and colour in a dietary revolution which was created by other causes. For how can we explain why we went crazy about French food when relatively few French arrived? (Don Dunstan detected in restaurants the "average Hungarian chef's idea of the French cuisine".) Even more of a problem, how can we explain similar upswings in the United States (where yoghurt consumption leapt 30 per cent during 1969), Canada, Great Britain, West Germany, Japan and even to some extent in France, when these countries enjoyed nothing like comparable influxes of labour?

The argument also ignored the historical "Continental" presence. Arnold Haskell wrote about it in *Waltzing Matilda* just before the war, claiming "Sydney has its Cafe Society", centred on the enormous Hotel Australia, with five restaurants at varying prices. Sydney already had Romano's and Prince's, "where, if you take the trouble to order your wine before six, or are known, you might just as well be in London." He said: "King's Cross has been taken straight out of Paris and dumped down in the middle of Sydney."

A volume proclaiming itself to be the *First Australian Continental Cookery Book* had been published in Melbourne by the Cosmopolitan Publishing Company in 1937. In those years cookery books often contained recipes for foreign dishes and advertisements for Sasso Olive Oil, and B.C., Rinoldi and even Kookaburra brands of "macaroni", as pasta tended to be known generically. Even earlier, Australia imported elements of "Continental" culture with its workforce. Making up for our lack of a peasantry, throughout the nineteenth-century French immigrants guided our vineyards. In SA, Germans were employed to get agriculture underway. The Spanish community started the tomato industry at Bendigo, using their old gravity irrigation methods.

To consider the case of Italians, they were deliberately sought, especially in Victoria in 1861 to establish wine, olive oil and tobacco industries. Ten years later Queenslanders employed them for the cultivation of the mulberry and olive. The Census of 1881 found 521 Italians in NSW, 947 in Victoria, 250 in Queensland, 141 in SA, 10 in WA and 11 in Tasmania. In 1905, the chairman of the NSW Fruit Exchange told a royal commission that Italian shopkeepers with their "splendid" window displays had captured the retail trade in fruit in NSW and Victoria. The 1920s saw a relative flood of Italian immigrants, with 7884 arriving in the peak year of 1927. Brought out for West Australian mining and the Queensland sugar industry, they tended to gravitate into catering industries. Before the war, the Italians came mainly from northern Italy, some buying into Griffith blocks in the doldrums.

In 1981, *Age* restaurant editor Claude Forell asserted that a "spaghetti mafia" of the Molina, Massoni, Codgnotto, Triaca and Virgona families "helped to establish civilised eating and drinking in Melbourne". These families traced their links with restaurants like the Florentino, Latin and Society back until the 1920s and 1930s, much earlier than the present "discovery" of good dining. Beyond Forell's recall, immigrants had opened great restaurants within years of Melbourne's foundation. A century of great Melbourne restaurateurs might have looked something like this: J. F. Gunsler, Vincent Fasoli, Calexte Denat, Rinaldo Massoni, Cammillo Triaca, Jimmy Watson and Hermann Schneider. A most un-British lot, and even "Jimmy" Watson was christened Calexte after Denat, who was his uncle, and his sister married Rinaldo Massoni.

Perhaps the most irksome obstacle for the immigration argument was the Chinese, whose food was gracelessly snubbed until their numbers had fallen to a "safe" low. For other reasons than their presence, ordinary Australians sought the novelty of odd ingredients, mysterious sauces and ritualistic chopsticks. Something more fundamental had also occurred.

The Big Trip

Frank Margan described in *The Grape and I* (1969) how, post-war, thousands returned from the "Grand Tour" with bags crammed with ebony elephants, maybe a fez or two, slides of Europe and memories of wine and food. Margan said he had discovered wine—an 11-shilling bottle of Médoc—when "bunging it on" at a London dinner. He told how other Australians had hitch-hiked around the vineyards of Bordeaux and the Bourgogne, had sat for lunch on the side of the road in some Italian village and eaten flour-dusted bread, salami and a bottle of unlabelled red. They had learnt there was more than steak-and-eggs and chips and tomato sauce—like the stinking cheeses in their little wooden boxes in the south of France and the hot scampi in little paper cones from the fantastic place on the corner in Venice.

Back in Sydney, he recorded, somebody found Lorenzini's wine bar and someone else had a letter to an Italian in Griffith who would sell bulk red in a barrel pretty cheaply. The women looked for Continental cook books and the men searched for the best wine at the cheapest price and you had dinner parties with the people you met on the ship and you tried to turn it on, with French salad in a beaut wooden bowl and antipasto from a great salami place in Leichhardt. "They had done the Grand Tour and it had cost them a packet and they had to take two or three jobs at a time and go without so many things to get to bloody Europe and they were bloody-well going to benefit from it and be sarcastic about the bloody plebs eating their steak and eggs..." he wrote.

Frank Margan didn't agree with the "official fictions" about the influx of migrants bringing their wine-drinking habits and teaching about food and wine. Nor with the other stories about our higher standard of living and more money in our pockets and greater sophistication. He didn't believe any of that, he said. It all happened because 25,000 of us were coming back every year, after tasting the Médocs and the Graves and the *vin ordinaire*. It wasn't the migrants, he concluded, "it wasn't them, it was us".

If Australians "streamed" to Europe in Margan's day, then with relatively cheap airfares in the mid-1960s, the numbers must rightly be described as "soaring". Margan spoke of 25,000 per year, presumably an estimate of holiday-makers among those 43,000 or so residents departing for a variety of reasons in the early 1950s. Ten years later this had more than doubled. Ten years later again, it had grown another six times, so that in 1972, Australian residents departed 500,000 times for overseas. By 1976, there were one million departures, which represented a healthy proportion of the population eating all over the world. Those taking the American guidebook then called *Europe on $10 a Day* could have noted a comment by H. R. Baker of Rockhampton, Queensland: "I have insufficient words to praise the Munich beer. It was wonderful. The food, too, was excellent, although I found the sausage skins a little too tough for my teeth." So that's another theory for what caused Australians to turn to garlic and the grape. And there's a further, influential-figure view of history.

Influential personalities

The burst of fascination with eating and drinking has been said to result from enthusiastic propaganda, a proposal usually advanced in praise of individuals who have done much to publicise wine and food. Think of writers like Elizabeth David and Robert Carrier and television demonstrators like "Galloping Gourmet", Graham Kerr. Then consider the effect of bon vivants like those operating in Sydney's business district, Johnnie Walker and Len Evans. Each of these has been acclaimed as leading a revolution.

During the gastronomically bleak immediate post-war years, there was a small audience for the books of Oscar Mendelsohn, for instance. He was a food chemist who settled for a while on a farm at Lara, outside Geelong, "to give our children an experience of good eating that they could carry through their lives". He published copious food and wine notes, starting just after the war with books like *The Earnest Drinker* and *Drinking with Pepys*. He devoted almost the entire *A Salute to Onions* to that subject, and then in 1965 compiled a *Dictionary of Drink and Drinking*.

A contemporary of Mendelsohn, and a more sensitive writer, was Walter James. James liked the cigars and brandy of the well-to-do gentleman who thought life was having enough "old wood to burn, old wine to drink, old friends to talk to and old books to read". James considered: "You can lead a woman to the altar but you cannot make her drink. At all events, not willingly and with joy, like a man". Yet beginning with the handsomely-printed books *Barrel and Book* (1949), *Nuts on Wine* (1950) and *Wine in Australia* (1952), his jottings praised fine wine, subsistence farming, Luddite philosophy and Rousseau's *Walden*. James despised, as a degradation of human personality, the "present way of living in unimaginative suburban uniformity with mass-produced food, clothing, furniture and everything else—and most of it both pretentious and shoddy". So he too shifted out to a vineyard and grew food. "Australians have a sweet tooth", he wrote. "Our beer is not so bitter as the English and we drink nine bottles of port, muscat and sweet sherry for every single bottle of dry table wine such as claret and chablis."

An intriguing chain of influence can be picked up with the Sydney publication in 1947 of the *Garrulous Gourmet*, a series of essays by an American businessman in Paris, William Wallace Irwin. The manuscript was brought to Australia by a J. Walter Thompson adman, Deke Coleman, who published the book with a Sydney member of the same agency, Ted Moloney. Noting the help of various French wives in the project, *Sydney Morning Herald* columnist Leon Gellert wrote about it under the headline, "Oh, for a French Wife". That became the clever title of a cookery book published in 1952 by Coleman and Moloney, with illustrations by George Molnar, and which by 1980 had been reprinted 18 times in three editions.

Oh, for a French Wife was balanced in 1957 by *Oh, for a Man who Cooks*, which included a delightful set of Molnar sketches of "eating around the world" (mainly Sydney) and was a charity production by the six-man Society of Gourmets, who included Ted Moloney and Johnnie Walker. Walker entered the business in 1926 with an hotel in East Sydney. In the late 1930s he established Rhine Castle Cellars in the stone basement under the Royal Exchange in Pitt Street. Business people, like woolbuyers Henri and Jeanne Renault, dropped in for French bread sandwiches and decided to form a food and wine society. With members subscribing various amounts, the Renaults opened the Hermitage in Ash Street and that became headquarters. Johnnie Walker went on to open his Bistro in June, 1957.

These were the sorts of names who formed the gourmet societies dedicated to keeping alive the guéridon flame of food and wine appreciation. Probably the oldest had been the Viticultural Society founded in 1920 by Victorian winegrowers. It limited its membership to 50 men, and built a cellar of thousands of bottles, many left in members' wills. The major fraternities, however, were the Wine and Food Societies, founded on the teachings from London of André L. Simon, who, like many principals in such bodies, was a wine merchant. These societies, attended by sometimes cliquish ritual, derived from century-old traditions of England and, as often happens, followers were not leaders and tended to worship French vintages and elaborate menus uninventively. The Wine and Food Society of Victoria, founded on August 5, 1936, was the sixth worldwide. It was for men only, and so the Victorian Ladies Wine and Food Society was formed in the late 1960s. There were dozens of others. Yet how could even this enthusiasm generate the tremendous boom?

Affluence

In other countries, the gourmet upsurge was given such explanations as increased travel, the opening of foreign restaurants, the decline of the Puritan ethic, households of fewer members, and more women working outside the home. However, at base, most commentators considered that the cause was affluence. In 1970, the economists at the OECD in Paris summarised the rapid changes in western eating habits as: "Rising consumer incomes awaken dormant desires for a greater variety of higher quality goods and services and give consumers the necessary economic power to use natural talents of selection more fully . . . Increases in travel, education, and communication stimulate consumer awareness of new products, improve knowledge of foods and nutrition, and reduce differences in eating habits among nations."

Simply stated, they suggested that more money, more movement and more textbook learning made a better life, dutifully provided by more industry. While this is reasonable, the argument of affluence needs refinement. The OECD reasons should apply to the relatively prosperous decades like the 1920s and 1950s, when dining was marked by conformity, and should falter in the less expansionary, more decadent 1890s and 1970s. Something further convinced us that on our working-class ship we all dined First.

Disruption by the food industry

I would argue that Australia has experienced three waves of gourmet interest, the first cresting in the 1850s. Although the effects were naturally slight in the newly-conquered continent, the rise of the English and French gourmet early in the nineteenth century was reflected, with a delay, in the gold-diggers' delight in champagne, the arrival of "cafe-restaurants" and Edward Abbott's cookery book. On December 4, 1888, the Melbourne *Argus* detected cookery as the lady of fashion's "latest and most engrossing fad". It was the beginning of the second wave of exciting restaurants and cookery books. The First World War was a notable gastronomic dehydrator, the drought lasting until the 1950s. And then, beginning with cocktail parties and cheap Chinese meals, came the third rise in fascination with eating and drinking.

In my view, these bursts of passion were produced by three periods of tremendous change in the food industry—the industrialisation of the garden, the pantry and then the kitchen. In the first step, the agricultural and industrial revolutions in England fed a newly estate-less bourgeoisie, who installed the first ranges, employed French cooks and enjoyed the groceries of other lands. By breaking down old links, the food industry stimulated experimentation. No longer tied to the local garden and artisan, the gourmet could enjoy culinary experiences with almost intellectual detachment.

A second step in the 1880s brought the great food companies based on the railways, roller-mills, refrigeration, brandnames and chain shops. Processed foods again shook preconceptions about eating and drinking. Some people reacted by turning to health fads and vegetarianism. With machine production, even the relatively impoverished Bohemian could afford the lively gustatory experiences of the abundantly-provided city. The gas stove, too, arrived to produce Escoffier's sauces.

Finally, considerable investment throughout the 1960s and 1970s took cooking out of the home and into the factory. The saturation advertising of multinational food corporations persuaded consumers to experiment once again with taste sensations. They featured the new style of "convenience" foods in the form of snacks, quick meals and "fastfoods", which shattered the family routine of three plain meals daily. The industry also provided the components of grander entertaining. This activity produced another generation of gourmets, vegetarians, dieters, and other food experimenters.

As it happens, our epicurean episodes followed key moments in immigration—the convict arrivals, the gold rush and then the post-war programme—but I prefer to believe that both resulted from the same industrial growth. It is also worth noting that the gustatory gusto synchronised with flourishing feminism in both the 1890s and 1970s, suggesting another link, both perhaps responding to inroads into the kitchen. It is certainly reasonable to suppose that the changes by the food industry brought renewed concern in nutrition. In 1975, the Nutritional Society of Australia was founded and, by

1978, the country's first two professors of nutrition had taken up chairs at Sydney and Deakin universities.

As an illustration of how the latest onslaught widened epicurean horizons, think of Electrolux's recommendation in 1951 that refrigerator buyers be "open-minded" to new cold drinks to replace "monotonous" water. Think of the work by Golden Circle to encourage experimentation with its prize-winning "Pineapple Gourmet Dessert". Think how Wynn's used the winecask to attract new drinkers. And think also about coffee. In the 1950s, this sophistication was attributed to American influence during the war. It was next credited to immigrants opening smart espresso bars. Meanwhile, in Britain, the same trend was explained as the result of tea restrictions during the war. In fact, the main reason was product innovation by Nestlé, which invented "instant" coffee in response to the Brazilian government's exhortations to find better ways to preserve the beans. Nescafé arrived here in 1939 and was manufactured locally from 1947. We tried coffee at the insistence of a food corporation, and then ventured onto percolators and cappuccinos.

We experimented with much more than that, as the supermarket systematically overthrew our conceptions of cooking. In the foreword to their *Mastering the Art of French Cooking* (New York, 1961), Beck, Bertholle and Child acknowledged: "The book could well be titled 'French Cooking from the Supermarket', for the excellence of French cooking, and of good cooking in general, is due more to cooking techniques than to anything else . . . Anyone can cook in the French manner anywhere, with the right instruction." The vanity of the supermarket replaced wonderful French ingredients, closeness to the soil and experience. The disorientation brought about by the food industry's invasion was even easier to perceive in the artificial rustic style of the myriads of lesser cookery books. The trendy little recipe books produced by Sydney's *Terrace Times* were labelled, "Minimum effort Maximum effect," a revealing slogan.

Adam Smith's economics foresaw that capital would seek new ways to save us kitchen time, to brighten the dinner table and to stop us for a roadside snack, but each time an investment saved a minute here, lifted a moment there, filled a gap in the market, it separated eaters further from the source of food. The "middleman" slandered agrarian values, insulated us from the seasons, took away the diversity of distance, compromised quality for price, and then distracted us from the deterioration with the baits of cheapness, convenience and gourmet entertaining.

The restaurant boom

The need for authorities to record precise numbers of licensed restaurants provided a dramatic picture of the boom. A growth rate in the numbers of licensed restaurants in NSW of around 12 per cent was established in the early 1960s and just kept going through the 1970s. There were 342 licensed restaurants in NSW in 1966 and 1622 in 1980. Other States "caught up", like Queensland and SA with 14 per cent rates through the 1970s. At the opening of the 1970s, there were 1000 licensed restaurants nationally and at the close there were 3000. Add the unlicensed "BYOs" (bring your own liquor) and the restaurant total was probably close to 5000.

By 1980, the States were disproportionately provided. WA had about 140 restaurants per million people, Queensland 170, Tasmania 190, SA 240, NSW 320 and the ACT 650, a figure approaching those typical of France and Italy. The different supply of eating spots might reflect the different proportions of tourists, might be an index of some kind of "sophistication" and might respond to different licensing laws. The figures for Victoria were considerably lower, representing a mere 80 licences per million, an indication of the preponderance there of BYOs. Add them, and the situation became close to that in NSW.

My memories of Sydney restaurants in the 1960s start with Paddington's "arty" Lantern, where Bill James and a Bohemian waitress served charcoal-grilled pork fillet marinated in honey and soy sauce. It was easy to find a table for a lazy lunch at the Ozone on the promenade at Watson's Bay, surely one of the world's best restaurant settings. This was later renamed Doyle's, its proliferating plastic seats and lengthening queue a year-by-year measure of eating-out. And for an elegant dinner, I remember La Causerie in Potts Point, Madame Yolande de Salis offering guinea-fowl in port, and raspberry soufflé. But with a few exceptions, restaurants of the boom were not stunningly memorable. To some extent, the least pretentious "ethnic" establishments were most rewarding. Otherwise, in place of good food well cooked, too many average restaurants, lacking quality ingredients and seriousness of purpose, presented garlic bread, stewed coffee and either a sad copy of the grand tradition or gimmicks.

At the pinnacle of success were men like Oliver Shaul and Charles Frater, who took their restaurants to extraordinary heights—detached in the clouds above Sydney. A Swiss immigrant as a teenager in 1939, Shaul found his first job in the bakehouse of Cahill's restaurants and, after the war, became chef at Le Coq d'Or and the Savarin. In 1947, he joined the management of the Federal Hotel in Melbourne and left, as managing director, a much expanded chain. He became a catering consultant, before, in January 1968, he opened the first of his own restaurants, the revolving Summit atop the Australia Square building in Sydney. He opened Flanagan's fish restaurants, another top-floor restaurant, Chattie's, on the North Shore, and next gained the lease of the dining rooms at the Sydney Opera House.

"People don't go out to restaurants because they are hungry," he revealed to the *Sydney Morning Herald* (February 13, 1973). "They go out because they want to enter a make-believe world, feeling good, experiencing hospitality." His staff were mostly European, the waitresses wore long black skirts, the prices were moderately expensive and the menus were written in French with unobtrusive English explanations. "When I opened the Summit, the favourite dishes were prawn cocktail, filet mignon and strawberries and cream," Shaul recalled in 1982. "Now, after all the food revolutions that are supposed to have hit Sydney, the favourite dishes are prawn cocktail, filet mignon and strawberries romanoff. They are safe, you see, and you don't have to chew too hard." He claimed to serve the food he liked at his latest restaurant, Central Park Bar and Grill.

Rising to even greater heights, Dr Charles Frater arrived from Hungary in 1948 with qualifications in economics and an interest in biscuits. Working in the baking and restaurant businesses, he eventually opened the Centrepoint Tavern in Sydney in 1972. A bust of Queen Victoria, labelled "Her Majesty", greeted guests as they descended from Pitt Street, for it was built on the site of the old Her Majesty's theatre. It had six rooms, all with a theatrical touch: the Don Carlos room, Victoria and her Hussar, the Pompadour Piano Bar, the Rigoletto Fountain Court, the Carousel Room and Her Majesty's restaurant. Lights were dim, music piped and the air-conditioned atmosphere bustling. On a tour with a reporter, Frater said: "You might call this kitsch. I would call it kitsch, but I've created a make-believe world. It has warmth, total freedom." To minimise the problems of hiring waiters, he used self-service. The meals were inexpensive and wines came by the glass and carafe. His turnover, he said in 1980, was $3·5 million, with an average of one million customers a year.

In September, 1981, Dr Frater opened the ultimate twin restaurants in an uprooted city, way above his tavern, on top of the giddy Sydney tower. Seating 250 on each of two revolving floors, he ascended from theatrical kitsch to total industrial unreality in one bound. After the opening, food critic Haruko Morita reported feeling gastronomically lost, as if "in a capsule flying to the moon". It was an apt culmination of a history of feeding as if on space rations. Office workers, tourists and shoppers could eat above the skyscrapers with a view straight down to the concrete-clad soil where once the Reverend Richard Johnson had established Australia's first private garden. There could be no more terrifying table from which to contemplate.

The food corporations supplied the "foodservice" industry, as they called it, with factory cheese, pellet-fed trout and quail and reconstituted orange juice. They offered special "pre-prepared" products like frozen French specialty bread, "ready-to-cook frozen deboned chicken breasts with various fillings" and frozen cakes and pastries. They also provided the "convenience" range of onion flakes, seafood extender, fish flavour enhancer, beef booster, "egg-wash substitute" (for breadcrumbing), dessert mix and aerosol "creme". Reading a trade magazine like *Hospitality* would have alarmed many restaurant-goers. The Dairy Corporation headlined its advertisement in the issue of July 7–20, 1982: "Two ways to increase the size of the bill . . ." The first was for pubs to change from pie and sauce. "Try a 'Ploughman's Lunch'," the corporation said, of bread, pickled onion and cheese. "It's simple, can be prepared at the bar and is loaded with profit." The second was for restaurants to say to every customer, "We have a special Australian cheese board this week, would you care for some?"

After writing for nearly a decade in favour of simplicity, restaurant critic Leo Schofield complained in the *National Times* (September, 1981) that restaurateurs persisted in setting before their paying customers "platefuls of over-accessoried, under-intellectualised junk". The trouble was that the full might of our biggest industry, the food industry, encouraged cooking which was labour-saving, used seductive new tastes, featured bizarre combinations and enjoyed immediate visual appeal. It was perhaps no coincidence that some of these attributes were shared by nouvelle cuisine, fashionable in restaurants from about 1978. As developed by a generation of French chefs like Paul Bocuse and Michel Guérard, it was a lighter and fresher style of great optimism. "Now the accent is on presentation and exotic combinations," Margaret Fulton explained to *New Idea* readers in January, 1982. Here again, slick novelty distracted us from the food industry's inability to provide honest old tastes. Fanned slices of duck breast on strawberry sauce, sorbets and crowns of Kiwi fruit had superseded the pineapple ring.

As D. H. Lawrence found, Australia's "rush for money had no real pip in it," because we lacked genuine culture to buy. "Money is a means to rising to a higher, subtler, fuller state of consciousness, or nothing," he declared. Restaurants provided a splendid example. We had plenty of money, but little to spend it on. In France, the affluent Australian could purchase a charming auberge meal with fresh herbs, peas and strawberries. We could afford a three-star restaurant with layers of sauce and tradition on the greatest ingredients. The moneyed traveller in Italy could find a dignified Parma restaurant with the best Parma violets, Parma ham and parmesan. In a raucous, unhealthy and depressed city by our standards, Naples, the Australian could still find staggeringly tasty tomatoes and sublime mozzarella from that morning's buffalo milk. We could buy that culture where it emerged from a rich agrarian tapestry. Back in Australia, short-term greed led to skindeep dishes.

But perhaps that is being too hard. Eating out and eating "well" meant that an increasing proportion of the family budget went on food—that was the point. Out of the fashionable, often trivial and thus passing fascination could come some genuine concern for fresh produce and democratic elegance. Dedicated restaurateurs, although they scarcely knew it, battled against the junk-food gale. Digging into our past, we could find fine examples of owner-chefs. And now people like Tony and Gay Bilson had shown that cooking could at last be regarded an honourable Australian profession.

CHEFS TO THE COURT OF WHITLAM

Gay and Tony Bilson at the Bon Goût, Sydney, 1974

"A GOOD RESTAURANT when it first opened," wrote Leo Schofield in his first guide to *Eating Out in Sydney*, "Tony's Bon Goût shows every sign of developing into a great one." Listing the specialities in mid-1974 as saddle of hare, shellfish, and homemade French pastries, he extolled: "Duck seems to be top of the pops and several of my *Sunday Telegraph* readers have found the Canard aux Cerises a stunner. Original soups, freshly made, are a feature of the daily board of specials. The Filet de Boeuf is so good that one lady of my acquaintance never has anything else. The Balmain Bugs get an unequivocal recommendation. And the Almond Charlotte is an original and scrumptious pudding. The restaurant is not specially attractive. In fact, it's rather plain. But it does have a pleasant atmosphere and a clientele to match." Two stars. Highly recommended. Average cost (for two, not including wine): $15.

That is how they ate at Sydney's most fashionable restaurant at the height of the Whitlam era (1972–75). It was a restaurant they wove legends around, its Friday lunch regulars forming a "cafe society". Perhaps we shouldn't encourage such self-indulgence, but this country's restaurants could do with more legend-making—and "Tony's" hasn't yet been written about to the extent of Fasoli's at the turn of the century. Secondly, the restaurant was important because its owners, Tony and Gay Bilson, were the first obviously Australian chefs ever granted public acclaim—previously only patronisingly accorded to foreigners. And, thirdly, the special relationship the restaurant enjoyed with the Whitlam circle denied the old labour ethos that we "only eat to live" and leave peasurable dining to the decadent classes.

Tony Bilson came from a reasonably well-to-do family—one side owning pubs in Sydney and the other stores in western Victoria, his grandmother having a pastry shop in Portland. He considered his mother a fantastic cook—making a hamburger of swans' breasts with orange sauce, the birds shot near their Colac home by his father. His father and a friend shot 500 quail in a day to send to the Hotel Menzies for a fundraising dinner for Sir Robert Menzies. Tony remembered great times dressing up for "red-plush" Melbourne restaurants and, when still a schoolboy, he had an account at the Balzac.

He dropped out of university when he was 20, to wash up, at the recommendation of the Balzac's Georges Mora, at Johnnie Walker's Bistro in Sydney. There he learnt the craft from an old chef, Paul Harbulot, at a time when there were few good chefs in the country. "I had been thinking about French cooking from the time I was about thirteen—I mean, really seriously, avidly, grabbing any book I could get my hands on. And Paul taught me the really professional things: how to use a knife; how you get around it when you have got more customers than food and still produce what's on the menu; how to use a frying pan." To earn more he moved to the Dee Why RSL club, then did some landscape gardening. Back in Melbourne, he worked with Stephanie Alexander at Jamaica House restaurant, before buying, with an inheritance, La Pomme d'Or, a not overly successful venture. Then he provided the "first haute cuisine" for counter-culture counter-lunches at the Albion Hotel in Lygon Street, Melbourne.

He met Gay Morris, a Melbourne University librarian, and, while they did not marry, she eventually also took the surname Bilson. Like Tony, she was born in 1944 and was also a university drop-out. An "earnest" amateur cook when in America with her husband, she let "romance" push her into the restaurant business. They set up in Sydney, opening the Bon Goût on May 21, 1973, having literally removed the chewing-gum under the tables of a "greasy cafe". Liz Fell and other friends in the Push, then drinking at the Criterion Hotel, started to come down after the pub. It was for them that it was called "Tony's", although this came to be an embarrassment in increasingly feminist times especially because Gay, if anything, came to contribute more. They commenced with quiches, asparagus with hollandaise ... and a fixed-price alternative for $2.50 of soupe du jour, oxtail and poached pear. Gay would later "shudder at the careless simplicity of it all" and the hard work needed for relatively basic dishes. It was a "rat-infested, cockroach-infested nest of naive idealism", she summed up.

The influential restaurant critic in those days, Leo Schofield, was born in

Brewarrina in outback NSW, where his parents had a pub. He too claimed to have enjoyed good home cooking and later helped Henri Renault at the Sunday lunches of Vaucluse resident, Jo Fallon. He visited "swinging" London, experimenting with Elizabeth David's cookery books, and decided to become rich and famous in advertising. Despite his wound-up snappy language, he showed good taste, from the start rating "simplicity of preparation and presentation, value for money and freshness of prime importance". Schofield took Tony's over with 39 other guests for his fortieth birthday.

By the end of 1975, when Tony's Bon Goût had a fixed price of $9.50 a head and specialities of duck's neck "en brioche", live local lobster with mussels and lemon soufflé, Schofield declared: "He simply can't put a foot wrong. Every dish he turns out is light, fresh and delicious. That's the way restaurant cooking is heading all over the world . . . It's pointless to select items from a menu as mobile as his. But if the trout stuffed with a mousse of whiting is ever on the night you're dining there, for God's sake and mine, have it. Behind every great chef there's a team and it would be churlish of me not to mention both Gay, who makes all the pastries and puddings, and that most ebullient and efficient of waiters and no mean cook, M. Alain Chagny."

The Bon Goût's extraordinarily-long waiting-list resulted from the lack yet of any real competition, a superior waiter and, most of all, outstanding food. Tony, who had studied under professionals, and Gay, the librarian, combined the best of both disciplined training and book learning. In periods of innovation, major contributions are often made by amateurs. "At the same time as we were teaching ourselves, we were educating the public," she recalled. When the couple made their first visit to France at the height of the Bon Goût's success, they were "amazed, inspired", and also gratified to find their direction had a lot in common with the new French style.

The restaurant had opened five months after the election of the Whitlam government, and soon became the haunt of a circle of advisers and journalists around the Labor ministers. George Negus, who worked in Attorney-General Lionel Murphy's office, "discovered" the place. He mentioned it to David White, a media secretary of the Prime Minister, and just old enough to have known the last years of the arts-theatre "salon" at Vadim's at King's Cross. White came to be acknowledged as a ring-leader at the restaurant, flying up Fridays on the seven o'clock plane to meet friends there, some of them journalists relaxing from irregular, tense lives by eating and drinking a lot.

At first the Bilsons had opened for six lunches and six dinners every week, but, with labour costs, they found they made more money just doing dinners, except for the famous Friday lunches. Nothing contributed to the Bon Goût legend like the Friday lunches. Leo Schofield was an habitué. For a long time laywers James Halliday, John Beeston and Tony Albert (who had started their Brokenwood winery in the Hunter Valley in 1970) brought fancy labels to their table. There were some people from the gas industry. Margaret Fink, whose husband owned the building, always took a table for two. Rudy Komon, who had loaned the paintings on the walls, was another regular. The editors of the *Financial Review* and *National Times*, Vic Carroll and Max Suich, shared a table. Paddy McGuinness, then a Hayden advisor, had a table, which he renounced every now and again, declaring the food was no good. The *Bulletin* fielded an occasional table. And the main table was "Lenore's", of *Herald* journalist Lenore Nicklin and packed with Labor people.

Nicklin would start out on Friday morning booking for seven. Then she'd have to ring back to say "it looks as if we'll be nine" and in the end it might be 12. She'd try to arrive first, getting there at ten to one for, customarily, a table along the front window. She'd seek Alain's idea on the food, he was usually witty and arch. The group often included David White, Dick Hall, Eric Walsh, Mick Young, Jim McClelland, Brian Johns and Virginia Osborne, if she'd sold a poem.

The table tended to talk politics, avoiding heavy ideological debates. A political "fundamentalist" like Senator Arthur Gietzelt was the butt of jokes. "It wasn't gossip," writer Dick Hall later said in all seriousness. "It was analysis of character, which is different. Cairns' motivations were worked over early, which was useful." Nicklin might pick up a story for her paper, maybe from Frank Moorhouse or Michael Thornhill, who told her what was happening with the movies. People swapped tables, bringing their bottle or coffee over. Donald Horne from the *Bulletin* might want to talk to Brian Johns and they'd go off to another table.

Tony and Gay themselves were interested in ideas, politics and books—a rare type of restaurateur, thought Lenore Nicklin. "They would come out at half past three; Tony's a sweetie and he'd carry a can of beer." When Liberal leader Billy Snedden came, he observed the front-of-house poise of Alain and snubbed the skinny boy looking in from the kitchen door, Tony. "Gay would sit and not say anything if in a bad mood, but when she did, she'd read more than anybody else," said Nicklin. Apparently Gay confided to a friend that her favourite vision of herself was sitting in the Bon Goût kitchen, on an upturned rubbish tin, reading the *New York Review of Books*. The Bilsons gave a copy of M. F. K. Fisher's translation of Brillat-Savarin as a Christmas present to an academic customer.

Tony's was a "bring your own", which suited the crowd, who would nick up the road as the afternoon drew on. They also had to pop out to a frightful lavatory in the down-and-out hotel nextdoor. It never had any paper, but Dick Hall always carried a paperback in his back pocket and you could use the first chapter. In summer, the airless restaurant could be stifling. At the end of lunch, they'd try to split the bill. Virginia Osborne might have just had soup and hand over a couple of dollars. "I'm paying for so-and-so", they'd say if they brought a guest. Hiding behind a nervous façade, Nicklin was always grateful if rugby-playing colleague Ian Frykberg was there because she thought he was good at fixing up money.

Writer Frank Moorhouse, a Friday regular, wrote about Tony's in *Conferenceville*: "So I went to Tony's to meet Dick with some gossip . . . He wasn't there when I arrived. I took out a book but didn't read it. Instead, I brooded about the great luncheon tables. The Punch Table, the Round Table at the Algonquin, David Astor's lunches around the pool for the *Observer* people. Surely they weren't all witty and clever at every lunch. I worked up a hypothesis that our lunches were in fact wittier and cleverer than those legendary tables because we competed with legend."

Those who cautioned against over-estimating the Bon Goût's importance— "any of the pubs near Trades Hall always had more political significance"— neglected the wider meaning of politics. A journalist like Lenore Nicklin, who could sense more shifts in society than who happened to "have the numbers", saw Tony's this way: "It was anti-posh and yet had good and interesting food, it had a lot of style without being red-plush. Generally, it was a time when there was a lot happening, the Nimrod theatre, films being made, Australian plays. The people were gregarious, enjoyed the boozy part of the Whitlam thing. We were open to new ideas about food. It was a time of change anyway. Just as the rules of food had previously been established by a well-heeled elite, the trendsetters became younger, more adventurous." She pointed to the Beatles, Mary Quant, it was a continuation of that. Just as you didn't have to work ten years as a cutter for Sportscraft to become a fashion designer, you didn't need to be sauce assistant at the Savoy to become a chef.

Although hotly defending cooking as a craft which required solid training, Tony Bilson shared the view that a lot of people were enjoying good food, good wine and eating out and didn't like the pomposity of the older-style restaurants. "Before, you had to go to Maxim's, where you were booted out if you didn't have a tie." Asked how socialists could drink champagne, Tony retorted: "You ought to see how the French and Italian socialists live". He compared Gay and himself to artists and performers. "We're presenting our act, as long as it's done well, then we've done our thing." It was an elite entertainment to the extent that it became expensive, but then bricklayers earned big money.

So, typical of the times, we had some Labor insiders and some cultural leaders beginning to dine pretty well, and even be proud of it. Yet, which is a paradox to be explained, they scarcely took the slightest interest in food at the political level. Australia's largest industry, the subject of more television ads, the most fundamental human activity, scarcely came under government notice. Food, concerned intimately with everything from survival to style, was not considered relevant. Where, we might well have demanded, did the Labor cafe society stand on the dining table?

Some Whitlam government decisions and attitudes were intrinsically positive. Labor inherited the consumerist rebellion against the chrome-plated fifties, inspired by American books like J. K. Galbraith's *The Affluent Society* (1958), and Vance Packard's *The Hidden Persuaders* (1957) and *The Waste Makers* (1960), and taken up by the Australian Consumers' Association magazine, *Choice*, the first issue of which appeared in April, 1960. The visit of US consumer advocate Ralph Nader in July, 1972, toughened the resolve, and, to take an instance, the government responded to the gale of throwaway technology with a parliamentary inquiry recommending taxes on one-way drink containers. Pressure was renewed on the retail industry to accept minimum standards on handling frozen foods. The government shook up the food additives committee of the National Health and Medical Research Council, hitherto dominated by the food industry. With the food companies actually drafting their own regulations, one committee member had proudly told me in 1971: "As far as I know about the rest of the world there is no other system which has sufficient confidence in its food industry to seek its opinion."

The CSIRO, responding to pressures to redirect research from profits to people, turned animal nutrition laboratories into a Division of Human Nutrition under Dr Basil Hetzel. Labor influence could be seen behind the decision of the CSIRO Division of Horticultural Research to breed a more succulent quandong. Found over half the continent, the acidic and astringent flesh of the "native peach", rich in vitamin C, had long been turned into pies and jam and its kernel was also edible. Dr M. S. Buttrose explained that the quandong was studied "when there was a definite encouragement from the government to help improve the quality of life, as the catch-cry was, and at a time when the public was suddenly becoming more conscious of Australia as an independent nation."

But the effect on eating was hardly based on any carefully considered food policy, or even any but the scantiest appreciation of eating. Labor introduced Medibank, but did next to nothing to improve nutrition. It worried about the feminist cause in the workplace, but not in the kitchen. It jumped up and down about foreign ownership, but failed to improve the Coca-colonisation of mass eating. It preached "quality of life", but neglected food in the suburbs.

Why the neglect? Perhaps socialists believed they had achieved their legendary ideal, the abolition of hunger? The Henderson Poverty Commission, fostered by Labor, calculated that about 10 per cent of incomes fell below an arbitrary poverty line, with 14 per cent in rural areas. Although this was not all "absolute" poverty, where physical deprivation threatened life, it was still "relative" poverty, the product of an unequal society. There were "hidden people", who needed help. However, the problem tended to be too much rather than too little. Nutritionists would soon favour an American-style national nutrition policy—to encourage us to eat less sugar, less salt, less fats, and so forth. Many of us became obsessive slimmers and joggers.

Perhaps the government did not want to enter kitchens on civil liberties grounds? Wondering if eating was something consenting adults did in private, Peter Wilenski, a Whitlam adviser, later told me: "If people want to eat sugar, they have the right to go to Hell in their own way. It's like the anti-smoking campaign." But while commerce had generally refrained from involving itself in the bedrooms of the nation, it had put a lot of junk on the table.

Perhaps food was relegated to State and local government because of a puritanical fear in Labor circles that dining was the preserve of the idle rich? On the contrary, a good and satisfying meal has been held to be a person's first right. Long ago, when discussing the opening of the city's first French restaurant in 1854, the *Illustrated Sydney News* had been prepared to barter the right to vote for a "wholesome and well-cooked dinner every day", being convinced that the "corporeal constitution" had priority over the political. The paper wanted to see some professor of gastronomy establish a college to contribute to health and resources economics, leading to a "gastronomic regeneration".

I believe that the Whitlam government neglected food because it inherited typical working-class indifference. That Australia is "classless" has been a widespread myth. Just as it seemed "too young" for culture, it lacked aristocrats, peasants, and its ruling-class tended to remain in London and New York. We have just been an unusually homogeneous, working-class society. Even the so-called "middle-class" who discovered pâté, dry wine and Tony's Bon Goût were, at least in relation to the means of food production, working-class—landless, servant-less and thoughtlessly earning their "crust".

The immediate purview of the thoroughly-urban labour movement—composed primarily of industrial workers and not of housewives, self-employed or even unemployed—did not include the politics of strawberries and cream. Food politics? The idea of food politics still did not beguile the Friday regulars of Tony's Bon Goût when I tackled them a few years later. Tony Bilson said that the secret of good food was buying well, good marketing. "Tree-ripened fruit isn't to do with political parties, it doesn't matter if it's under socialism or capitalism," he said. On the contrary, apples are highly political, and challenge the rampant industrialism of both East and West.

Trade union socialists, themselves the product of capitalism, brought up to believe that food is for "feeding" and dining for idleness, have not always been sympathetic to the gardeners, fisherfolk, shopkeepers and restaurateurs—small business people—who make for good eating. They never came to terms with the waiter's skills, odd hours and attitudes too easily mistaken for subservience. They learnt to scorn the labour-intensive values of the suburban rustics on their quarter-acre blocks. But of all the Labor cafe society's sins of omission the most tragic was ignoring farmers. After the 1940s, the labour movement proved too urban, too incorporated into industrial civilisation, too committed to improving the "cities", too fattened on archetypal working-class fare to care about the subjugation of agriculture.

Historically, the Labor Party had an ambivalent attitude to the country. On one hand, populists in the party had favoured, for example, marketing in an "orderly", centralised fashion and, keeping up the long struggles against the graziers, closer settlement of the "little man". In 1945, the activist B. A. Santamaria advocated "independent farming", and also used the words "self-sufficiency", in his book *The Earth—Our Mother*. Interpreted by others as a society of "Catholic peasants", his movement actually set up a number of cooperative farms before Santamaria became increasingly coopted into the defence of, rather than the resistance to, capital.

On the other hand, the party also inherited the meat-eating contempt for both the aristocratic squatter and the foolish "stringy-bark cockatoo". The side which resented rural gullibility and perks became dominant in the Whitlam era. Rural policy makers fell in with the faith in unaided market forces to construct utopia. If an industry was "inefficient", if it needed propping up, even against considerable destructive pressures, then it served no useful purpose. So we witnessed the puzzling confrontation of an individualist Country Party fighting to retain bureaucratic supports, while a socialist party unleashed free enterprise. Perhaps the Country Party's role was largely as a vote-catcher for monopoly capital, while the Labor Party promoted bigness of both government and business. In the end, whatever either party might have claimed, particularly during the Menzies era and again under Whitlam, any Australian claim to a rural way of life was destroyed.

Through ignorance of food politics, the Whitlam government gave primary production a last kick. Very early, the government, in the overall rather than primary export interest, revalued the Australian dollar, followed by readjustments which led to the "floating" of the dollar on the economic oceans. The government supported "rural readjustment", which meant assisting hard-pressed farmers to "get big or get out". The government got economic wizard Dr H. C. Coombs to whip out a report on cutting rural assistance and by June, 1973, he had named more than 40 items.

The policies were somewhat inept, considered the cafe society's David White: "Labor wasn't good enough or quick enough to get the message across." Dick Hall observed: "The destruction of the smaller farmers—in the NSW dairy gullies, for instance—was too far gone; they're all dead." Lenore Nicklin: "The Labor Party was realistically brutal to the farmers, and paying them back." Good eating, according to the gastronomic perspective, requires a blessed agriculture. The Whitlam group paid attention to the original Australia of Aborigines and nature conservation. They elevated the theme of the industrial "cities". But they overlooked the middle, cultivated ground.

Although Whitlam was only able to dine at Tony's Bon Goût occasionally, he apparently had a healthy interest in food. Speechwriter Graham Freudenberg later described Whitlam's childhood household as: "full of good cooking, good books and good public servants; it was notably lacking in drink, tobacco and profanity. Ever since, Whitlam has been at home with good food, good books and almost any public servant and uncomfortable with drinking, smoking and swearing."

In the eventual hate-Labor days, a culinary rumour cut his stature. A restaurateur spread the story that the Prime Minister had asked for garlic bread at the Tour D'Argent in Paris, and this was printed in the *Bulletin*, much to the annoyance, among others, of Dick Hall. "For a start, Whitlam had never been there. For another, he doesn't like garlic bread, and, even if he did, he's not dumb enough to ask for it." Within minutes of being sacked by the Governor-General, Whitlam summoned Freudenberg, who found him "sitting alone in the small, glazed breakfast room beside the Lodge dining-room. Whitlam was eating his customary steak. There is perhaps something to be said about a man who can eat a steak minutes after the greatest shock in his life."

The gourmet boom outlasted Whitlam. By the time in 1979 that former Governor-General Kerr was publishing his memoirs and dining in France, Clifton Pugh's portrait of him hung in the Latin Cafe in Lonsdale Street, Melbourne. When Labor had taken power in 1972, there had been 36 licensed restaurants in Canberra, although it seemed much less. Now there were 137. To echo La Reynière's reasons for post-guillotine France, the "sudden inundation of undomiciled legislators" had drawn all Canberra to the cabaret. Describing a lunch at Paddington in Sydney, the English journalist Peregrine Worsthorne wrote: "If the food in this restaurant is any guide, then a miracle has been wrought, since there was nothing like it when I was last here some 15 years ago." He dined with Leo Schofield, who claimed to have played a part in transforming the city's eating habits. "That is what is such fun about living in a place where there are so few traditions," the food columnist said. And he also had an eater's imagery for describing the political past. "On the whole Gough did a good job. After 20 years of unbroken Liberal rule, the Australian body politic had become so constipated that it needed a purge, even if this did cause the country to have a bad case of the squitters."

Meanwhile, Tony and Gay Bilson had moved to the Berowra Waters Inn, on a glorious stretch of water outside Sydney, and generally held to be the "top temple of gastronomy" in the country. They now charged $40 a head, customers occasionally dropped in by seaplane, waiters polished Christofle cutlery, Tony was beginning to choose food to go with great wine and Gay had started a second career of writing about food. But could such a revolution be permanent without an agricultural base?

15

Hard tomatoes for hard times

The sacrifice of family farms to agribusiness left us to eat hard tomatoes, pale eggs and stale apples cosmetically coated with wax

IN THE 1930s, agriculture accounted for about one-quarter of Australia's employment and gross domestic product. Although in some ways agriculture had been over-promoted, and many farms struggled, it provided a semblance of rural society, and an escape route for urban unemployed during the depression. Then labourers left for the Second World War, along with many farmers' sons, and not all returned to the land. Immediately after the war, one-sixth of male employment and of the economy remained rural. In good years through the 1950s and 1960s farmers invested in machinery, chemicals and more prolific varieties. By the 1970s, rural industry accounted for one-tenth of employment and of the economy. Agriculture was becoming, as we shall see, capital-intensive "agribusiness", until, in the 1980s, no more than one-fifteenth of Australian society was rural.

Our continent is the driest, it's the flattest and its soils the tiredest. The hot sun, even climate and long distances have suited a highly industrial farming, in which the grazing of sheep and cattle enjoyed a distinct logic. So Australia has also remained the least cultivated continent. Our position was put into an international perspective by a report to the US President in 1967 on the *World Food Problem*. According to its figures, about one-fifth of Australia and New Zealand had potential for growing crops. However, only about 2 per cent of our arable land was actually cultivated. This compared with Europe (88 per cent), Asia (83), USSR (64), North America (51), Africa (22) and South America (11). We weren't a rural nation.

A moment of truth came in 1973, when Britain entered the European Common Market, closing a century-old market, the rationale of our agriculture. We found other openings, and wheat sold well in communist countries. But transport costs were rising, competition was keen and many nations endeavoured to return to self-reliance. The sudden revival of mining meant that rural exports, which had made up more than 80 per cent of exports in the 1950s, fell to 50 per cent in the 1970s. Rich and powerful friends had turned Australia from a source of cheap food and fibre to a source of minerals. Australia dismounted from the sheep's back—with a bump, according to Professor R. G. Gregory of the Australian National University, who estimated in 1976 that the "over-exporting" of minerals had been equivalent to a doubling of rural tariffs. Now there were no farms for those out of work to escape to. We were resource-rich, and resourceless.

An influential Canberra scientist, Dr Telford Conlon, revealed a chilling future for agriculture. "We don't take families out in the Timor Sea and create social problems on the oil rig," he told a conference in 1977. "We leave the families in Broome or Darwin and fly the men out there for five days on, then fly them back for five days off . . . If we really took our technology seriously, we need only have about five country towns in NSW. We could run our farms on a commuting basis." That was the direction of agriculture—of both the export sector and most especially of the real concern of this book, the cultivation of what we ate.

Governments assisted the "unsettling" of Australia with the removal of death duties to prevent fragmentation of large estates, with loans for the amalgamation of "uneconomic" farms into more "efficient" units, with relaxation of maximum block sizes in irrigation settlements, with the removal of farmers from "inappropriate" dairy regions, with the offer of debt-wiping to ease the pain, and with the deliberate withholding of facilities from small towns. Dyed-in-the-wool Professor Keith Campbell scoffed in 1977 that "a farmer can even get a sustenance grant for 12 months while he makes up his mind whether he is going to leave his farm or not."

Economists like Campbell acclaimed a device called the "cost-price squeeze", one of the collection of "invisible hands" with which to organise society. It was simple: the farmer's costs rose (for fertiliser, fuel and the family's own food), while the prices the farmer received fell. One result of the squeeze was expressed popularly in the 1960s as "get big or get out". Economists loved it for making farmers more "efficient": they had to raise their "productivity" to survive. It might do terrible things to rural living, the countryside, employment and the taste of food, but that was economics.

The cost-price squeeze hastened "mono-culture", sheds and fields incorporating economies of scale. More fertiliser created more pollution seeping from bigger fields. More pesticides were needed to repel plagues in overcrowded hectares. Battery production brought quicker carcass returns. Of course, these new techniques added to costs, squeezing harder. Larger, often multinational, buyers were in a strong bargaining position to force down prices because they could turn to cheap substitutes, tie up farmers in contracts and buy elsewhere. While processors could add extra services—like further preparation, more packaging and fancier recipes—farmers generally kept turning out the raw product and so could not charge for extra "value added". The more productive farmers became, the faster they went out of business. Satirist Jonathan Swift had said we would honour the person who makes two blades of grass grow where one grew before. The tragedy was we needed only half as many farmers.

Agricultural economist Dr H. P. Schapper told a conference of agricultural science students in 1977 that their purpose would be "ridding society of some of its farmers". The process whereby they would cull them was "silent, anonymous, unplanned and often painful," he said. The cost-price squeeze was a "thoroughly good private enterprise mechanism, yet thoroughly disliked by farmers despite their alleged commitment to private enterprise". Almost every economic change worked in favour of the richer, larger farmers, as it did for more prosperous and larger companies whatever they produced, he said. It would not be hard to paint a realistic scenario in which the entire farm output was produced by a small, highly-skilled, well-paid labour force guided by a hundred farm-managers backed by a computer network, he said. "It may not be the sort of agriculture anyone wants. But it may be the sort of agriculture Australia will get if the policies of farmer governments and farmers' organisations continue to be more agricultural bigness for ever."

In 1976, the Kellogg corporation backed a Kellogg Rural Adjustment Unit at the University of New England, Armidale, to study compassionate means to ease farmers into new fields, and to facilitate the entry of this centralised agriculture. Farmers had lost their independence not from the dreaded socialists, nor from the thoughtless city slickers, but from corporate capitalism. In egging on the industrialisation of agriculture, so-called "agribusiness", the Country Party eroded its own basis of support, and changed its name to "National Party".

In the 1970s, we saw the eclipse of the hills orchardist, the market gardener, the traditional "man on the land". Some small-scale vegetable growers still produced close to city markets, but urban expansion, rising land prices, faster transport, irrigation and more freezing dispersed production to specialised centres. With machinery and chemicals, one gardener could look after perhaps 12 to 20 hectares. On top of this, company operations emerged, exploiting hundreds of hectares, and often integrated with suppliers, distributors and processors. Fewer, bigger enterprises meshed in with the supermarket chains.

The remaining farmers, committed to the growth which served their ancestors well, were "brainwashed on the virtues of scientific agriculture, profit maximisation and the adoption of materialistic goals and conspicuous wealth as measures of status and prestige", Armidale sociologist Professor John S. Nalson noted in 1979. He foresaw family farmers surviving in some wildly fluctuating export industries, while "agribusiness" succeeded in the intensive production of eggs, poultry, pigmeat and vegetables, geared to the stable local market.

On the face of it, city people should have been pleased. We spent less of our income shopping for food. In 1972–3, Australians devoted 16 per cent of after-tax household disposable income on food. Ten years earlier, it had been 21 per cent. At the beginning of the century, it had seemed miraculous when only 37·5 per cent. In France, England, Germany and Japan the average was still around 38 per cent of income spent on food, in most countries more. In another way of looking at it, the Bureau of Agricultural Economics estimated in late 1978 that one farmer fed 70 Australians. This could be thought a tremendous economic triumph. The trouble was that hard-pressed farmers, wringing out every drop of the crop, often wrung out quality.

By 1981, the consumer magazine *Choice* found it impossible to buy commercially a genuine free-range chicken anywhere in Australia. The "efficient" grower locked chickens up to stop them wasting energy by moving, fed them minimal rations and dosed them with antibiotics so that bug-free digestive tracts let them grow faster. The battery fowls emerged bloated and tasteless. By 1978, Victoria's senior poultry officer, Bill Stanhope, suggested that more farmers try guinea fowl, pheasant, quail and squab pigeon, for "special occasion" dinners when the public wanted "something different, something tastier—even at higher prices". He said that Australia was one of the few countries where the pheasant was bred straight for meat and not shooting. Guinea fowl had been adapted to intensive broiler-growing conditions, he said, the extraordinarily fertile Japanese quail was at full lay at seven weeks, and the remarkable squab pigeon, fed on a new pellet, was ready for market at only 28 days of age. We had battery "game".

While early this century autumn and winter brought scores of commercial apple varieties in sequence, orchardists now grew little other than Granny Smiths, Delicious and Jonathans for a season extended by "controlled atmosphere" stores. Supermarkets demanded that growers provide unblemished, even-looking fruit, waxed to look nicer. Taste was sacrificed, which buyers only noticed when they got home. Fresh figs and persimmons were just too delicate to handle.

A typical victim of the cost-price squeeze was the tomato. The customer used to be served the small, soft, ugly and sweet-tasting varieties like Rouge de Marmande. But tomatoes had to be re-designed in the 1970s for the self-service industry. They had to be over-si   reduce handling costs, uniform to fit foam trays, and tough to withstand a long shelf-life. The supply had to be reliable, and growers tried to provide them year-round, usually to the detriment of quality. Instead of growing them in hot-houses in winter, farmers tried the dry Queensland tropics at Bowen. They had to pick them unripe to withstand transport to Sydney and Melbourne, where they were "de-greened" with ethylene gas. The trouble was that Bowen tomatoes, when gassed, remained hard and without flavour.

In addition, farmers could avoid high labour costs by using mechanical pickers. But to reduce bruising, the tomatoes had to be cropped when even harder. In 1967, machine harvesters had picked Murrumbidgee tomatoes, where damage did not matter so much since they were used for processing into soup, sauce and the like. About 1978, mechanical harvesters arrived in Bowen and with them the "MH-1" variety of specially hard tomatoes direct from Florida.

The seasons tormented not just tomato growers, but the entire food industry. In 1981, speaking to newspapers about the forthcoming ABC television program, "Towards 2000", reporter Sonia Humphrey enthused: "Technology is being able to have oranges in winter." Her statement showed how technology kept us ignorant of food. Oranges normally arrive in winter, with handy supplies of vitamin C. However, since we like our thirst quenched in the hot months, growers jumped at preservation, making all-season orange juice a boom industry of the 1970s. Juice concentrate was conveniently stored and transported, which also encouraged imports from South America, besetting orange growers with further anxieties.

Factory farms

Our early agriculture was dominated by the industrial approach. Grazing was capital rather than labour-intensive, especially after the minor exertions of shepherds were replaced by fences. Wheat was soon adapted to all manner of machinery, dragged by extraordinary teams of horses and then horse-power. Similar industrialisation occurred with sugar-growing, speeded up after the repatriation of cheap, Kanaka labour. Considered the province of Asians working in paddy-fields, rice-growing arrived in the Murrumbidgee Irrigation Area as a highly-mechanised and chemicalised industry. A booklet produced in the 1970s by rice growers claimed it to be one of our "most efficient and capital-intensive" rural industries; aeroplanes dropped germinated seed, harvesting was done with giant implements and milling removed the husks and germ for stock-feed, leaving "Sunwhite".

Commercial mushroom culture commenced in the early 1930s, after the chief biologist of the NSW Department of Agriculture, Dr R. J. Noble, published a booklet on overseas methods. Previously, we collected mushrooms only from the fields, even if top dressing reduced our chances. Mushrooms soon sprouted in sheds, cellars, railway tunnels, in the old brick kilns at Ryde and under the pylons of the new Harbour Bridge. After the war, those early methods came to be called labour-intensive and low-yielding. Mushrooming moved onto the production-line. The growers cultivated them on trays, which could be shifted from spot to spot for soil pasteurisation, introduction of spawn and growing. The temperature, humidity and ventilation could be so finely tuned that harvesting could be organised for weekdays, with Saturday and Sunday off. Over the years, each stage was given more attention until the growing of spawn was mechanised at specialised firms. The making of compost was cut from six weeks to one, and again different firms specialised, one offshoot being formulated compost for the home grower. Indeed, such was the increase in efficiency that mushroom prices fell relatively every year. Finally, in the 1970s, mushroom culture became fully automated—waste organic material could be fed in one end of a machine and boxed mushrooms appeared at the other. The technological intervention in the growing of food seemed to be total.

During the 1970s, according to fact sheets published by the Victorian Department of Agriculture, apple orchards were planted more densely, to utilise land and sunlight more effectively. Not only that, trees wouldn't grow as tall, making pruning, spraying, thinning and harvesting less time-consuming. The denser orchard also favoured pests. So along came more insecticides to control codling moth. The tractor-pulled spray made its many passes, showering the trees against fungus diseases. Other sprays reduced the need for pruning and thinning, or the fall of fruit, and improved apple colour. Ethephon ripened and coloured them. Bulk handling, grading equipment and cool stores further reduced labour needs, although demanding capital. Fruit for the "controlled atmosphere" stores could not be picked later than the green-yellow stage, and deteriorated as fast as Dorian Gray when let out six months later.

The purple flowers of a pineapple open one day only. Researchers found that the chemical "alpha napthalene acetic acid" induced flowering. By spraying so that all pineapples flowered the same day, they would mature uniformly some 180 days later. This simplified harvesting, so that all pineapples could be picked together and put on a conveyor belt to a truck. Spraying the maturing fruit again with the hormone at the right time delayed ripening by about a fortnight, so that the fruit would grow 20 per cent heavier. While the hormone treatment was popular among growers, the Golden Circle factory rejected the distinct drop in quality for its fruit.

It had been an earlier discovery of food preservation scientists in Australia that the rotting of eggs could be slowed sufficiently for export by not washing the eggs. This might be regarded as a neat result in the science of "post-harvest" agriculture, made fashionable in the 1970s by the supermarket demand for greengroceries. It was partly a science of food cosmetics. To take the case of lemons, post-harvest scientists with departments of agriculture recommended to growers in the 1970s that, as soon as the fruit was harvested, a sterilising fungicide dip was "vital" to prevent mould. Perhaps a

30-second dip in a tank of Benlate, Bavistin, Thiabendazole or Topsin. Then the lemons might be "pre-sized and pre-sorted". This was followed by washing and then more fungicide. The fruit was now waxed, perhaps in dip tanks, by sprays, flood or foam. A wax coating kept citrus fruit from drying out and shrivelling—and gave an attractive shine (the only reason why apples also came to be waxed). The fruit was possibly "de-greened" by a gas, bringing colour to the cheeks. So, to keep the "buttons" (stalks) of the lemons a natural-looking green during dipping, the wax contained amine 2,4-D. Now the fruit was sorted and sized, perhaps proudly stamped with brand-name, stored and then sold, fresh from the chemical Eden.

Post-harvest scientists calculated that the distribution cost of fruit and vegetables—that is, from harvest to retail sale—was five to nine times the production cost. To cut this, they worked out an "integrated" distribution system on a national scale, featuring standardised, returnable crates, for which plant breeders would need to develop short-stalked celery to fit. Here mechanical handling might be gentler on produce. "An important concept in improving the handling system is that we can control machines but not people," two Queensland researchers, D. Schoorl and J. E. Holt, reported in 1977.

By the late 1970s Australia spent about $150 million a year on agricultural research. About 85 per cent of the cost came direct from the taxpayer. Perhaps a clearer idea of the magnitude of this effort—which supplemented vast research in corporations—came from the statistics of the number of scientists employed—3000 of them, not including support staff. The scientists and agricultural corporations protected us from honest food by a barrage of patented hybrid seeds, hormones, formulated feeds, pesticides, mechanical harvesters, fungicide dips and bulk-handling techniques. Profitable tree shakers and CA sheds wedged themselves firmly between people and nature. What a paradoxical paradise, so proud of its technical fortunes, and which found it virtually impossible to provide a fresh apple.

In what we might call the food-conscious countries like France and Italy, pigs and poultry usually fended for themselves and cattle were kept in stalls, improving taste by making white meat less fatty and red not too lean. Quite the opposite happened in factory-farm Australia, where grazing of sheep and cattle was cheap, but where fowls and pigs came to be imprisoned in sheds and fed on pellets. This led to lean red meat and fatty white. When I asked the CSIRO's meat research laboratory about any inferiority of our butcher's meat, an official wrote: "there is little nutritional difference if you ignore the obvious differences in fat content." That rather begged the question.

Did freezing of meat affect quality, I also asked? "Prolonged storage at −18°C for up to 12 months is possible with little nutritional loss." Note the stress again on nutrition rather than gastronomy, and then the reply explained: "The fat will eventually become rancid due to a slow chemical combination with oxygen and may cause off-flavour." Asked to comment on changes in techniques of bacon curing, sausage-making and other smallgoods manufacture, well, present-day methods "differ little from older techniques, with the exception that all stages of the process are now highly automated, the curing ingredients used are much more efficient, and the use of emulsifying agents etc enable many more products to be created." If these minor changes were made to farm production, what had happened to farmers?

The Unsettling of Australia

Ten local features made the country fine,
The farmers bought their tractors and then there were nine.

Nine local features—rural life still great,
They centralised the local school, then there were eight.

Eight local features in our rustic heaven,
The local dance petered out and then there were seven.

Seven local features on which the township ticks,
The exchange went automatic and then there were six.

Six local features managed to survive,
The supermarket stole the trade and then there were five.

Five local features—we wished that we had more,
The local Show folded up and then there were four.

Four local features, all important you'll agree,
The trading bank closed its doors and then there were three.

Three local features—sadly it is true,
The parish church closed down and then there were two . . .

When the church closed down, the poet of the above, the Reverend Jim Stuckey, left for the coast, and so it was not necessarily discretion which prevented him recording the fate of the town's last two "local features". An officer with the NSW Department of Agriculture, Gordon Yabsley, took up the story when he re-visited the unnamed spot (somewhere near Maitland), writing in the April, 1977, issue of his department's *Agricultural Gazette*.

"There is some bare ground about, it could be for summer crops," Yabsley thought, as he drove into the old town. "Someone's told me cropping's a year-round job now in places. Perhaps that's why they need those big tractors. Or do they need to crop twice to pay for them?" He wondered who lived in the old *Caroona* homestead and recognised what seemed to be Santa Gertrudis under its trees. "They must have been son Henry's idea," he decided. "That's his long low bungalow built during the wool boom. The trees have grown a lot. Henry's son did law at Sydney Uni. I'll bet he doesn't come back to run the place when Henry gives up. Still, the old place lasted through three generations."

Looking around the town, he confirmed that several "local features" had gone the way of the blacksmith's. The school had given way to the school bus. The Post Office looked much too big for a town this size. "I wonder what they did with the old exchange at the back? It provided some job opportunities for the girls leaving school in my day." The general store stood empty, its big wooden wall along the lane carrying a fading sign, DRINK KINKARA TEA. "Their delivery truck had a regular run round the farms. The farmers appreciated the credit readily extended to them . . . It couldn't have been for want of overdrafts that the bank closed down. Perhaps more than the convenience of banking locally the farmers miss the local bank manager . . . Invariably he was treasurer of at least two organisations."

When Gordon Yabsley recorded this experience in the *Agricultural Gazette of NSW*, he could have described any number of country towns. About 70 per cent of Australians now lived in the eleven urban conglomerations and, with the expansion of favoured "growth centres", nobody much wanted the small communities. The decline of towns in the "sheep-wheat" districts was poignantly paralleled by suburban smothering of near-city gardening and orcharding communities. Country people had clamoured for highways; it had seemed a good idea to transport produce, to socialise, to go into the supermarket more often and, after all, the dust had been covered on metropolitan streets since last century. The main trouble with this tyranny of movement, like most "free" exchange, was that it favoured centralisation. But that was just one symptom of the sacrifice of an entire way of life. The cost-price squeeze wrung out any peasant-like tendencies of farmers.

Among the most haunting of rural contradictions was that few groups adopted supermarket eating faster than country families. As we've seen, they really were never set up for self-sufficiency, just for getting the commodities to the market, and so were a ready market for packaged feed. When Golden Circle conducted its first market survey, it found its cans better stocked in country stores than in the city. Soon no self-respecting country kitchen went without a freezer, or two, justified in terms of the gluts, but more likely convenient for buckets of icecream and sliced bread. In country districts it was desirable to have a suburban house and garden, with the utmost labour-saving kitchen and certainly no chooks, lemon tree or cabbages visible from the road. The farmer no longer offered fresh cream, dairy butter, bacon or even eggs. The noted country cooking did not sustain itself, thanks to smaller families, no hungry hired labour to feed and all that supermaket "convenience" within a half-hour drive. And for this loss of independence few country housekeepers were honestly thankful; they'd witnessed progress in their own time, but food prices crept up, and country folk paid more.

A FRESH START

Gil Wahlquist plans Botobolar vineyard, Mudgee, 1971

WE HAD NO great love of the cultivated landscape and, as a consequence, lost touch with a pre-requisite of good eating. Instead of getting brown in the fields, we lay motionless on the beach. Instead of clambering around orchards, we jogged through the lunch-breaks. And instead of encouraging market gardens, we planted quick-growing, low-maintenance native shrubs. We neglected the arts of the farmhouse: milking cows, killing pigs, smoking fish, baking bread, making cheese, brewing beer and bottling with our Fowler's Vacola.

However, there were in the 1970s signs of renewed interest in getting back to the land. With a festival in 1973, the far-north coast NSW town of Nimbin, a small and decayed dairy centre, victim of rural adjustment, was suddenly revived. Farms were taken over by city drop-outs, who were often young and with little money, but often older, sometimes professional and occasionally with a fair amount of capital.

The impulse had been heralded by the "alternative" movement, originating in California and forming an international youth culture in the late 1960s.

Sometimes the alternative, resembling a sect rather than the promise of a new civilisation, seemed even more plastic, make-shift and derivative than the "straight" society which it allegedly rejected. While professing "back to the earth" values, members supplemented the industrial society's food ignorance with imitation Third World cuisine—herbal teas, exotic seaweeds, harsh cakes, lukewarm beans, crank pills and expiatory fasts. The 80-year-old Scotch ovens at the Feedwell Foundry in Prahran began to bake 100 per cent wholemeal bread from "organic, granite-ground" wheat, sugarless cakes, slices and takeaway food, and provided tables for relaxing with musicians, chess, soups and vegetarian savoury dishes. Ceres wholefoods nearby had "macro, organic and biodynamic" food, which was nevertheless edible.

And while it is easy to be cynical, readers might notice that the jean generation shared the cheap blue durable uniforms of two cultivating heroes, the Dungaree settlers and the Chinese gardeners, and they shared the impulse which had been strong in our history towards closer settlement. Behind the costumes by Levi's and music by RCA lay the often attractive ideas of John and Sally Seymour, Ivan Illich and E. F. Schumacher, who in *Small is Beautiful* (1974) proposed an "intermediate technology of tools and not machines". In Tasmania, Bill Mollison and D. Holmgren advocated "Permaculture", planting a self-sustaining, productive garden. Melbourne biologist Peter Singer campaigned with *Animal Liberation* (1977) against battery confinement of poultry, among other abuses.

In 1971, Sydney journalist Gil Wahlquist and his wife Vincie took their family to Mudgee in NSW to found the Botobolar vineyard, which boasted a love of birds and natural winemaking. In 1975, *Age* reporter Roger Aldridge moved with his wife Jo to an old mill at Malsbury, 95 km north-west of Melbourne, where they opened a restaurant. At the end of 1978 a few government officials and academics advocated teaching subsistence agriculture to the large body of unemployed, and the *National Times* saw a new class of "middle-class peasants".

A Labor Premier who kept his own chooks couldn't be all bad. Revealing in his brave cookery book in 1976 that his fowls clucked only three miles from the centre of Adelaide, Don Dunstan advocated commonplace chicken as the "basis of Australian cuisine", which he foresaw would be "inevitably derivative, but which will take the best from elsewhere". He catalogued his own backyard herbs, vegetables and fruit trees, an impressive list. In 1966, a French survey showed that "auto-consumption", as they called growing your own food, accounted for 35 per cent of food budgets on farms, 12 per cent of provincial family food expenses and 1·6 per cent in Paris. United States estimates were 8 per cent nationally in 1929, 2·6 in 1956 and under 1·0 per cent by 1966. The degree of self-sufficiency would not seem to have been a handy statistic for anyone in Australia, since the figures appear never to have been collected, but if close to the American, it made Dunstan a rare bird.

Yet the do-it-yourself, quarter-acre rustic has always been an unrecognised Australian anomaly, and a thoroughly under-rated social protester, since self-sufficiency, more than going on strike, represents withdrawal of both labour and market. Since 1895, *Yates Garden Guide* has been an essential household reference book. A Victorian government survey in 1978 found that gardening was our biggest single pastime, with 28 per cent of adults giving it as their main recreation. In 1981, the director of the Royal Horticultural Society, Neil Williams, estimated that more than one million Victorians were hobby gardeners. "If we were to field a candidate for Parliament on a gardening ticket, we would probably have him elected," he said. But such was our concern to elevate ourselves above peasants that the gardeners showed off their leisure by cultivating mainly unproductive ornamentals. Epicurean gardening was still very much an exception.

We no longer grew our own food, and we lost contact with the producers. The passing of the Parramatta orange groves, the Adelaide celery patches, the suburban Chinese gardens, the near-city vineyards went largely unlamented. Governments at first seemed little concerned at the decline of growers' and central markets and in their place the impersonal system of refrigerated transport, bulk-handling and supermarketing in plastic films. The wholesale markets of Brisbane, Melbourne and then, in 1975, Sydney (as with Les Halles and Covent Garden) were relocated and transformed into massive corner-cutting operations. Despite this, a committee during Dunstan's reign recommended against shifting Adelaide's East End market out of the centre of the city. It remained a direct meeting place between retailers and almost 400 growers, whose properties ringed the city. In 1977, the NSW government set up a "Food Marketing Working Party", which supported the coming together of producer and consumer. Shorter marketing chains could mean "food reaching the consumer more cheaply and more quickly and hence in fresher condition," it declared. By 1982, the Collingwood council in Melbourne had established a community farm for city people to see farmyard animals, and several other metropolitan councils had opened community vegetable gardens for those with no plot of their own.

New crowds appeared at Sydney's "Paddy's" market, Adelaide's Central market and the city and street markets with which Melbourne had thoughtfully kept itself supplied. "Organic" fruit and vegetables, which essentially meant using more traditional fertilisers and pesticides, appeared at the stalls. But for all to enjoy post-revolutionary strawberries, we would need to construct rural society. This enormous task, at which we have been failing for 200 years, would require the faith of monks, the tenacity of peasants, the solidarity of unions and the nimble-mindedness of the cafe society. To overcome the cost-price squeeze would require the joint action of both consumers and producers, of both town and country, of the wielders of both the mallet and the scythe.

16

The art of eating in Australia

Not left to establish agrarian roots, Australians have suffered the world's worst cuisine. The hope is a consumer revolt towards fresh, local produce

NOBODY has ever been terribly complimentary about Australian cuisine. By November, 1788, the Reverend Richard Johnson had decided that this promised to be a "poor wretched country where scarcely anything is to be seen but Rocks, or eaten but Rats". After 50 years, when the squatters held us in their grip, Louisa Ann Meredith found: "Meat can run about and feed itself in the wild hills, and flour they can buy; fruit and vegetables they 'don't heed', as they would demand some little labour to produce." In 1856, W. W. Dobie disparaged the "muttonous ideas" of the bush aristocracy.

In 1883, when Chinese gardeners and railways brought produce into the cities, young Frenchman Edmond Marin La Meslée wrote: "No other country on earth offers more of everything needed to make a good meal, or offers it more cheaply, than Australia: but there is no other country either where the cuisine is more elementary, not to say abominable." In the same year, Richard Twopenny suggested our food was all show and no substance, a "Barmecide's feast". This referred to the Arabian-Nights prince who taunted a beggar by setting before him empty dish covers. "It requires the tongue and the pen of a Brillat-Savarin to give flavour to a Barmecide's feast," Twopenny wrote.

In 1893, despite cheap white flour, refrigerated milk and lager, Dr Philip Muskett found that we were "largely carnivorous and addicted to tea" and the "state of affairs in the culinary arts with the bulk of the people is simply deplorable." In 1903, when enjoying farm kitchens at their peak, Ada

Cambridge wrote: "Living, ie feeding, in Australia is proverbially good, although the cooking is often unworthy of the material."

The Great War crushed vineyards and the fleeting pleasures of some fine restaurants, replacing them with processed cheese, cornflakes, cocoa nightcaps and six o'clock closing. "One does not dine in Sydney nowadays," G. F. Everett said in 1928. "One merely pays to eat." George Meudell lamented: "Our women can't cook and our men do not know the art of good eating. There is no epicurism in Australia, no fine sense of gastronomy as the prop of happiness." In 1940, Arnold Haskell declared: "The gastronomic mission of Australia seems to be to preserve the good old-fashioned English cooking, the grills and roasts that it is becoming impossible to find in England." Professor D. W. Brogan from Cambridge reported in 1947: "The food in public places in Australia would shock the traveller used to Ireland or the Deep South. Even dealing with a potato is beyond the culinary resources of an Australian hotel."

In 1981, with supermarkets in full swing, a United Nations tea-drinking survey put the race of great tea-addicts in their place. The report said the constant pressure to "blend down to a price" had discouraged a concept of quality in the Australian tea market. "The average quality of tea drunk, viewed objectively, is probably the lowest of any tea market—including Poland . . . and a tea connoisseur or a tea 'elite' simply does not exist," it said. While former CSIRO food chief J. R. Vickery had seen a "golden age of food supplies" with an unlimited choice "at all times of the year", my contemporaries commiserated that a book on Australian food would be exceedingly short. For two centuries, Australian cuisine has been judged to be plenty of food poorly selected, grown and cooked. It has left a very meagre list of national culinary boasts.

The tuckerbox cornucopia

Our Christmas dinner is inappropriate, butter melts in a climate where oil wouldn't, hops does not fare as widely as the grape, and even wheat might be replaced here and there by other grains. It is more than a majestic error of British heredity that we have attempted to eat at variance with our climate. We have belonged to a global food industry, the flag of which had been planted by stoic captains like Cook and Phillip. We have eaten prefabricated food, comparatively little tainted by local flavour.

After 200 years, the only indigenous plant cropped commercially is the macadamia. A handsome tree from coastal northern NSW and southern Queensland, it produces what some consider the world's finest nut. And how typical that not we but Americans in Hawaii, where it was planted last century, recognised the prospects in the 1930s. So what about the quandong, geebung and native cherry, genetic resources which could expand the world range of food species? What about our fungi? Why import frozen fish fingers when we are the world's largest producer of abalone meat and export squid, octopus, cuttlefish and lobster tails?

In all this time, we've developed no typical cheeses, cured meats or local wines; although the Rutherglen muscats—evaporated under corrugated-iron roofs—deserve greater recognition. Our proudest names tend just to be the heaviest advertised: Foster's, Vegemite, Violet Crumble and Milo. As for our cooking, we have almost no coherent style, except perhaps for a proud preponderance of beef and lamb and now a widespread obsession with short-cuts. The only even modestly famous dish has been the pavlova, an invention we adopted from New Zealand. Otherwise, it's lamingtons, Anzac biscuits and lamentably little else.

So what can we nominate as the typical Australian meal? Damper, steak and tea? A baked dinner and pudding? Prawn cocktail, filet mignon and strawberries and cream? A barbecue in the great outdoors? Our sardonic humour, unable to take this society seriously, holds our national dish to be the meat pie and tomato sauce. And it has everything—it's borrowed, it's crude, its contents are dubious, it's portable, it's factory-made and even the manufacturers are now mostly foreign.

Introducing their *French Cuisine for Australians* (1981), Gabriel and Angie Gaté listed the secrets of good food as "freshness, simplicity and love". These have come in peasant societies through an intimate, daily relationship with food production. Little is eaten that is not grown within walking distance. Animals are killed by those who eat them. Much is consumed the day of picking. The preparation of familiar ingredients becomes expert. The seasons provide harvest rituals and the pleasures of anticipation.

Our food has gained the three opposite attributes—it is portable, pretentious and profitable. The basic flaw is that our eating has not come from the soil, seasons, or familiarity, but from factories. While agrarian societies tilled their valleys, Australians just ringbarked. We shunned the Dungaree farmers and Chinese gardeners. Without agrarian tradition, we never developed knowledge of natural resources, experience in cultivation and cooking, nor a self-respecting national cuisine.

Our eating and drinking can usefully be regarded as "one continuous picnic". It is an expression that Australians seem to know, mothers having cautioned us that life was not like that. The only reference I have found is in the bush ballad, "Australia's Happy Land" (*Tibbs' Popular Song Book*, Sydney, c. 1887), which appears to credit the phrase to novelist Anthony Trollope. Other observers have witnessed a big picnic, Rudyard Kipling finding "leisured multitudes all in their shirtsleeves and picnicking all day". It is apt, since we were despatched into the unknown with packed provisions of salt pork and ships' biscuits. The squatters paid in rations for damper, billy tea and slabs of meat, continuing the cheap and convenient cornucopia. The railways sent us jaunting off with a litter of tins and bottles of jam, condensed milk, camp pie, tomato sauce and lager. More recently, semi-trailers shifted in Coke, Nescafé and Big Macs.

A picnic highlights a most essential characteristic of our food—portability. Picnickers carry ample supplies, and might get a superficial kick out of eating and drinking. Yet they never establish close contact with the soil, never take food seriously. The picnickers' cuisine is lightweight. In comparison with other traditions, Australia's cuisine must be a contender for the world's most artificial and careless. To be more than amply provided has not prevented our eating and drinking being impoverished. On the contrary, until now relative or periodic scarcity has stimulated the resourcefulness to bring about great cuisines like the Chinese. But if necessity mothered culinary invention, then the corollary is that history's easiest cuisine became the world's worst.

The promise a century ago

Only during one period did any number of Australian writers optimistically propose elements of a national cuisine. That was around the turn of the century when the gourmet interest in food was at its highest. The diversity and freshness of our cuisine had been improving and the urge to plant fruit trees was not yet overwhelmed by the processing industry. Those were the days when Yates' Reliable Seeds advertised: "Good vegetables and beautiful flowers are essentials to a good dinner." The intricate supply of city markets rewarded shoppers. Domestic science was hoping to bring about social reforms. Especially in the 1890s, we had some exuberant restaurants. The importation of French champagne reached a peak. Queenslanders explored the culinary wonders of their coast. And with the Centenary and all the talk of Federation, back then writers felt nationalistic stirrings. It might not have amounted to much, but the food romantics deserve the final word.

Mina Rawson's *Queensland Cookery Book* (1878) included recipes for wallaby soup, baked bandicoot, pigweed salad and boiled thistles. Her interest in the possibilities of the bush was enforced by "two hard years" on the coast of Wide Bay, 16 miles from Maryborough. Until she went there with her husband and his partner, no woman had put foot, "save, of course, blacks". She was thus dependent on Aborigines and Kanakas for relief from salt beef and bread. Fish and crabs she had in plenty, she said. Vegetable delicacies included bush yams and the tender shoots of the wild fig. By far the Kanaka's favourite, she said, was a rank-looking mushroom on trees and logs. For a large party, a Kanaka suggested flying fox, which was excellent because it lived on fruit, grain and honey. Good too was baked scrub turkey and "fruit birds", she didn't know the name. A great deal was to be learned before the rapid work of extermination had "swept all the blacks who possess this wonderful bush lore off the face of the earth", she wrote.

In Rosa Campbell-Praed's romantic novel, *Sister Sorrow*, published in 1916 and set on the Great Barrier Reef in the 1890s, a vegetarian mystic called Torvald Helsing inhabits an isolated paradise, growing an Aboriginal narcotic, pituri. In a culinary climax, his Chinese cook serves a lovers' feast. "We had turtle soup served in the carapace," describes the heroine. "We had roasted eggs of the scrub turkey and a vegetable course of sweet yams: also the heart of a certain palm dressed with coconut and native ginger—a glorified sort of cabbage. Broad beans, too, with a nutty flavour: then curry . . . Fruit to end with, one of that early variety of flesh melon, sweet, small figs, the colour of an orange, and another fruit something like a strawberry outside, but hot and spicy within. A poetic repast . . ."

In the city, the fishmonger displayed curious fish on marble slabs, E. C. Buley reported in *Australian Life in Town and Country* in 1905. There was pink schnapper, hideous flathead, silver barracouta and piles of tiny garfish. The gameseller sometimes festooned the shopfront with bright plumaged parrots, useless as food, but attractive to the eye, he said. Game included wild duck, magpie geese and black swan, with a wallaby or two and kangaroo tails. The wild turkey—which was really a bustard and very shy—was the finest game bird the country produced. While other Australian shops were like shops elsewhere, Buley said: "The gameshop and fruit-shop serve best to remind the visitor that he is in an Australian city."

Just before the First World War, the otherwise-prosaic *Official Yearbook of Australia No. 6* published a 12-page guide to mineral springs. Included were Hepburn Spring in Victoria, on Crown land and fitted with a pavilion for public use, and Queensland's Helidon Spa, both of which were promoted in later years. Among the NSW table waters was Zetz Spa, bottled by Tooth's Brewery at Ballimore Spring, a coal-search drill hole put down in 1886 north of Dubbo. But how exotic it would be, for instance, to sip water from the unusual "mound springs" around the fringe of the Great Artesian Basin. An important group, the Dalhousie Springs, lay 75 miles north of Oodnadatta and could be reached from the railway line. The surroundings were apparently "not, as a rule, picturesque in the conventional way, but have a certain weird fascination of their own," the government yearbook said.

The eccentric journalist Nehemiah Bartley published some "stray notes" at the end of last century listing regional specialities of fish and fruit. He considered the trumpeter of Hobart was "*the* champion smoked fish of the world, salmon, haddock, and herring being a bad 'second'". The giant crab of Queensland had "all the flavour and twice the digestibility of the English lobster". Being a "warm-blooded and milk-bearing and not a cold" fish, the dugong of southern Queensland combined the flavour of the veal sweetbread and the turtle steak, and had a "melt-in-the-mouth" delicacy that surpassed both.

As to the fruits, admittedly exotic, Bartley considered that the peaches of NSW were as good as the French, and he commended Hobart cherries and

New Zealand strawberries. Chestnuts and walnuts grew to perfection in the French climate of Tasmania. Ribstone pippins were also as "perfect" there as in Devonshire. Grapes of world-challenging merit were exported from Adelaide, and the dry climate there imparted a "keeping" quality to its products. Victoria was ahead on its kitchen vegetables—tomato, asparagus and the like. We could learn from the regional variety of Bartley's time. But along came Federation, the legislative step to an unimpeded national market. Not so easily could we be divided, with somewhat culinary nick-names, into Cornstalks (of NSW), Bananalanders (Queensland), Cabbage Patchers (Victoria), Apple Islanders (Tasmania) and Croweaters (South Australia).

The art of eating in Australia

Finally, let's glance at the writings of a prominent Sydney medical educator, Dr Philip E. Muskett, who was a prolific advocate of a national cuisine. In nine works, and enunciated least lugubriously in *The Art of Living in Australia* (1893), he advocated well-ventilated bedrooms, six miles of walking daily, cookery instruction for the formation of female character and some bizarre medical advice. With his quirks went a deal of good sense. "Australia will only reach the zenith of her possibilities," he declared at the height of Queen Victoria's reign, "when her people conform to her climatic requirements." Complaining about the "struggle between our Anglo-Saxon heredities and our Australian environment", he explained that the mean annual temperature of Melbourne of 57·5°F corresponded with Marseilles, Bordeaux, northern Italy and mid-United States, Sydney's 62·9° with Naples, Lisbon and central California, Adelaide's 63·1° with Sicily and Brisbane's 67·7° with Algiers and New Orleans. He claimed: "All the world over, except in Australia, the food of different nations is suited to their climatic conditions."

And what was Muskett's solution? "Market gardens innumerable, and a healthy and lucrative life for all concerned; the development of deep-sea fisheries, and employment, direct as well as indirect, to thousands; the cultivation of the vine, with all the wealth pertaining to smiling vineyards; the growth of the olive and other fruits . . ." Market gardening was a healthy and profitable calling, settled people on the land, and created a class of small landed proprietors—the very bone and sinew of any population, he wrote. Instead of this, we knew we were "the greatest meat-eating and tea-drinking race on earth".

To replace the "monotony in an endless recurrence of boiled potatoes, boiled cabbage, boiled this and boiled that", he ran through the merits of globe artichokes, Jerusalem artichokes, asparagus, brussels sprouts, the cardoon, celeriac, eggplant, kohlrabi, salsify, scorzonera, sea kale and sweetcorn. The same recognition that had at last come to the tomato could surely come to sweetcorn, a great favourite of Americans, he said. While many Sydney butchers had attractive shops, those devoted to greengrocery were dingy-looking with an apologetic collection of faded vegetables, he said. As well as the Halles Centrales, Paris had nearly 60 local provision markets, and he advocated that every suburb should possess its own.

Wine, which should be the beverage of everyday life, was at table almost a curiosity, Dr Muskett said. He calculated that Paris consumed in 12 days all the wine which Australia took 12 months to make. Wine was thus a valuable export, a wholesome national beverage, employed "thousands upon thousands" and decentralised the population. He was especially keen to see fine cellars built—not corrugated iron sheds—since, as the French said, "the cellar makes the wine". He also related the Aesop fable of the sons who dug up their vineyard in search of their dead father's promised treasure—this tillage yielded a finer vintage than ever before.

Muskett pondered why we had no national dish. Although tea and damper came to mind, he hoped we would all repel such an "accusation". He had seen a cookery book dub a compote "Pêches à l'Australienne", but he believed this was simply a name. He preferred a "*macédoine* of vegetables, or a vegetable curry, or some well-concocted salad". The salad deserved to "meet favour as a national dish". He devoted a chapter to the "seabreeze of the table", passing on the chef of the Cosmopolitan Club's advice on making a proper mayonnaise. Luncheon offered opportunity for a distinctive repast, lending itself to the requirements of the semi-tropical climate. He urged a little soup, the choice of one or two vegetables, and a salad, with bread, butter and cheese to follow. This might be varied with oysters, fish, cooked or fresh fruit. Such a lunch would give most people a "sensation of buoyancy in the afternoon they never before experienced".

The present lunch was at either extremes of the bulky, ponderous meal or the tea-room variety. The uninviting character of ordinary luncheon places in the city was to be deplored, with the exigencies of ground space leading to small, stifling rooms, he wrote. Balconies and French windows would be preferable and it was curious that roof gardens were virtually non-existent. One of the most praiseworthy features of Brisbane was taking a delightful luncheon in the Botanic Gardens, he wrote. And it was gratifying that a kiosk, with 14-foot wide verandahs, had been erected in Hyde Park, Sydney. The verandahs gave such kiosks their peculiar charm and Australian attractiveness.

So many of Muskett's points apply today. We still need market gardens, fishing-boats and cellars. Fresh street markets would serve us well. Every visitor has expected to dine beside Sydney Harbour, yet we've locked our typical restaurant in an air-conditioned capsule. Our food is rarely taken on verandahs overlooking crops, vineyards and fishing-waters. Perhaps we have become a little less "carnivorous and addicted to tea", but we still gorge on white sugar and fats. Our rich and unsuitable food cannot be labelled "Australian".

Cultivating a continent

Almost no other culinary experience can match, say, a freshly-picked bowl of the almost lost varieties of strawberries that our great-grandparents enjoyed. It looks better and tastes better than anything agribusiness offers. We can hardly get decent honey anymore, let alone anything as complicated as bread, wine and cheese. Nothing is so simultaneously fundamental to survival and yet so embroidering of civilisation as food, and so cuisine is a great Australian catastrophe. We can make a choice.

Either we can eat strawberries selected patiently for lusciousness, or new varieties bred for profit. We can choose tomatoes ripened on the bush or picked green to suit mass distribution. We can eat vegetables freshly-harvested or squashed in cans and deteriorating in slow-motion in ice. We can keep persimmons, raspberries and fresh herbs or accept that they are simply too delicate to supermarket. We can care how our chickens live, pigs are fed and cattle butchered, or leave it to economic dictation. We can either cook to enhance natural textures and flavour or we can hide our ignorance under a cloak of complexity, and a foreign name. We can let our eating be dominated by cars and television, or rebuild cafe cities. We can enjoy the everyday tasks of living or leave them to factories. We can have good food, or the cheap substitute.

The right direction can be stated simply: towards the use of the freshest ingredients. Fresh, natural food is usually more nutritious, tends to be more rewarding in taste, is a better teacher, encourages less pretentious dishes to suit what is available, magnifies the appreciation of the seasons and reduces the steps between producer and consumer. Using fresh food also means using local food, perhaps even home-grown. It means a move towards what is patronisingly labelled the "simple" life, and which is more richly-rewarding.

In 1864, Edward Abbott, the "Australian Aristologist", quoted the opinion of the *Magazine of Domestic Economy* that: "Home-made good bread is full of flavour—that of the baker comparatively tasteless. The former is firm, of a strong, compact substance, goes far, and keeps well (from three days to three weeks), and, indeed, improves after the three first days; the latter is light, very white and spongy, does not satisfy the appetite, and can scarcely be kept in an eatable condition for four days." And so the solution, available to Abbott and those who cared about their bread before and since, was to bake your own.

It is not hard to study labels on fruit cases, engage in a mutual education campaign with the butcher, avert our eyes from the frozen food cabinet, experiment with our own yoghurt, tend a row of peas and maybe, with enough room, keep a cow. Such simple affirmations, when repeated enough times, create a cuisine. Relying on the carefully-grown, fresh article is the way to authentic cooking. This might explore the local fish and foods of the land. It might well be based on the beef and lamb of our unique spaces. It might also exploit the fruit our climate provides for the picking, as our forbears began to appreciate.

And so, perhaps one day food chauvinists will blacklist foreign names like Birds Eye, Heinz and Tip Top; Kraft workers will seize back the Vegemite factory; a youth wearing a "cabbage-tree" hat will gallop up to a MacDonald's barn and set fire to it; members of the coffee society will translate the French on "Bills of Fare"; and a Prime Minister will be seen dining on wallaby stew, quandongs, macadamias and Anzac biscuits. As for provincial pride, Tasmanians might refuse bananas and Queenslanders turn their noses up at apples. To some this would seem like moving to mismatch the railways once again, but this too, if it relieved us of some of transport's tyranny, would bring us closer to our food. We Australians might yet worship our gardeners, grape-pickers and fisherfolk, reward the artistry of shopkeepers and put our cooks on a pedestal. In the face of automation and unemployment, we can encourage food as a craft rather than an industry. We might grow basil at the backdoor and tomatoes at the front. Despite our historical disdain, we might yet get to love our food.

"Tell me what you eat, and I shall tell you what you are," the French philosopher of food, Jean Anthelme Brillat-Savarin, wrote early last century. Weekly rations of mutton, flour, tea and sugar made us a mobile army clearing a whole continent. Tins of jam, condensed milk, camp pie and bottles of tomato sauce and beer turned us into early suburbanites. By the time of screwtop "riesling", takeaway chicken and frozen puff pastry, we were hypnotised consumers. Good food has never come from factory farms, process lines, canteens, supermarkets and fastfood chains. It still belongs to careful vegetable gardeners, painstaking cheese-makers and dedicated chef-patrons, meeting in the bustling market-place. Good food comes from "smiling vineyards" and lunch on verandahs. So, when we enjoy a healthy diet of fresh, local produce treated with proper respect, when we learn from peasants, Brillat-Savarin might venture that we have at last found a national cuisine, and cultivated a continent.

Select bibliography

Abbott, Edward, ("An Australian Aristologist"), *The English and Australian Cookery Book: Cooking for the many as well as the 'Upper Ten Thousand'*. London, Sampson Low, Son & Marston, 1864. (Rearranged as Burt, Alison (ed), *The Colonial Cookbook*. Sydney, Paul Hamyln, 1970.)
Acton, Eliza, *Modern Cookery for Private Families*. London, 1845, 1855.
Atkinson, James, *An Account of the State of Agriculture and Grazing in NSW*. London, 1826.
Aron, Jean Paul, *The Art of Dining in France: Manners and menus in the nineteenth century*. London, Peter Owen, 1975.
Australian Institute of Political Science, *Rural Australia: The other nation*. AIPS 43rd summer school, January, 1977.
Bate, W. A., *A History of Brighton*. Melbourne, MUP, 1962.
Beeton, Mrs Isabella, *Book of Household Management*. London, 1861. (The third edition in 1888 introduced an Australian section.)
Birch, A., and Macmillan, D. (eds), *The Sydney Scene: 1788–1960*. Melbourne, MUP, 1962.
Blainey, Geoffrey, *The Tyranny of Distance: How distance shaped Australia's history*. Melbourne, Sun, 1966.
———, *Triumph of the Nomads: A history of ancient Aust.* Melbourne, 1975.
Bligh, Beatrice, *Cherish the Earth: The story of gardening in Australia*. Sydney, Ure Smith, 1973.
Booth, E. Carlton, *Another England: Life, living, homes and homemakers in Victoria*. Melbourne, 1869.
Boyd, A. J. ("Old Chum"), *Old Colonials*. London, 1882.
Briggs, D. H., and Smyth, R. L., *The Distribution of Groceries: Economic aspects with special reference to Western Australia*. Uni of WA Press, 1967.
Brillat-Savarin, Jean Anthelme, *La Physiologie du Goût*. 1825 (many editions).
Buley, E. C., *Australian Life in Town and Country*. London, 1905.
Burnett, John, *Plenty and Want: A social history of diet in England from 1815 to the present day*. London, 1966.
Cambridge, Ada, *Thirty Years in Australia*. London, 1903.
Campbell-Praed, Rosa, *My Australian Girlhood*. London, 1902.
———, *Sister Sorrow: A story of Australian life*. London, 1916.
Cannon, Michael, *Who's Master, Who's Man?* (Australia in the Victorian age trilogy). Melbourne, Nelson, 1971.
———, *Life in the Country*, 1973. ———, *Life in the Cities*, 1975.
Chang, K. C. (ed), *Food in Chinese Culture: Anthropological and historical perspectives*. Yale Uni Press, 1977.
Choi, C. Y., *Chinese Migration and Settlement in Australia*, Sydney, SUP, 1970.
Clowes, E. M., *On the Wallaby through Victoria*. London, 1911.
Cole, Colin E. (ed), *Melbourne Markets (1841–1979)*. Melbourne Wholesale Fruit & Vegetable Market Trust, 1980.
Commonsense Cookery Book (compiled by NSW Public School Cookery Teachers' Assoc). Sydney, 1914 (numerous editions).
Cribb, A. B. and J. W., *Wild Food in Australia*. Sydney, Collins, 1975.
Crowley, Frank (ed), *A New History of Australia*. Melbourne, Heinemann, 1974.
Cummings, Richard O., *The American and his Food: A history of food habits in the US*. Chicago, 1940.

Davidson, Caroline, *Woman's Work is Never Done*. London, 1982 (housework).
Drummond, J. C., and Wilbraham, A., *The Englishman's Food: Five centuries of English diet.* London, 1939 & 1957 (a classic).
Dunman, Jack, *Agriculture: Capitalist and Socialist.* London, 1975.
Dunsdorfs, Edgars, *The Australian Wheatgrowing Industry, 1788-1948.* Melbourne, MUP, 1956 (very detailed).
Dunstan, Don, *Don Dunstan's Cookbook.* Adelaide, Rigby, 1976.
Farrer, K. T. H., *A Settlement Amply Supplied: A history of food technology in Australia up to the year 1900.* Melbourne, MUP, 1980.
First Sixty Years, The. Associated Bread Manufacturers of Aust & NZ, [1967].
Fitzpatrick, Brian, *The British Empire in Australia, 1834-1939.* Melbourne, 1941 (economic history).
Fowler, Frank, *Southern Lights and Shadows.* London, 1859.
Fox, Len, *Old Sydney Windmills.* The author, Potts Point, Sydney, 1978.
Freeland, J. M., *The Australian Pub.* Melbourne, MUP, 1966.
Freeman, John, *Lights and Shadows of Melbourne Life.* London, 1888.
Fulton, M., *Margaret Fulton Cookbook*, Sydney, 1968 (successful author).
Gallati, Mary, *My Low-down on Down-Under.* London, 1953.
Gilmore, Mary (ed), *The Worker Cook Book.* Sydney, Worker Trustees, 1915.
Gollan, Anne, *The Tradition of Australian Cooking.* Canberra, ANU Press, 1978 (most serious recipe history to date).
Hancock, W. Keith, *Australia.* London, Ernest Benn, 1930.
Harris, Alexander ("An Emigrant Mechanic"), *Settlers and Convicts: Or, reflections of sixteen years in the Australian backwoods.* London, 1847.
Harrison, Molly, *The Kitchen in History.* London, 1972.
Haskell, Arnold, *Waltzing Matilda: A background to Australia.* London, 1940.
Hayward, Abraham, *The Art of Dining: Or, gastronomy and gastronomers.* London, 1852 (reworking of *Quarterly Review* masterpieces).
Hess, John and Karen, *The Taste of America.* US, 1977 ("full-scale attack").
Hightower, Jim, *Eat Your Heart Out: Food profiteering in America.* 1975.
Hobsbawm, E. J., *Industry and Empire: Economic history of Britain from 1750 to the present day.* London, Pelican, 1969.
Hutchinson, R. C., *Food for the People of Australia.* Sydney, 1958 (nutrition).
Inglis, K. S., *The Australian Colonists: An exploration of social history, 1788-1870.* Melbourne, MUP, 1974.
James, J. S., ("The Vagabond"), *The Vagabond Papers.* Melbourne, 1877.
James, Walter, *Barrel and Book.* Melbourne, 1949. *Nuts on Wine*, 1950. *Wine in Australia*, 1952. *What's What about Wine*, 1953.
Kelly, William, *Life in Victoria.* London, 1859.
King, C. J., *First Fifty Years of Agriculture in NSW.* Sydney, 1950.
Kingston, Beverley, *My Wife, My Daughter and Poor Mary Ann: Women and work in Australia.* Melbourne, Nelson, 1975.
—— (ed), *The World Moves Slowly.* Sydney, Cassell, 1977.
La Meslée, E. Marin, *L'Australie Nouvelle*, Paris, 1883. (trans London, 1973).
Lang, J. D., *Historical and Statistical Account of NSW.* London, 1875 (4th).
Lawrence, D. H., *Kangaroo*, London, 1923.
Layton, R. A. (ed), *Australian Marketing Projects (Hoover awards)*, Sydney, 1961–.
Mackenzie, Eneas, *The Emigrants' Guide to Australia.* London, 1853 (includes Caroline Chisholm's "Bush Cookery").
Maclurcan, Hannah, *Mrs Maclurcan's Cookery Book: A collection of practical recipes specially suitable for Australia.* Townsville, The author, 1898 (2nd).

SELECT BIBLIOGRAPHY

McNair, W. A. (ed), *Some Reflections of the first 50 Years of Market Research in Australia, 1928–1978.* Market Research Soc of NSW.
MacRobertson, *A Young Man with a Nail Can.* Melbourne, 1921 (promotional).
Mendelsohn, Oscar, *The Earnest Drinker,* 1950. *Drinking with Pepys,* 1963. *A Salute to Onions,* 1965. *Dictionary of Drinks and Drinking,* 1965. *From Cellar to Kitchen,* 1968.
Meredith, Mrs Charles (Louisa Anne), *Notes and Sketches of NSW during a Residence in the Colony.* London, 1844.
Meudell, George Dick, *The Pleasant Career of a Spendthrift.* London, 1929.
Mollison, Bill, *Permaculture: A perennial agriculture.* Hobart, 1978.
Moloney, Ted, *Oh, for a French Wife!* Sydney, 1952 (influential cookbook).
Moore, William, *City Sketches.* Melbourne, 1905.
Muskett, Philip E., *The Art of Living in Australia.* London, [1893].
OECD, *Food Marketing and Economic Growth.* Paris, 1970.
———, *The Formation of Food Prices in Times of Inflation.* Paris, 1973.
Pearson, Margaret, *Cookery Recipes for the People.* Melbourne, 1888.
Pike, Douglas, *The Quiet Continent.* Cambridge, 1962.
Pownall, Eve, *Mary of Maranoa: Tales of Aust pioneer women.* Sydney, 1959.
Pringle, John Douglas, *Australian Accent.* London, 1958.
Quong-Tart, Margaret, *The Life of Quong-Tart.* Sydney, 1911.
"Rashleigh, Ralph", *The Adventures of Ralph Rashleigh.* London, 1929 (exciting novel written c 1840).
Rawson, Mina (Mrs Lance), *Cookery Book and Household Hints.* Rockhampton, 1878 (several editions and titles).
Reader's Digest, *Australia's Yesterdays.* Sydney, 1974.
"Rita", *Cottage Cookery, Hygienic and Economic.* Melbourne, [1897?].
Root, Waverley, and de Rochement, Richard, *Eating in America: A history.* New York, William Morrow, 1976 (excellent).
Russell's Useful Family Receipt Book, Sydney, 1878.
Salaman, Redcliffe N., *The History and Social Influence of the Potato.* Cambridge, 1949 (monumental).
Sawkins, D. T., *The National Diet.* Sydney, 1922 (statistical).
Schauer, M., *The Schauer Cookery Book.* Brisbane, 1909 (numerous editions).
Schofield, Leo, *Eating out in Sydney.* Sydney, 1974 (annual restaurant guide).
Serle, A. G., *The Rush to be Rich.* Melbourne, MUP, 1971.
Sherer, John, *The Goldfinder in Australia.* London, 1853.
Tannahill, Reay, *Food in History.* London, 1973 (excellent world survey).
Trollope, Anthony, *Australia and New Zealand.* 1873 & 1967.
Twopenny, R. N., *Town Life in Australia.* London, 1883 (good chapter on food).
Ward, Russel, *The Australian Legend.* Melbourne, 1958.
Wheelhouse, Frances, *Digging Stick to Rotary Hoe: Men and machines in rural Australia.* Melbourne, Cassell, 1966.
Wicken, Harriet F., *The Kingswood Cookery Book.* London, 1885.
———, *The Australian Home: Handbook of domestic economy.* Sydney, 1891.
Wilkes, G. A., *Dictionary of Australian Colloquialisms.* Sydney, SUP, 1978.
Wilkinson, Alfred J., *Australian Cook.* Melbourne, 1876.
Wood, Beverley (ed), *Tucker in Australia.* Melbourne, Hill of Content, 1977 ("multicultural" recipes, and includes "The Hungry Years, 1788–1792").
Wynn, Allan, *Fortunes of Samuel Wynn.* Melb, 1968 (1920s restaurants).
Yong, C. F., *The New Gold Mountain: The Chinese in Australia, 1901–1921.* Adelaide, Raphael Arts, 1977.

Notes on sources

MANY REFERENCES have been made clear in the text. Useful books have been included in the select bibliography. Other details are found in standard references, especially the *Australian Encyclopedia* and *Australian Dictionary of Biography*.

The following notes provide clues to further sources, especially to handy specialist items. The single-name entries refer to the bibliography.

Introduction: The uncultivated continent: Root & de Rochement. Gould RA, 'Progress to Oblivion: Aborigines of the Great Western Desert', *Ecologist*, 2, 2, 1971. A gastronomic study reinforces such other historical interpretations as: JW McCarty's description of Australian cities as '"pure" products of the nineteenth-century expansion of capitalism' (*Aust Ec Hist Rev*, Sep 1970, p 110) and JB Hirst's argument that Blainey 'diverts attention from the mobility which has made the Australian experience distinctive' (*Hist Studies*, Apr 1975, p 447).

1: The English heritage: Birch & Macmillan, Drummond & Wilbraham, Dunman, Hobsbawm, Tannahill, Lang. Davey L, MacPherson M & Clements FW, 'The Hungry Years: 1788–1792', *Hist Studies*, 3, 11, Nov 1947 (reprinted in Wood). 'James Wright our First Baker', *A'asian Baker*, Jan 31 1938. *Black Dwarf* from Thompson EP, *The Making of the English Working-Class*, London 1963. **Taste for home:** Polya R, *Nineteenth-century plant nursery catalogues: bibliography*, La Trobe Uni 1981. Hutton HB, 'Two nurseries in Mt Macedon', *J Aust Garden Hist Soc*, 2, 1981. Thomas EK (ed), *Diary & Letters of Mary Thomas*, Adelaide 1925.

2: Meat three times a day: Harris, Lang, Ward, Wilkes. Hainsworth DR, 'Iron men in wooden ships: Sydney sealers 1800–1820', *Labour Hist*, 13, 1967. Ward, Russel, 'Billy: early tribute to royalty?' *Meanjin*, Sep 1972. King CJ, 'First 50 years of agriculture in NSW', *Rev Mark & Ag Ecs*, 16, 8, Aug 1948 etc (also King). Hoban, Mary, *Fifty-one pieces of cake: Caroline Chisholm*, Kilmore 1973. Hain, Gladys, 'Dr Daniel Curdie's Grand Tour in 1851', *Vic Hist Mag*, May 1961.

3: The Aristologist: Abbott's obituary: *Tasmanian Times*, Mon Apr 5 1869. Farrer KTH, 'Historical perspectives of food in Tas', *Food Tech Aust*, 24, 3, Mar 1972. Howeler-Coy JF, 'Account of food and drink in Tas 1800–1900', *Roy Soc Tas Papers*, 100, Apr 1966. Reynolds, Henry, 'Men of substance: Tas gentry 1856–1875', *Aust J Pol Hist*, 15, 3, 1969. **How we entertained a prince:** McKinlay, Brian, *First royal tour 1867–68*, Rigby 1970.

4: Metropolitan paradise: Cannon, Kingston (1975), Serle. **The city markets:** Cole. Campbell WS, 'Some old cries . . .' *Roy Aust Hist Soc*, 14, 2, 1928. Greig AW, 'Old Melb's markets', *Vic Hist Mag*, 11, 1, 1926. Delessert E, *Souvenirs d'un voyage à Sydney*, 1847.

5: The Chinese exception: Many leads from Yong. Also Chang and Choi. Rotary hoe: Wheelhouse.

6: The tyranny of transport: Dunsdorts, Fitzpatrick, Farrer. Dallas KM, 'Fallacy of remoteness', *Tas Hist Res Assoc Procs*, 16, 2, Sep 1968. **Granny Smith:** Rumsey HJ, *Farmer & Settler*, Jan 25 1924. Spurway, Benjamin, *Bathurst Dist Hist Soc Ann Mag*, 1968. McAlpin DM, *Fruit World & Market Grower*, Jun 1976.

7: The first food factories: Drummond & Wilbraham, Farrer, *First Sixty Years*, Kingston (1977), Serle. Parsons TG, 'Technological change in Melb flour-milling & brewing 1870–1890', *Aust Ec Hist Rev*, 11, 2, Sep 1971. Farrer KTH, 'Adulterations of all descriptions', *Food Tech Aust*, 31, 8, 1979. *Aust Brewers' J*, Oct 20 1888 & Mar 20 1889. **Mr MacRobertson:** MacRobertson. Taylor, George, *Making it happen: rise of Sir MacPherson Robertson*, Melb 1934.

8: Bohemian restaurants: Readers Digest. Various commercial directories. Wathen GH, *The Golden Colony*, 1855. Everett GF, 'Ghosts of gastronomia', *New Triad*, Jun 1 1928. **Let's go to Fasoli's:** Clowes, Moore. Brady EJ, 'Let's go to Fasoli's', *Focus*, Aug 1947. Croll RH, *I Recall*, 1939.

9: Family goodness: Drummond & Wilbraham, Dunsdorfs, Fitzpatrick, Hancock, Root & de Rochement. Correspondence from various companies. Thanks to VicRail librarian (Maureen Carroll) for copies of annual reports, magazines concerning Clapp. **Vegemite:** Farrer KTH, 'CP Callister: pioneer of Aust food tech', *Food Tech Aust*, 25, 2, Feb 1973.

10: Dainty cooks and sudden drinkers: Judith Wright and JD Pringle have acclaimed Lawrence's *Kangaroo* and Hancock's *Australia* as the two most 'profound' books about this country. Both were written after sojourns in Italy. Hardy, Frank, 'How the Melb–Sydney argument was settled', *Airways Inflight*, Qantas, Nov/Dec 1977. Clarke, Percy, *The New Chum in Aust*, London 1886. Clarke, Marcus, 'Bohemian eating', *Australasian*, Jul 3 1869.

NOTES ON SOURCES

The pavlova: Personal communications from Ellen M Sachse, Bill Plowman & Tony Motion. Esplanade history: *Weekend News*, Oct 18 1969. Schmitt, Hugh, 'The man who whipped up the world's first pavlova', *Woman's Day*, Aug 27 1973. Ellen Sachse told me that on the first day the pavlova was served, the proprietress asked Bert Sachse to give the recipe to a guest. A month later it won £2 in the *Aust Women's Mirror*, where I have found only the meringue cake recipe.

Sliced white: *First Sixty Years*. Kelly JT, 'Baking Trade Reviewed', *Aust Baker*, Dec 31 1909. Vogel: *Aust*, Mar 22, 1980; *Sydney Sun*, Dec 14 1981. The use of the Kelleher commission indicates the fund of detail contained in scores of inquiries into food.

11: The first munition: McNair. *Official Yearbook of Aust*, Nos 35, 36 & 37. Cramp KR, 'Food: The first munition of war (American–Aust cooperation)', *Roy Aust Hist Soc J*, 31, 2, 1945. McEwan, Kitty, 'Aust Women's Land Army', *Vic Hist Mag*, 38, 2, May 1967. Loveday camp: *Adelaide Advertiser*, Dec 4, 1945. Hay camp: File provided by CM Clift, Hay, NSW. **Coca-colonisation:** Two booklets from Coke, 'An illustrated Profile of a worldwide company', Atlanta 1974; 'The First 40 Years in Aust'.

12: Carpark shopping: Briggs & Smyth, OECD (1970 & 1973). 'Merchandising revolution', *Curr Aff Bull*, 31, 11, Apr 15 1963. Symons M, 'Super Planning', *Outlook*, Dec 1965. 'Shopping Centres', *Curr Aff Bull*, 40, 2, Jun 19 1967. 'Notes on food retailing industry', ANZ Bank, Jul 1974. 'Energy down on the farm', *Rural Res*, 85, Sep 1974. Glasson B, 'Aust Retail Scene', Coles res notes, Feb 7 1978. Ruthven, Philip K, 'Future of food retailing', *National Bank Monthly Summary*, Feb 1978. Sutherland AM & Davies T, 'Supermarket shopping behaviour' & 'Influence on tape and time in supermarkets', Dept of Marketing, Caulfield Inst Tech, Aug 1978 & Jan 1979.

Golden Circle pineapple: Layton. Seale PE, 'Pineapples & progress', *Food Tech Aust*, 19, 10, Jul 1967. 'Aust Unlimited: report on the Aust marketing of Golden Circle products 1954–61', Golden Circle (presumably submission to Hoover award).

13: The industrial kitchen: Layton (1975/76), McNair, OECD (1970 & 1973). Special issue of *Food Tech Aust* (Aug 1970). Wightwick IM, 'Vanilla' & 'Flavours in Dairy Products', Bush Boake Allen. _____ , 'Future of Flavour Research', *Food Tech NZ*, Aug 1973. Farrer KTH, 'Food additives: for and against', *Food Tech Aust*, 27, 379, 1975. Kenny, Peter, *Our Everyday Community*, Sydney, Peter Kenny P/L 1973. Holden, Pauline, 'How advertising affects food habits', *Food Nutr Notes Rev*, 28, 7 & 8, Jul/Aug 1971. Marshall, Anne, 'Food information & media', *Food Nutr Notes Rev*, 33, 1976, 28. Boas, Max & Chain, Steve, *Big Mac*, New York 1976.

Frozen food: Sykes, McCarthy & O'Reilly, *Food Tech Aust*, 2, 5, May 1950. Sykes SM, 'Freezing in Aust', *Aust Inst Ag Sc*, Mar 1954. Thompson PC, 'Frozen Foods', *Food Tech Aust*, Aug 1970 & Nov 1977. 'Frozen Food Revolution', *National Bank Monthly Summary*, Jan 1977. Nicholson, Vic, 'New product development', Aust Dairy Corp Marketing Conf, Mar 1977. Conlan KR, 'Frozen fish distribution', Fishexpo '76, Canb, Dept Prim Ind 1977.

The great wine dinner: Smart, Richard, 'Table wine quality in Aust', *Epicurean*, Dec 1979/Jan 1980. Dry P & Smart R, 'Need to rationalise wine grape variety use', *Aust Grapegrower & Winemaker*, Apr 1980. Symons M, interviews with Brian Croser, Robert Hesketh & Orlando, *National Times*, Aug 23–29, Sep 13–18, Nov 8–14, 1981. Dingle, AE, 'Truly Magnificent Thirst', *Hist Studies*, 19, 75, Oct 1980.

14: Oh, for a French wife!: Halligan, Marion, 'Writing about food', *Quadrant*, Jan 1977. Shaul: *Syd Morn Herald*, May 20 1971; Feb 13 1973. Frater: *Fin Rev*, Apr 24 1980; Sep 11 1981. **Chefs to the court of Whitlam:** Wynhausen, Elisabeth, 'It is tiny & cramped but the cafe crowd call it their own'. *National Times*, Jan 12–17 1976. The previous most celebrated of our 'own' chefs was perhaps Hannah Maclurcan.

15: Hard tomatoes for hard times: AIPS, OECD (1970). Various department of ag bulletins. Gruen FH, 'Trends in food marketing in US', *Aust J Ag Ecs*, 12, 1, Jun 1968. McKay DH, 'Small-farm problem', *Aust J Ag Ecs*, 11, 2, Dec 1967. Farrer KTH, 'Impact of food tech on primary production', *Food Tech Aust*, 23, 3, Mar 1971. Campbell, Keith, 'Rural reconstruction', *Curr Aff Bull*, 48, 3, Aug 1 1971. Whitelaw RA & Simpson PC, 'Benefits from efficient agriculture', *Ag Gazette NSW*, 87, 5, Oct 1976. Schapper JP, 'Farmers, ag scs & ecs', *J Aust Inst Ag Sc*, Mar/Jun 1977. 'The tomato tragedy', *Nat Times* Apr 26–May 2, 1981. Nair NG, 'Mushrooms', *Ag Gazette NSW*, 89, 1, Feb 1978. Many thanks to Rev Jim Stuckey

16: The art of eating in Australia: Readers Digest. UN tea survey: *Aust Gourmet*, 14, 4, Aug–Sep 1982. Leverington RE, 'Macadmia Nut Industry', *CSIRO Fd Res Q*, 31, 4, Dec 1971. Bartley, Nehemiah, *Australian Pioneers*, Brisb 1896.

Index

For the names of individual restaurants, see Restaurants; similarly, for particular markets, see Markets

Abalone, 256
Abattoirs, 62
Abbott, Edward ("Australian Aristologist"), 42–51, 52, 59, 63, 102, 137, 181, 200, 228, 261, 263
Aborigines, 5–7, 10, 27, 31, 45, 95, 240
Acclimatisation societies, 25
Accum, Frederick, 102
Acton, Eliza, 51, 52, 54
Additives, 102–3, 161, 195, 200, 218
Adelaide, 25–6, 59, 65, 146, 252; markets, 76, 253, 259
Adelaide Steamship, 205, 206
Adulteration, 49, 102, see also Additives
Advertising, 101, 127, 155, 165, 172, 179, 185, 195–6, 199, 202, 228
Aeroplane Jelly, 141
Affluence, 193, 227, 238
Afternoon tea, 136, 138, 139, 142, 194
Agribusiness, 242, 244, 245
Agricultural machinery, 60, 88, 89, 170, 244, 246; see also Mechanical harvesters, Tractors
Agricultural research, 88, 244, 247–8
Agricultural revolution, 22, 37
Agriculture (Australian), 95, 179, 242; early, 17–9, 27, 32–4, 46–7; for export, 86–7, 95, 126–7; Second World War, 166–7, 170; recent, 212, 240, 242–9, 251, 252
Albury, NSW, 81, 136, 160
Alexander, Stephanie, 234
Alfred, Prince, 57–9, 87
Allied Mills, 160, 205
Amatil, 197, 205
America (North), 10–11, 22, 177, 204
American influence, 60–1, 104, 114, 128–9, 162–3, 168–72, 175, 176, 191, 229; see also Imports
Antill, Harvey, 205
Ants, 40, 94
Anzac biscuits, 140, 256
Appert, Nicolas, 89
Apples, 17, 25, 26, 39, 46, 72, 96–7, 146, 191, 199, 245, 247
Ardmona, 91
Aristology, 42, 45
Arnold, Joseph, 20
Arnott's, 100, 201, 205, 206
Art of Living in Australia (Muskett), 53, 259
Artificial flavours, 198–9, 200

Ashby, Sylvia, 201
Asparagus, 42, 119, 143, 171, 207, 234, 259
"At homes", 53, 144
Atkinson, James, 34, 263
"Australian Aristologist", see Abbott, Edward
Australian cuisine, see Cooking, Judgements, National cuisine, National dish
Australian Dairy Corporation, 198, 231
Australian Gourmet, 216
Australian Labor Party, 163, 235, 236, 237–41
Australian Women's Mirror, 140, 143, 145, 150–1
Australian Women's Weekly, 140, 173, 190, 191–2, 193, 196, 201, 203

BYO ("bring your own"), 230, 236
Baby foods, 128, 203
Backyards, 62, 138, 142, 252
Bacon, 35, 94, 103, 165
Bakers, 19, 47, 48, 65, 99, 102, 155–61, 261; see also Bread
Bananas, 17, 80, 85, 94, 259, 262
Banks, Joseph, 24
Barbecues, 137, 256
"Barcoo rot", 21
Barossa Pearl, 216
Barossa Valley, SA, 148, 216, 218, 219
Bartley, Nehemiah, 258, 267
Bate, Weston, 78, 263
Batlow, NSW, 207
Battery chickens, 160, 209, 243, 245
Beaney, James George, 119
Beckett, Richard, 161
Beef, 28, 60, 87, 89–90, 162, 256, 262; see also Roast beef
Beer; English, 20–1, 41, 48, 51; early difficulties, 19, 30, 32; nineteenth-century, 43, 58, 65, 111; period of triumph, 7, 104–5, 128, 136–7, 144, 167, 168, 169, 220; Melbourne, 104–5, 136–7; Sydney, 105, 136–7; see also Lager
Bees, 46; see also Honey
Beeton, Isabella, 52; see also Mrs Beeton's
Ben Ean moselle, 216
Bendigo, Vic, 209, 224
Beri-beri, 128
Big Ben pies, 160, 206
Bigge report, 27

INDEX

"Billy", 31, 63, 94, 169, 177
Bilson, Gay, 232, 233–6, 241
Bilson, Tony, 232, 233–6, 237, 239, 241
Birbeck, E. J., 99
Birds Eye, 131, 196, 207–8
Biscuits, 15, 49, 99, 100, 103, 142, 159, 206
Black, John, 211
Blainey, Geoffrey, 95, 263
Bleasdale, J. I., 58
Bligh, Governor William, 24, 32, 34, 70
"Blow my skull", 45
Bodalla, NSW, 90
Bodley, George, 63
Bond, E. E., 159, 161
Bonox, 132
Booth, E. C., 74, 111, 263
Boston, John, 19
Botobolar vineyard, NSW, 251, 252
Bournvita, 130
Boyd, A. J., 75, 92, 263
Brady, E. J., 99, 121
Brandnames, 100–1, 157, 165, 228
Bread, 7, 15, 16, 33, 41, 48, 50, 60, 73, 155–61, 261; brown, 41, 155, 161, 200, 252; crusty, 156; sliced, 159; white, 41, 99, 146; wrapped, 125, 157–8, 161
Bread Manufacturers' Association, 155
Bread Research Institute, 159, 161
Breakfast, 8, 93, 110, 116, 142, 194, 196
Breakfast cereals, 128, 131, 157, 185
Breweries, 19, 48, 104–5; see also Beer
Briggs, D. H., 181, 185, 263
Brighton, Vic, 78
Brillat-Savarin, Jean Anthelme, 1, 44, 68, 236, 254, 262, 263
Brisbane, 59, 174, 188, 189, 260
Britain, 5, 21–3, 75, 85–6, 87, 162; see also England
Brogan, D. W., 255
Brooke Bond Ltd, 206
Brown, J. F. S., 189
Brunton, Thomas, 98
Buley, E. C., 63, 64, 78, 111, 150, 258, 263
Bull, John Wrathall, 89
Bulletin, 80, 87, 92, 119, 122, 236, 241
Bully beef, 31
Bunge, 160, 206
Burnett, John, 115, 263
Bush Boake Allen, 198
Bushell's, 206
Butchers, 7, 47, 62, 92, 142, 259
Butter, 28, 49, 60, 63, 72, 87, 88, 91, 146, 165, 178, 198, 255
Buttercup bread, 159, 160
Butterine, 102
Buttrose, M. S., 238

CA (Controlled Atmosphere) stores, 247, 248
CSIRO (Commonwealth Scientific Industrial Research Organisation), 108, 137, 179, 198, 208, 211, 218, 238, 248, 255
CSR Ltd, 92, 149, 205, 206
CWA (Country Women's Association), 127, 139, 140
"Cabbage patch", 91, 259
Cabbage tree palm, 30
Cadbury-Schweppes, 109, 129, 130, 195, 196, 197, 205, 206
Café-Bar, 194
Cafe society, 121, 223, 233, 253
Cafes, 64, 115, 143, 221
Cakes, 68, 94, 140; frozen, 209; mix, 202; see also names of individual cakes
Callister, C. P., 132–3, 134
Cambridge, Ada, 69, 76, 151, 255, 263
Camp oven, 38, 63, 64, 93
Camp pie, 7, 86, 90, 132
Campbell, Arthur, 145
Campbell, Keith, 243
Campbell, Walter, 72–3, 266
Campbell-Praed, Rosa, 94, 257–8, 263
Canberra, 241
Canning, 21, 89, 91, 163, 170–1, 184, 188, 189–90
Carba, 212
Carlton & United Brewery (CUB), 105, 132, 205
Carpetbag steak, 54, 137
Cars, 123, 126, 158, 160, 162, 171, 178, 217
Cascade brewery, 48
Cattle, 17, 90, 92; see also Beef
Cellars, 9, 141, 218, 220, 260
Centralisation, 99, 185, 205, 250
Chaffey, George & William, 91
Chagny, Alain, 235, 236
Chain stores, 100, 160, 178, 182, 191, 228
Champagne, American, 61; French, 45, 58, 60, 66, 109, 114, 117, 215, 228, 237, 257
Chang, K. C., 77, 263
Charlotte Russe, 54, 109
Cheapness, 21, 180–1, 182
Cheese, 15, 28, 42, 88, 122, 123, 131, 139, 146, 163, 165, 177, 232, 256
Cheesecake, 114, 209, 210
Cheval, Timothy, 114, *frontispiece*
Chicken, 110, 144, 209, 210; see also Fowls, Poultry industry
Chiko Roll, 209–10
Chili con carne, 162, 171, 176
Chinese, 71, 74–84, 136, 148, 224, 252, 253, 258; in China, 76–7, 257
Chinese food for Australians, 81, 203, 209, 228

Chisholm, Caroline, 35–6, 42, 201
Chocolate, 106–9, 130, 196
Choi, C. Y., 81, 263
Choice, 133, 238, 245
Chokoes, 64, 143
"Chooks" (fowls), 142
Christensen, E., 206
Christmas, 26, 40, 203, 212, 255
Christmas, H. P., 182
Cider, 47, 49, 70
Clapp, Harold, 124–9, 145, 158, 176
Clarke, Marcus, 138
Clarke, Percy, 137
Clements, F. W., 16, 158, 161
Clifford Love & Co, 84, 102
Climate, 259
Closer settlement, 86–7, 240
Clowes, E. M., 76, 78–9, 121, 122, 263
Clubs (gentlemen's), 53, 114, 115, 119, 145
Cobbett, William, 20, 43
Coca-Cola, 162, 168, 173–6, 184, 186, 197, 201
Cockatoo, to "cook", 31
Cocktails, 61, 162, 228
"Cocky's joy", 87, 168
Cocoa, 17, 108, 130, 255
Coffee, 17, 60, 115, 122, 136, 144, 168, 169, 194, 199, 229
Coffee-barrows, 138
Coffee-houses, 20, 114, 115
Coghlan, Timothy A., 69, 87
Coles supermarkets, 153, 182–3, 185, 196
Collins, David, 17, 19
Colonial oven, 63
Commetant, O., 119
Common Market (EEC), 243
Commonsense Cookery Book, 140, 142, 143, 144, 150, 201, 263
Condensed milk, 8, 86, 130, 181, 257
Confectionery, 99, 103, 106–8, 164, 186, 199; *see also* Lollies
Conlan, K. R., 212
Conlon, Telford, 243
Consumers, 62, 139, 227, 238
Convenience food, 20, 100–1, 129, 194, 196, 211–2, 228, 231
Cook, Captain James, 11, 21, 255
Cookery books, 8, 42, 44, 51, 52–4, 67, 69, 140, 145, 150, 166, 201, 229
Cooking; early, 26, 28, 33, 36, 38, 40–1, 50; in cities, 53–4, 63, 66, 67, 68, 101, 123, 140, 143–5, 151, 166, 188, 191–2, 195, 197, 228, 232, 256; *see also* Country cooking
Cooks & chefs, 48, 53–4, 66, 111, 112, 113, 114, 115, 137, 148, 232
Corned beef, 111, 112, 143; *see also* Salt meat

Corner store, 73, 135, 143, 177, 178
Cornflakes, 131, 132, 157, 196, 255
Cost-price squeeze, 243, 244, 245, 250, 253
Cottee, Spencer Milton, 150
Counter-lunches, 112, 137, 234
Country cooking, 53–4, 94, 95, 250
Country Party of Australia, 93, 127, 129, 240, 244
Country towns, 92, 243, 249–50
Cowley's pie carts, 71
Crab, Queensland, 54, 258
Cramp, K. R., 162, 170, 171
Crayfish, 70, 136, 208
Cream, 28, 117, 144, 165, 231, 256
Cream separator, 8, 90
Croll, Robert H., 121
Croser, Brian, 218–9
Cuisine nouvelle, *see* nouvelle cuisine
Cunningham, Allan, 25
Cut-lunch, 142, 157

Daintiness, 138–9, 141, 144, 149
Dairying, 88, 90–1, 130, 149, 171, 243; *see also* Butter, Cheese, Cream, Milk
Damper, 7, 28, 29–30, 36, 41, 50, 63, 66, 111, 256, 260
Dangar, Henry, William & Richard, 89
Darling Harbour, NSW, 71, 91
Davey, Governor Thomas, 45
David, Elizabeth, 222, 226, 235
Davis Gelatine, 141, 150
Day-baking, 157, 160
De Bavay, Auguste, 105
Deer, 47
Delessert, E., 70
Delivery carts, 63, 73, 136, 157, 158, 177, 179; *see also* Hawkers
Denat, Calexte, 119, 224
Dennis, C. J., 103
Depression (1929–1932), 126, 146, 148, 149, 177, 242
Dickens, Charles, 23, 68
Dieting, 195, 228
"Dilly-bag", 94
Dim Sims, 169
Dingle, A. E., 200
Dinner, 93, 143, 145, 168, 194
Dirty Eaters' Club, 137
Disraeli, Benjamin, 85
Dixon Street, Sydney, 79
Dobie, W. W., 29, 254
Doilies, 138
Domestic science, 53, 67–68, 127, 140, 192, 257; *see also* Home economists
Domestic servants, 40, 48, 53, 66–67
Dried fruit, 91, 125, 217
Drinking, excessive, 19, 30, 33–34, 38, 40, 41, 45, 66, 220

INDEX

Drummond, Jack, & Wilbraham, Anne, 23, 264
Dugong, 258
Dungaree settlers, 32–4, 176, 252
Dunsdorfs, Edgars, 126, 264
Dunstan, Don, 222, 223, 252, 253, 264

Edgell's, 170, 201, 206
Eggs, 7, 30, 72, 111, 196, 247
Elders-IXL, 205; *see also* Henry Jones
Electricity, 62, 124, 127
Elliott, Sizar, 89
Email, 127
Empire Marketing Board, 127
Emu, 6, 46, 49, 57
Energy resources, 10, 179
England; diet, 15, 19, 20, 22, 23; industrial revolution, 21–3, 85
"Englishness" of Australian eating, 2, 17, 19–20, 24–6, 46–7, 64, 108, 123, 162, 255
Epicurean, 203, 216, 220
Escoffier, Auguste, 115, 140, 228
Eskimo Pie, 130–1
Esky, 179
Esplanade hotel, Perth, 147–9, 152
Evans, Len, 215, 216, 220, 226
Everage, Edna, 138, 188
Everett, G. F., 116–7, 255
Expenditure on food, 69, 181, 187, 245
Exports, 86, 90–1, 95, 131, 149, 163, 189, 243, 247, 260
Extended family, 22, 36

Fanta, 175
Farrer, K. T. H., 88, 200, 264
Farrer, William, 89
Fasoli, Vincent, 121, 123, 224
Fastfood, 138, 194, 204–5, 228
Fayle, Ann, 203
Federation, 54, 92, 109, 148, 151, 257, 259
Feedwell Foundry, Prahran, 252
Fertiliser, 78, 88, 89, 95, 165, 170, 189, 243; *see also*, Manure, lack of
Feuerbach, Ludwig, 37
Fireplaces (for cooking), 10, 16, 26, 29–30, 33, 38, 49, 63, 64; *see also* Stoves
Fish, 16, 39, 49–50, 54, 75, 91, 111, 116, 139, 144, 145, 210, 258; markets 71, 80
Fish-fingers, 208, 212, 255
Fitzroy, Vic, 62, 107
Flavour chemistry, 198–9
Floater, 138
Flour, 16, 19, 27, 36, 41, 65, 94, 98–9, 143, 146, 156; stone-ground, 48, 156, 252; white, 7, 41, 98–9
Flour-millers, 48, 99, 158, 160; *see also* Flour, Roller-mills, Watermills, Windmills

"Flying Pieman" (William King), 72, 137
Food; *see* Additives, Convenience food, Frozen food, Meals, Rations, etc
Food companies, 100–1, 139, 185, 195, 205–6
Food consumption, 146, 165–6, 168, 220
Food industry, 8, 10, 19, 103, 195, 205, 228–9
Food preservation, 10, 20, 88, 170, 207, 212, 247
Food prices, 46, 60, 65, 72, 164, 250
Food processing, 98–109, 130–1, 132–3, 194–212
Food stylists, 203
Food technology, 48–9, 171, 195–200, 205, 218
Food workers, 100, 103, 107, 157, 195
Foodservice industry, 195, 209–10, 231
Forell, Claude, 224
Foster Clark, 196
Foster, William M., 104, 176
Foster's, 104–5, 256
Fowler, Frank, 61, 62, 72, 113, 115, 264
Fowler's Vacola, 251
Fowls, 17, 47, 88, 135; *see also* Chicken, "Chooks", Eggs
France, 44, 118, 219, 224–5, 232, 235
Fraser, Malcolm, 215
Frater, Charles, 213, 230, 231
Free Banquet, Melbourne (1867), 58–9
Freeman, John, 71–2, 73, 80, 110–1, 112, 264
Freemason's Arms, Parramatta, 112
Freezers, 202, 209, 212, 250
Freezing, 90, 171, 248; *see also* Frozen food
French Club, Melbourne, 119
French cuisine for Australians, 64, 112, 113–4, 223, 229, 256
French in Australia, 20, 112, 113, 114, 224
French revolution, 12, 44
Freshness, 21, 196, 212, 256, 261; lack of fresh food; 7, 15, 21, 28, 256
Freudenberg, Graham, 241
Frozen food, 196, 207–12, 238; chickens, 209, 210; sales, 209; *see also* Freezers
Frozen Food Industries, 210
Fruit, 19, 25, 25, 32, 39, 42, 54, 64, 65, 70, 73, 88, 121, 124, 125, 168, 258–9, 262; *see also* Apples, Grapes, Oranges, Passionfruit, Pears, Pineapples, Watermelon
Fruit industry, 91, 163, 247
Fruit salad, 136, 144, 189, 192
Fruit shops, 39, 73, 224, 258
Frying pan, 28, 41, 63, 64, 234
Fulton, Margaret, 201, 203, 232, 264
"Furphy", 73

Galbraith, J. K., 193, 238
Gallati, Mary, 221, 222, 264
Game, 6, 49, 91, 117, 143, 245, 258
Gardens, home & kitchen, 18, 28, 40, 47, 62, 65, 93, 135, 165, 253; *see also* Backyards
Garlic, 43, 225
Garlic bread, 230, 241
Garrulous Gourmet, 226
Gas, 62, 63, 65, 69, 127, 140, 151, 228
Gaté, Gabriel & Angie, 256
Gates, Charlie, 119
Gellert, Leon, 226
Gem scones, 140
General Foods (corporation), 131, 198, 207
General Motors, 133, 178
George Weston, 160, 205, 206
Gepp Commission, 158
Germans in Australia, 76, 114, 167, 224
Gifford, Roger, 179
Gilmore, Mary, 143, 264
Ginger, 170
Golden Circle, 188–93, 212, 229, 247, 250
Goldrush; NSW & Vic, 59, 60, 74, 75, 85, 91; WA, 6, 148
Goodrich, Carter, 11
Gooseberries, 25
Goulburn Cookery Book, 54, 84, 150, 265
Goulburn Valley, Vic, 91
Gould, Richard, 5–7
Gourmets, 44–5, 117, 227, 228
Grace, 137, 144
Gramma, 64
Granadilla, 54, 64
Grand Tour, 224–5, 266
Granny Smith apple, 96–7, 245
Grapes, 17, 65, 94, 125, 219, 259
Grazing, 11, 27, 35, 179, 242, 246; *see also* Cattle, Sheep, Squatters
"Greeks, The", 137
Green & Gold cookery book, 140
Green apricot pudding, 43
Greengrocers, 177, 259–60; *see also* Fruit shops
Gregory, R. G., 243
Griffith, NSW, 166, 224, 225
Grocers, 40, 49, 53, 99–100, 157, 177–8, 180, 183, 185
Grog shanties, 30
Guest, Thomas, 100, 103
Gundagai, NSW, 31, 76
Gunsler, J. F., 119, 224

Hall, Dick, 236, 240, 241
Halliday, James, 235
Hallstrom, Edward, 127
Ham & eggs, 40
Hamburgers, 162, 169, 204, 205

Hancock, W. Keith, 12, 126, 162, 264, 266
Harbulot, Paul, 234
Hardy, Frank, 136–7, 138
Harris, Alexander, 29–31, 31–3, 34, 59, 70, 264
Harrison, James, 58, 88, 90
Haskell, Arnold, 145–6, 217, 223, 255, 264
Hawkers, 72–3, 76, 113, 179
Hawkesbury settlement, NSW, 19, 24, 32–4
Hayward, Abraham, 44, 264
Heinz, 129, 144, 176, 196, 201, 205, 217, 219
Henry Jones (IXL), 49; *see also* Elders-IXL
Herbert Adams, 206
Herbs, 43
Hesketh, Robert, 219
Hetzel, Basil, 238
Hitler, Adolf, 208
Hoadley's, 100, 164, 206
Hobart, 45, 48, 258
Hodges, Thomas D., 113–4
Holden, Pauline M., 202
Home economists, 195, 202, 210
Homebush, NSW, 40, 62
Honey, 25, 26, 46, 72, 136, 144, 261
Hoover awards, 197, 264
Hops, 19, 48, 104, 105, 255
Horses, 71, 73, 78, 87, 89, 95, 108, 158, 246
Hot dogs, 169
Hotcross buns, 73
Hotels, 50, 68, 112, 114, 128, 146, 148, 169; *see also* Publicans
Housewives' Association, 127
Howard, Cliff, 81
Hughes, W. M., 149, 163
"Hungry Years" (1788–92), 16, 265, 266
Hunter-gatherers, 5, 7, 10
Hunter Valley, NSW, 57, 216, 217, 222

Ice, 49, 61, 63, 73, 88, 104, 105, 130, 177
Ice-chests, 49, 63, 127, 141, 177, 178
Icecream, 54, 125, 130, 195, 199, 200, 203–4, 209, 210, 221
Iles, H. G., 119
Illich, Ivan, 252
Immigrants, 35, 171, 222–4, 225, 228; *see also* Chinese, French, Germans, Irish, Italians
Imports, 16, 60–1, 86, 104; from America, 60–1, 129, 130, 131
Indian corn, 18, 19, 259
Indigenous foods, 6, 11, 16, 25, 30, 49, 53, 64, 255, 257–8; *see also* Kangaroo, Macadamia, Quandong, Turkey (native)

INDEX

Industrial Revolution, 12, 21, 23, 44, 241
Inghams, 205
Inglis, K. S., 26, 264
Ireland, 36–8
Irish, 32, 34, 36–8, 66, 77–8
Irrigation, 76, 81, 91, 243
Italian food in Australia, 9, 121–2, 210, 223–4
Italians in Australia, 73, 167, 224
Italy, 1, 8–9, 95, 232

J. Walter Thompson, 133, 202, 226
Jam, 49, 67, 91, 99, 100, 103, 165
James, J. S. ("The Vagabond"), 110, 111, 112, 264
James, Walter, 226, 264
Jelly, 101, 141
Jogging, 239, 251
"Johnny Appleseed", 25
Johnson, Rev Richard, 18, 231, 254
Jubilee cake, 140
Judgements of Australian cuisine, 12, 28–9, 51, 64–6, 75, 111, 123, 145–6, 221–2, 232, 254–5, 257

Kanakas, 92, 246, 257
Kangaroo, 6, 16, 42, 46, 50, 54, 64, 94, 169, 258; "steamer", 50; kangaroo tail soup, 57
Kelleher inquiry, 160–1
Kellogg's, 129, 131, 176, 196, 205, 244
Kelly, J. T., 156
Kelly William, 60, 61, 113, 114, 137, 264
Kelvinator, 127, 178
Kenny, Peter, 201, 267
Kentucky Fried Chicken, 204
Kerr, Graham, 226
King, Bernard, 201, 202–3
King, Betty, 210
King, C. J., 34, 264
King, Governor Philip, 24
Kings Cross, NSW, 222, 223
Kingsley, Henry, 62
Kingston, Beverley, 66, 196, 264
Kipling, Rudyard, 256
"Kitchen tea", 145
Kitchens, 26, 63–4, 141, 195; test, 191
Kitchiner, William, 44
Kraft, 129, 131, 133–4, 176, 184–5, 196, 200, 205, 206

Labour costs, 92, 103, 158, 180, 189, 192
Lager, 48–9, 104–5
La Meslée, Edmond Marin, 29, 76, 86, 111, 254, 264
Lamb, 9, 42, 72, 142, 146, 222, 256, 262; see also Mutton
Lamingtons, 94, 139, 140, 166, 256

Land League, NSW, 86
Lang, John Dunmore, 16, 25, 35, 36, 38, 264
La Reynière, Grimod de, 44, 241
Larra, James, 112, 114
Lawrence, D. H., 135–6, 138, 145, 181, 232, 264, 266
Lawson, Henry, 87
Lederer, Andrew, 223
Lemons, 17, 25, 247–8
Leverhulme, Lord, 108
Licensing laws, 38, 128, 169, 221, 222, 230; see also Six o'clock closing
Liebig, Justus von, 89, 104
Lievain, Gaston, 116
Life Savers, 129
Lindemans, 216, 217, 219
Little Bourke Street, Melbourne, 79, 82
"Lollies" (confectionery), 86, 107, 141, 168
Lolly shops, 67
Loquats, 39, 64, 143
Lord, Simeon, 28
Lorenzini's wine bar, Sydney, 225
Lucky Country (Donald Horne), 12, 62
Lunch, 8, 9, 142–3, 194, 235–7, 260; see also Cut-lunch
Lygon Street, Melbourne, 223, 234

Macadamia nut, 255
Macaroni, 53, 122, 224
Macarthur, John, 27, 31, 34
McCarthy, E. J., 207
McDonald's, 204, 205, 262
McEncroe, Frank, 209–10
McEwen, Kitty, 166–7
McKay, Hugh Victor, 89
Mackenzie, Rev David, 28–9
Mackenzie, Eneas, 36, 264
Maclurcan, Hannah, 53–4, 162, 264–5, 267
MacRobertson's, 106–9, 206, 265
Mail-order selling, 100
Maize, 17, 19, 31, 32, 34, 41, 93; see also Indian corn, Sweetcorn
Mandarins, 39
Manure, lack of, 17, 32
Margan, Frank, 224–5
Margarine, 102, 136, 160, 172, 198, 200
Market gardens, 32, 76, 78–9, 80, 244, 250, 251, 259
Market research, 172, 190, 195, 201
Marketing, 155, 159, 160, 163, 185, 190–1, 194, 197, 198, 202, 217, 218
Marketing boards, 127, 163; see also Australian Dairy Corporation, Meat Board

MARKETS, 70–2, 80, 253, 260
  Adelaide, 253
  Brisbane, 253
  Hobart, 46
  Melbourne, 71–2; Eastern, 70, 71; Queen Victoria, 71–2; Western, 71
  Sydney, 31, 39, 70; Flemington, 71; Haymarket, 70–1; Queen Victoria, 70, 83
Marshall, Anne, 203
Marx, Karl, 21
Massoni, Rinaldo, 224
Master Bakers' Association, 155
Mastering the Art of French Cooking (Beck, Bertholle & Child), 229
Matra, James, 22, 75
Mauri, 202, 205
Meadowlea, 205
Meals on Wheels, 8
Meal-times (typical), 29, 64, 136
Meals (typical), 29, 64, 66, 93, 136, 142–6, 168–9, 194, 221–2; *see also* Breakfast, Dinner, Lunch, Tea
Meat, 15, 27, 36, 41, 65, 69, 70, 72, 88, 90, 92, 137, 143, 165, 168, 171, 248–9, 259; *see also* Beef, Butchers, Chicken, Lamb, Mutton, Pork
Meat Board, 90, 163
Meat pies, 72–3, 137–8, 169, 206, 256
"Meat three times a day", 36, 132, 194
Mechanical harvesters, 89, 170, 212, 218, 246, 248
Mechanisation; agriculture, 10, 92, 170; bread, 155–9; food processing, 107, 164, 212, 248; *see also* Agricultural machinery, Food technology, Labour costs
Melbourne, 58–9, 60, 64, 67, 76, 100, 117–8, 124–5, 129, 136–7, 138, 169, 259; beer, 104–5, 136–7; markets, 71–2, 80; restaurants, 79, 110–2, 113–4, 119, 121–3, 224, 234
Melville, Henry, 46–7, 50
Mendelsohn, Oscar, 226, 265
Menzies, R. G., 162, 234
Meredith, Louisa Anne, 39–41, 48, 50, 63, 70, 254, 265
Meringue cake, 149, 150
Metropole hotel, Sydney, 116
Metropolitan hotel, Sydney, 117
Meudell, George Dick, 117–9, 123, 255, 265
Milani, Lawrence, 205
Mildura, Vic, 91
Milk, 15, 28, 47, 62, 73, 86, 88, 91, 102, 124, 125, 129–30, 131, 145, 149, 177, 194, 198–9
Milk bars, 131

Millington, Dick, 179
Milo, 130, 141, 256
Mineral water, 258
Minties, 141, 206
Mittagong, NSW, 86, 90
Mollison, Bill, 252
Molnar, George, 226
Moloney, Ted, 226–7, 265
Monopoly, 34, 158, 206
Moore, William, 116, 121, 265
Moorhouse, Frank, 236, 237
Mora, Georges, 234
Morita, Haruko, 231
Morning tea, 116, 142
Mort, Thomas Sutcliffe, 73, 90
Mrs Beeton's, 52, 64, 76, 90, 192, 263
Muesli, 194
Murray River, 81, 91, 217
Muscat of Rutherglen, 217, 256
Mushroom industry, 246–7
Muskett, Philip E., 53, 63, 67, 162, 254, 259–60, 265
Mutton, 28, 40, 51, 60, 65, 66, 89–90, 111, 113, 143, 162, 169; *see also* Lamb
"Muttonous" diet, 29, 254

NHMRC (National Health & Medical Research Council), 134, 146, 166, 238
NSW Fresh Food & Ice Co, 91
Nalson, John S., 245
National cuisine, 12, 64, 256, 257, 259; *see also* Judgements
National dish, 137, 148, 256, 260
Nationwide caterers, 210
Native foods; *see* Indigenous foods
Neilsen (A. S.) market research, 190
Neolithic revolution, 10
Nestlé, 109, 129, 130, 138, 164, 181, 205, 229
New South Wales (NSW), 34, 39–41, 75, 86–7, 160, 182, 183, 229–30, 255, 259
New Zealand, 148, 150–1, 256
Nicholson, Vic, 191, 201, 211, 267
Nicklin, Lenore, 236, 237, 240
Nightclubs, 168, 221
Nimbin, NSW, 251
"Nobbler", 61, 65
Norfolk Island, 19
Nouvelle cuisine, 232
Novarra, Virginia, 196–7
"Novel Industries" clause, 87
Nurseries (plant), 25
Nutrition, 17, 21, 28, 99, 196, 228–9, 238, 248
Nutritionists, 161, 166, 171, 229, 238

OECD (Organisation for Economic Cooperation & Development), 227, 265

INDEX

Oh, for a French Wife! (Moloney), 226, 265
Oligopoly, 183
Olives, 9, 49, 87, 224, 259
Omelette Soufflée, 114, 116
"One continuous picnic", 3, 12, 256–7
Orange juice, 125, 162, 194, 246
Oranges, 17, 18, 25, 39, 128, 199, 246, 253
Orlando, 216, 217, 218
"Orr, Sam" (Richard Beckett), 161
Ovens, 9, 19, 49, 63; bread, 28, 63, 64, 156; *see also* Camp oven, Colonial oven
Overseas Corporation, 171–2
Oyster saloons, 23, 113
Oysters, 23, 57, 70, 72, 117, 138, 139, 145, 222

PMU (Pick-Me-Up Co), 142
Packaging, 100–1, 184, 185
Packham, Charles Henry, 97
Papa Giuseppe, 196
Parkinson, John, 215
Parma, Italy, 232
Parramatta, NSW, 17, 18
Passiona, 150, 198, 201
Passionfruit, 54, 64, 65, 136, 142, 144, 149–50, 151, 198, 221
Pasteurisation, 91, 104
Pavlova, 12, 140, 147–52, 256, 267
Peach Melba, 136, 140–1
Peaches, 25, 65, 144, 188, 190; abundance of, 32, 33, 34, 39, 46, 125, 258
Peacock, George, 49
Pears, 17, 25, 26, 65, 97, 144, 191, 234
Pearson, Margaret, 53, 67, 265
Peas, 16, 17, 18, 71, 170, 261; frozen, 207, 208, 211
Peasants, 8–9, 10, 11, 12, 22, 34, 69, 87, 93, 127, 175, 212, 216, 240, 256
Penfolds, 217
Permaculture (Bill Mollison), 252
Péron, François, 112
Perth, 59, 147, 151, 152, 179–81
Pesticides, 243, 247
Petaluma winery, 219
Peters, F. A. B., 130, 176, 206
Peters(ville), 129, 206, 196, 205, 210, 211, 223
Phillip, Governor Arthur, 15, 18, 19, 255
Photographing food, 188, 193, 202, 203–4
Pickles, 99, 142; factories, 100, 103
Picnics, 57–8, 109, 144, *see also* One continuous picnic
Pigs, 9, 17, 32, 33, 34, 37, 40, 45, 46, 72, 74, 88, 93, 160, 248; *see also* Pork
Pineapples, 54, 64, 188–93, 247
Pinkness, 139, 144, 146
Pizzas, 194, 204, 223

Pleasant Career of a Spendthrift (Meudell), 117, 265
Ploughs, 19, 32, 47, 89
Plum pudding, 26, 36, 47, 50, 57, 113–4, 212
Poehlman, John, 114, *frontispiece*
Pork, 7, 16, 28, 33, 34, 162
Portability (of food), 20, 94, 95, 172, 217, 256, 257
Portable soup, 21
Potatoes, 18, 36–8, 40, 46, 65, 72, 93, 164, 165, 169, 170, 171, 211, 255
Poultry industry, 142, 160, 166, 209, 245, 248; *see also* Battery chickens, Chicken, Eggs
Poverty, 67, 181, 238
Pownall, Eve, 94, 265
Prawns, 72, 231, 256
Pressure-cookers, 172
Price control, 163, 164
Prickly pear, 17, 39, 94
Pringle, John Douglas, 11–12, 221–2, 223, 265
Prisoners-of-War, 167
Procera, 159
Prohibition, 128; US, 134
Publicans, 30, 38, 66
Pudding, 54, 66, 99, 110, 111, 143–4, 168, 256; *see also* Plum Pudding
Pumpkin, 11, 33, 34, 94, 143, 196

Quandong, 6, 238, 255
Quarter-acre block, 62, 239, 253
Queensland, 80, 92, 94, 160, 183, 224, 230, 255, 257–8, 259
Quong-Tart, Mei, 82–4, 265

Rabbit, 6, 43, 57, 90, 111, 143, 165
"Rabbit-oh", 8, 73
Radio, 127, 166
Railways, 59, 85, 86, 87, 88, 89, 91, 93, 115, 124–7, 228, 256, 262
Rainbow cake, 139, 140
Raisin bread, 125
Rankine, B. C., 218
"Rashleigh, Ralph", 29, 33–4, 265
Rationing, 133, 165–6, 177
Rations, 172; Aboriginal, 5, 7; First Fleet, 11, 15–6; convict, 15, 47, 135; bush, 27–9, 35, 36, 94, 146, 256; dole, 146; war-time, 165; military, 164, 169
Rawson, Mina (Mrs Lance), 53, 257, 265
Recipes, 53–4, 63, 191–2, 193, 201, 202, 203; *see also* Cookery books
Reckitt & Colman, 205, 217
Refrigeration, 61, 88, 90, 91, 104, 115, 130, 216, 218, 228; *see also* Freezing
Refrigerators, 49, 63, 127, 171, 178–9, 212, 216, 217, 229; *see also* Ice-chests

275

Renault, Henri & Jeanne, 227, 235
Resale price maintenance, 180
Resch, Emil, 105
RESTAURANTS, 12, 29, 69, 74, 79, 110–23, 221, 222, 229–32, 233, 241, 257
  Melbourne, Balzac, 234; Café Anglais, 119; Café Bohemia, 123; Café de Paris, 119; Crystal Café, 119; Fasoli's 120–3, 233; Florentino, 224; Latin Cafe, 224, 241; Maison Dorée, 119; La Mascotte, 119; Pension Suisse, 121, 123; Society, 224; Two Faces, 223; Union hotel, 113–4; Vienna Café, 119
  Sydney, Adam's Café, 115; Aux Frères Provençaux-Café Restaurant de Paris, 114–5; Baumann's, 116; Berowra Waters Inn, 241; Café Monaco, 116; Café Restaurant, The, 114 *frontispiece*; La Causerie, 230; Centrepoint tavern, 231; Chinneries, 116; Dîner Parisien, 116; Doyle's, 230; Hermitage, 227; Hotel Australia, 223; Lantern, 230; Ozone, 230; Paris House, 116; Pfahlert's Grill, 116; Prince's, 222, 223; Rainaud's, 117; Romano's, 222, 223; Summit, 230–1; Sydney Tower, 213, 231; Taiping, 81; Tony's Bon Goût, 233–7, 239; Trocadero, 116; Vadim's. 235; Bill Walker's, 116
  Various overseas, 118
Retail World, 183, 184, 209
Reuter, F. H., 171
Rice, 17, 43, 66, 94, 142, 144, 145
Rice industry, 129, 246
Richmond, NSW, 24, 32, 34
Ridley, John, 89
Rita, 67–8, 138, 139, 265
Roast beef, 20, 26, 37, 57, 145, 146
Robertson, Sir John, 83, 86
Robertson, MacPherson, 106–9
Roller mills, 98, 157, 228
Rosella, 100, 162, 203, 206
Rotary hoe, 81
Rothbury Estate, 220
Rowland, Percy, 20
Rowlands, Evan, 100
Rum, 30, 32, 33, 34
Rum rebellion, 34
Rumford, Count (Benjamin Thompson), 21, 63
Rural life, 47, 92, 240, 249–50
Ruse, James, 18
Russell-Clarke, Peter, 202
Russell's Useful Family Receipt Book, 53, 265

Rutledge, Jean, 53, 54
SPC (Shepparton Preserving Co), 91
Sachse, Herbert, 147–52
Safeway, 185, 186
Sago, 66, 142, 144
Salads, 121, 139, 144, 146, 202, 260
Salaman, Redcliffe N., 37, 265
Salt, 7, 28, 133, 195, 198, 238
Salt meat, 15, 16, 28, 92, 94; *see also* Corned beef
Samphire, 16, 25
Sandwiches, 58, 142–3, 145
Santamaria, B. A., 240
Sara Lee, 204, 209, 210
Saveloy machine, 73
Savouries, 145
Sawkins, D. T., 128, 265
Schapper, H. P., 244
Schauer, M., 140, 265
Schneider, Hermann, 223, 224
Schofield, Leo, 232, 233, 234–5, 241, 265
Schumacher, E. F., 252
Scurvy, 21, 95
Seale, P. E., 189, 190, 192
Sealers, 28
Seeds, 17, 24, 46, 167, 170, 248, 257
Self-service, 177, 178, 182, 184, 185, 190–1
Self-sufficiency, 5, 7, 11, 19, 69, 240, 250, 252–3
Servants, *see* Domestic servants
Seymour, John & Sally, 252
Shaul, Oliver, 230–1
Sheep, 17, 27, 90; *see also* Lamb, Mutton
Sherer, John, 38, 64, 265
Shopping behaviour, 185–7
"Shout", 61, 168
Siebers bread, 160, 161
Simon, André L., 227
Simplicity, 45, 67, 235, 256
Sinclair, Upton, 102
Singer, Peter, 252
Sirius, 16
Six o'clock closing, 128, 216, 255
Sixpence, price of drinks, 65, 111–2
Sixpenny restaurants, 64, 110–2
Slavery, 21–2, 92
Slezak, N., 223
"Slippery-Bob", 50
Sloan, William, 159
Smart, Shelley, 202
Smiles, Samuel, 109
Smith, Adam, 21, 22, 229
Smith, L. L., 58, 59
Smith, Maria Ann (Granny), 96–7
Smyth, R. L., 181, 185, 263
Snacks, 30, 126, 129, 194, 195, 228
Soda fountains, 126, 129

INDEX

Softdrinks, 61, 86, 92, 141, 175, 186, 195, 197, 201
Solo, 197
South Australia, 89, 98, 183, 230, 259
Soyer, Alexis, 52, 67, 68, 114
Specials (supermarket), 181, 183, 190
Spider (drink), 61
Spirits, 30, 58, 66; *see also* Rum
Spits (roasting), 63, 64
"Spree", 30
Squatters, 75, 87, 222, 240; *see also* Grazing
Squire, James, 19
Stabler, Rosetta, 113
Standard of Living, 69, 157
Stevns, Niel, 161
Sticker-up cookery, 50
Story, F. Fawcett, 54, 67
Stoves, 12, 21, 28, 49, 63, 64, 68, 94, 115, 179, 192; *see also* Fireplaces, Ovens
Strathleven, 90, 91
Strawberries, 17, 18, 65, 117, 139, 199, 210, 231, 239, 256, 261
Streets icecream, 130, 203
Stuckey, Rev James, 249
Sugar, 7, 27, 28, 60, 94, 146, 149, 165, 176, 239; as raw material, 104, 105, 107, 198–9
Sugar industry, 17, 90, 91–2, 94, 149, 165, 246
Sultana-grape, 217, 219
Sunkist juice extractor, 125
Sunshine milk, 130
Supermarket trolleys, 184
Supermarkets, 7, 160, 177–87, 188, 190, 194, 212, 229, 245, 250
Suttor, George, 24–5
Swallow & Ariell, 100, 103
Swan, 46, 49, 234, 258
Swan Brewery, 205
Sweetcorn, 162, 259
Swift, Jonathan, 37, 244
Sydney, 17–8, 19, 20, 31–2, 57–8, 59, 61, 62, 64, 67, 72–3, 83–4, 103, 112–3, 115, 115–7, 136–7, 158, 159, 161, 168, 182, 215, 220, 221, 222, 223, 225, 226–7, 259, 260; beer, 105, 136–7; markets, 31–2, 39, 70–1, 253; restaurants, 114–5

T-bone steak, 138
TV dinners, 209
Takeaway food, 8, 195, 204–5; *see also* Chiko Roll, Fastfood, Hamburgers, Hawkers, Meat pies
Tariff protection, 105, 137, 189, 243
Tasmania, 46–9, 109, 208, 230, 259
Tasmanian trumpeter, 42, 49–50, 115, 258

Tea (drink), 7, 16, 20, 28, 41, 60, 64, 65, 66, 83–4, 102, 144, 162, 164, 165, 169, 221, 255; tea-bags, 194
Tea (meal), 64, 93, 136, 143, 168, 194
Tea-rooms, 69, 83, 84, 127, 143, 260
Television, 8, 182, 194, 195, 196, 197, 204
Temperance, 57, 68, 86, 128
"Ten, ten, two & quarter", 27, 35, 146
Tench, Watkin, 18
Thomas, Mary, 25–6
Tin cans, littered about, 8, 79, 135, 184
Tip Top, 160
Tolley's, 217
Tom the Cheap, 179–81, 182–3
Tomato sauce, 72, 86, 100, 137–8, 206, 256
Tomatoes, 12, 65, 162, 200, 245–6, 259, 261
Toohey's, 105, 205, 217
Tooth's, 105, 171, 217, 258
Tractors, 170, 172, 249
Trademarks, 84, 101
Transport's effect on food, 2, 71, 72–3, 95, 178; *see also* Cars, Railways
Triaca, Cammillo, 224
Trockenbeerenauslese, 215, 216
Trollope, Anthony, 12, 62, 256, 265
Tuckerbox, 31, 255
Turkey, native, 12, 49, 117, 257, 258
Turtle, 111, 116; soup, 12, 42, 57, 258
Tuscany, 1, 8–9, 10
Twopenny, Richard, 1, 64–6, 87, 102, 254, 265
Tyranny of Distance (Blainey), 95, 263

USA, *see* America
Unemployment, 149, 164, 242
Unilever, 108, 130, 190, 203, 205, 206, 207, 208
Union hotel, Melbourne, 61, 113–4
Usher's hotel, Sydney, 145
Utensils, 28, 41, 63–4, 68, 142

Vacherin, 152
"Vagabond", *see* James, J. S.
Value added, 195, 205, 244
Vanilla, 199, 267; icecream, 116
Vegemite, 131, 132–4, 165, 206, 256
Vegetables, 18, 25, 26, 31, 33, 64, 65, 70, 72, 76, 143, 167, 170, 259–60, 261; *see also* Potatoes, Pumpkin, Tomatoes
Vegetarians, 115, 228, 257
Vichyssoise, 176
Vickery, J. F., 255
Victoria, 74, 87, 88, 91, 98, 126, 157, 166, 216, 227, 230, 253, 259
Vinegar, 15, 49, 53, 150

Vineyards, 39, 57, 87, 251, 252, 259; see also Grapes, Wine
Violet Crumble Bar, 100, 141, 143, 164, 206, 256
Vitamins, 17, 126, 128, 133, 158, 161, 169
Vogel loaf, 161

Wahlquist, Gil & Vincie, 251, 252
Waiters, 110-1, 221, 235, 239
Wakefield, E. G., 22, 35, 75
Walker, A. R., 63
Walker, Fred, 131, 132-4
Walker, Johnnie, 226, 227, 234
Walker, Thomas, 44-5
War, 172; (1914-18), 107, 123, 127, 128, 131, 149, 166, 255; (1939-45), 158, 159, 162-72, 174, 178, 242
Ward, Kirwan, 152
Ward, Russel, 28, 31, 265
Wardle, T. E., 179-80, 182
Warrnambool, Victoria, 151
Water (drinking), 5-7, 15, 58, 62, 63, 65, 73, 94, 135, 179, 229
Water-melons, 33, 34, 39, 72
Watermills, 48
Wathen, G. H., 114
Watson, Jimmy, 224, 227
Way, David T., 110
Weight Watchers, 196
Wentworth hotel, Sydney, 54
Wentworth, W. C., 49, 59
Western Australia, 148, 149, 230
Wheat, 17, 18, 31, 46, 87, 89, 126, 148. 159, 243, 250, 255; soft-grain, 89, 159
White, David, 235, 236, 240
White, Patrick, 139
Whitlam, Gough, 81, 233, 241
Wicken, Harriet, 53, 67, 101, 139, 265
Wightwick, Ian, 198, 267
Wilenski, Peter, 239
Wilkes, G. A., 137, 265
Wilkinson, Alfred J., 53, 63, 265
Windmills, 19, 31, 48, 99
Windsor, NSW, 32, 34
Wine, 9, 18, 38, 42-3, 49, 50, 51, 57, 58, 66, 86, 89, 91, 121, 145, 146, 169, 215-20, 222, 226, 256, 260; consumption, 216
Wine & food societies, 145, 227
Wine & Spirit Buying Guide, 215, 220
Wine labels, 219-20
Winecask, 217, 222, 229
Woman's Day, 190, 193, 196
Women, 6, 9, 66-7, 69, 164, 166-7, 196-7, 226, 228; factory work, 67, 103, 107, 189; imbalance of numbers, 33, 35, 48; in retailing, 180, 184; suffrage, 68

Women's Land Army, 166-7
Woolworths, 182-3, 185
"Working-man's paradise", 12, 59, 62, 69, 110
Worsthorne, Peregrine, 241
Wright, Dave, 121, 122, 123
Wright, James, 19
Wrigley's gum, 129, 165
Wynn's, 217, 229

Yabbies, 70, 138
Yabsley, Gordon, 249
Yates seeds, 253, 257
Yoghurt, 201, 222, 223, 261
Yong, C. F., 81, 265

Menu.

Potage.
Tortue.

Poissons.
Saumon à la Royale.
Filet de Sole, Crême des Anchoies.   Schnapper à la Maréchal.

Entrees.
Les Pâtes à la Reine.
Salmi des Perdrix.
Chaud Froid de Volaille.

Releves.
Dinde Rôti à la Perigord.   Dinde Bouilli, Sauce aux Champignons.
Jambon de Yorc, Langues de Bœuf.
Selle d'Agneau, Haut de Bœuf.
Bœuf en Preserve.

Gibier.
Faisans, Sauce au Pain.
Pâte de Foie Gras en Aspic.
Salade à la Russe.
Mayonnaise des Crevettes.

Entremets.
Gelée à l'Australienne.
Gelée des Oranges.   Gelée au Ponche.
Charlotte aux Fraises.
Pouding à la Princesse.   Pouding aux Amandes.
Crême à la Vanille.   Crême au Fleur des Oranges.
Crême au Chocolat.
Nougat au Crême.
Fanchettes.
Bouchés des Dames.   Tartelettes au Crême.
Pouding Glacé à la Nesselrode.
Eau Glacé aux Oranges.

Dessert.

Café.

Wines.

SHERRY.

HOCK.

CHABLIS.

AUSTRALIAN WINES.

CHAMPAGNES.

Ruinart.

Irroy.

Pommery & Greno.

CLARETS.
Mouton de Rothschild,
Latour.

PORT.

LIQUEURS.
Curacoa.
Maraschino.
Old Brandy.

UNDER THE CONTROL OF MR. W. G. CASSIDY.   CATERING BY MR. BAUMANN, PITT STREET.